THE STRUCTURE OF EVIL

*An Essay on the Unification
of the Science of Man*

The Structure of Evil

An Essay on the Unification
of the Science of Man

ERNEST BECKER

George Braziller · New York

For information address the publisher:
George Braziller, Inc.
One Park Avenue
New York, New York 10016

Library of Congress Catalog Card Number: 68-12890
Printed in the United States of America

TO THE MEMORY OF

Saint-Simon, Comte, Fourier, Lester Ward, Dewey,

and the many others who died waiting

ACKNOWLEDGMENTS

This manuscript has been relatively long in search of the light of published day. During its career, it had the good fortune to come across the desk of Professor Norman Jacobson, who made very incisive and extremely helpful comments on the revision of it, and who gave it his characteristically generous encouragement, which extended even to points of view he may not have agreed with personally. This encouragement was very important to me, coming when it did, and I am grateful for it. I also want to thank Martin Hoffman for active help.

It is a pleasure, too, to acknowledge a grant from the Wenner-Gren Foundation, which helped me take time off for writing the book. It was a "manly" grant, so unusual in our time, and so necessary to aspiring scholars: it was given in a straightforward manner, to me as a person and not to a "parent" institution; and it was given with no strings attached, for frankly speculative, theoretical work. No other foundation or national scientific organization—out of the many to which I applied—was willing to do the same. Actually, what I had sought was a grant to do a year's work in the Archives at Paris, to steep myself personally in the climate of the eighteenth century— but this was unobtainable. I hope that this at least partly explains my reliance on secondary sources for that period.

Indications we do see in other countries and in our own, signs infinitely cheering to us, that Mechanism is not always to be our hard taskmaster, but one day to be our pliant, all-ministering servant. . . . If Mechanism, like some glass bell, encircles and imprisons us; if the soul looks forth on a fair heavenly country which it cannot reach, and pines, and in its scanty atmosphere is ready to perish,—yet the bell is but of glass; "one bold stroke to break the bell in pieces, and thou art delivered!"

THOMAS CARLYLE *(1829, p. 244)*

Thus the divorce between scientist facts and religious facts may not necessarily be as eternal as it at first sight seems, nor the personalism and romanticism of the world, as they appeared to primitive thinking, be matters so irrevocably outgrown. The final human opinion may, in short . . . revert to the more personal style. . . . If this were so, the rigorously impersonal view of science might one day appear as having been a temporarily useful eccentricity rather than the definitively triumphant position which the sectarian scientist at present so confidently announces it to be.

WILLIAM JAMES *(1902, p. 491, note)*

PREFACE

꙰

*In recent years I have come to the conclusion that the best
way of finding out what sociology is, and what it is worth, is
to approach it historically. . . . Until 1917 I had not acted on
this later belief. I had started my own treatment of sociology
each year in the graduate school with . . . an introduction to the
technique of sociology. . . .*

These are the words of Albion W. Small, who helped American sociology become a going discipline. They were written near the end of his
long and active career (1923, p. 389). Today we ignore the experience
that Small drew from an entire lifetime; and Auguste Comte's advice
to employ a historical approach in pursuing the science of man,
which I have quoted as an epigraph to Chapter Three, seems antiquarian to many. Besides, we are fond of referring to Comte as a
"glorious madman"—and sometimes with much less flattering epithets,
such as "second-rate" thinker. In part, these views are defensible:
styles of science change, the heroes of one epoch are replaced by those
of another. History is not popular in the human sciences today,
largely because the various disciplines imagine that they have "arrived" finally at true "scientific" stature, and that this exempts them
from the need to dwell on their infantile past.

Yet, today, we know something very serious is wrong with our
science. We thought we could get clear about the nature of it, like
Small, by concentrating on its method. Instead, we find ourselves

hopelessly confused about what a science of man is, or should be. The disciplines are again having trouble with their self-images; witness, for example, the current turmoil in psychology and sociology. Psychology is again flirting with philosophy, which she once renounced with great scorn. And sociology, comfortably in step with what C. Wright Mills called "The Great American Celebration," finds herself now accused by some of turning her back on the world.

Rivalry, confusion, accusations—these are all part of the history of science; most scientists might call them "growing pains." Science is, after all, a somewhat cumulative, historical activity: it does not have to give an account of itself at any one period, does not have to justify its activities like a profit-and-loss business operation, or open its books to public audit. But in the second half of the twentieth century we are witnessing what seems to be a pervasive change in attitude. The social sciences have always aped the physical sciences, and now they are finding that in the physical sciences there is great stirring; many physicists are seeking precisely to give an account of themselves, to open their books and their hearts to the public. They are discovering, in other words, that the growing pains of science do not necessarily benefit man.

What is the social scientist to say? For over a half century he thought he was growing, and now he is not sure; his own struggles may be meaningless, he may have nothing to give the world an account *of*. Was the separation from philosophy a mistake? Is value freedom a fallacy? If so, what is the relation of social science to public policy? The social scientist wants to be liked, admired, perhaps even rewarded by mankind, and the only way of meriting this is to show that what one knows and does has some real relationship to human wants and needs—if not now, at least in some imaginable future. This sentiment is especially characteristic of great crisis periods of social change, such as we are undergoing today. The social scientist has a conscience, and if he judges his work by this standard he is pervaded by a real malaise. Measured against the needs of the times there is nothing remotely resembling a science of man: there are only mountains of disciplinary journals, and hordes of busy specialists; what is their effectiveness in relation to the momentous problems of survival and human dignity in our time? To ask the question is already to answer it: taken separately, most of the disciplinary activity in the social sciences represents trivial work. True, it is hard-working, certainly well-intentioned, at times deeply hopeful and anxious—but still somehow very much beside the point of the problems of man in contemporary society.

Many social scientists are of course stoically unconcerned about relating science to the problems of their time. They cling to the faith in disinterested, cumulative science, and believe that science will somehow automatically benefit man, if only it is left alone and heavily subventioned. Judged by the needs of the times this faith seems arrogant; judged by the evidence of history, it is naïve—and science judges on evidence. Even more, judged by history, this faith in some future apotheosis of science is a teleology that is absolutely and blindly in error. The physical sciences took three hundred odd years to demonstrate it; the social scientists have been trusting in their future for over a century and a half. Meanwhile, the world continues to be manipulated by politicians in power, by warlords and special-interest groups who scoff at social science, or use what they know to further their own profit, and by hate and fear.

But let me stress that I am not writing a book that intends to argue partisan issues, or to take a negative view of the possibilities of a science of man. On the contrary, if the alternatives were helpless malaise, or hopeful teleology, there would be no reason to write a book at all at the present time. If the work is to be true to its title and inspiration, it should be a clarifying and unifying one, should help reconcile divisive interests, and should allow us to see how science can be made humanly significant—in our time if we wish. I hope to show that if the long and patient disciplinary quest is beside the point of the problems of today's world, the quest has not been in vain. In the science of man we seem finally in a position to capitalize on our history.

WHAT KIND OF HISTORY?

We know that the kind of history one writes depends very much on the kind one wants. History shares a quality with all scientific classifications: it is composed for some specific *purpose*. So long as it does not willfully distort facts and events, it must be judged on the basis of whether it meets the historian's intentions. No history can be true or false in an abstract or absolute sense. Consequently, it is very important to be explicit about one's aims.

The history of the science of man that I draw in these pages is based on the following assumptions, and seeks to support them:

In order to understand the problem of a unified science of man today, we must go back at least to the decline of the medieval cosmology, and to the more or less decisive break from the old order that took the form of the French Enlightenment and, subsequently, the French Revolution. We could conceivably go back further than this, to the earlier flourishing of anarchic, divisive society in the West—the morally alarming situation that prompted Plato's *Republic*. But I think that the decline of the medieval cosmology repeats this same problem for the modern Western world, and that we can justifiably begin our history there. This allows us to see something that we have almost quite forgotten, and to explain why our conceptions of a science of man are so relatively sterile: the science of man is a problem *in society* and *in history*. It is not an abstract, logical, or "objective" problem primarily. Saint-Simon understood this, as did Comte, and more recently Dewey saw quite clearly that the problem of the unity of science in the largest sense is a social problem.

In the second place, each rereading of history is occupied with "new" facts, even if it uses facts that have been used time and time again. As Dilthey saw, the latest rereading of the historical past *gives something* to these past events, gives them a richness and added meaning that they did not have either at the time they took place, or at any of the other subsequent times in which they were examined. The new perspective that one brings from his vantage point in history offers a partly new vista over the familiar landscape. Thus, we must look again at the ideas of theorists like Fourier, Comte, Lester Ward, and others, and reassess their places in the science of man. I think we can see better than ever before where and why they fell short of the needs and possibilities of their own times, as well as what they have uniquely to offer us today, toward understanding what a unified science is and should be.

The specific vantage point that I use for this rereading of history is a new, unified theory of human behavior. The theory has been very long and very slow in the making, and it is only now that it has become possible to articulate it. This means that my endeavor is a circular one, but I hope a justified, self-reinforcing circularity: a new reading of history that derives from a new theoretical understanding; and a new theoretical understanding that is substantiated by a new reading of history. The circularity, then, is not a "vicious" or sterile one, but rather an incremental one of enhanced logical consistency, and added insight and meaningfulness.

Finally, since the history is drawn up for a specific purpose, here are some of the ideas it intends to promote and to highlight:

—That disciplinary fragmentation without some superordinate

unity is not only decreasingly productive, but has today become posi-
tively harmful and hindering to the progress of science; we are becoming mired in data, and devoted to triviality.

—That the idea of progress must be reintroduced into the science
of man, and it must be properly interpreted—as Comte, Ward, and
others intended.

—That the separation of fact and value is a historical anomaly
that has no place in contemporary science.

—That, consequently, the science of man in society must be a
superordinate value science; one which has opted for human progress,
and which has a clear and comprehensive, compelling idea of what
constitutes such progress. The task of such a science would be the
incessant implementation of human well-being.

—Finally, that we now have achieved a comprehensive theory
of human alienation that we can use to help us design a clear ideal
of progress.

These ideas will be strange to many; to others they will be deeply
hostile. But there is nothing in ideas themselves that violates man's
nature. The strangeness and the hostility are due to the fact that in
our graduate schools today we simply do not approach science in
these terms. As a product of one of these graduate schools, I too was
trained to believe that a unified theory of action was a remote possibility—hardly an immediate one; I was taught the strict separation
of fact and value, enjoined to shun philosophy and ontology as utterly
alien to the science of man. The notion that a science of man might
have to be a superordinate value science was a notion that only one
teacher—Douglas G. Haring—permitted me to glimpse. Yet I was
trained as a scientist, which means that I had to look at the data on
man, and try to fathom their uniqueness and interrelationships. As a
result, ideas that I had entertained reluctantly at first gradually
became more and more compelling, and finally I had to give in to
them. What had seemed strange and unacceptable was exactly what
put problems in a new and productive light, so that, despite the
strangeness of these perspectives, I was led to push my study further.
This is a biographical record of my work in a sense: I have been forced
to reach out for and justify ideas that seemed the most productive,
but that the science of man had not been entertaining for over a
half century at least. Finally, I found that the ideas that were most
compelling seemed to me to be justifiable from all points of view, and
from history most of all. These perspectives, I found, had been held
before, but in our time we had allowed them to lapse. Thus was re-

served for me the most gratifying experience of scientific investigation, the sense of being part of a true and living historical community.

This book, then, is actually the third of a trilogy, which records the development of my ideas and the substantiation of the early perspectives I reached for. In the first work, *The Birth and Death of Meaning: A Perspective in Psychiatry and Anthropology*, I pulled together an abstract scheme for conceptualizing human behavior, and offered a suggestion for a new orientation for the science of man. The book was directed partly against the ascendancy of medical-psychiatric explanations of human behavior, including Freudian, instinctivist ones. Thus it stressed the largely fictional nature of human meanings, the uniquely linguistic aspects of human experience, and the wholly social-psychological genesis of the self.

In a second work, *The Revolution in Psychiatry: The New Understanding of Man*, I attempted to fill out this perspective by elaborating comprehensive, social-behavioral theories of mental illness. This second book sought to provide a broader and more detailed explanation of human action and its failures, and to see them as grounded in total, organismic functioning—and not merely in symbolic, linguistic modes. On the one hand, it had to do this without losing the truth of the symbolic approach, specifically, of the social-psychological explanation of the origin and nature of the human self, and how it functions in social interaction. On the other hand, it had to accomplish this total organismic restatement without resorting to the facile reductionist and Freudian-instinctivist explanations of total biological functioning. These two works supplied, I think, the necessary basis for a unified theory of action.

The present, third work, finally, complements the first two, by rounding out and substantiating historically a unified theory of action. Its task is to place the whole understanding of human nature into the historical perspective of the past two centuries, during which time this understanding was gradually being developed. Furthermore, it continues the task begun in the second book, which is to introduce frankly ideas from philosophy and naturalistic descriptive ontology and to attempt to show their indispensable place in a science of man.

The overall result, I dare to hope, is an integral framework for setting in motion a socially experimental science of man—something we have been building for over two centuries. Whether the framework is sufficient to this ambitious task is now for others to say. No one feels the inadequacy and unfinished nature of this trilogy more than its author. Every thinker reaches beyond his competence by the very act of thought: as Comte and Feuerbach taught us, thinking is a community affair; and I have reached much further beyond my competence than was safe to dare. But I was intrigued, and had to follow where the data led me. Should I have studied certain matters longer, attempted a more thorough and detailed examination of certain questions? Should I have avoided some areas where my competence was just too obviously thin? Should I have let my work rest and "mellow" for a few years, and attempted a more careful, more broadly substantiated documentation for the ideas that today seem so strange? Needless to say I have turned these questions over in my mind increasingly as the work developed, but continued to publish the trilogy as it was put together. The major reason is the indisputable achievement, in scope and solidity, of the vast work which has preceded our time, and on which I have been able to lean so confidently and heavily—Baldwin, Freud, Adler, Comte, Lester Ward, Dewey, Merz, Scheler—to mention only a few. Another reason is the sheer pressure of the times: so much is being said, and so much of it is beside the point of either the needs of the times or those of science. A scientific work is, after all, inseparable from its social and historical context: the context is part of the intellectual and editorial fabric of the work itself. To me this means that urgency has just as integral a claim as does further study and precision—something with which, I was happy to find, A. O. Lovejoy somewhere agrees. And Toynbee's considered comments on the need to dare in scholarship (*A Study of History*, vol. 13), put me almost at ease. There seems sufficient justification for our work today if it can be stimulating to the younger generation of thinkers, lead them to again ask broad and basic questions, to grapple with the biggest and most difficult problems. The great ages of human creativity were ages which did these very things. Perhaps I may be judged less harshly for hurrying somewhat to get these views down in print in an epoch which is far from great on the level of critical ideas, and which is dangerously tottering for lack of them.

E.B.

Rome, Spring, 1964
Berkeley, Fall, 1966

CONTENTS

PART III
THE IDEAL-TYPE:
THE INDIVIDUAL AND THE COMMUNITY

PART IV
THE NEW SCIENCE OF MAN:
RETROSPECT AND CONCLUSION

PART I

The Science of Man as a Moral Problem:

A Brief History

> *Science must be humanized, which means among other things that it must not be permitted to go on a rampage. It must be an integral part of our culture and must remain a part of it subservient to the rest. The best if not the only way of humanizing it is to consider it historically. . . .*
>
> GEORGE SARTON *(1962, p. 185)*

THE BEGINNING OF
A SCIENCE OF MAN

*. . . si l'on bannit l'homme . . . l'univers se tait; le silence et la
nuit s'en emparent. Tout se change en une vaste solitude où les
phénomènes inobservés se passent d'une manière obscure et
sourde. C'est la présence de l'homme qui rend l'existence des
êtres intéressante. . . . Pourquoi n'en ferons-nous pas un centre
commun? . . . L'homme est le terme unique d'où il faut partir
et auquel il faut tout ramener. . . . Abstraction faite de mon
existence et du bonheur de mes semblables, que m'importe le
reste de la nature?*

*(. . . if we banish man . . . the universe becomes quiet; silence
and night take over. All is transformed into a vast solitude, where
unobserved phenomena take place, in darkness and deafness. It
is the presence of man that renders natural existence interesting.
. . . Why should we not make of man an agreed center? . . . Man
is the unique end from which we must begin and to which everything must return. . . . If I omit my existence and the happiness
of my fellows, what can the rest of nature mean to me?)*
　　　　　　　DIDEROT, "Encyclopédie" *(in Lough, 1954, pp. 55–56)*

The science of man, like almost everything else we know, began with
the Greeks. But it was interrupted in its main development by the
Middle Ages. It was not until the medieval world view itself began its
slow but sure decline that the groundwork could be laid for the
emergence of an authentic science of man in our time. This occurred

between the sixteenth and the eighteenth centuries, and since that time a distinctive science of man has been slowly taking shape.

The great theological system of the Middle Ages has fascinated many social thinkers, mostly conservative ones like de Maistre, de Bonald, and Auguste Comte. But since their time historians have been uncovering increasing evidence that the fabulous medieval synthesis was never much of a synthesis at all. Whatever social order there was, was based on power and privilege, on tyranny, coercion, benevolent paternalism; society was composed of more-or-less fixed classes; and from the earliest feudal times the whole structure shifted on the sands of abortive social movements, of economic and industrial change that would eventually undermine it completely.

We are all familiar with the Copernican Revolution, the Baconian and the Newtonian, that gradually ushered in a new world picture to replace the medieval one. But, as Lovejoy has so well reminded us, the matter was not simple, it was not merely a question of replacing a geocentric universe with a heliocentric one (1960a, pp. 101–102). Man did not lose geocentricity in a spatial sense, he lost it in a psychological sense. In the medieval hierarchy the Earth was the vile cellar of the universe; it was furthest from God. What gave it distinction was that it was a breeding ground for souls and rational beings whose destiny was not yet settled. The great meaning of the medieval world view was that the Creator, in His design, had a stake in the Earth: the Earth was a staging ground for salvation. As Lovejoy so aptly put it, God was so actively concerned with human destiny that, when man ate an apple in Mesopotamia, God was led to assume the form of flesh in order to provide him a way out of the blunder of original sin. Little wonder that these centuries of great social and intellectual ferment made men so anxious: they felt that the universe was in a progressive state of decadence and ruin, and that the world would soon be doomed (cf. Harris, 1949; Haydn, 1950).

The great significance of the Newtonian world picture was that it put an end to this whole period of anxiety—at least on a conceptual level, for the more sensitive and advanced thinkers. By mechanizing nature Newton actually reversed the gloomy vision of a chaotic universe cold to man's fate; instead he offered man the comfort of a new harmony and security. Here was an automatic clockwork structure that did not even need God's continuing providential surveillance; God need only have given it its first push, and it would tick on surely to eternity, governed by its own inexorable and regular laws. With the advent of Newton the world became "friendly" to man, in a quite different sense from that in which the late medieval world had been. A new age gradually took form, an age which Basil Willey has aptly called the age of physico-theology (1961, p. 43). And it was summed up in the famous observation of Locke: "The works of Nature everywhere sufficiently evidence a Deity." But it was a new kind of deity, a "gentleman God"—to use another famous aphorism by Shaftesbury—a God who ran the universe in regular, lawful ways, not angry, cataclysmic ones.

The new adjustment seemed excellent. Descartes drew a firm line between man and the animals by asserting that only humans had reason and hence an entirely unique nature in the chain of being. If the new nature was now to be God's pride, then reason was man's pride—and his freedom. The religious conflicts of the sixteenth and seventeenth centuries helped to provide support for the new confidence: when so many credos surrounded the Bible, man had nowhere to turn for revelation except to his own inner powers of reason.

THE NEW RATIONALISM

The rationalism of the French Enlightenment is well known, and I do not propose to retrace the story of the spread of Cartesian philosophy, of Newtonian mechanism, the long influence of the centenarian Fontenelle among the French intelligentsia, the voyages of discovery, the new-found optimism, or any of the familiar world pictures of man's awakening to his own powers. Rather, I want to stress the reverse side of this revolution, and for a reason that may at first seem strange: it is precisely the reaction *against* the Newtonian ascendancy that is important for understanding the birth of a science of man.

The rationalist adjustment to the decline of the medieval cosmology had a major defect—a defect which, as we shall see, was bound to undermine it eventually: it was *intellectual* and not supported by necessary *social* adjustments. Thus it was to suffer much the same fate as the German idealist solutions which were quickly eclipsed by the hard social realities of the nineteenth century. The medieval world view, after all, had had considerable social institutional support; but the new Enlightenment rationalism was built on the continuing decay of organized society, the increasing tempo of social disruption and institutional change.

As we shall see, it was in France that the problem was most sharply etched. Thinkers of the time were striving for a new unity with which to replace the medieval one. Man's urge during those times was the same as ever: the urge for order, social harmony, happiness. But the new rationalism by itself seemed only to aggravate the problem at worst, or, at best, it served to adjust the intellectuals only, and not the rest of society.

Among the upper classes the new rationalism often became a social faddism. There was a new devotion to scientific gadgetry, a "teasing" of nature for her "secrets" that shuts off the larger problems of everyday social reality, exactly as it does today. Class conflicts and inequalities remained, or grew even sharper, while the new scientific spirit served to feed a new kind of easy, secular pride that aggravated these social and individual differences. Lovejoy has called attention to the significant fact that the most influential and representative writers of the early and mid-eighteenth century were those who castigated the vice of pride and the exaggerated claims of reason (1960b, p. 68). Thinkers of the stature of Spinoza and Pascal were also caught up in the problem of pride, and ruminated whether one could educate children effectively without stressing it (Lovejoy, 1961, p. 241). (This is an argument worthy of contemporary interaction and identity theory, as we shall see in Part III of this work.)

What is the point of this historical preoccupation with intellectualism and pride? Why were the most influential and representative writers occupied with it? Probably because the problems of pride and intellect are derivative problems of social disruption and rapid change —they become serious and sharpened precisely at those times. Man then begins to ask, what socially beneficial goals does intelligence serve? Comte, Marx, and Dewey, who were concerned much later with these same problems, problems of narrow analytic intelligence and urgent social change, levied a criticism against the selfishness of the scientist who seeks only the resolution of his intellectual puzzles, without any thought of social gain or good. The important social question, during troubled times, is simply this: What should a person properly be proud of? A voyage of discovery that imports the plague? A shipload of exotic spices that only a few households can afford? The discovery of a new star that multiplies activity at the elite Royal Academy? But this discovery does not diminish famine in the countryside—and, even worse, it distracts attention from the problem. (Exactly as space probes distract attention from domestic and international problems today.) The medieval knight was often ludicrous in his pride, but he was at least socially responsive. Now, in the new science, pride had a new mystique, and it became possible for a man to act dignified on the basis of even more inverted and esoteric games than those played in knightly times.

It will be obvious to many that this line of reasoning anticipates Rousseau's poetic and heartfelt assault on science. But this is getting ahead of the story. Furthermore, in order to understand the anguished problems of the time, it is important not to give Rousseau credit for any original protest against science. The medieval world view did not decline "all at once." There were several centuries of transition from the synthesis of Aquinas to the new world view of Newton, and these centuries were characterized by an anguished search for the true sources of human salvation (Haydn, 1950). Man saw vanity in science as well as in rational theology. The Renaissance Humanists did not look with favor at a study of nature which would downgrade man (Cassirer, Kristeller, and Randall, 1948, pp. 19–20). And the great skeptics like Machiavelli, Montaigne, and Cornelius Agrippa could not stomach the facile scholastic coexistence of reason and morality that was being continued by the Renaissance Humanists themselves. Haydn calls this later movement the "Counter-Renaissance," and Catholic writers have termed it the "false" Renaissance; it was part of the great seething of the time: where was man to look for true and dependable morality and dignity? In the sciences, in philosophical religion, or in pure faith? The "vanity of the sciences" continued to be attacked by Pascal in the seventeenth century, and he also echoed the familiar harangue against the institution of private property: it is obvious that these centuries of transition from one reasonable intellectual system to another were depraved in a thoroughgoing social sense—and neither man's reason nor his personal acquisition of knowledge and goods was helping the matter. By Rousseau's time, of course, the nadir had been hit, and when Jefferson saw pre-revolutionary Paris he knew that traditional European civilization was at an end. The French Revolution was merely the formal funeral for a centuries-old change of system.

THE PROBLEM OF A UNITARY VISION

The dilemma of new optimisms and old nostalgias, of intellectual gains and continuing social disruptions, seems to reveal the heart of this whole period. But let us pause and project for just one moment, and we will see the full implications of the late Renaissance and Enlightenment dilemma: *the problem of that period is the same problem we have today*, namely, how are we to reconcile science with the larger designs of human life? Can science alone give us a unitary vision in which man has a prominent place? We are only just answering these questions, so we can hardly expect a solution from thinkers of that time. But they launched several different attacks on the problem, approaches which contain heavy and urgent intelligence for our efforts today; let us glance at them briefly.

The problem of the unity of knowledge in Western society dates from the rise of knowledge with the Greeks, and since Plato various thinkers have attacked it (cf. Flint, 1904, for an excellent survey). The undermining of medieval cosmology merely signaled a redoubling of energy on the problem, since the theocentric unity was now lost. The very thinkers who were responsible for this loss had to address themselves to the old problem, and had to offer schemes for the unification of the new scientific thought. And the need for unification was felt more keenly precisely because the times were out of joint, and man was not at home in the world.

As we would expect, in such times, with the old medieval unity still fresh in mind, the fragmentation of knowledge was seen in all its destructiveness. Thus, when Descartes offered his new system, it was a logical unity, without any diversity of the various sciences. He made some biting criticisms of the division of subject matter and labor in science. To his mind, to isolate a science according to its subject matter was to deprive it of its scientific character, and to reduce it to a mere collection of detached truths (McRae, 1961, p. 7). In a word, Descartes was alive to the moral background of science, as was that other unitary thinker, Leibnitz. Leibnitz did not at all like the arguments that were raging among the Cartesians, the theologians, the mathematicians. The luxuriance of individual philosophers and schools was to him a symbol of the universal conflict of his time (Meyer, 1952, p. 113). To remedy this Babel, he projected his design for a scientific-religious Academy which would group all learning. Leibnitz' aim was nothing less than to recapture the lost medieval order in a new synthesis. Thus, in the age of absolute monarchism Leibnitz reacted strongly against Hobbes and Locke and the absolute state, and longed to see the reinstitution of the medieval Empire—of a commonwealth of intellects and a harmony that would be timeless and supranational (Meyer, 1952, p. 37). Today we are in a position to realize that Leibnitz had a vision of a new scientific universalism that is now almost entirely lost; and we can also judge that this loss is much to our sorrow. In our national statism we are Hobbesian with a vengeance; and in our fragmented science we are scientific without a vision. Historians of the future will very likely mark us as the true *fins de race* of the Newtonian Revolution.

The ideas of system, unity, interrelatedness, academies were very much in the air a few hundred years ago, and formed a vital part of the strictly scientific preoccupation. Fontenelle too agreed with Leibnitz that a certain solidarity ought to unite all the sciences, and he too championed the creation of academies that would trace the lines of communication between the various sciences, and centralize the results. Today we are still stirring in this direction, and the motives are basically the same: the unity of science had to answer intellectual problems *only in order to come to grips with moral and social problems*. Certainly this is very clear in Leibnitz. It becomes even clearer as the Enlightenment progresses. The purely intellectualistic quest of science becomes increasingly a source of discontent, and has to be attacked again and again, from different approaches.

The approach of certain of the French Enlightenment thinkers contains some very distinct emphases that we do not find in either Descartes or Leibnitz. In the first place, there is no nostalgic longing after a medieval Empire as with Leibnitz, largely because there is less tolerance for the organized Church. Furthermore, the idea of God that formed an inseparable part of Descartes' systematic thinking nearly drops out. The result is new and curious: Newtonian science itself comes to occupy the whole stage; and, when it is seen in its stark nudity to be inadequate to a solution of the problems of man in society, it suffers a heavy devaluation and attack. The Leibnitzian tolerance—which merged religion with science—is gone. But, as we shall see, the very intolerance of certain of the French Enlightenment thinkers, to both the Church and to Newton's monopolistic ascendancy, permitted them to devise uniquely new solutions to the central problems of a science of man in society. Thus we will be able to say that a distinctive science of man begins with them.

THE BEGINNING OF A SCIENCE OF MAN

To name the founding father of a science is a shorthand for saying "this is what I think the science is"—it establishes an option for its character. To choose the Abbé de Saint-Pierre as the beginner of the science of man is to announce frankly that it is a superordinate value science in the service of human betterment, and this is exactly the position I intend to elaborate from many different points of view, I hope cumulatively, all through this work.

A science, of course, is a complex affair—it never "begins" with

any one man, as knowledge never begins in one human mind. But
Saint-Pierre did give the problem of man in society a distinctive cast:
he outlined the active program for a science of man, for which Diderot
was to provide the conceptual argument. In Saint-Pierre we see the
social protest against a science divorced from human affairs; in
Diderot we see the human protest against a science which would take
the universe, and not man, as a center. But the two protests, of course,
are inseparable, even though Diderot did not perhaps see the peculiar
character of a science of man as clearly as Saint-Pierre and Rousseau.
Saint-Pierre was one of the very first to hold that man should consciously plan a better future by applying social science to human
affairs. He was the first to call for a Political Academy and an Ethical
Academy to do for politics and ethics what the Scientific Academies
do for science. The great experiment was tried during the French
Revolution, in the form of the *Institut national,* but Napoleon quickly
snuffed it out by suppressing the social scientists. And, much to our
sorrow, we have not again tried to implement this daring vision, since
that time. At least part of our imponderable social and political
problems are due to this failure to institute a guiding "Scientific
Brain" over our national life. We can say of Saint-Pierre as the great
sociologist Albion Small remarked of Karl Marx (1911–12): the longer
we refrain from taking him seriously, the longer will his name and
criticism remain and grow.

Along with his vision, Saint-Pierre did exactly what we are
beginning to do today—or should be doing: he put forth a criticism
of the overvaluation of the physical sciences. Later thinkers thought
the idea so presumptuous that they dismissed the Abbé as a naïve
visionary, out of touch with the real world. But in our time we have
seen him vindicated, and his justifiers are none other than the editors
of the *Bulletin of the Atomic Scientists*—the physical scientists
themselves (see especially Max Born's historically crucial essay,
1964). We have lived to see how truly Saint-Pierre probed. In his
eyes the overvaluation of the physical sciences represented an
incredible naïveness on the part of the Titans of the scientific revolution; as he put it:

> It is a grave misfortune that Descartes and Newton
> did not devote themselves to perfecting these sciences
> [ethics and politics], so incomparably more useful for
> mankind than those in which they made their great
> discoveries. They fell into the prevailing error as to the
> comparative values of the various domains of knowledge,

an error to which we must also ascribe the fact that while
Academies of Sciences and Belles-Lettres exist there are
no such institutions for Politics or Ethics (Bury, 1955,
p. 139).

Imagine attacking Descartes and Newton. J. B. Bury says that the reason Saint-Pierre depreciated mathematics and the physical sciences
was his "crude utilitarianism" (p. 141). But this betrays the very
overvaluation of science that Saint-Pierre attacks. During Saint-
Pierre's time science had not accomplished what it was to accomplish
after the industrial revolution, so that he was justified in being disre-
spectful on purely utilitarian grounds. And today, in the full Age of
Terror, we see once again that we must become "crude utilitarians"—at
least in the sense in which science cannot be seen apart from life.
We return, in sum, to the Abbé de Saint-Pierre with our compliments,
and with our deep and hopeful respect.

Diderot and some of the Encyclopedists were also dissatisfied
with Bacon and Newton, thus too anticipating our present belated
discontent and disillusionment. It is really striking to compare
Diderot's *cri du coeur* against the Newtonian imperialism with our
similar stirrings today—it is as if two hundred years were effaced
from the history of science, as if they had contributed nothing to
solving its central problem. When Diderot complained so eloquently
about the meaninglessness of the natural order if man was banished
from the earth, he raised the echo which still haunts us: Where
exactly is the place of a science of man in a Newtonian world? Or, more
courageously and radically: What is the place of physical science in a
science centered on human values?

The Encyclopedia was an attempt to bring some order and
relation into the mass of accumulated knowledge of the scientific
revolution. But it would be wrong to see this in the same light as
similar "collections" of our time: it was not simply an attempt "to do"
more science. (Diderot was already appalled at the volume of books
which was collecting, and he uttered a heartfelt groan for future
ages which would be literally swamped by the sheer numbers of
volumes; he predicted that it would one day be easier to get facts
by going directly back to nature than by addressing oneself to the
library with its swollen stacks; have we already arrived at such a
time?) The animating spirit of the Encyclopedia was not only a call
to science—it was that, and something more: it also contained a
fundamental protest of the Enlightenment spirit *against* Newtonian
science (Gillispie, 1959, p. 280). It would be difficult to overstress this

point. Of course there were earlier and continuing protests against the new science, as we noted above, protests characteristic of every age of social disruption—reaching back even to Seneca and the Stoics. But the attempt of the Encyclopedists to remedy this carried something new, a step that we should be taking now, but are reluctant to: namely, the frank *option for man as a center from which all sciences radiate.*

Voltaire reflected this spirit in a letter to D'Argental: "I liked physics as long as it did not attempt to oust poetry; now that it is crushing all the arts I refuse to consider physics as anything else than an unsociable tyrant" (in Green, 1950, p. 4). Newtonianism was skewing the esthetic sensibilities of the time, and that was a serious matter, if one rightly considers poetry and art as the basis of what is distinctively human. But Diderot and d'Alembert were more explicit in accusing the new science of skewing the whole natural order. The Encyclopedia took its inspiration from and honored Bacon, while at the same time it attacked him on a fundamental point: d'Alembert wrote that he did not understand why the celebrated Bacon, who served as the guide for the Encyclopedia, *had placed nature before man* in his system. The Encyclopedists thus executed the first "Copernican shift" in the human sciences, by placing man *before* nature. But they overlooked the fact that Bacon did not need to make this shift: he retained God in his system, thereby assuring to man an automatically privileged place. Only when the French had effectively disposed of Providence was it necessary to affirm man in a new way.

How does one make science significant? Diderot had the answer upon which we cannot improve today: The sciences should be centered on man, and the various sciences would be considered in relation to him and his needs; lines would radiate out from man to all the sciences. Instead of being woven at random, like an afterthought design, into an alien fabric, man would be the central line on a switchboard (as in Albion Small's later model [1910]).

This original centering of the sciences on man was a far greater revolution than the Renaissance had been. J. B. Bury, who seized on its true significance, thought that the closest analogy in history to this radical anthropocentrism was fifth-century Athens with its concentration on man and his works, its turning away from the cosmos and its ultimate problems (1955, p. 160). Newtonianism, we are led to conclude, carried over some of the otherworldliness of medievalism. Diderot, by recentering science on man, adapted man to the astronomical revolution in the only way he could be adapted: by turning his gaze upon himself rather than upon the stars. Man kept possession of the psychological center he had enjoyed in the medieval cosmology, but with none of the burdens of otherworldliness. The Enlightenment thus carried through a change that neither the Renaissance nor the scientific revolution could manage: after over a century of fumbling it inaugurated a true Athenian celebration of man.

We could understand most of the intellectual thrust of the time as a protest that man had a place in Newtonian nature. Thus, as E. A. Burtt points out (1932, p. 25), modern metaphysics, beginning with Berkeley and Leibnitz, is not only an exercise in epistemology: its really significant connecting thread is that it represents a series of unsuccessful protests against the new view of man and nature. From Pascal on, philosophers could tremble at a vast cosmos that dwarfed man, and they all wanted to carve out an important place for him and his unique spiritual claims: Berkeley, Hume, Monboddo, Kant, Fichte, Hegel, James, Bergson, Alexander. Seen in this way, idealism is directly related to Diderot's protest; it is a philosophical *cri du coeur* against a science which gives primacy to the physical world.

One of the main things I hope to show in this work is how we have gradually succeeded in solving the idealist protest, but on a purely *scientific* level; this was the great challenge that remained to be worked out. For now, let us merely stress the far-reaching nature of this early protest that sought to find a place for human values in a mechanical cosmos; it was a protest that included thinkers like Turgot and Condorcet in France, Herder and Kant in Germany, and practically the whole school of Scotch philosophy. Herder saw man as being just in the bud, a creature of possibility who would one day flower into something unrecognizable. And Hume lamented the century lag from Bacon to the beginning of a true science of man, and saw that only such a science would make the others meaningful. The brilliant and colorful Lord Monboddo, for his part, damned everyone who would mechanize the human spirit: Locke, and even Descartes.

But it is important to pause and etch some basic differences in these laments. A protest without a program is little more than sentimentalism—this is the epitaph of many of the great idealisms. It is one thing to call for a man-centered science; it is quite another to show what a man-centered science is, and how it should be brought about. One thing that made Kant so lastingly prominent is that we have still not been able to realize the vast program that his thought mapped out: he saw what needed to be done in the Newtonian world, but practically, nothing could be done in his time. Thus he opened the way for endless speculation instead of immediate remedial action. He was firm enough that "knowledge remains forever incomplete and haphazard in character unless the various scientific disciplines are brought into some intelligible relation with each other and directed toward such ends as will serve to give them purpose for human well-being" (Smith, 1957, pp. 18–19). Then, the real problem, and the one that the French thinkers tried to cope with, was exactly how this was to be done on a concrete level: Saint-Pierre wanted an Academy of Political Science and one of Ethics; d'Holbach called for repeated social experimentation over a long span of time (Bury, 1955, p. 170). They had, in other words, the good sense and the correct vision of posing the problem as one of social action. But with the advent of Napoleon after the French Revolution, there was no possibility of implementing such a program. In Germany, there was no revolution, and most of the academic philosophers who followed Kant worked on an abstract metaphysical level, and obscured Kant's man-centered activism. Thus, Marx had to attack Hegel with a new urge to social action. In other words, post-Kantian philosophy only delayed coming to grips with the practical problems; little wonder that Marx had to explode with greater promotive vehemence: a vital tradition had almost been buried.

This has been the theme of the science of man down to this very day; perhaps at last we can be convinced that delay is no longer necessary. This is the case I hope to present with this work. I am very much aware that this is a mighty ambition, and if I undertake it confidently it is because of a long preparation by many scientists, and because of ripe historical circumstances, and thus is hardly due to the sorely limited powers of any one individual.

CHAPTER TWO

THE PROBLEM OF
A NEW THEODICY

. . . this throng which has indiscreetly broken into the Sanctuary of science, and occupied a place of which they are unworthy . . . One could only wish . . . that they would have been thrown back right at the entrance, and directed into arts useful to society.

ROUSSEAU *(1750, pp. 158–159)*

Kant's program could not have any immediate effect on the social problem; it was a long-range vision that had to be painfully worked out. His synthesis was an attempt to save science and knowledge in the face of Hume's skepticism; and, at the same time, it wanted to secure a place for morality in a deterministic Newtonian world. Even though man could never know "things in themselves," since he was transcended by nature, he could learn enough about the world to manipulate it to his purposes. And, even though he could not find moral principles in the workings of nature, man could fashion morality and introduce it into the world.

To mention Kant's attempted solution helps us see what the true problem of that time was: *it was basically a moral one.* The fundamental criticism of the times was that the pursuit of Newtonian science had done nothing to promote social morality. This must be repeated again and again.

Perhaps nowhere is this more evident than in Rousseau, who sums up in his very being the moral dilemmas of science for science's sake. He believed in reason, yet he lashed out against the pathetic trust in the blind following of science that still mesmerizes us today.

15

Rousseau more than anyone else saw the disparity between the new intellectual faddism and the social disruptions and continuing abasement of the mass of men. Science had become a fad, degenerated from the vision and powers of its earlier leaders. It promised automatic advance, no matter how meager and ritualistic the efforts of the throng of its second-rate devotees. In Rousseau's own words, the uncritical pursuit of science might actually waste good talent:

> Someone who would all his life be a...second-rate geometrician, might have become a great producer of fabrics... Man's nature subtly adapts itself to the objects of his preoccupation, and it is the great opportunities that make great men (1750, p. 159).[1]

Rousseau is not saying that science is bad—hadn't he once gone down on his knees to kiss the threshold of the illustrious Buffon's doorway?—only that it is trifling when not put into talented and responsible hands, in the service of the people. The pride and self-sufficiency of the philosophers and scientists was unmerited if it derived from the pursuit of science for its own sake. For Rousseau the vital issue was very clear: science was meaningful only if it subserved virtue and morality. Knowledge must support the social order; "a sure and clear formation of the moral world must precede the construction of the scientific world" (Cassirer, 1955, p. 273).

It seems that the more the sciences developed, the more these anxieties grew, not for Rousseau alone, but among many of those who were concerned about the breakup of the old traditions (cf. Leming, 1952). Rousseau gave expression to one of the basic underlying anxieties of this age of rapid change, exaggerated hopes, increasingly fragmented thinking. Why were the stirrings so anguished, why Rousseau's attacks so heartfelt? What exactly was the problem of this time that these thinkers could react to it so totally and so emotionally? It was the problem of Leibnitz and Kant, the problem of science divorced from life, the same one that we are struggling with today. But then, why are we so comparatively stoic about it, even after Hiroshima? The Lisbon earthquake, after all, was followed by Voltaire's *Candide* to show that this was surely not the best of all possible worlds; we have had no work of comparable stature and biting self-scrutiny after Hiroshima. Is it only because there is only one Voltaire?

Perhaps. But the reason could be more thoroughgoing than that. The fact is that 350 years ago, at the end of the decline of the medieval world view, man still knew right from wrong. If he belonged to the minority that distrusted the simple enjoinders of the Church, if he did not believe in the Fall, in the inevitability of Sin, in the whole theodicy of why God permitted evil in the world—if he had grown away from all this, still he was vitally concerned with the loss; he was personally very sensitive to the problem of good and evil. By the time of Hiroshima, it is fair to say, not only was the medieval theodicy long since dead, but the burning problem of good and evil was remote from most people's lives. At best, overcoming evil was a "job to be done"—someone else's job; it was not a way of life for everyone to heed. And how could it be otherwise?—the world was so matter-of-fact. In the missile age man finally crowned Newton's beginning, and completely secularized the stars; now we yearn toward the moon in order to plant a national banner. The external world is deprived of all inherent meaningfulness; and with the philosopher Sartre we all feel some nausea. Man having lost the capacity to marvel, it was inevitable that good and evil should have become merely an affair of technical calculation. As we know, the great prophet of this outcome, of the bureaucratization of good and evil, was Max Weber; he saw that man's own organized efficiency would threaten to degrade him completely.

In the medieval cosmology, as we noted in Chapter One, man had a psychologically important place. Evil existed in the world because of Adam's Fall, and that was that. But God took all this to heart, and exercised a Providential direction over man's salvation. Even if the earth was a decaying, ugly, and hostile place, man's ultimate happiness was not affected. Thus, the idea of the decay of nature, which held sway from the late medieval times through the sixteenth and seventeenth centuries, was itself a moral force, and had moral significance (Harris, 1949, pp. 1–3). That is to say, one could be an optimist even though the world was going to pot. By contrast, in the troubled times of our Age of Terror, when instant annihilation is a constant possibility and background anxiety, we can see what we have lost with the loss of the medieval cosmology. As someone remarked, in Saint Augustine's time the best thing that could have happened to worthy souls would have been atomic annihilation so they could leave the blighted earth and mount up to heaven and claim their rewards. But today, as the late Pope John's Encyclicals make clear, even the Church has become this-worldly.

With Bacon and his followers something strange occurred in the revaluation of nature. When they denied the cyclical nature of change and turned the cosmos into a harmonious mechanism that had timeless beauty, they actually attacked the Christian morality. By rehabilitating nature they weakened morals. The idea of decay had kept man's mind focused on the primary value of otherworldliness, and it thus kept to the fore the notion of Providential concern about man. It didn't matter that the world was accursed, so long as it was the center of God's preoccupation. The new Newtonianism, by rehabilitating nature, gravely weakened the old cosmology. If the world was physically better off, then psychologically man was not. This whole reversal was the source of Leibnitz' comment on the rashness of nonreligious optimism. As we shall see below, the French Enlightenment completed the destruction *by actively attacking* the idea of Providence; the job was so complete that they placed themselves in a moral dead end, from which they could only extricate themselves by painfully and gropingly fashioning a science of man in society—but this is getting ahead of the story.

The central problem posed by the Newtonian revolution was not long in making itself felt. This was a momentous new problem; it is still ours today—so we must realize what a formidable new challenge was thrown out to the mind of man. I mean of course *the problem of a new theodicy*. If the new nature was so regular and beautiful, then why was there evil in the human world? Man needed a new theodicy, but this time he could not put the burden on God. Something entirely different had to be done to explain evil in the world, a theodicy without Divine intervention. The new theodicy had to be a natural one, a "secular" one. The challenge was all the greater because the human mind was not prepared for such ingenuity: the idea of a "secular" theodicy was a contradiction in words and in emotions. Yet it describes exactly what was needed: an "anthropodicy." Evil had to be explained as existing in the world apart from God's intention or justification. Furthermore, as God was gradually eliminated from science as an explanatory principle, the need for a complete theodicy also finally vanished. There could be no sensible explanation for *all* the evil to which life is subject, apart from a belief in God—certainly no explanation that mere mortals could attain. Consequently, man had to settle for a new *limited* explanation, an anthropodicy which would cover only *those evils that allow for human remedy*. The only way to achieve this new explanation was gradually to shift the burden from reliance on God's will to the belief in man's understanding and powers. This was a shift that was to occupy the whole Enlightenment, and it was not accomplished easily. In fact, it is still not accomplished today. The separate national traditions each had their own kind of ingenuity, and fashioned quite different notions of "secular" theodicy, or "anthropodicy." Thus there emerged quite different types of "social science," which we know as the French, English, and German schools.

At first this search took the form of a new "reading" of nature to try to discover the sources of evil, but this did not mark any sharp break with medieval practice. The shift was merely from God-centered to man-centered interpretations. In the Middle Ages man read nature to try to divine how the various creatures served God's purpose. In the Enlightenment they likewise read nature, but to try to discern what *man* should do. They tried to find "natural laws" to which man should conform. In one sense, the new worship of science was really a new way of *finding support* in God's nature. After all, weren't the rationalistic-deductive and mathematic-geometric methods God's divine gift to man? And wasn't the new experimental-descriptive method the key to nature's secrets? We can see that the historical tradition was unbroken in one key sense: man never ceased to seek independence from helplessness and natural caprice (cf. Randall, 1940, Chapter 11, esp. pp. 276–279). He had to find new meaning in nature.

THE PASSIVE "SECULAR" THEODICY

But this raised another problem. How much active interpretation could man allow himself to assume? Locke's *Essay*, for example, by showing that man had no inner depraved nature, still left open the question about why some people were depraved—did God allow the environment to cause this? (C. Becker, 1959, p. 66). The questioning was anguished. Why isn't everything natural, even custom? Pascal asked. And, if customs contain evil, is it the fault of custom, or is it man who is "out of harmony"? Pope was particularly sensitive to the possibilities of human meddling in customs and morals—so he decided there was no evil in the world that man could or should do anything about. The famous phrase "whatever is, is right," did not reflect blind callousness, but deep-seated anxieties about morality. This was a way of saving the new natural theodicy, without taking the radical step to human agency—it was a "Cosmic Toryism" to use Basil Willey's fine phrase. Man simply reads the world for new clues to morality, and what he finds will lead him to conform to it. One of the most succinct summaries of this view is Lovejoy's, and he is worth quoting in full here:

> ... for two centuries the efforts made for improvement and correction in beliefs, in institutions, and in art had been, in the main, controlled by the assumption that, in each phase of his activity, man should conform as nearly as possible to a standard conceived as universal, uncompli-

cated, immutable, uniform for every rational being. The Enlightenment was, in short, an age devoted, at least in its dominant tendency, to the simplification and standardization of thought and life—to their standardization by means of their simplification ... The struggle to realize this supposed purpose of nature, the general attack upon the *differentness* of men and their opinions and valuations and institutions—this, with the resistance to it and the eventual revulsion against it, was the central and dominating fact in the intellectual history of Europe from the late sixteenth to the late eighteenth century" (1960a, pp. 292–293).

In other words, it seems as though the Enlightenment was trying to order the chaotically pluralistic world of rapid social change, the breakup of the medieval world, in a purely formal, intellectual way. And, for the most part, we have been continuing this very tradition: our medical reductionist research into human behavior has about as much relevance to our ponderous social problems as the atomistic psychology of the eighteenth century had to theirs. We are still trying to standardize and simplify life by stressing conformity to what we find. Instead, we should be shaping the world to our own imaginative purposes.

Thus, when we criticize the complacent and confident Enlightenment rationalism that Hume and Rousseau struck out against, we are really condemning its passivity, as Rousseau later did. His great importance as a figure of that time stems partly from the deep dissatisfaction that he expressed with the Enlightenment, precisely because of its *passive acceptance of "reading" nature by simply developing reason.* Rousseau saw that this intellectualistic "puzzle solving" was no way to approach the dilemmas of human morality. Both he and Hume stand out of the eighteenth century, because neither of them accepted its reigning fad. Both were to deal it death blows, each in his own unique way: Hume with merciless logic; Rousseau with poetic images. But both were looking for the same thing, for a way of overcoming evil. Ordinarily we learn that Hume "destroyed the notion of causality" when he showed that we cannot really know what is going on in nature. But what Hume did was even more devastating: by showing how subjective and uncritical all our perceptions and feelings are, how they are hopelessly separated from all that is going on in the external world, Hume did nothing less than *destroy the naïve rationalist trust in reading nature for moral precepts.*

Did Spinoza in his *Ethics* say that the concept of evil is a human invention, and that therefore morality is a human problem? Well, Hume showed unanswerably that mankind was stuck with this problem in its entirety.

This attack on the passive posture of reading nature in the service of morality had one definite result: it pointed to a new activism, a pragmatism: one now had to actively *correct* reigning evils. Most important of all, this new pragmatism shifted the arena of action from reductionist psychology and physical medicine; it was a pragmatism that would focus on society itself. And it shifted the problem of morality to mankind at large, and not only to specially gifted or strong persons, where it was confined with Spinoza, and even Kant.

THE TRANSITION TO AN ACTIVE "SECULAR" THEODICY

We can better understand this whole development to activism by glancing at what actually happened to Hume, and to Diderot. One popular image of Hume is that he was a cold, cynical dissector of human folly and egotism, and yet not himself immune to the basic human ambitions. But I like Carl Becker's more sympathetic portrayal of him as a man concerned with the problem of morality, and sharing the "eager didactic impulse" of his age.[2] Hume's philosophical speculations, as Carl Becker noted, "left him quite without illusion . . . since they led him to the conclusion that the ultimate cause of things 'has no more regard to good above ill than to heat above cold' " (1959, p. 38). But being without illusion is just what the thinker needs in order to come to grips with the dilemmas of man in society. Hume was obliged to seek more positive approaches to the problem of morality precisely because he could not push it to any positive conclusion on the philosophical level. The result was the new moral pragmatism, that went beyond Jenyns' and Pope's Cosmic Toryism. Hume took the "Whatever is, is right" thesis, and restated it, so that it became the foundation for the utilitarian philosophy: Whatever is, is *relatively* good because relatively *useful*.

We shall see later on that this utilitarian pragmatism had both strengths and weaknesses, and its weakness was its accommodation to the social world, even while pretending to reform it. The utilitarian dress only made Cosmic Toryism *seem* pragmatic, as Bentham's failure was later to attest. The English did not really want to change the basic structures of their society. But Hume's program, like that of the

Encyclopedia, offered the English an inspiring vision, whether they wanted to see it or not. Let us listen to his own words from his famous *Treatise of Human Nature*:

> It is evident, that all the sciences have a relation, greater or less, to human nature; and that, however wide any of them may seem to run from it, they still return by one passage or another. [We must] march directly up to the capital or centre of these sciences, to human nature itself; which being once masters of, we may everywhere else hope for an easy victory. From this station we may extend our conquests over all those sciences. . . . There is no question of importance, whose decision is not comprised in the science of man; and there is none, which can be decided with any certainty, before we become acquainted with that science. In pretending, therefore, to explain the principles of human nature, we in effect propose a complete system of the sciences, built on a foundation almost entirely new, and the only one upon which they can stand with any security . . . the science of man is the only solid foundation for the other sciences (1739, pp. xii–xiii).

When Hume lamented the delay of the new sciences in coming to grips with man, he compared the century lag from Bacon to Locke and Shaftesbury with the original lag from Thales to Socrates. It is evident what Hume was after: to complete the Socratic search for a new secular morality. His *Treatise* was just what its subtitle indicated— an attempt to introduce the experimental method of reasoning into moral subjects. It would do for the science of man what Newton's *Principia* had done for physics. The passions could be studied like any natural phenomena, for were they not also linked with their objects and with one another?

We will see again and again how various thinkers styled themselves after Newton, Galileo, or Bacon. I am purposely pausing each time to note this self-classification, because in Chapter Fourteen I outline my own retrospective summary of the development of the science of man, using the same analogy of figures in the physical sciences. In this way we can perhaps more exactly compare our present perspective on the problem with the views that each of the innovators held in his time. Also, it is important to note this self-designation because it reflects the scientific optimism of the time, and shows the explicit consciousness of the immaturity of the human sciences.

Today we rarely use these single-founder appellations in historically reconstructing the science of man. On the one hand, we have learned that a science is much too complex a development to take definitive shape in the mind of any one man, or at any one point in history. On the other, we seem to have thrown up our hands: we have no clear idea of what the science of man now is, or what it should be—we have not been able so far to trace any agreed history of its exact identity; we think we have arrived, but we are not sure how, or where.

Thus it was easy for Hume, in this age of unlimited scientific horizons, to imagine himself the Newton of the moral sciences. He aimed to repeat Newton in the moral sphere, by finding laws like those of the principle of gravity. The associationist psychology of the time set itself the ambitious task of studying how morality was deterministically developed, according to regular and universal principles of human nature; hopefully, it could be broken down to its simplest constituents. The vision was a grand one, and although the reductionist atomistic psychology was wrong, the problem remained—as we shall see—until Freud.

Here was Hume's program of moral pragmatism—utilitarianism—based on a man-centered science, and working with regular, lawful principles of human nature. And here too was his dilemma: he wanted a morality based on a simple principle like deterministic association; but, unlike a Hartley, for example, he could not be satisfied with this fragmentation, this breaking of man down into simple compartmentalized elements. Like Rousseau he struck out for the whole man; he saw that logic is an illusion that dupes instinct; he condemned reflection because it paralyzes action (Halévy, 1960, p. 11). And Hume, as we noted earlier, shared the "eager didactic impulse" of his time: he saw that associationist reductionism would lead to skepticism and inactivity, to the worship of reason over emotion—and, like Rousseau, he could admit neither. The result of all this was that Newtonianism in the moral sciences failed to satisfy him; man needed a free and active morality; and the slavish aping of Newtonian methods and concepts simply would not do. It was only in the nineteenth century that thinkers became more comfortable with reductionism and determinism; but by that time the moral meaning of the science of man was being lost.

If we look now at Diderot, we see a problem similar to the one that troubled Hume—how to get a new scientific morality in the Newtonian world. The new accent was on naturalism, not on supernaturalism: man had to be understood as an emergent in nature. But then, this placed man firmly in a deterministic, physical world; as a part of this world, man's action would be determined beyond his control. And, since society too is natural, it too is determined, and . . . whatever is, is right. On the philosophical level Diderot was inclined to accept this—but the price was too great on the level of morality since it left no room for free human acts; and Diderot was very moral (C. Becker, 1935, pp. 280 ff.). He wanted to read morality into nature, but Newtonian mechanics would not allow it. It was the same dilemma that Montesquieu was in: the philosophy of objective determinism was very compelling, but if one accepted it there was no way to preserve a subjective morality for man, a freedom of the moral world (Vartanian, 1953, p. 316). The whole new program of science was at stake because without a synthesis between determinism and freedom man would be no different from other natural phenomena, and the recentering of the sciences on man would make no sense.

We have already noted Diderot's proposal that the sciences be centered on man, and we have also seen how similar it was to Hume's. Now we must note something further, namely, that Diderot's revolt against the Newtonian world picture was double-edged. Not only did it place man at the center of the physical world; but at the same time it saw that mechanistic science could not allow for the primacy of free, moral man. And it was with this second edge that Diderot dealt the crippling blow to the Newtonian mystique. For one thing, he downgraded mathematics, the queen of the sciences, by accusing it of falsifying nature since it deprived bodies of their *qualitative* existence. Diderot attacked the very stronghold of the new scientific fetishism, and made a new and shattering proposal: that science had to have a *threefold* object, and not a *single*, mechanistic one: existence, qualities, utility—this was the comprehensive realm of a mature science (Gillispie, 1959, pp. 261–262). Little wonder that Sainte-Beuve called Diderot "the most synthetic genius of his century" (Vartanian, 1953, p. 316). His vision of a mature science—one that unites quality, morality, and quantity—is one that only now we are beginning to comprehend. Goethe later continued the attack against Newton for leaving quality out of science, and generations of "true" scientists have softly chuckled at the poet's perversity (see Heller's excellent essay, 1959).

THE NEW "SECULAR" THEODICY

Diderot did not complete the transition, he only posed the problem comprehensively. He remained, like Hume, in a peculiar dilemma; he saw the need for a new secular morality, but could propose no practical solution; he had a proper vision of the broadness of the new man-based science, but could not suggest its peculiar constructs. Thus, both Hume and Diderot typify the problem of critical reason that is divorced from a program of action. At heart they were among the first modern moral pragmatists, and they were subject to the same criticism that their later descendant, Dewey, was to encounter: a pragmatic approach to morals has to start out from *some* moral imperatives—what were they to be? Dewey could have more courage because, as we shall see, social science had already pointed out many secular evils that man could adjust. But in Diderot's and Hume's time, to be a moral pragmatist was equivalent to stepping into an existential void. They had no compelling moral precepts to support them, and the problem had to remain at the stage of compromise: How far can reason be pushed before we have to fall back on revealed truth (C. Becker, 1959, p. 86)? Diderot was obliged to retain the belief that men *naturally* form judgments of right and wrong (cf. Crocker, 1963, pp. 198 ff.). And the utilitarian philosophy that stemmed from Hume remained a moral pragmatism that exempted the pre-existing state—just as Machiavelli's was obliged to do. The point is, simply, that moral relativity had to stop somewhere, and support something solid and beneficial that itself was beyond question. All these early modern moral pragmatists were up against this same problem: how to be wholly pragmatic and still leave some kind of ordered social life.

Yet, this was hardly the foundation upon which a thoroughgoing "secular" theodicy could be built. The French wanted flatly to get rid of the notion of God as an active, solicitous, Providential agent in the world; they were not prepared to compromise with any remnants of the medieval belief in Providence. Having done this, they could then build a new "secular" theodicy, but the question still had to be—how? This was a problem that existed throughout the century that extended from Saint-Pierre to Rousseau. Carl Becker says that after 1750 a certain sentimentalism started to pervade the air (1959, pp. 41-42). I wonder whether this resulted partly from the felt strain between cognitive powers and the power to do—a tension that we would now label in Deweyan terms as a dichotomy between "knowing" and "doing"? Rousseau, who tried to carry his beliefs into action, went to idiosyncratic personal extremes, and we might expect that his contemporaries would be appalled at his eagerness to bring about active changes in the world, on what seemed quixotic premises. But hadn't they also guffawed earlier at the projects of Saint-Pierre?

THE IDEA OF PROGRESS

The French thinkers bridged the gulf between reason and action in two very distinctive ways. The first was the gradual evolution of the secular "Idea of Progress." This proved to be a primary component of the new "secular" theodicy. It had been in the making for some time, and grew partly out of the same general protest against Newtonian mechanism that we have outlined so far.

We noted earlier that the medieval habit of "reading" nature to divine God's purpose was carried over into the Enlightenment, transformed into a reading of nature in order to find out how *man* should act. In a similar way, the idea of progress did not spring full-blown onto the Enlightenment scene, without antecedents. In the Middle Ages God progressed toward the perfect, and carried mankind along with him. The idea of progress existed in this form, but it was a passive creed. Instead of man pulling the strings via science, God pulled them via the creatures of His creation. The Middle Ages' faith in God was a faith in the perfectibility of nature according to God's peculiar vision (Randall, 1940, p. 100). The Enlightenment, in other words, had to turn a passive God-centered credo into an active, man-centered one.[3] In still another way, then, the Enlightenment sought to keep the unique position that man had enjoyed in the medieval hierarchy, while radically changing the theological accent. How else could it launch its New Athenian Celebration?

At first glance it might seem that the Enlightenment reacted to the Newtonian devaluation of man by re-establishing contact with the medieval tradition, and adopting a ready-made idea of human uniqueness. In large part, of course, man draws conceptual inspiration from the past. But the French could no longer allow themselves to formulate basic notions in theological terms. When Diderot and the Encyclopedists reacted against Newton and recentered the sciences on man, the distinctively human kept its superior valuation, but this time in a wholly secular way. It was then very logical for Turgot to contrast man and matter, and find a special distinction for man, a distinction that matter does not have—namely, the idea of infinite and steady perfectibility, constant change rather than sameness; Newton's scientific objects certainly lacked this. The Enlightenment idea of progress, then, was arrived at by *empirical* contrast with contemporary science; the medieval idea of progress was simply metaphysical fiat.

Thus was born a secular idea of progress that rehabilitated man in the face of nature, much as Bacon had rehabilitated nature in the face of the late medieval doctrines of decay and cyclical change (Harris, 1949, p. 132). Furthermore, this idea of progress made the science of man as progressive as the rest of the sciences, including it in Bacon's vision of scientific progress. In one sense the French were *forced* to devise the idea of active progress: having rid themselves of the notion of God as an active, solicitous, Providential agent in the world, there could be no one who would want the world to remain as it is. And since the French were committed to changing the abuses of the *Ancien Régime,* the new secular theodicy had to be progressive.

The evolution of the idea of active progress was of course not an overnight development. The change from the passive optimism of rationalism to the progressive optimism of activism could not take place unless there was first built up a current of disillusionment. We saw above that during this transitional stage thinkers like Hume and Diderot were caught in a frustrating bind. Only a fully developed idea of progress could unplug the situation. But what were the components of a fully developed idea of progress? Only when we cut apart this problem can we see the truly great acquisitions of this period, that form the basics of a science of man.

In the first place, progress could not be conceived as the progress of reason alone. Again, this is the dilemma in which we left Hume and Diderot. Reason had to be taken off her perch on the abstract level, where she towered divorced from the real problems of man in society. Only in this way could criticism hope to formulate the basis for a new morality. But how to go about this? It is important for us to note that, with the exception of Rousseau, the Enlightenment thinkers never could quite succeed in bringing reason down to earth in talking about man *in* society and *in* history. Several lines of thinking provided the basis for doing this—Vico, for example, Helvétius and Holbach; but it was not until the cataclysm of the Revolution that the idea of progress could be seen fully as a problem of social change.

Vico first advanced his epochal *New Science* in 1725, and considered himself the Galileo-Newton of the human sciences. He wanted to create a science of human society that would do for the "world of nations" what Galileo and Newton had done for the world of nature. He admitted that the natural-law theorists and Hobbes had tried to found a new science, but he held that they had failed precisely because they modeled their efforts on the other science. (How can we fail to be thrilled today by such a superb and courageous insight?) Vico

considered his own efforts successful because he found the true key
to the new science in a painstaking restudy of Homer, and of the
historical development of human institutions. What was Vico's great
advance and the core of his system? It was the radical new idea that
the social world is the work of man, and that the earliest layer of
human culture is that of myth and poetry. In other words, Vico put
his finger right on the pulse of human novelty—on the culturally
created nature of human institutions (1744). Long before Auguste
Comte, Vico offered a three-stage theory of the progress of reason.
And before Diderot he saw that the sciences should be centered on
man, specifically on man's mind as a creation of history. Thus he was
the direct forerunner of Herder, Hegel, Dilthey, Croce—down to
Huizinga in our time (cf. Flint, 1904, pp. 128–129).

Vico's work supported a full, man-centered activism. If human
institutions and beliefs were self-styled, why should man stand still?
The influence of Vico on French thought is still unclear (cf. Fisch and
Bergin, 1944, pp. 72 ff.), but the French never needed Vico's discovery of culture in order to have a theoretical mandate for human
manipulation: thinkers such as Condillac and Helvétius had arrived
at a purely environmentalist explanation of human behavior, using
Locke's *tabula rasa* model of human character and perception. By
the time of the Revolution the problem could be taken completely out
of the metaphysical realm, where it still rested with Vico, and placed
squarely on an environmental and manipulative basis. It was no
longer necessary to confine one's efforts to the study of history; one
could begin actively to change society. But in its long development
from Bacon, Fontenelle, Turgot, to Condorcet, the secular idea of
progress remained somehow disembodied from the institutions of
society. It was the shock of the Revolution itself which connected the
idea of progress firmly with the possibility of social change. With all
their beginning work in history and sociology (Montesquieu, Voltaire,
Vico), and psychology (Condillac, Helvétius), the Continental thinkers of the Enlightenment could not quite bring the idea of progress
down from the abstract level of reason and turn it into a broad
social-science concept that would refer distinctively to the progress of
human institutions, of man immersed in an ever-changeable society.
That is, none of the thinkers but one.

THE EQUALLY CRUCIAL NOTION OF AN IDEAL-TYPOLOGY

The idea of progress provided only one potential pillar for the new
secular morality. But, taken by itself, Condorcet's final expression of

the idea, in the shadow of the guillotine, seems like a lonely, consoling and very personal hope. On the level of reason alone, the idea is not very convincing: it could never lead to an option for a new morality. Man has literally to squeeze his morality out of actual human suffering, and not out of the dictates of reason. Thus even the slow discovery of history and culture, of the formation of man by his environment, of the changeability of human institutions, of the desirability and possibility of progress—none of this was enough to constitute a critical, moralistic canon. And so we must go back to Rousseau, who gave the idea of progress "moral body" by tearing at the mask of conventional morality with all the equipment that his person and his talents disposed. Thus it was to be Rousseau who earned, from Kant, the title of "Newton of the moral world" (Cassirer, 1955, p. 280).

What exactly did Kant see in Rousseau that made him deserving of such an august title? What had Rousseau done to give morality the status of a basic science? It was clear that Newtonian science was based on a firm law; consequently, in order to be a Newton of the moral world one would have to find the law *within human nature*, on which a new scientific morality could be based. Furthermore, it would have to be a peculiar kind of "law." It would have to be a law which showed that man as he now was, was not man as he should be; it had to provide a standard of criticism and the hope of betterment. In a word, it had to hold up to view a constant image of man by which he could be measured against the present. Rousseau provided just this by setting up an ideal-typical "primitive" man, living in a "state of nature." Thus, at one stroke, he achieved what Diderot wanted and had glimpsed, but could not bring himself decisively to do: he brought reason down from its advanced abstractions, and applied it to *an analytically scientific problem*: the problem of showing what human nature *really is*, so as to provide a sound program for a regenerated society. The discrepancy between reason and action was overcome in the only way it can be overcome—by becoming analytically scientific, and finding an ideal model *upon which to predicate new moral action*. This would give the much-needed pragmatic moral imperative upon which to begin action. And, what is best, one would have to fall back upon nothing absolute or unquestioned, but could follow the very canons of science itself.

The ideal of the primitive or of the pastoral life has a habit of recurring throughout human history, from classical times on, whenever man is not happy with the present; it expresses a natural longing for an uncomplicated life, for the pleasures of the peaceful forest and countryside (cf. Haydn, 1950, chap. 8; Huizinga, 1957, p. 108; 1959). Rousseau has been accused of this simple romantic use of the idea, of reviving an unreal notion, so as to relieve his own maladjustment and discontent with the times. He has also been taken to task for either ignoring or not reading Hume when he held to the idea of a "social contract" that Hume more than anyone else so effectively demolished.

But it is very clear that Rousseau never held to the idea of the primitive, or the social contract, as "real happenings." He used these ideas exactly as Plato had used his *Republic*, and as Renaissance thinkers did later: as a way of formulating a moral critique. For Rousseau, these ideas were what they had to be in order to found a new scientific morality: they were "ideal-types" which held up a new image of man. As Rousseau declared, in his use of the term *"l'homme de la nature"* he did not aim to make man a savage relegated to the woods, but rather a man truly fit for free and equal society— what we would today call an "autonomous" man: responsible, strong, a source of spontaneous values and not automatic social ones (1762, pp. 306, 606, and Intro., pp. v–vi, and note *e*.). Rousseau did not have to read Hume on the fallacy of the social contract simply because he did not take this as a real, historical event. He saw the place of fictions in the science of man a full hundred years before Vaihinger. Rousseau may have leaned on what had mostly been sentimental ideals, but it is supremely important for us to realize that he introduced them at a time when they would make *scientific* sense, as they could not have done earlier, even at the time of the Renaissance. Linked with the idea of progress and the directiveness of human reason, Rousseau's notions on the "state of nature" and the "social contract" could thus serve as a "prospective prophecy" (Cassirer, 1961a, p. 10): it showed society *not* as it *had* been, but *"tel qu'il peut et doit devenir"* ("as it can and ought to become"), as Alfred Fouillée understood long ago (Fouillée, quoted in Merz, 1914, vol. 4, p. 524 note). It was a *"critique indirecte du présent"* upon which to base a manipulative science of man. Rousseau saw that a science of man was a science that had as its primary task that of changing society, so that it became a product of human freedom rather than of blind necessity (Cassirer, 1955, p. 272). Many thinkers in the nineteenth century understood exactly the kind of ideal-real science that Rousseau championed; but in the early part of this century we lost this vision, and so Rousseau had to be rediscovered in his original meaning—largely by Lovejoy and Ernst Cassirer, and now by the new anthropologists (cf. Lévi-Strauss, 1961, pp. 389–392; Diamond, 1964, p. xxii). Today there is no longer any mistake about what Rousseau meant. Man, instead of continually and blindly following his passions in the social sphere, could begin to exercise free direction over human affairs. Thus he would eliminate the last obstacle to true and full human freedom, once and for all, by choosing and *creating* the kind of world he wanted to live in. Rousseau joins Saint-Pierre as one of the first since Plato to see what "social science" really must mean. From Rousseau the ideal-type passed to the great humanist Wilhelm von Humboldt, to Kant, and on to Feuerbach in the nineteenth century. There could no longer be any question but that it belonged to man in society to liberate himself, to move from the individually actual to the socially possible. In von Humboldt's words: "The purpose of comparative anthropology is to measure out in their whole ideality the possible differences of human nature or—which is the same thing—to investigate how the human ideal type, which no individual is ever adequate to represent, can be represented by many" (1963, p. 110). The science of man had assumed its indelible humanistic form.

CONCLUSION

With Rousseau the early Enlightenment was capped and we can now judge with striking clarity what the Enlightenment achieved. It laid the basis for nothing less than a fully "secular" theodicy: a program for analyzing and remedying the evils that befall man in society. What began as a heartfelt stirring against the ascendancy of Newtonianism, and as a protest for a place for man in a mechanistic and perhaps Godless universe, ended with a new "secular" theodicy to replace the lost medieval one (see Cassirer, 1954, pp. 76–77). The shift to order, progress, and human purposiveness is thus all of a logical piece with the ultimate breakdown of the medieval cosmology. Vico and Diderot saw how to make science humanly significant, and they performed the first "Copernican shift" for the human sciences, by centering all the sciences on man. This recentering on a science of man then had to be elaborated to take account of the social nature of human behavior: the science of man had to become a science of man *in society*.

To meet this need, the threefold idea was gradually evolved: *liberty, progress,* and the *ideal-type*—an interdependent conceptual scheme that put progress under the control of reason and that brought reason down to the happenings of the real world. It cannot be over-stressed that the basic triad, progress, liberty, and moral ideal, are inseparable notions (Delvaille, 1910, p. 731); they establish the true character of the science of man as a special science wholly different from Newtonianism. They link the individual to social life in a non-deterministic and open way: they declare that the science of man is a science that must be based on the possibility of freedom. They thus link science inextricably with democracy and possibility, as we in the West have always known; but at the same time they announce that a science of man in society cannot do without the guidance of imagination and vision, of planning and control, purposive experimental manipulation and reasoned intervention—as we so constantly try to overlook. Thus, this simple triadic notion is the indispensable framework for an analytic and activist science of man. The science of man, in other words, as the Enlightenment gradually realized, had this peculiar character that none of the other sciences had: it was a critical, "projective," moral science, an anthropodicy within the vision of man and potentially under his control.

We will see how much this framework is still ours today, how we have to fit our accumulated knowledge into it. We will also see why it was not adequate, in its early Enlightenment form, to command the scientific allegiance it needed in order to become an agreed paradigm for the human sciences. For now it is enough to hail Rousseau as the first critic of alienation, the first unmasker of culture, who established the basic character of a science of man that a succession of later thinkers were to elaborate into a superb and compelling edifice. Today, thanks to the Enlightenment and two hundred years of accumulated effort and ingenuity, we have what might be called "a full-field theory of human alienation." Rousseau's idea of the primitive was sorely inadequate and largely erroneous: it now seems like a Ptolemaic model—which is just as it should be in the advance of a science. Let us now see what the nineteenth century did with this heritage.

CHAPTER THREE

THE GREAT MORAL GROPING
OF THE NINETEENTH CENTURY:
The Systematic, Scientific Attempts
to Design a New Morality

*A new science must be pursued historically, the only thing to
be done being to study in chronological order the different works
that have contributed to the progress of the science.*

AUGUSTE COMTE

There were many reasons why the basic Enlightenment framework
for a science of man in society was not put into operation. One reason
was the immense cataclysm of the French Revolution. It had an effect
upon social activism abroad similar to that of the Stalinist period
in our time. It was easy to conclude that if an activist optimism
could so miscarry, cause so much bloodshed, dislocation, and misery,
and still leave society palpably no better off than previously, then it
would be better to be passive in the face of even serious injustice.
The "science of man" seemed like an impostor, or a devil. We are
familiar with the climate of opinion at that time, with Burke, Carlyle,
de Bonald, de Maistre, and the others who protested against the
cataclysmic change—a change they thought was given its focus by
destructive critical intellect. Even the great Auguste Comte misunderstood Rousseau, and scorned him for the disruptive effect of
his ideas.

I think it is safe to say that in the judgment of history the
catastrophes of the nineteenth and twentieth centuries can hardly be
laid at the feet of the Enlightenment. They were groping for a reasoned
moral code which they hoped would free man. The failure of reason

33

that is so much lamented today is not that reason itself became a tyranny over the human spirit: rather, the lamentable failure of our times is that we have not given reason enough sway in human affairs. We are still stretched out upon the rack of uncritically functioning social institutions; which means that we have never really heeded the Enlightenment program. Let us look at some of these men and their visions, so that we may judge how great the promise was that ushered in our modern epoch.

ADAM SMITH

Like Hume, Adam Smith too saw himself as the Newton of the moral world (Barnes and Becker, 1961, vol. 2, p. 530). He saw life as a moral affair, and tried to come to grips with it as a whole. The system he presented was really that, a system, in two great parts: it tried to show man "in the round," in terms of all his motivations. Thus, the first part of his system, the *Theory of Moral Sentiments*, laid stress on the sentiment of sympathy which held society together; the second part, *The Wealth of Nations*, accented man's propensity to barter and exchange for accumulation and gain. But for Smith this two-sided picture was not in conflict; everything was under the sway of a higher regulative principle, the principle of justice as Smith conceived it (cf. Merz, 1914, vol. 4, p. 458 and note).

It was posterity that forgot the roundness of Smith's system, and placed the accent on economic man. To Smith, economics represented merely a section of life, a logical detail in an overriding moral process. Like anthropologists today, Smith understood that economics was enmeshed in a larger web of social relationships. The economic philosophy of laissez-faire was merely an arbitrary separation of half of Smith's system—the human barter motives—which he thought might be allowed to run their natural course without the historically crippling restrictions of mercantilism. And the famous "invisible hand of God" that guided the whole fabric of society was something very real to Smith, who believed in Divine Providence; it was not a cynical apology for immoral economics.

It was Smith's followers who lost sight of the fundamentally moral nature of human action. So much so that in atomizing economics they were led to object to Smith's introducing social dimensions into the economic domain. Smith's separations had been provisional; the systematic, methodical, and strictly deductive approach was the work of his followers—especially Ricardo. They were the ones who were prone to analytic separation and deduction, and they separated economics more and more from the larger context into which Smith had placed it. As in today's world of fractionated science, this gave rise to an enormous literature which tried to systematize and introduce logical rigor into the new discipline. Ricardo had a real talent for it, and attained great celebrity on the basis of it (cf. Merz, 1914, vol. 4, p. 459).

The whole subsequent development of economics in the nineteenth century was a reaction to the abstractions of Smith's followers. But Smith can hardly be held guilty for what was done to him by his successors—just as Comte, as we shall see, was not guilty of the narrow positivism that came to be championed in his name. Later sociologists such as Albion Small and Franklin Giddings placed a high value on Smith's effort at a systematic treatment of society: Giddings even agreed that Smith *was* the Newton of the moral sciences, on the sole basis of his theory of sympathy (which Giddings took over, and overworked, as the principle of "consciousness of kind"). Small, perhaps more than anyone else, attempted to reinterpret Smith in his larger moral dimensions, and wrote a whole book to show that Smith's moral philosophy had been suppressed for a century by the narrow-minded search for the production of economic goods alone. He went so far as to say that if Smith had been writing at the end of the century he would have been more disposed to the socialists than to the capitalists.

Smith's vision may have provided a framework and a stimulus to professional sociology, yet there is no question that it was wholly inadequate to the moral dilemmas of his time. The Smithians in England, as well as the Physiocrats in France, were quite beside the basic problems of their society: the Code of Nature would not automatically solve them.

JEREMY BENTHAM AND BRITISH DEDUCTIVE HEDONISM

What was needed was less trust and hope, and more pragmatic meddling; and this is where Bentham entered the scene with something new. He tried to unite abstract social analysis with a direct pragmatic approach to the ponderous problems of society in his time. Thus he borrowed from Smith and Hume, as well as the French. No exception to the time, he posed his candidacy for the honorific post of Newton of the moral world, applying one simple positive principle to a wealth of phenomena just as Newton applied the principle of gravity. Newton's principle of universal attraction was replaced by the principle of

utility based on the association of ideas. With Bentham, ideas that
had been at work for some time took definitive form as the Utilitarian
doctrine, and were applied consciously and systematically to judicial,
economic, and political matters. Bentham wanted to develop an
experimental, scientific approach to moral and legal theory, a practical
ethics in the spirit of Newtonian science, but one which would serve to
reform society in the profound crisis of that time (cf. Halévy, 1960).

Like Hume, Bentham wanted a science that would be man-
centered, but his option for man was very Continental: he had no
automatic respect for traditional English law and legal and social
fictions. As Graham Wallas succinctly put Bentham's thought: "We
have no duties to abstractions, like states, and constitutions, and
natural rights, and parties, and churches, but only to actual human
beings who can feel actual pains and pleasures" (1923, pp. 50–51).
Bentham carried on where Hume left off—the same man-based option,
the same respect for the passions over the abstractions of reason. There
would be, he thought, no obstacle to the reform of society in the
service of human happiness, once we had discovered a framework
for analysis and the operation of simple principles on which all men
would be able to agree. Science could thus frankly serve hedonism,
and transform itself into the art of social life.

Bentham's work is very significant for the history I am etching.
It was a superb vision. It pulls together the Newtonian method and
all the scientific optimism of the time, and applies them to the constructive analysis of moral, social problems. Yet it failed. In judicial
matters Utilitarianism was way ahead of its time—or rather, the laws
were very much behind; in economics it went along with the times;
in politics it lagged very much behind (Halévy, 1960, p. 4). The
philosophy petered out finally with John Stuart Mill, and we must be
clear about why it failed.

Experimental morality on the Newtonian model failed for
several reasons. In the first place, association psychology was a bogus
psychology, as the latter part of the nineteenth century was to find
out: the human mind does not function on the basis of atomistic
sensations. On the contrary, ideas are formative—they impose their
own order and partly dictate perception; they are not simply mechanically reactive to the sensations of the external world. In the second
place, as we shall see in another chapter, and as the debacle of Bentham's Panopticon venture proved, in order to apply simple deductive
principles to human behavior one has to know considerably more
about the range, forms, and dimensions of that behavior than was

possible to know at Bentham's time. To use simple hedonism as the basis for deductive prediction was bound to err because it was based on the shallowest understanding of the complexity of human behavior. Finally, and not least important, Utilitarianism was used in the service of liberal parliamentarianism, laissez-faire economy, and to secure the final formation of bourgeois society. The English had ultimately to make the same discovery as the French, namely, that the science of man cannot be in the service of a government representing vested-interest groupings. Parliamentary government was a spoils system, dividing up in a new way the benefits of the new Industrial Revolution. As Saint-Simon and Comte were to see very clearly, there is no science of man unless it is able to work actively counter to the vested-interested groupings of parliamentary society. The reason is simple: if the science of man takes man as a center, then government becomes peripheral in the service of man, and the most hallowed institutions must be adapted to the ever-new flow of knowledge about man. Scientists cannot be mere technicians in the employ of government, but must be powerful advisors, actively influencing it, as Saint-Pierre and Rousseau understood. Choosing to work within the parliamentary spoils system, Utilitarianism proved to be little more than a naïve hope, quickly abandoned when it proved to be "unrealistic"—unrealistic, that is, to the everyday needs of the times, which are never necessarily *man's* needs. Carlyle was among the first to thunder out its betrayal of the real task of total social reconstruction.

Thus, at the conclusion of this very brief sketch of the English venture to construct a Newtonian science of morality, we are brought right back to where Rousseau and the French left off. As systematic attempts, the English efforts all failed to provide a framework for a science of man. Hobbes began the tradition when he opted for the state over the individual, and used the metaphor of gravity to define moral determinism; Bentham and Mill ended it, with a failure supporting Hume's misgivings: any moral science worthy of the name must grant man the freest possible choice to change any social forms. We might also mention Carlyle's plan for total social reconstruction: a plan instrumented by a charismatic elite who would bathe the world with transcendental powers. (If only there *were* such an alternative!) Carlyle was the mighty conscience of his age, one of the few in England who saw clearly that the science of man was a moral problem. But whatever was good in his suggestions for reorganizing society was probably inspired by the Saint-Simonians—he was interested in their doctrine until his mentor Goethe called him off with alarm. Let us then turn to continuations of the French Enlightenment development in Saint-Simon, Comte, and Fourier.

NEW RESPONSES TO THE TWO REVOLUTIONS: THE GREAT FRENCH SYSTEMS

What was the world like in the decades after the French Revolution? What exactly were the problems raised by it, and by the related revolution—the industrial? We do well to lend a very attentive ear to accounts of the time because its problems are still ours. With the French Revolution some of the major institutions of feudal society came down with a crash, and the way was cleared for building industrial society on new governmental models. England had started this some time before France, but vast changes in industry and parliamentary democracy were to come during these same decades of the early nineteenth century. All the goods and most of the evils that we now enjoy were then trumpeted into the Western world. The goods were loudly heralded: the luxuriant variety of consumer commodities, freedom from tyranny, representative government—they promised a new world of human integrity, dignity, comfort, continuing novelty and excitement. The evils, on the other hand, were somewhat less apparent, and took some time before they became fully understood. *Homo sapiens*, who a short fifty years before had to be castigated for excessive pride, gradually was to lose anything to be really proud of—family and heredity, a feeling of one's place in history, a coherent and critical world view, most of the special craftsmanlike skills, an agreed preserve of inner dignity—it all gradually vanished with hiring lines, time-clocked work, efficiency, and dedication to production and profit. The critical intelligence of all but perhaps a privileged minority of scholars was gradually shaped by this new dedication, so that by and large proud *Homo sapiens* has today (in Western society) become the finicky peruser of brand names, the coveter and consumer of gadgets and junk.

The important freedom to be left alone, to acquire what one thought worthy of acquiring, to live the kind of life one designed for oneself—these never really had much of a chance, as Alexis de Tocqueville observed in the first revolutionary, postfeudal society— America. Today there are no longer even Thoreaus or Emersons to give us the needling enjoinder that we can and must be ourselves.

The rub is that man needs models of dignity and excellence if he is to pursue them. Without any specifications about things worthy to acquire, models really worthy to follow, things worth doing when alone, man was thrown back upon the collective myth: he was harangued from all sides to "enjoy, enjoy." He could only give in. As Chekhov lamented, the "art of enslaving" was being gradually refined. So was launched a race for status based largely on consumption of ever-new goods, a pride of ownership alone and not of excellence—the story is so well-known and so constantly aired that it seems hackneyed to repeat it. But it *is* our story. Worst of all is the gradual disengagement from the sense of community, from shared dedication to larger spiritual goods and common worthwhile goals, from real social challenges, and from the possibilities of continuing interhuman dignity. Responsibility, in a word, is gone. Modern man has learned that acquisitions are fundamentally unsatisfying; that freedom without the knowledge of real choice is a contradiction; that living for one's own pursuits, surrounded by others doing likewise, is not community. The result of all this is that representative democracy has become a Platonic idea without real, everyday substance. In the 150 years since the beginning of this drama of gradual degradation, we have failed to lay the groundwork for real democracy: we have omitted the thoroughgoing and continuing critical education of the whole population, upon which alone responsible representative government can be based. In consequence, public elections have become little more than a big national ritual, at best the uncritical celebration of the mediocre, the struggle to keep the status quo, and, at worst, the vicious tug of self-interest, the unobtrusive rallying of hate and fear, of faction against faction, man against man. At one extreme, bland immorality; at the other, deliberate fraud; in between, the confident proclaiming of the mediocre, the two-party system with the single program. Dedication, where it exists, is a dedication to the cheerful smile and the serious look that commands the empty-headed vote; more than anything else it tries to rally support for sound currency; beyond this, its greatest vision is the destruction of enemies, large or small. The American abroad is today embarrassed when asked about his program, his aims for the future. The promise of industrial democracy is now almost a secret vision, locked in the hearts of a few men, some of them, happily, still among the leadership. All in all we can say that today, 150 years after the New Promise, we are instead celebrating the New Roman Potlatch, where agreed community responsibility is envisioned and heeded only as a call to global war. When C. Wright

Mills put forth this thesis in his books *The Power Elite* and *The Causes of World War III,* most of the academic community turned their backs on him or carped at details of his presentation. They have yet to show that he was wrong, or offer a more convincing thesis in its place.

We are in a rare position today to savor the climate of opinion in Europe just after the French Revolution, and during the dilemmas of the Industrial one. In two-thirds of our world we are re-experiencing the same dilemmas, the same hopes and fears. What price order? What price industrialization? What should one keep of the beneficial order of traditional society while attempting to do away with its injustices and inequalities? How can one keep what is good, and reject the bad? Is industrialization an unmitigated good—can its ill effects be foreseen or remedied? What directions shall it take—under what kind of government? What exactly does the free vote contribute to this process—what does it really mean in the hands of an ignorant peasant? Is an uninformed vote a fetish—or, perhaps worse, an active obstacle to intelligent change? What kind of commodities are fetishes, and who is to proscribe them if people "really want" them?

The questioning is anguished—and it is often very well informed, informed by the lessons of our own failures and successes during these 150 years of our history in the West. But the new elite of the two-thirds of the world who are asking these questions are often better informed about our own problems than we are ourselves. Thus, they go back again and again to questions that we have stopped asking: "When hereditary class privilege and aristocracy—the first pillar of feudalism—are destroyed, is it enough? Doesn't the second pillar of feudalism also have to be eliminated, namely, the private ownership of land? If both pillars of traditional society are not removed, can one really make an effective transition to industrial democracy in the service of the common good? Without this twofold change, isn't parliamentary democracy merely a new kind of spoils system—with new owners and new classes redividing the old and the new privately owned wealth? If this is true, then isn't industrial democracy merely a new kind of domination, a quick change of costume that leaves fundamental problems untouched? If not—if industrial democracy is really making more and more wealth available to more and more people—is this enough? Is it enough just to spread more and more goods, thoughtlessly, to turn man into a clever consumer ape, eying greedily the dangling things?" These are anguished and urgent questions. We do not examine the French Revolution and its aftermath, the Industrial Revolution, in these terms today, in our schools and colleges. Is it because, in the West, we have abdicated facing up to the problems which two-thirds of the world now has to face? The answer is that we have, and that only a thoroughgoing science of man in society can begin to remedy our default. Saint-Simon and Comte understood this right at the beginning of the modern era, as I noted at the end of the previous section. Let us now turn to them.

HENRI SAINT-SIMON

The French Revolution, then, and the new industrial expansions brought into sharp relief all the questions that we posed above. Europeans suddenly realized that they lived in an "emerging area"—to use today's jargon. Only they did not have Russian, Chinese, or American industrialization models, but merely their own instincts, ingenuity, and prejudices. At a time like that the premium is on good instinct, much ingenuity, and a minimum of prejudice—so that very few thinkers can qualify to point the way. Saint-Simon's distinction is that he was just such a thinker, had just those qualities. In many ways he resembled a Rousseau who had suddenly come upon the post-Revolutionary industrial scene. He cut right to the heart of the matter, saw that industrialization was good, that the new reshuffling of classes—with its new immorality—was bad, that morals were relative, that human happiness was supremely important. First he put his trust in science, but then, like Rousseau, saw that the scientists cared not one hoot about the state of society, that all they wanted was "to do" more disciplinary science. At first he took a house near the Academy of Science and invited leading scientists to fine suppers, in order to "pick their brains," as we would now say. The attempt was not rewarding and he had to observe: "These gentlemen eat a lot, but they don't talk much."

His experiences led him to fume in rage at their lack of social responsibility; he was even less restrained than Rousseau—perhaps because he was less poetic, and even more because the post-Revolutionary crisis was infinitely more alarming than social morality had been at Rousseau's time. Like Diderot before him, he turned on the scientific elite, the mathematical scientists, "those sorry calculators ensconced behind their rampart of X and Z" (Manuel, 1956, p. 137); they had turned their backs on the social problem, something an Enlightenment man of large vision could not comprehend. Listen to his passionate words, just as thrilling and relevant today as they were then:

> . . . My blood boils, rage possesses me. . . . What right
> have you [mathematicians] at this point to occupy the
> position of scientific advance guard? The human species
> is involved in one of the severest crises it has ever
> experienced since the beginning of its existence. What
> efforts have you made to terminate this crisis? What
> methods have you adopted to reestablish order in human
> society? (Quoted in Manuel, 1956, pp. 137–138.)

Frank Manuel, in his outstanding work on Saint-Simon, sums
up his attitude toward the scientists, and the problem of the time,
in a few well-chosen words:

> He began to see in the leaders of contemporary science
> the indifferentists, men blind to the catastrophe of the
> European continent and the chaos of society, proceeding
> with their trifling experiments unconcerned for the
> consequences. They held the clue to the salvation of the
> continent—the integration of scientific thought and the
> imposition of a uniform system of knowledge and morality
> upon society, but they shirked their duty, letting the full
> weight of the burden fall upon his shoulders alone. In his
> rage at beholding the egotist scientists, each pursuing
> petty experiments while the world which needed their
> spiritual leadership was bleeding itself to death, Saint-
> Simon drove them from the eminence to which they had
> been raised in his ideal society a few years before. First
> he denounced the physical-mathematical scientists, then
> the physiologists. They had refused to formulate a general
> scientific theory which would lead to the Science of
> Man (Manuel, 1956, p. 248).

Thus they could properly be called "anarchist scientists" (p. 83),
fully worthy of their modern descendants.

The whole problem of science and morality that occupied the
Enlightenment after the decline of the medieval cosmology—the
story we sketched in the first two chapters—is summed up here.
Saint-Simon posed the problem of science and morals in rational
industrial society, of unitary science and a unitary world view which
would give a reasoned morality to replace the collapsed one, a
problem that began with Descartes, Leibnitz, Saint-Pierre, Diderot,
Rousseau, and has continued through Marx, Ward, Veblen, Dewey,
down through C. Wright Mills in our time. He stepped into history at
a time when it offered a commanding height from which to survey

its problems, a time when a sensitive, courageous, and critical mind could tower over its whole sweep. In post-Revolutionary France he could see the problem of conquest, class, order, change, in a manner which was previously not possible. Everything had precipitated into a transparent solution. Like Rousseau before him—but living at a time that made Rousseau's seem innocent and halcyon—Saint-Simon's originality lay in bringing together all the previous currents of thought into a new critical unity, and suggesting a definite program of remedial action. He brought the whole Enlightenment to bear on the problems of industrial society after the collapse of the feudal-theological synthesis, and suggested a new, rational, thoroughgoing social reconstruction: a secular community under the supreme guidance of a Science of Man in Society. He thus posed the problem that is ours today, and ranks as one of the classic founders of sociology, a truly great and original figure in the history of the science of man.

AUGUSTE COMTE

Saint-Simon, however, is not usually acknowledged to be the "father" of sociology in any direct sense; this distinction is usually reserved for his disciple, Auguste Comte, who coined the word "sociology." Comte elaborated in full all of Saint-Simon's ingenious insights, and put them into a systematic form and framework that Saint-Simon had merely sketched. Thus it was Comte who was to be the towering theorist of the "emerging" society, who put critical intellectual order and scientific body into Saint-Simon's passionate vision and daring suggestions.[1]

It is one of my principal theses in this book that we need to proceed to a thoroughgoing reappraisal of Comte's work. Specifically, we must look at his systematic effort anew, from the vantage point of all the knowledge in the various disciplines that we have acquired since his time. In the present section I want to show what Comte really tried to do before suggesting some reasons why he failed. In a later section I would like to bring our accumulated knowledge to bear within the same framework that Comte outlined, and to show how this framework can be brought up to date and why it is supremely relevant to a science of man today.

Comte has been accused by many second-rate thinkers of being one of their kin. He was badly enough handled in his lifetime, by being either neglected or misinterpreted. Posterity has handled him even worse. Freud says somewhere that since he created psychoanalysis he had the right to define it as he chose. Comte created Positivism, but very few have granted him the right to his own definition. Let us be clear about this once and for all: Comte intended Positivism to be a *complete system of morality,* not merely a technical scientific method for the analysis of social facts.

His life's work is normally considered to fall into two distinct phases: the early phase of the six volumes of *Cours de philosophie positive* (1830–1842), and the later phase of the four-volume *Politique positive* (1851–1854). The first work was a treatise on all the sciences, putting forth the striking new proposal that sociology followed logically in the history of the development of the sciences: that consequently it was the natural superordinate science for the analysis of social facts; that not only was scientific method possible in treating human affairs, but that it was most desirable, being the final and consummate achievement of science. The second work enunciated the "Religion of Humanity" based on love: in the new community sociology would subserve social order and be used to promote social interest instead of the private selfish interest that was rampant. Science would be guided by love in an orderly society dedicated to the worship of man.

Stuart Mill, Littré and other notable admirers of Comte based their admiration on the first work, and considered that the second work was done in the grip of some kind of dementia or senility. Often they explicitly indict Comte's love affair with Clotilde de Vaux. We shall return later to the reasoned and necessary unity of Comte's system; suffice it to say for now that, contrary to the opinion of many superficial commentators, Comte was well aware of what he was doing—the two "phases" of his work were one integral whole. The first period was a systematization that he undertook on a positivistic, scientific basis in order to avoid charges of mysticism which he knew might be leveled against his guiding ideas. The second period was a frank predication of his life work on feeling, love, and morality, which he felt were the basis of his whole position (see Lévy-Bruhl, 1903, p. 13). But his whole position, as Henri Gouhier (1933, p. 18) and others have seen, was explicitly outlined in his early—1818–1828— work, which was a precursor for everything that came later. What seems to have happened to many interpreters of Comte, during his lifetime and later, is that they were inspired by the vision of a scientific sociology, and, under the sway of the mechanism and materialism of the mid-nineteenth century, simply overlooked the last part of his system—that is, they overlooked the vision upon which the whole was undertaken. The positivists disemboweled Comte (cf. also Simon, 1963; Manuel, 1962, p. 267). They were not concerned, as was he, with the fundamental moral problem posed by the Enlightenment and brought into sharp relief by the French Revolution.

Comte was a late Enlightenment thinker who intended to answer once and for all the problem of replacing the lost medieval morality in a new scientific and moral synthesis. Like Saint-Simon he was a child of the Revolution, who saw both its tragedy and its opportunity. By his own definition, Positivism meant *the subordination of politics to morals* (1848, p. 420). Science enters the picture *only to provide the basis for an agreed morality*. The use of reason in all spheres carries its own conviction, thought Comte; science could thus provide what man needed most, namely, a "demonstrated faith." Positivist science, that is, would bring scientific analysis to bear on all social questions and social problems, and not merely on the realm of inanimate nature. In this way scientists could analyze the causes of human unhappiness, and agree about what those causes are. This would automatically "indicate the right path of duty" (1848, p. 403) and the question of morality would be solved.

"Automatically?"—the philosopher of science and the logician may shudder at this facile transition from facts to moral imperatives. The answer to this is that Comte based the interdependence of science and morality on exactly the framework that he inherited from the Enlightenment, namely, to recap briefly, that a science of man in society is the central science to which all the others are contributory and peripheral (Vico, Diderot, Rousseau); that its guiding principle is the idea of progress (Turgot, Condorcet). Thus, if science is centered on man and subserves him, and if progress is its goal, then, logically, when we find out the social causes of human unhappiness, we will have an automatic directive to an agreed solution. This is how the Enlightenment—as we saw—finally crowned the earlier idea of reading nature as a guide to morality. Only in this version man takes from morality its theological imperative and makes it subserve human betterment. He reads nature under the aegis of his own will, and in his own service, by extending rational, scientific analysis into all domains—human and social as well as physical and natural. He then has an anthropodicy. This fusion of science and morals is still our legacy in sociology today; we ignore it simply because we ignore the Enlightenment framework in which alone it can be operative—that is, the framework of an active, progressive, ideal-typical superordinate science of man.

The average philosopher of science, who ignores this too, delights himself with the fallacy of those who merge the "is" and the "ought." He says that one cannot logically deduce an "ought" statement from an "is" statement—what "is" does not carry any necessary transition to what "ought" to be. Having thus logically separated fact and value, "is" and "ought," he proceeds to prove his contention by saying that once you change an "is" statement into an "ought" directive, then you *lose* the "is." Now this is very neat; logically, of course, it is unassailable. But man lives *in* the world, subserves it to his own use. Might it not occur to the logical analyst that perhaps this is precisely what a superordinate value science of man in society should seek to do?—that is, to merge the "is" into the "ought"—to seek continually to reshape the actual into a vision of the desirable, to implement progress in the service of man. The science of man is characterized precisely by its continual attempt to promote value; any fact is a guide for value-laden action.

Comte saw and understood this, which is why he placed such a high premium on the idea of progress and insisted that a science of man cannot exist without it. Thus, he dates the radical new direction of the Enlightenment precisely from the debate of the "ancients" and the "moderns" at the beginning of the eighteenth century (1830–1842, vol. 4, pp. 120 ff.). This was the debate in which cyclical and static views of history were finally largely abandoned; people came to accept the idea that perhaps man at that time was actually better than the ancients had been, and that there was no longer any need to look longingly to the past, but instead one could begin to look to the future. Comte insisted that the great positive value of the French Revolution for a science of man lay in the fact that it pushed to the very fore the idea of progress, because it held up before humanity the vision of active social change as something humanly achievable. He also stressed the negative effect of the Revolution on a science of man, namely, that it blocked the *scientific* development of the idea of progress by opposing every rational view of the past and every cumulative approach to the development of social institutions (1830–1842, vol. 4, p. 135). This was one of the reasons Comte valued Montesquieu over Condorcet, and especially over Rousseau, whose ideas gave impetus to the Revolution; Comte considered that Rousseau had effaced Montesquieu's law-like approach to social phenomena. In our time, the Russian Revolution of 1917 had the same twofold effect: it elevated the possibility of radical progress, but at the same time Marxism-Leninism-Stalinism-Maoism downgrades a cumulative, scientific approach to human progress. Our academic social scientists, who quite rightly objected to the second effect of Marxism-Leninism, quite wrongly overlooked the importance of an active implementation of progress.

Comte also understood that the science of man had to be a central science upon which all others revolved. With his immensely knowledgeable analysis of the progress of the various sciences, he in effect wrote a new Encyclopedia and brought up to date Diderot's contention. At a time when considerable progress had been made in such sciences as chemistry and biology, he reperformed Diderot's "Copernican shift," and again centered the sciences firmly on man. Comte echoed strongly the whole Enlightenment diatribe against fragmentation, separation, disciplinary particularism (1830–1842, vol. 4, pp. 220, 282), and saw that the remedy was to take man as center. But now he could profit from the considerable advance that had taken place in the Enlightenment view of science since Diderot, namely, the maturing of the idea of progress, and he could support it with his own elaborated theory of the mental evolution of mankind through the famous "three stages"—theological, metaphysical, positivist. As he saw it, there could now be no logical or rational objection to a complete man-centering of all the sciences. With sociology as the superordinate science serving human progress, all the disciplines would take their natural place *in the service of man*. The natural and physical sciences would become *subsciences* of the science of man in society. Nothing could be clearer or simpler; in Comte's own words,

> . . . all scientific speculations, of whatever kind, as human endeavors, must perforce be subordinated to the idea of progress, to the true general theory of human development (1830–1842, vol. 4, p. 274).

Now it is worth pausing on this because the whole dilemma of disciplinary fragmentation, the place of science in society, the separation of fact and value—all that plagues our most ingenious thinkers today, is *solved on this simple basis*—that is, it is solved by man-centering the science in the service of human progress. All the disciplines become subordinate, are downgraded, and are to be judged only in terms of what they *actively contribute* to man. Comte understood something that we are only today again beginning to realize, namely, that our picture of the whole history of modern science has somehow been perversely inverted. In other words, Comte brought up to date Saint-Pierre's criticism of Descartes and Newton

and their overvaluation of the physical sciences, by making exactly
the same criticism at a considerably later date in the development of
the various disciplines, and making it with considerable acumen and
knowledge. In Comte's own inspired words—which are today well
worth studying:

> Let us say, by a chimerical hypothesis, that the general
> theory of human progress becomes, one day, so perfected,
> that there is no obstacle to the most precise deductions.
> Then it would be quite clear that the hierarchy of the scien-
> ces, *up to then totally inverted,* would, *a priori,* then present
> the different sciences as simple parts of this new, unique
> science (1830–1842, vol. 4, p. 274, emphasis added).

But of course!—a fully deductive science in the service of man would
reverse automatically the seniority of the physical sciences. The
reader may object that this radical man-centering in the service of
progress is wholly unconvincing at this point; he might well say that
both the idea of progress and the possibility of a deductive science of
man are indeed chimeras. This is a valid objection, and the remainder
of this work is devoted to meeting it. But for now, it is important to
note that Comte had no illusions on the difficulties of elaborating a
full-scale theory of human progress or on the remoteness of a fully
deductive science of man. He says:

> The feebleness of our intellect at such an extremely
> complicated study, will perhaps never permit us to
> realize such a situation; nevertheless, this supposition
> [about reversing the hierarchy of the sciences] is apt to
> make us immediately understand the legitimate general
> intervention of a true social science into all possible
> orders of human speculation (1830–1842, vol. 4, p. 274).

What could be more realistic? Comte is actually proposing that the
man-centering of the sciences is an "ideal-typical enjoinder," so to
speak, but very necessary and even urgent, in order to put some
kind of unity and reason into the world of scientific investigation. He
sees that there is a discrepancy between what is immediately convincing, based on persuasive knowledge, and what is ideal—what
ought to be done. I call this discrepancy between the actual state of
knowledge and the ideal-typical vision the "Enlightenment paradox,"
as we will see in more detail later on. An adumbration of the discrepancy started with Saint-Pierre and Rousseau but was only given

explicit scientific voice by Comte. Comte saw that analytic criticism was not enough—indeed this was the lesson that the destructive French Revolution brought home. The divisive quest of the single sciences was all right only so long as they had to dislodge the old superstitions. It could then be tolerated; but now some kind of new organic unity was necessary. Comte repeats this problem of necessary analysis versus necessary synthesis throughout his work. Besides, if science is to become positive and leave behind forever the old theological and metaphysical gropings, it must assert *its own* organic unity. To fail to do so, he saw, was to leave open a large place for theology and metaphysics right within science. "By rejecting any new general discipline, modern scientific men would unknowingly tend to re-establish the system which they seemed to have shattered forever" (Lévy-Bruhl, 1903, p. 114). To discredit the theological and metaphysical systems by the advance of disciplinary science is not enough; they would not have replaced these systems *qua* systems, and consequently would not have fully superseded them. Peirce saw that modern science is ridden through with metaphysics. Comte understood that the reason for this is precisely because it remains in a state of disciplinary fragmentation. Accordingly, Comte's plea for man-centering is a perfect solution for ridding the disciplines of unconscious metaphysics:

> Considered in its object, each one of our sciences reaches, so to speak, to infinity, far beyond our limited horizon. If then, in order to satisfy us, a *single* conception of the world is necessary, we shall never obtain such a conception from the objective point of view. But if we change our point of view, if we refer the whole of the sciences to man, or better, to humanity, as a center, we shall then be able to realize the unity which we seek. This is precisely what is made possible by sociology, by subordinating the hierarchy of the positive sciences to the final science of humanity (Lévy–Bruhl, 1903, p. 116).

There can be no better statement for us today of the scientific, human, and historical problem of a unified science. It is the perfect consummation of the Enlightenment vision of science in the service of man—a thoroughgoing empiricism in the service of human values, a mature and controlled idealism of the most realistic kind (cf. Miller, 1949, p. 406). Although in Comte's day the Enlightenment vision of the beauty and majesty of a fully-deductive all-disciplinary science in the service of man was only a vision, it remains to haunt us today:

The perfect spontaneous unity of such a subject despite its immense extension, the more pronounced solidarity of its diverse aspects, its characteristic movement from general questions to more gradually special researches, finally, the more frequent use, and more important use, of a priori considerations furnished by the anterior sciences—especially by the biological theory of human nature—all this must make us conceive of the highest hopes for the speculative dignity of such a science (1830–1842, vol. 4, p. 282).

In this great unity the Leibnitzian problem would finally be resolved, science and morals would coexist in intricate interdependence; but Comte's vision goes beyond Leibnitz; it is a unity without the necessary intervention of theology or any unreasoned belief.

Comte's Positivism, in sum, solved the problem of science and morals by using science to support a man-based morality. With all the force at his command he showed that life is a moral problem, and science only a tool whose unity would serve the larger unity of life. Like de Maistre and de Bonald, and like Carlyle in England, he looked approvingly on the Middle Ages. But he did not pine nostalgically for their institutions; he saw the Middle Ages as possessing what man needed most, and has since lost: a critical, unitary world view by which to judge right and wrong, good and bad, by which to subordinate personal desire to social interest. But, instead of basing this knowledge on theological fiat, man could now settle it firmly on science. In this way, the Enlightenment could achieve what the Middle Ages almost possessed; but it could do this on a much sounder footing than could ever have been possible during the earlier time, namely, it could achieve the subordination of politics to morality on a scientific rather than on a theological basis. Social order and social harmony would be the call of the new day, and human progress could then be progress in social feeling, community, and love—all of it based on the superordinate science of man in society, serving man, elevating humanity. Science, morality, dignity, order, progress—such was the vision of the one who has been called a "glorious madman."

But today we are sane; we have separated science and morals, abandoned any critical, reasoned notion of progress, largely given up trying to instrument dignity, attacked the concept of order as a Platonic reactionism, scoffed at the possibility of a unitary world view. That is to say, since the Enlightenment we have gradually drifted into a position of what amounts to calculated self-abasement, by actively forfeiting what the human animal needs most: a unitary, critical world view, infused by continuing moral awareness. Having lost this—and indeed having lost even the awareness that it is necessary—we should not wonder that we in the West are repeating too, almost exactly, the experience of the earlier time in which this was being lost: the fourteenth to sixteenth century experience of the decay of nature, the gradual petering out of life, the end of man on earth. But, unlike this earlier time, our present disillusionment cannot be turned in the service of otherworldliness or religious morality. It is instead in the service of the new cynicism, blind to both spiritual and human values, a headlong, consumer race to "enjoy" while there is still time. Carl Becker tried to show that the idea of progress was actually the Enlightenment version of the City of God of medieval times— it was a new futurism, a deferment for the failures of the present. Again, the implication is that they were naïve, but that we are mature. A maturity that renounces the past and that fears for the future is, however, no maturity at all, as our present-day world so eloquently attests. Perhaps for all these reasons, and others, a "neo-Comtean" or "neo-Wardian" movement in the human sciences is a very urgent idea—as I hope to show cumulatively throughout this work.

FOURIER AND FRENCH DEDUCTIVE HEDONISM

With Fourier we arrive at something quite new in social-science theory. Like Bentham, he wanted a fully deductive science of man in the service of human pleasure. But now the new Newtonianism has a peculiarly French accent: the fully deductive science of man, centered on the human personality, would be based on a thorough reorganization of society—a building up of entirely new institutions on the vastest possible scale. Thus, like Saint-Simon, Fourier had a Utopian socialist vision for the new industrial society; but, unlike Saint-Simon, he offered what he considered a comprehensive theory of personality which would put the vision on a firm scientific footing. While all his other imaginative and fantastic ideas are dead, Fourier's theory of the passions still merits our close attention, as I hope to show more fully later on.

Again, like Bentham, Hume, Condillac, Hartley, Helvétius, and the rest, Fourier was moved by the beauty and perfection of Newtonianism, and wanted to coordinate the facts of the moral world just as the principle of gravitation had coordinated those of the physical world. It was in 1808 that he claimed to have found the secret, the law of

"Passional Attraction" that he thought entitled him to be called the Newton of the moral world; moreover, he was so impressed by the originality of his discovery that he considered himself a Newton for whom no Kepler or Galileo had paved the way (Bury, 1955, p. 279). Accordingly, he also called himself the Columbus of the social life, maintaining that his theory of the passions was the basis for the new science of social man (Manuel, 1962, p. 230).

J. B. Bury gives short shrift to the theoretical background of Fourier's work, and considers him merely as one who helped familiarize the world with the idea of indefinite progress (1955, p. 281). But for a history of ideas this brushes Fourier off much too lightly. Fourier understood the problem of social science with an acuity that today deserves great respect. Renouvier was one of the few to appreciate this, and he especially noted Fourier's attempt to shift the problem of a theodicy to that of an active anthropodicy (1883–1884, pp. 215–220). Fourier wanted a science of man in society that would be naturalistically based, and for this he suggested a study of the workings of human nature, specifically of the twelve human passions as he conceived them. He sought to discover the laws of order and organization of social life, taking the individual human actor as the point of departure. In the clear words of Albert Brisbane, his American disciple, Fourier's basic program amounts to this:

> Man must first obtain a knowledge of his nature, of the law which regulates his passions, to organize a true society; and this law he must discover by his own observation and investigation, precisely as he has to discover those which regulate the solar system, to obtain a knowledge of its mechanism:—for the human mind comprehends none of nature's law intuitively and without labor. . . . This study has been prevented by the inveterate prejudice respecting the depravity of human nature, which has turned the minds of men from this primary object of investigations. . . . Fourier followed a different route . . . proceeding on the principle of *absolute doubt* of pre-existing scientific doctrines. . . . Possessing, through Fourier, the theory of the passions and that of a true social organization, we should found an agricultural Association and see whether agricultural, manufacturing and household occupations, organized in Groups and Series, could not be rendered attractive. If the experiment succeeded, the greatest and most gigantic of social problems would be solved (quoted in Bernard, 1943, p. 674).

I quote this at length to bring home two major points about Fourier's system. The first is that it is a system, that it aims to introduce a fully experimental social science with no preconceived notions about morality and taking *nothing for granted* about human nature. It is thus wholly within the secular Enlightenment tradition. The second major point is something we have completely lost sight of in social science today, as we blindly continue our plodding everyday fact gathering in the hope that one day all the bits of knowledge will fall together and form a fully mature science. Fourier understood that the subject matter of social science was much too complicated for a trust in simple inductivism; he saw that only an experimental, deductive science would give a comprehensive grasp of human nature similar to that which the physical sciences had of inanimate nature. Brisbane outlines Fourier's views on this problem very succinctly:

> Social science is a vast and complex science; it cannot be discovered and constituted by the aid of empirical observation and reasoning; the *inductive method* can not do its work here. The laws of order and organization in nature must be discovered, and from them the science must be deduced. In astronomy, in order to solve its higher and more abstruse problems, it is necessary to deduce from one of the great laws of Nature; namely, that of gravitation. It is more necessary still in the case of the involved problems of Social Science.... If Fourier has failed, if he has not discovered the laws of natural organization; or has not deduced rightly from them, he has opened the way and pointed out the true path.... He has shown how the human mind is to create a Social Science and effect the Social Reconstruction to which this science is to lead.... Possessing like Kepler, a vast and bold genius, he has, by far-reaching intuition and close analytic thought, discovered some of the fundamental principles of Social Science, enough to place it on a scientific foundation, and to constitute it regularly, as did Kepler in astronomy (in Bernard, 1943, pp. 675–676).

This was the justification for Fourier's attempt to begin at once social reconstruction, to set up an orderly society for the continuing observation and interpretation of the human passions. Fourier wanted to cut through the endless induction and patient speculation, divorced from any vital connection to social life. He wanted an experimental society in the service of man. Furthermore, like any true scientist, he was willing to admit that he might be wrong about the passions, but he saw it was necessary to begin deducing from some kind of comprehensive theory. He repeated: "I *deduce*. If I have deduced erroneously, let others establish the true deduction." In other words, if we hark back to our previous discussion of Comte, we can see that Fourier wanted immediately to implement the Enlightenment vision of a fully deductive science in the service of man. He did not put off the "speculative dignity" of such a science to some distant future day, as had Comte. Thus he could assign to Comte a lesser rank in the history of the science of man: he called him the Tycho Brahe of social science, "learned and patient, but not original" (Brisbane, in Bernard, 1943, p. 676).

To Fourier, Comte's system must have seemed too plodding, too much under the sway of old scientific preconceptions. It would certainly not have offered the world a daring new hedonism, nourished and encouraged by science. In Comte's system the social had a primacy over the individual; man had to curb his self-seeking nature in the interests of social harmony. In Fourier's, society was organized to give each individual the maximum possible pleasure for which nature had amply equipped him: it did not matter that man was hellbent for his own pleasure; if only he followed nature instead of twisting it, individual pleasure could never have socially harmful effects. In Comte's system, man would have to be enjoined gradually, by the findings of science, to be more reasonably social; in Fourier's, man could begin at once to give full indulgence to the primitive capacity of his nature for unadulterated pleasure—it sufficed to set up a society designed according to Fourier's model, where children could always eat the sweets they preferred, instead of the perverted dry bread.

CONCLUSION: THE CENTURY IN RETROSPECT— THE VICISSITUDES OF IDEOLOGY AND PREMATURITY

Utopian social communities on Fourier's models were attempted, but they all failed. The lesson they taught was not necessarily the erroneousness of Fourier's reading of the "passions"; but rather, like the lesson of Robert Owen's New Lanark, they showed that one does not immerse a social experiment within a larger ideology that is hostile to it and expect it subsequently to thrive. Comte, despite the

spread of his ideas to the New World, never was to see his Positivism
put into effect as a system of social morality subserved by science.
Thus, we have to conclude that the great French Utopian systems
that sought to answer the social and moral dilemmas of the post-Revolutionary time were obviously insufficient to the task of designing and
effecting a persuasive new scientific morality—just as the British
empiricist moral systems had been.

The reasons for this failure were many. In the first place, we must
be realistic and acknowledge that the thinkers we are dealing with were
just that—thinkers. The vast movement of everyday cares, hopes, and
fears, and the slow plodding of encrusted institutions and vested
interests carried the nineteenth century along, just as all other centuries are carried. The thinkers are buoys on the waves of humanity,
tossed along with it, swamped by it, occasionally charting the way
for a new generation of leaders—but all of them move with the ocean,
rather than move *it*. The image is certainly a commonplace one,
but perhaps at no time was it more true than in the course of the
nineteenth century, which moved along under the power of its own
confused diversity and industrial promise. Of course, thinkers such
as Darwin caused a great stir, and Marx made considerable intellectual
movement, but Darwin's effect was theoretical and Marxism really
incubated until the great revolutions of our day.

THE "OFF-CENTERING" OF THE IDEA OF PROGRESS

The epitaph for a science of man in society, in the nineteenth century, can be written in the jargon of the institution which flourished in
its place: The new parliamentary liberalism would simply "not buy"
the great systematic schemes for founding a new scientific morality.
The English, as we saw, wanted reform attached to parliamentary
tradition; they never did have any taste for Rousseau (Delvaille,
1910, p. 545). Thus, British deductive hedonism failed as a systematic
attempt. And the French, after 1848, made it clear that their revolution would never be proletarianized: they would follow the model of
British gradualism, retaining the last pillar of feudalism on which to
base a new division of the spoils, operating under the legitimation of
representative government. England, in 1649 and 1689, had begun
to undermine the first pillar of feudalism—the hereditary class and
aristocratic legal privilege; France toppled it more decisively in
1789, Germany in 1848, Russia in 1905. But the second pillar of feudalism, the monopolization of land in private hands, remained in

all these countries. Thus we refer to these revolutions as "bourgeois" revolutions and not "proletarian" ones. The problem that we inherited from the decline of medieval society was never resolved. The ill-fated leaders who wanted to extend the various revolutions to the abolition of private ownership of land—Gerrard Winstanley, Babeuf, Blanqui, for example—were effectively suppressed. In the 1871 Commune, thirty-thousand men and women were machine-gunned in the sewers of Paris, and that was the end of that. It is important for the student of social science to keep in mind that while this butchery went on Herbert Spencer was elaborating his serene, gradualist social theory, which allowed no room for any human influence over the "progressive evolution" of society. Only in the twentieth century have we seen accomplished what these earlier times could not do, namely, the toppling of both pillars of feudalism in a single revolution, permitting the complete reconstruction of society on a wholly new basis, without any hereditary privilege remaining—in Russia, China, and Cuba. Thus, the nineteenth century bypassed complete social reconstruction in the two ways available: by suppressing proletarian revolution as well as by ignoring the systematic efforts of the scientific thinkers of the time.

For the social scientist today, it is important to realize that this twofold refusal to come to grips with rational social reconstruction cannot be covered over by the dodge of liberal parliamentarianism. There was nothing "political" about the new industrialism, just as there had been nothing "political" about the feudal institutions. Feudalism was a social and legal system, political only indirectly. In fact, as Comte understood, the Middle Ages presented a desirable model precisely because they tried to subordinate politics to morals. Today, as in the nineteenth century, industrialism is a social and economic system, only indirectly political (Kariel, 1961, p. 6). As C. Wright Mills analyzed very recently (1959), politics in industrial society is on the "middle level" of power. No one would have denied the desirability of this subordinate position of political power in the Middle Ages, but we deny it stridently today, simply because we function under another myth—the myth of control of industrial society by a representative parliament. But the social scientist must penetrate beneath the myth, to the actual forces at work in society, which is what Marx, Weber, Veblen, Mills, and a whole succession of social analysts sought to do. As far as we have been able to learn, these forces have always been social and economic primarily. The question for the social analyst in each new epoch is, exactly how and in what new ways do the social and economic forces exercise their ideology, by which they move society? In this sense the function of sociology is at all times a de-mythologizing one.

When we understand the nineteenth-century evasion of these basic problems, we also understand the fate of the guiding idea of the science of man—I mean, of course, the idea of progress. Refusing to come to grips with thoroughgoing social reconstruction, the nineteenth century had to emasculate radical social theory. The most immediate way of accomplishing this was to dethrone the idea of progress, in any manner it could—and this it did effectively in several ways.

It is significant that the most serious early blow to the idea of progress came from England, delivered by Robert Malthus. The English, as we noted several times, could not stomach French radicalism, and with an occasional striking exception—such as the anarchist Godwin—insisted that a science of man be kept firmly subordinate to traditional institutional forms. It is further significant that we continue to overvalue Malthus, partly because, I think, we still share his prejudice against an active science of man developing its own new morality.

Malthus disposed of the idea of progress in the most effective way, namely, by divorcing it from Rousseau's ideal-typology, which alone had given it body. Having done this, it was an easy matter to "off-center" it completely; that is, *take it out of the realm of human implementation,* and make a passive rather than an active instrumental notion out of it. Thus isolated, the idea of progress almost automatically fell back into its previous skeletal immaturity, where it had been with its early formulators. Malthus, in other words, falsified the idea by ignoring it in its mature form; it was then an easy matter to tear to shreds a straw idea of progress. Malthus reduced his adversary from the start, and today we are still falsely discussing the notion of progress as a passive, objective principle.

Malthus, like Adam Smith, wanted to "follow the law of nature." But he was not concerned, as were the French, in finding out what nature was up to; the fact is that he prejudged the case—he was a clergyman who believed in Original Sin (Randall, 1940, p. 328). The whole story of his dismissal of the idea of progress is contained in this prejudgment: he was not looking for a new "secular" theodicy, as were the French. He was thus really a medieval and not an Enlightenment figure. The most one could hope for in social betterment, he thought, was palliatives—the removal of obstacles in the path of the natural progress that God had marked out (Teggart, 1960, p. 89). He wanted to oppose any radical social change, and reacted directly to

the anarchism of Godwin and to the Rousseauism of his father
(his father had been a personal friend of Rousseau's) (Merz, 1914,
vol. 4, p. 460). Malthus, in other words, was not the sophisticated
debunker of sentimental French notions: he was a conservative
figure with his own personal, emotional vested interests in the
status quo, and he completely missed the spirit of the new science.
The aim of his celebrated *Law of Population* was not to put the discourse about the problems of the new science on a higher level—far
from it. He wanted to show that any kind of socialism is purely
Utopian and anti-natural; that the attempt to abolish class formations
is foredoomed to failure.

The English economists insisted that the reason class differences
existed at that time was because of different degrees of talent in individuals throughout history. It was claimed that everyone had
started in the "primitive state" with the same amount. Differences in
talent and energy led ineluctably to the formation of wealthy classes,
and since this uneven accumulation was based on natural differences,
it gave a "law of primitive accumulation" which man had to respect.
Marx was later aptly to call this law a "nursery tale." Malthus wanted
to support this nursery tale not only in the past, but also in the future.
Hence his celebrated *Law of Population*. If any attempt was made to
restore the state of economic equality, he maintained, the workings of
his *Law of Population* would soon render this attempt futile, and
classes would be inevitably restored to their present state. Thus,
Malthus actually projected the myth of "primitive accumulation"
into the future (Oppenheimer, 1922, pp. vii–viii). In place of constructive clarification in the science of man, Malthus offered his own
wishful historicism. Furthermore, he did not want it tampered with:
he was averse to contraception.

With this kind of distortion, it is small wonder that the idea of
progress became a debatable and discredited notion in some quar-
ters. In others, it also became a fact for "objective" study, but in different ways. A good deal of the history of ideas of the nineteenth
century is summed up in the various approaches to the objective
study of the idea of progress, once it was removed from the central,
active place that the Enlightenment had given it.

HISTORICISM AND EVOLUTIONISM: VARIETIES OF "OFF-CENTERING"

Thus, what began originally with **Turgot and Diderot** as a protest of
the uniqueness of a man-centered science in a world of physical

objectivity was subverted: by looking objectively at the idea of progress, the nineteenth century again off-centered the science of man. Diderot's work was reversed, man was again dethroned from his central place, and transmuted into an object to be studied with Olympian scientific detachment. The nineteenth century reforged its link with Newton, and forced man into the background of nature. Only an occasional voice rose in protest (cf. Thomas, 1883–1884, pp. 102–103; and Lavrov, 1891), but it was to no avail.

Several traditions contributed to this. The German tradition, which we have so far not discussed, had drawbacks and important advantages for the full development of a science of man—as we shall see in another section. For one thing, the Germans contrast sharply with the French; whereas the French accent was always on the individual and his motive power, the Germans tended to talk of "species," to affirm the idea of man immersed in nature, of "organic development," of a "continuity which engulfs all the manifestations of existence." The Germans had a view of progress, but one which we could properly call "pantheistic" (Delvaille, 1910, p. 726).

The German tradition resulted in exactly what we would expect. Kant urged that we discover a "law" of the movement of civilization, but in his time how could such an enjoinder be brought down to the concrete level of everyday historical reality and social analysis? This kind of comprehensiveness thus led quite naturally to a passive, metaphysical historicism in Hegel. Man had only to read history philosophically in order to find the new moral order. Thus, instead of a natural determinism, as in Newton, the German philosophical approach to a science of man bogged down into a philosophical-historical determinism. And although Kant had opted for man as a free center and moral agent, his inability to carry through critically on any but a philosophical level had its expected issue. Hegel could then maintain that "philosophy is theodicy"—that one could interpret the past and the historical movement of thought in order to see what will and should happen. This is quite different from reading nature to see what *man should do*. It was a new determinism that sacrificed individual ethical freedom, allowing no room for personal decision and choice. Hence Hegelian historicism, as developed out of German metaphysical organicism, could lead easily to totalitarian social forms (cf. Baillie, 1950, pp. 122 ff.). In this tradition, others saw more clearly than did Kant and Hegel: Fichte, for example, espoused an activism that placed him in the French—rather than the German— spirit (cf. Charlton, 1959, pp. 108–112). Herder kept his anthropological analyses on concrete cultural and historical situations so that his idea of man was never swept up into abstractions like Kant's view of evolution toward the "modern rational State" or his preoccupation with "races" (see Clark, 1955, pp. 321 ff.). In fact, Herder summed up the basic weakness of the whole abstract movement from Kant to Hegel: he said that the ideal philospoher is the cultural anthropologist. And finally, Wilhelm von Humboldt also chafed at Kant for slighting the individual—exactly as Kierkegaard was later to fume at Hegel. We may not agree that this is at all justified as regards Kant, the man who more than anyone else is responsible for championing the full development of individual powers, the man who placed a primary value on the depths of the individual subjectivity. Yet the dispute helps us to see what was at stake in the problem of human progress: the instrumental scientific advancement of man, by getting down to actual social facts, versus abstract philosophical views that tended to place man in the background of social and historical movement.

As for the English, their theories of natural evolution gave another kind of serious twist to the idea of progress. They took the new Olympian objectivity toward progress and put it on a firm scientific footing. And this was done by combining the mechanism and materialism of the mid-century with Darwin's and Spencer's view of evolution. The result was that man was firmly and scientifically locked into the background of nature. Darwin really aggravated the problem of a science of man, as I understand its development, by reviving Malthus and breathing new life into him—a life that he never deserved. Malthus' historicism was scientifically legitimated by being woven into a new mechanistic naturalism. In Darwin's version, the pressures of population on limited environment resources contrived to assure the "survival of the fittest," according to the automatic principle of "natural selection." Thus, one could look to Darwin to substantiate social class and economic inequality as natural products of the life struggle. True, the evolutionist view of progress was certainly less dim than the one offered by Malthus and Ricardo, but it was well within their tradition: man was moved by a new dismal fate, by natural laws which worked themselves out at their own sweet pace— and he could not meddle.

Spencer, it is true, offered a doctrine of perfectibility, but one which rested on entirely different premises from those the Enlightenment proposed. As Bury so well said, it is one thing to stress human perfectibility on the basis of a psychology which holds that human nature is unresistingly plastic in the hands of the legislator and the instructor; it is quite another thing to argue that human nature is subject to some implacable general law of change (Bury, 1955, p. 340). This was the great warning that Helvétius had laid down in the concluding paragraphs of his treatise *On Man* (1772). It was the necessary philosophy of science for all the human sciences—but Spencer had not heeded it.

On the contrary, Spencer's system offered a view of human development in which the major changes take place in an unconscious realm, entirely separate from the possibilities of creative human intervention. Thus, with Darwin and Spencer, the science of man became the science of fatalism, a curious monstrosity: man now reads nature for its laws, but in order to do nothing but continue to read nature! The Enlightenment tradition expired without benefit of better purpose or new promise. The new view of progress did not serve morality in any way—which is perhaps one reason why the clergy reacted so violently to Darwin. A tradition of objective science took over completely the science of man—a tradition that should have had only a subsidiary place there. The century saw a redoubling of emphasis on method, and those like Buckle and Quételet sought to use statistics to "tease out" the general laws of progress, which operate independently of the acts of individual men. The historical method was born, and the comparative one, and the psychological one, and ethnological classification. Sumner's laissez-faire sociology was born, on the Spencerian model. Other disciplines were born, and they each went their separate ways. They have accomplished much indispensable work in the last hundred years, but the point of this whole story is that they have shirked the central task of a science of man: the active implementation of human progress.

I said above that the science of man expired with Comte, and without new promise, but this is not exactly true. It expired without any new *scientific* promise: the fact is that the *science* of man was replaced by the *ideology* of laissez-faire industrial society, into whose hands Spencer and Sumner so well played. It is not without deep significance that the dispassionate study of sociology replaced the active science of man at about the same time as the impressive results of science were applied, via the new industrialism, to the conveniences of life. The trumpets *did* blare forth a successor, and with proper pageantry, and the big show was the Great Exhibition of London (1851) which displayed the consumer commodities of the new "scientific" society. *This*, it was claimed, was the "new, intelligent, moral movement" in world history—the movement that would provide peace with plenty! (Bury, 1955, p. 331.) It took over a half-century before the mask fell with a thud in 1914. The apt observation on the whole fiasco is Whitehead's: the famous Crystal Palace, which housed the great international Exhibition, has very symbolically been burnt down (in Johnson, 1959, p. 58). Today, who can fail to see that the moral promise of commercial-industrial society has literally become ashes—and in our time, in Buchenwald and in Hiroshima.

The idea of progress was thus "off-centered" in several different ways and in several different countries—in England by Malthus, Spencer, and Darwin, and in Germany by Hegel. In France, Comte himself contributed to this off-centering by his own reliance on history, by objectifying it in his system. This gave "scientific historicism" wide currency, and the rest of the nineteenth century, as we know, went ahead full steam to try to find "objective" laws of historical progress. Ethnologists, sociologists, historians—all looked to reconstruct the stages of development of humanity in a single line. This would give them an easy key to the secret of social dynamics (Teggart, 1960, pp. 116–117).

As a result, the idea of progress became a political appendage of the new liberal parliamentarianism. It began to be argued solely in terms of political events and political opportunities. In other words, it began to be falsely argued: "Is personal liberty or state authority the most efficient means of progressing?" (Bury, 1955, p. 314.) And so on, with the comedy lasting down to the present day. When the idea of progress was off-centered from its superordinate position as an active guiding principle for the science of man, its fate was sealed. We could then become sophisticated or cynical about it, live without it, or simply hope for it, by doing our daily plodding duty. We need no longer take the trouble to frame an active design for a better life, but could let things grind their course, like primitives who trust that the institutions of their ancestors will assure the future. J. B. Bury, the noted historian of the idea of progress, nears the end of his famous study with this cynical and inappropriate comment:

> ... does not Progress itself suggest that its value as a doctrine
> is only relative, corresponding to a certain not very ad-
> vanced stage of civilization; just as Providence, in its day,
> was an idea of relative value, corresponding to a stage
> somewhat less advanced? (p. 352.)

But it is precisely because the idea of progress was taken out of its Enlightenment context as an actively implemented principle, insepar-

ably connected with ideal-typical models, that it could then resemble
the idea of Providence, so that in the nineteenth century man again
became a passive plaything of fate, trusting his future to parliament
as well as to God. Ernest Renan, who summed up in his person so
much of the movement of the century, could finally criticize himself,
at the end of his life in 1890, for falling into the error of assigning
to man an unduly central place in the universe (Bury, p. 322). Renan
was really expressing the modern disillusionment with science, with
a universe built wholly on brash intellectual meanings: he wanted to
give back to nature its great mystery—exactly as we must do today (cf.
1890, pp. xiii ff.). But, in any case, it is clear that at the end of the nineteenth century the noble vision of a New Athenian Celebration of
Man had been allowed to lapse. And it is also clear that man himself
was not to blame for Renan's second thoughts: but rather, the
ignoble alliance of naïve mechanistic science and trusting laissez-
faire democracy.

KARL MARX: THE ATTEMPT TO KEEP THE ENLIGHTENMENT ACTIVISM

There was, however, one figure who tried to end the nineteenth
century as Rousseau had tried to end the eighteenth—in complete
and utter protest against its fantastic hopes and its simple trust.
Just as Rousseau attacked the exaggerated trust in reason, Marx
spoofed at the visions and plans of the Utopian socialists, at the "crank
cults" of Saint-Simon, Fourier, Owen, Proudhon, at Comte's new
"Religion of Humanity," as well as at Feuerbach's; he cut mercilessly
through the intricate, deductive "laws" of the British economists, and
revealed the metaphysical principles on which their "scientific"
doctrines rested, as well as in whose service these doctrines operated;
he saw that parliamentary democracy was a new spoils system, and
that to believe that it could solve the problems of industrial society was
a naïve hope. Thus, like Rousseau, he threw his whole being into a
powerful protest against all the current foibles of his century, understanding their utter inadequacy to the problems and needs of the
time. Today there are many who reproach Marx for his stridency, his
relentless argumentation, even against those with whom he had only
minor differences—like Moses Hess—his biting satire and denigrating
name coining (he called Max Stirner "Saint Max," and "Sancho,"
and Mazzini "that everlasting old ass"). But, without aiming con-
descendingly to justify his personality, I daresay that much of Marx's
tactics was a variation on Rousseau's unsettling costume: he had to

actively shock his age out of its complacency, and this meant pouncing loudly on the luxuriance of hopeful visions, opening a broad wedge into the subtlest differences of opinion, to show exactly where the naïve fallacy lay.

Marx, in other words, was a late Enlightenment figure who held fast to the Enlightenment version of the idea of progress and rejected the new bourgeois variety: he believed that man could and should make himself (cf. Ginsburg, 1953, p. 13). And he saw further that the great variety of effort being expended in politics, industry, and theory was all beside the point of the necessary real solution: the toppling of the second pillar of feudalism. He wanted radical social reconstruction, like the Utopians; but unlike them he put no trust in the good will of the industrialist—he wanted a proletarian revolution once and for all. His program is familiar, and so is the failure of his prediction that the advance of industry will inevitably lead to proletarian revolution. But let us grant that during the nineteenth century this seemed like an eminently correct reading of the process of history. The revolutionary spirit and worker discontent were a continuing undercurrent of the time. Only toward the end of the century did he and Engels, glancing over at America, have misgivings about the inevitability of proletarian discontent. After all, it was Marx who coined the brilliant insight "fetishism of commodities"; how could he fail to take into account this new and subtle form of slavery? The contradiction has often been pointed out (cf. Baillie, 1950, p. 133) in Marx, between his urge to activism and his faith in historical inevitability. But perhaps in this too he shares a quality of the Enlightenment: there was so little that could be done in his time, it was natural to make an emotional investment in posterity. He shares the futuristic optimism of the thinkers from Leibnitz to Condorcet—an optimism that was partly a reflex of powerlessness; for him it was the proletarians who would build the "Heavenly City," to borrow Carl Becker's notion.

Albion Small, who knew more about sociology than most sociologists of today, thought that Marx would occupy a place in social science similar to that of Galileo in the physical sciences (1911–1912, p. 810). What was the basis for this judgment? Simply that Marx provided the mature insight into the influence of economic institutions on the form and content of social beliefs. Thereby Marx pointed the way to the potential liberation of human consciousness: man could put the basic modes of production and distribution under the control of reason, and free himself from slavish response to their vagaries. Thus society would become a product of human freedom rather than of blind necessity.

We will recall at this point that this is exactly what Rousseau saw—that instead of blindly following his passions in the social sphere man could begin to exercise free control over human affairs by choosing and creating the kind of world he wanted to live in. And it was precisely for this option for man that Rousseau earned from Kant the title of Newton of the moral world. In a word, the central figures who form points of reference for the authentic science of man must be those who have opted for man over the constraints of social institutions. The most recent figure in this tradition is, of course, C. Wright Mills, whose life was so lamentably cut short in the flower of its productivity and at the height of his courageous and defiant criticism of his own society.

Mills lashed out, Marx-like, at the colleagues who did not favor his "big-range" sociology, and so provided striking support for Albion Small's contention that Marx will continue to live on until we begin to act on the insights he had. "Big-range" sociology is still compelling and urgent precisely because, in the century since Marx, we have done nothing actively to take control of even the most obvious of those institutions which call the tune to our blind social passions. Mills was merely bringing up to date the same enjoinder that Small had earlier put forth in his evaluation of Marx:

> There is [said Small] an irrepressible conflict in modern society between the presuppositions of capital and the paramount values of humanity. Our academic social scientists would serve their generation to better purpose if they would diminish the ratio of attention which they give to the refinements interesting only to their own kind, and if they would apply the saving to tackling this radical moral problem of men in general (1911–1912, p. 819).

Thus, we might say that Marx brought Rousseau up to date by providing a post-Revolutionary critique of human alienation. He added to Rousseau's (and Herder's) accusation of "civilized" society the nineteenth-century knowledge of history, of the social context of economic theory, as well as the activist example of the Revolution. Marx summed up all that the nineteenth century had learned about alienation, about the social constraints and subjugations of free human powers. Unfortunately, in his time Marx had to strive so hard to show that man's nature was social and historical that he could no longer approach man from within, as Feuerbach had so well done. As a result, he could not proceed to formulate a truly complete

theory of alienation, one that would rest on a thoroughgoing phenomenology of individual striving. Equally serious, in his scorn for
Saint-Simon's "New Christianity," and for Comte's "Religion of
Humanity," he missed appreciating how these systems embodied
potentially the full achievement of Enlightenment science. In Saint-
Simon's system, the "New Christianity" was an *ideal factor*, set over
and against the new industrialism, which was the real factor. By insisting on this duality, he kept the whole Enlightenment framework—
man-centering, ideal-typicality, and the idea of progress. Comte,
too, kept a suggestion of dualism in his system, by stressing that the
problem of achieving altruism and negating egotism, was a continuing one: man had to try to recapture the community feeling of
the medieval time, but this would not happen automatically. Thus,
there was the suggestion of a moral ideal in these systems. True, it
was a *rational* moral ideal, and not the beginning of an empirically
based psychological moral ideal, as it had been with Rousseau—but
it was an ideal all the same.

With Marx, the suggestion of a dualism based on an ideal-type
gets pushed even further into the background. Not only did he suffer
like all the others in his time, from the immature state of psychology,
but Marx had even further reasons for subordinating the ideal
element. In the first place, he was influenced by Hegel's effort to
systematize and to reduce things to monistic principles; in the second,
he was influenced by Feuerbach's naturalism. As a result, when he
came up against French thought in its dualistic nature—in Saint-
Simon's and Comte's systems—he reacted negatively. From Feuerbach
he learned that religion, and the ideal forces in human nature and
history, were merely idealizations of natural and material processes—
that is, logical abstractions. Thus, if Marx wanted to adopt this naturalism and also keep the monistic emphasis he learned from Hegel, he
had to subordinate the ideal elements that constituted such an
important part of the French dualistic systems, as well as of Feuerbach
himself. He subordinated, in sum, the *active ideal element* of social
life (Merz, 1914, vol. 4, p. 540). But this very devaluation skews the
full Enlightenment framework that is indispensable for a mature
science of society. We might say that Marx boiled the threefold
Enlightenment framework down to two elements: instead of the
dualism of an ideal-type with its idea of progress and its active, man-
centered orientation, Marx made the ideal vision a twofold dynamic:
he threw the whole burden of perfectibility and progress into an
automatic law of history, aided by the continual class struggle.

In his own way, Marx thus proved to be as hasty as the Utopians in his ambition to see social reconstruction accomplished once and for all. The price had to be paid: in Marx's later work man turned out to be an objective thing, offered up passively to the forces of society and history. Unwittingly, the ideas of the humanist Marx drifted to a social and historical determinism, and so he left himself open to a judgment which he despised: his "system" turned out to be as unrealistic and as cultist as that of the Utopian socialists: the problem of the whole, thinking, feeling, acting man was sacrificed to an ideology.

As we will see more fully as our story progresses, it was simply not possible to offer up anything like a complete theory of alienation in Marx's time, despite the brilliant beginnings of a Fourier and a Feuerbach. Marx could and did make a powerful synthesis of insights that went considerably beyond Rousseau's and Feuerbach's idealtypology, and his general views on alienation are still thoroughly valid (cf. E. Becker, 1964b; H. L. Parsons, 1964; and see below). So we can hardly accuse Marx of shirking the task, or of failing to do what could not possibly be done in his time. But, in championing the objective forces of society and history at a time when a thoroughgoing theory of the individual personality still did not exist, he had to succumb to the danger: he left the study of moral subjectivity in favor of a deterministic scientific objectivity (Easton, 1961–1962). And in this way he performed one striking disservice for social theory: he obscured its fundamentally moral nature—the very thing with which he himself began. With all his Enlightenment humanism, his incredibly informed moral outrage, he helped draw a veil of nineteenth-century mechanistic scientism over the science of man, so much so that at the beginning of the twentieth century a thinker as acute as Sorel had to struggle to see that socialism was part of a great historical moral problem—and not a narrowly scientific one (cf. also Izoulet, 1895, for a view of the dilemmas of the time). Sorel had, in sum, to find the science of man where the nineteenth century had picked it up, and not where it left it—closer to where the great Mazzini, rather than the later Marx, had said that it was. As Martin Buber has so penetratingly argued in his *Paths in Utopia*, Marx failed precisely where he abolished the earlier Utopian element in social theory.

Today we are very clear on the nature of the problem and on where it began. Our new dilemma will be what to do with it.

CHAPTER FOUR

LESTER WARD AND THE
TWO SOCIOLOGIES IN AMERICA

None of the most outstanding achievements in the history of science can be understood without recognizing the essential place which the demand for system occupies in scientific thinking. The world, as science conceives it, is always the best integrated order that can be established consistently with the known facts.

E. A. BURTT *(1946, p. 414)*

American sociology incorporated the scientific and moral struggle of the nineteenth century and has continued it down to the present day. For this reason alone its history is rich and most instructive. The Spencerian laissez-faire approach to progress was continued by Sumner and Keller. Lester Ward, on the other hand, tried to begin American sociology by by-passing this current and rejoining the French Enlightenment; he was not enticed into the English detour, and sought to revive the science of man from where it had remained with Comte and Fourier.

Ward was directly inspired by the Enlightenment, so much so that, as one reads him, it is possible to say that he was a post-Revolutionary Enlightenment theorist. He pulled together all the ideas of the Enlightenment on progress, education, human plasticity, the need for science to be man-centered; like Saint-Pierre, Leibnitz, Rousseau, and Saint-Simon, he called for an Academy of Political Science in Washington which would serve as a direct influence on legislators as

68

they used it to guide them in the shaping of governmental policy; he used utility as the pragmatic principle of action; he saw hedonism as a goal. He culled every positive insight and creative proposal that the Enlightenment fashioned, from England and Germany as well as France, and offered his own systematic synthesis of *Dynamic Sociology* (a work that Small once wished he could have written). He has been called the Darwin of the social sciences (Chugerman, 1939, p. 37), but he is really a latter-day Comte with a distinctive American modification. His system is more tentative and open than Comte's, more pragmatic, more experimental, more trusting in the individual. It is like the difference between Jefferson and Adams. But Comte was a child of the Revolution, and Ward an optimistic member of a society that had almost no past.

Ward's primary importance, as I see it, lies in the fact that he proposed a firmly man-centered sociology at a time when man-centering was being gradually eclipsed as an ideal. One has only to recall Ernest Renan's sentiment, cited earlier, in order to capture the flavor of the time. Mechanism, unconscious evolutionism, full-blown laissez-fairism—these were formidable adversaries for Ward. It is fair to say that it was far more difficult to man-center the sciences at the end of the nineteenth century than it had been in Diderot's epoch— and the fate of Ward's short-lived attempt supports this speculation. But Ward's framework is important precisely because it is a unique blending of everything the Enlightenment achieved, as well as what Fourier and Comte specifically aimed for. In other words, it is still a model framework for a superordinate value science of man in society —perhaps the best model we have.

Ward saw very clearly what his task was: to breathe new life into a sociology that was becoming an objective science—or, in his words, a "polite amusement," or "dead science" (1883, p. xxvii). This was the anti-Spencer manifesto. "The real object of science is to benefit man" (quoted in Ellwood, 1938, p. 536). It is almost as though one were listening to Diderot and Rousseau on the Newtonian world picture— and it is quite apt: as we saw, Darwin and Spencer did the same thing to man that Newton did: locked him in the depths of nature. How did Ward propose to rehabilitate sociology? By frankly making it subserve human happiness and pleasure, as Fourier and Bentham had wanted. Sociology would be the science of the "social forces," of the feelings and desires of man, the feelings which move him and move the social world. To study the social forces is to study all that is vital in man; to promote the social forces or human desires is the primary task of any science of man worthy of the name. "The problem of social science is to point out in what way the most complete and universal satisfaction of human desires can be attained, and this is one with the problem of greatest happiness" (Ward, 1893, p. 74). Sociology, in other words, had to take its point of departure from man's subjectivity, from his feeling; this was the "great heart of nature" as Ward so beautifully called it (1893, p. 81). "In fact human desires . . . seeking their satisfaction through appropriate activity, constitute the only good from the standpoint of sociology. They are the *social forces*" (p. 115).

The social forces were thus the unmistakable core of Ward's system, but it was not easy to get agreement on this vision of sociology. In a letter to Giddings in 1896 he wrote:

> . . . I think neither you nor Small have yet fully seized my doctrine of *feeling and function*, of the *dynamic agent*, of the *social forces*, or of *dynamic sociology*. I want your criticisms so that I can see where I fail to make these principles clear, but there seems little hope of my yielding them. To do so is to yield all I stand for (1896).

Just as Fourier had bemoaned the blind prejudices with which society had always regarded the human passions, Ward urged that we study human feelings to see what they were really like. His enjoinder could have been written by Fourier, as he calls for a new science of the human passions:

> Civilized man has made no progress with the social forces, and looks upon the passions precisely as the savage looks upon the tornado. . . . Manifestations of social energy are still looked upon as necessary inflictions which may be preached against but must be endured. We have no science of social psychology or sociology that teaches the true nature of human motives, desires and passions or of social wants and needs and the psychic energy working for their satisfaction (1909, p. 110).

Ward offered a "law of parsimony" for sociology, by which the individual would try to get the greatest pleasure for the least pain (1909, pp. 59 ff.). But Ward's understanding of pleasure was not the naïve hedonism of Bentham, but rather the broader insight of Fourier. The human animal lives in a psychic world; pleasure takes rarefied symbolic forms; most of all, pleasure occupies time—it is a complex spatio-temporal phenomenon. Man can deprive himself on earth for expected rewards in heaven. Ward criticized both Bentham and Schopenhauer for failing to realize this, and he scored Stuart Mill for his attack on hedonism, which devalued Utilitarianism in the eyes of its enemies. All that was needed, thought Ward, was to abandon its simplistic formulation (1918, vol. 6, pp. 4–5). Again, Ward proves himself a child of the Enlightenment, but one who lived at a time when he had to attack the subtle nineteenth-century perversions of the central tenets of a science of man. As Marx tried to keep alive the active implementation of progress, Ward tried to keep the eyes of the scientific world focused on the proper function of a science of man—the incessant implementation of human well-being and pleasure. Like Marx, Ward had to show the errors of his time, especially those of Spencer, Bentham, and Mill. But, unlike Marx, Ward fastened on no historicism. He had, instead, a very clear idea of what a systematic sociology should comprise; he saw that it should be an active science, but a systematic, exploratory, and careful science.

He was thus closer to Comte than to Marx, if we want to use affinities to help define his orientation. He saw science as a continuing moral problem, as a problem of social reconstruction and direction. He was against the disciplinary quest for its own sake, the blind subservience to fact gathering, the aimless piling up of more and more information—in sum, he was against the post-Enlightenment version of science, the reading of nature for the sole sake of reading nature. He saw that sociology was not a descriptive science in search of facts, and he understood better than we do today that facts by themselves can impede the progress of a science. The job of descriptive fact gathering belonged to the "ancillary, special social sciences," that is, to the various disciplines such as ethnography, demography, history, statistics, etc. Like Gumplowicz he held that this kind of scientific fact gathering represented a rudimentary stage in science (Gumplowicz, 1963, p. 135). It was the job of sociology to transcend this stage, and take its place as a mature science, that is, using, correlating, generalizing, synthesizing the work of the various disciplines (Ward, 1901–1902). In Ward's view, sociology called for broader, deeper, keener, more synthetic intellectual powers than did the various ancillary disciplines. When Ross wanted to leave economics and become a sociologist, Ward encouraged him, saying that he had a big enough mind for it. Needless to say, we are far from this view of sociology today; practically anyone who can come in off the street and master its techniques can pass as a sociologist—synthetic mental powers would even be a positive disadvantage in most of our graduate schools.

In sum, Ward called for nothing less than a systematic, super-ordinate science of man that would be in the continuing service of human happiness, of the passions, of the "great heart of nature," of the marvelous organisms which have sprung up and evolved on our globe. He called for a Comtean synthesis, but for an open, tentative, pragmatic one, serving not the social over the individual good but, like Fourier, the full expansion of natural individual pleasure.

Thus, from 1883 on, there was an attempt to launch American sociology on a full and mature Enlightenment footing. But it failed. In his declining years, Ward's ideas were no longer central at professional meetings; and, after his death in 1913, academic sociology hastened to forget him. Its image subsequently changed almost entirely from the one Ward had championed. It rejoined the Spencer-Sumner current with a gush, and, as we shall see, nearly drowned with it.

EIGHTY YEARS OF AMERICAN SOCIOLOGY:
THE SUBSTITUTION OF DISCIPLINARY FOR MORAL SCIENCE

What exactly had happened to the current of thinking represented by Ward? Luther and Jessie Bernard, in their outstanding history of early American social science (1943), have shown exactly what took place at that time. Social science in America went through several distinct phases. At the time of Fourier and Comte, America was the scene of an Association Social Science Movement; this was a frank Utopian aspiration and humanitarian idealism, seeking to experiment with communal colonies on Fourier-type models, and attempting to systematize a science of man for human betterment. It was a wide-open, optimistic time, with unlimited horizons and visions fit for Wilhelm Meisters. This movement was succeeded by a more conservative phase represented by the American Social Science Association. The emphasis shifted from theorizing and Utopianism to a search for more "realistic" working principles upon which to base social welfare and reform. The new Association wanted to work within the limits of the existing social structure. The shift was comparable, in a way, to a change from the French to the British parliamentarian direction—from Saint-Simon and Fourier to Bentham and Mill. It was a response to the impossibility of Utopian communities and the implacable currents of laissez-faire society.

With this kind of change the inevitable happened. The social reform ideal, having lost its Utopianism, degenerated into social-welfare work under the reigning ideology, disdaining "impractical" theory. When theory separated from practice, and practice disdained theory, there was nothing left but to work within the ongoing social ideology, gathering data and hoping to patch things here and there. (Today, even psychoanalytic social work is in the service of the system—and psychoanalysis began by being potentially very radical.) The lesson is that when we cut off an applied science from close intercourse with its theoretical base there is no longer anything to feed and shape the theory. The superordinate scientific ideal, then, freed from practical necessity, abandoned the effort to fashion a guiding theory and gradually turned into the fact-gathering, descriptive research of the various disciplines. Among them, the new academic discipline of sociology was formed (see Bernard, 1943, pp. 527, 529, 591, 599, 835). Eventually, with this fragmentation, not only the Association Social Science Movement had to fold up, but also its more conservative successor, the American Social Science Association. There was no longer any possibility for the kind of superordinate social science that Ward had championed, and all hope of a unifying, active moral vision and control died.

The death did not go unlamented. In 1886, when the seceding disciplines were about to scuttle the aim and vision of the American Social Science Association, John Eaton uttered his eloquent and heartfelt plea, a plea that should grip us today more than ever: "Let the warning cry fill the air of scientific associations, from meeting to meeting, that science is our means, not our end. . ." (Bernard, 1943, p. 599). The spirit of the Enlightenment still hung on in America of that time, but we know what fills the air of our scientific meetings today: cigar smoke and grant-money boasting, and incredibly narrow-focused papers, and the inauguration of new publications, and hiring, and building, building, building. Science *has* become the end, as Eaton knew it would.

But sociology, even as a discipline, was powerfully influenced by Ward and it was in the guiding hands of Small. The platform on which was launched *The American Journal of Sociology,* one of the first journals of sociology in the world, by Small, in 1895, read, in part:

> [To]. . . assist all intelligent men in taking the largest possible view of their rights and duties as citizens . . . [it] will attempt to translate sociology into the language of ordinary life, so that it will not appear to be merely a classification and explanation of fossil facts . . . to so far increase our present intelligence about social utilities

that there may be much more effective combination for
the promotion of the general welfare than has thus far
been organized . . . and [be] an element of strength and
support in every wise endeavor to insure the good of
man (AJS, 1895, pp. 13–14).

If this platform were to be printed on the cover of the *Journal*
today it would appear grotesque to its readers—the contents of most
of the *Journal* would mock each sentence. But we must not be unjust;
how was sociology to stand alone as a humanitarian discipline, without
a superordinate unity to guide it? With the breakup of the early
vision and the death of Ward, it had "to do" science just as the other
disciplines were doing. By 1920 sociology had undergone a startling
change, and opted for methodological rigor after the model of the
physical sciences, aided by a sharp impetus from behaviorism in its
sister discipline, "scientific" psychology. Ward was completely forgotten; and even his disciple Ross, in the 1930 edition of his popular
1920 textbook, did not mention Ward (Burnham, 1956, pp. 10–11).

By 1929 sociology, striving for the height of imagined scientific
respectability, hit its nadir as a humanly relevant activity. W. F.
Ogburn, in his presidential address to the American Sociological
Society, had this to say:

Sociology as a science is not interested in making the
world a better place in which to live, in encouraging
beliefs, in spreading information [sic] in dispensing news,
in setting forth impressions of life, in leading the multi-
tudes, or in guiding the ship of state. Science is interested directly in one thing only, to wit, discovering new
knowledge. . . .(Quoted in Burnham, 1956, pp. 10–11.)

This was the new disciplinarian speaking, traveling unen-
cumbered in the way that had been prepared for him; it is obvious
that the new men had grown up in a new atmosphere. Small had
begun American sociology in the service of human betterment;
Ogburn firmly enunciated science in the service of no one.

The sentiment has governed sociology to this day. The social
problems of the 1930's were a threat to this detachment; but in the
1940's war once again saved the day for science, against the need for
social reconstruction that had seemed imminent in the 1930's. Again,
the "new moral movement" of commercial-industrial society bore
forth its hideous fruit, and stole the day from its nineteenth-century

adversary. An apparent social unity and full production were again artificially forged, and could continue to support a disinterested science. By the decade of the 1950's, this disinterest became almost total: the disciplines became fully "professionalized," and a mass of describers and observers plied away at ordering the value-free facts. Only a few thinkers arose to disturb this halcyon calm—R. S. Lynd and his *Knowledge For What?*, Pitirim Sorokin and his *Fads and Foibles in Sociology and Related Sciences*, C. Wright Mills and his *Sociological Imagination*. But, aside from perhaps some personal bitterness, these works caused only a minor ruffle on the surface of the discipline; the few critics grew old or died, but the "profession" carried on. Only today, in the 1960's, it begins to appear that sociology is about to undertake a fundamental reappraisal of its disciplinary image.

PENALTIES FOR THE LOSS OF A SUPERORDINATE UNITY: THE EXAMPLE OF GIDDINGS

This history of the abandonment of humanitarianism for the ostensible advance of science is perhaps all the more curious when we examine the men who made American sociology. They were all idealists who saw human betterment as an integral part of the very conception of a science of man. Ward, Small, Ross, Giddings, the conservative Sumner—they all agreed that sociology should serve man, however much they may have differed on exactly how and what the findings of sociology should contribute. Small had deeply religious sentiments, Ross was a social reformer at heart. These men were still scientists in the original Baconian and Newtonian vision of the quest, and not "laboratory managerialists"—to use Lewis Feuer's (1963) apt description of the breed today.

What happened to their efforts, why couldn't they guide sociology into an activist posture, and maintain its basic humanitarian intent? I think the simple answer is the one we have just considered—that sociology became a discipline, and lost its superordinate social science orientation. Consequently, these men were caught in a bind: they had "to do" disciplinary science, but did not have any way of bringing the findings of their discipline to bear on social life. When action is frustrated and becomes impossible, the only thing to do is to let it slide into the background of one's preoccupations, or put it off for some future date. The Enlightenment problem seemed again to be repeated: when one can reason but is unable to act, the only

thing to do is to invest in posterity. Giddings put his faith in the future
of inductive science, just as Condorcet had put his in progress, and
Marx in the coming proletariat.

Giddings reacted to the "do-gooder" social-problem sociology of
the early years of the century. In his view, mere sentiment about
"problems" would have to give way to objective attempts to see just
what was going on in society, to determine its basic patterns. But he
did not abandon the humanistic intent—it runs through all his
writings: "The function of society is to develop and to safeguard the
higher types of human personality . . ." (1922, p. 291). "The rational
improvement of society proceeds through a criticism of social values"
(quoted in Northcott, 1918). Giddings held to Plato's and Rousseau's
emphasis on ideal-typology, and said that a society which does not have
ideals is as good as dead (1922, p. 230). But he wanted to be more
scientific about what progress was. He sought to find out what kind of
progress would be an acceptable minimum to people of different
cultures. What would it cost in human energy, time, worry, money,
sacrifice, to produce whatever kind of person is deemed adequate in the
society under study? What would be, in sum, an observably definable,
minimum definition of progress that would make sense to nearly all
thoughtful humans of good will, to social planners who might use this
definition to provide standards for social betterment?

Now this is a straightforward humanitarian program such as we
do not see in sociology today. The criticism of social values and
furtherance of progress is exactly what Ward too had championed.
But when we move from Giddings' aims and desires to his means and
methods, we experience an ominous change of air. What is the
standard for this criticism of social values? Giddings wanted to determine how much restraint, liberty, conformity, and variation are con-
ducive to the general welfare. This he thought was supremely important for issues of public policy. How does one determine this?
By finding, says Giddings, the "normal social constraint in a given
community, at a given stage of its evolution. . ." (quoted in Northcott, 1918, pp. 22–23). What is the method to be used? The same one
which Giddings resolutely championed for sociology, and in which
he trained many devotees of rigorous techniques: the method of
analysis by statistics, for the "purpose of discovering ratios, modalities,
coefficients of variation, and correlations" (1922, p. 300). What
facts were to be analyzed in this fashion? Those which arose out of
the random social experimentation that is always going on in society;
the sociologist has to observe and analyze the continuing natural social

experiments of group living. Thus, for example, Giddings would study the inductive data on the plurality of birth rates over death rates, health and plenty over sickness and poverty, and so on. The object of this study, to repeat, would be to attempt to put the human sciences on a sound footing, to try to get some objectively verifiable index of progress in place of the starry-eyed notions of the earlier generation of social do-gooders.

Well and fine. But now emerges full force the fallacy of this kind of scientific futurism in sociology (I have dealt with Giddings at some length in order to demonstrate it because it is still the fallacy of most sociology today). In reacting to the "social problem" sociology, Giddings slighted its main preoccupations, namely, *contemporary history* and *urgent social problems*. These are of immediate concern to sociology, in addition to the regularities that Giddings wanted to study inductively. The point is that, whatever regularities one might find, they will be modified by history and by human purpose. Like Sumner, who learned from his own concept of folkways, Giddings was ultimately to see where his own thinking led him: that social facts are psychological in nature, and not physical, and that his rigorous concepts of "law," "contingency," and "correlation," if defined dynamically, would not represent most of the data of the social sciences. The logical step to take, then, would be to plead for an activist sociology, in addition to an analytic one, but Giddings—like Sumner—never took it, and neither have most of his students.

It is easy to sum up Giddings' fallacy: by lifting an activist humanitarianism to the detached scientific heights of an opportunistic inductivism, we have lifted it right out of the world of contemporary social problems. The program is entirely incommensurate with its aims, and by its cautious, restricted scope it has undermined them. The humanistic criticism of social values—radical in intent—bogs down practically into a conservatism of method that is self-defeating. The data that one would gather from random social experimentation would be largely outmoded and by-passed by events. As Franz Boas had urged: "All social data become historical data almost as soon as they can be recorded" (cf. also Haring, 1956, p. 117). Sociology would thus be in business as a disinterested discipline for a long time, and life would go on—and right by it. This is exactly what is happening today—Giddings' own legacy confirms the criticism of his orientation, and the penalty of the loss of an active, superordinate social science.

Furthermore, what happens to the search for higher values in this kind of program? As a scientist Giddings tried to refrain from putting anything other into nature, in terms of valuations, than is there in the first place—he wanted to study objective data. But this is a value program that really side-steps the issue of values. Human ideal valuations, in a word, are hardly so simple as birth rates and adequacy to exist and achieve. Human valuings must take cues from the natural order—this is the Enlightenment heritage, as we have noted several times. But the other part of this heritage is that we must inevitably transcend the natural order in our values: otherwise, we do not have *human* valuations. Giddings died before the full Nazi upsurge, when bouncy babies and healthy adequacy were a social standard. On the other hand, a high abortion rate and a low birth rate may be a sign of superb national health, as in present-day Japan. Giddings, of course, with all his broadness, would probably have been quick to agree with these comments, and he would have been able to cite his own work in support: as we noted, he himself said that a society which has no Utopian ideals is as good as dead. But the fact is that in his program for sociology he broached an artificial gulf between man and nature, and he left us looking for inherent criteria of "normal" that must really be human valuations.

Finally, and not least, Giddings' search for an agreeable minimum definition of progress was one that objectivized man. He wanted, as we noted, to provide a scientific guide for producing whatever kind of human person was "deemed adequate" in any particular society. This was all of a piece with his belief in deterministic social laws and measurable regularities: it would allow a science that would control man. Thus, Giddings continued the nineteenth-century off-centering of the idea of progress, well into the twentieth, disguising it in more scientific garb. But today we can see that this does not hide the fact that it places man at the disposal of society instead of using man as a central measure of value. Giddings' science was ultimately as con- servative as Comte's, and, despite its similar intentions, it equally lost man.

There is certainly more respectability in belonging to a going discipline, possessing a definite technique, than to continue trying to reconstruct history in order to find out who one is. The latter procedure is hard on the self-image, especially when one's sister disciplines are cockily proclaiming how closely they can follow physics. So much so that the brilliant historian of sociology Harry Elmer Barnes late in life dedicated a small book on historical sociology to George A. Lundberg, with a tribute to his furthering of sound scientific method in sociology. Lundberg was a disciple of Giddings' approach, a "resolute champion" of "rigorous techniques," who thought that sociology had "arrived" at the full stature of a science and no longer had any need of history. In his words:

> The history of social thought will be relegated approximately to the position that the history of chemistry, physics, and biology occupies in the training of students in these fields. That is, advanced students will be expected to be familiar with the main outlines *in the light of contemporary knowledge*, in which they will first have a firm grounding (Lundberg, 1944–1945, p. 508).

So Lundberg could accept Barnes' dedication in complete serenity. The only thing Lundberg did not see was that the Giddings' tradition would end in almost utter sterility on the level of theory, and that he himself would represent its conceptual *fin de race*. He did not see that sociology was still in its prehistory, was not yet a mature hypothetico-deductive science, working along agreed paradigms, as were the physical sciences which he hoped to ape. Its history was not yet antiquarian or anecdotal because sociology did not possess a cumulative, experimental body of knowledge. That day was still far off. Sociology was not, in sum, a superordinate, experimental science of man in society.

The failure to realize what sociology was and what its history showed it should be was responsible for considerable confusion and argumentation in the eighty years after Ward. Some voices, such as Sorokin's, resolutely held out for sociology as a synthetic, generalizing, theoretical, superordinate science, and deplored the new narrow-gauge sociologist who had become "chilled by the fact-finding mode" (1936–1937). So too did Karl Mannheim, who wanted sociology to be the basic, unifying social science which would give a complete theory of the social process (1953, pp. 203–204). In the 1920's there had been some movement toward a possible synthesis in the social sciences: a Social Science Research Council was set up, an *Encyclopedia of the Social Sciences*, and a *Journal of Social Philosophy* were put under way.

In the 1930's, the decade of great social needs and new hopes, the debate about what sociology really is was reanimated. Stuart A. Rice's article "What Is Sociology?" and the anxious questions it raised were typical. Rice concluded that sociology was not a single, unified subject matter, but a plural number of subject matters, grouped ambiguously under a single name (1931–1932, p. 319). He was firm about one thing, however: that whatever sociology was, mixtures of philosophy or other disciplines or what not, there was one thing it definitely was *not* and should not be, namely, "ethical valuations . . . which are ultimately beyond the reach of science" (p. 325). Sorokin answered Rice and claimed that sociology was not a grab bag of mixtures, but a "clear and logically consistent science" (p. 327). C. A. Ellwood, another of the broad thinkers in sociology, held that ethical valuations can be made reliable by science (p. 328)—thus restating the familiar Enlightenment credo that science reads nature in the service of human action and is based on consensus. But all of this hardly represented any agreement among sociologists, and reflects truly the vicissitudes of a discipline in search of itself, a discipline which originally had a clear idea of its function, but which had narrowed its focus down in the interests of the scientific quest. So that today, in the 1960's, we are once again hotly joining the issue of the proper image of a science of man. Perhaps, owing to sociology's historical default, another discipline may move in to fill the breach, for example, anthropology—which Kroeber and others have seen as the generalizing, unifying, humanitarian discipline par excellence. Unhappily, anthropology is moving away from Kroeber's broadness with the same relentlessness with which sociology moved away from Ward.

THE LESSONS OF THE AMERICAN EXPERIENCE: THE TWO PATHS TO A SCIENCE OF MAN

I have used Lester Ward and the American experience as a sort of shorthand paradigm of the problem of the science of man. Now that we have sketched the example in a short space, let us probe a bit more into the background. The men who fashioned American sociology into a discipline were not naïve or ill-willed. Those who allowed it to dissipate into an objective, fact-gathering pursuit were under the impulsion of strong motivations, motivations which at all times must have seemed reasonable. What I mean is that American sociology was not merely swept blindly along by the fact that it was immersed in laissez-faire society. Ward's sociology, like Fourier's and Comte's systems before, was simply not adequate to the task of compelling enough allegiance to proceed to design and build a new morality. The social context was wrong, the times were wrong, and the system was inadequate.

From our present historical vantage point, we can see that there were two paths to a science of man. The first was that of an activist, systemic, superordinate social science. This kind of system would begin almost immediately to build a mature, hypothetico-deductive experimental science of man in society, on the model of the Enlightenment. We saw that this was Comte's hope, and Fourier's immediate ambition, as well as Bentham's vision. The second path was the passive, objective, disciplinary quest. This approach would attempt to clarify as much as possible the various areas of specialized knowledge so that one day a directive science would have sound data upon which to base its action. It was the second path which won out in all cases, and we can now see that the reason for this was not wholly the social or ideological pressures against an actively manipulative science. Let us examine the background to the problem in more detail; it is the paradigm problem for a science of man.

THE MAN-CENTERED APPROACH TO A SYSTEMIC, SUPERORDINATE SCIENCE OF SOCIETY

In the nineteenth century, many people saw the need for social reconstruction, and looked to a radical reform via sociology. The Association Social Science Movement and the American Social Science Association reflected this wide stirring. There was no lack of imaginative, independent thinkers who could seize on the systemic idea of Comte and Spencer. Many have dropped out of history who deserve to be remembered and whose thought is well worth perusing today; for example, Robert S. Hamilton, another self-styled Newton of the social sciences—earlier than Ward (1874)—saw the need for an agreed synthesis and offered his own reconciliation of Comte, Spencer, and Buckle. Also before Ward, the noted W. T. Harris knew that the new society would have to have universal, critical education as its core, an education that would aim at the gradual emancipation of man from blind social constraint.

Not only in the United States, but also abroad, there was great ferment for social reconstruction and for a new scientific society, mostly using Comte as a model. In Russia there were several great sociologists whose work still rewards reading, especially Peter Lavrov and Nicolai Mikhailovsky. Lavrov was the one who adopted Kant's famous challenge to the nineteenth century, the paradoxical challenge that still haunts us today: to promote maximum individuality and maximum community at the very same time. Lavrov saw that the danger of the times was the absorption of the individual in the "new social good," just as Dostoievsky feared. And for this he was critical of both Kant and Comte, who aimed for the good of the individual, but actually risked submerging him in some larger entity called society. He tried to make Kant's work more historical, and Comte's more critical, and thus allow for a more developmental and pragmatic approach to social reconstruction. He actually recaptured the spirit of the Enlightenment in its pre-Revolutionary groping, and could thus oppose not only Comte's conservatism but also Bakunin's anarchism and Marx's communism. In other words, he wanted a science of man in society and not new ideologies (cf. Barnes and Becker, 1961, vol. 3, pp. 1036 ff.; and see Lavrov, 1891).

When we learn that Comte's motto "Order and Progress" still decorates the flag of Brazil, we can understand that he was championed precisely in those countries which envisaged a new social order as a possibility. In the nineteenth century both the Americas and Russia shared this vision, while in France and England Comte's Positivism tended to be interpreted as a narrow method. It seems that in the nineteenth century, as today, the outlying or the frontier countries to which the new struggles for social reconstruction were carried could not afford to fall victims to a fad—narrow positivism then, narrow Marxism or disinterested American academic sociology today. It is significant that the critical sociology championed by C. Wright Mills has won more attention in Asia, Africa, and Latin America today than it has in the academic community in the United States.

Of course, there were individual thinkers even in England who held to a Comtean, systemic view of social science—Hobhouse is the outstanding one. He saw that a science of society had to be synthetic and all-embracing. Hobhouse is interesting for us here because he had to fight in England against the same things Ward fought in the United States; that is, he had to keep Enlightenment social science alive in a post-Darwinian world—exactly as Ward had to try to do. Thus he kept the idea of progress to the fore, and fought Spencer's notion that progress is unconscious by insisting that progress is deliberative and based on chosen values. He promoted the rational control over the conditions of social life, and had to fight the new anti-intellectualism and the overvaluation of biological factors in human life, which Darwin had made popular.

One of the things that gradually emerges, then, from the history I am sketching is that the whole post-Darwinian development of the

science of man is a struggle to get back to the pre-Darwinian, Enlightenment good sense. Hobhouse and Ward did to Darwin and
Spencer what we in our day have had to do with Freud—go back beyond him to a more plastic, open, broadly social view of human
striving. In our day this is easier than it was in Ward's and Hobhouse's,
because we are further from Darwin; but it is also more difficult—because we have practically completely lost the Enlightenment tradition.

When we turn to Germany we see that there, too, the systemic
approach to sociology was kept alive, but for reasons quite peculiar to
that country. Ever since the political economy of Cameralism in the
sixteenth century and since Leibnitz and the later idealisms of
Fichte, Schelling, and Hegel, the social problem was seen on a total
organic and increasingly national basis. The Germans, in other
words, had a comprehensive approach to the science of man that
stemmed naturally from their own social and metaphysical traditions.
It was this same orientation that led them to criticize the English
deductive economics and to develop instead broadly historical and
contextual views of narrow economic problems, in the work of Roscher
and his followers. In sociology it gave rise to what we call "organicist"
theories of society, a current that developed through the nineteenth
century in the work of Schaeffle and Lilienfeld, and into recent decades in the work of Othmar Spann. The sociology of Spann, for all
its distortions and inadequacies, was social critical and social reconstructionist in spirit and intent. Here was the familiar criticism of
the "overdevelopment of the exact sciences," of the "concentration
on economic pursuits," of the "artificial popularity of individualism"
(Landheer, 1948, p. 397). In Spann's work there was an inherent
moral protest, albeit blunted by an archaic, backward-looking anti-
industrialism. Perhaps if German organicism had been more international instead of national in scope, it could have avoided the
archaic accents. Certainly it was attempting to answer a real and
deep-felt need, as the twentieth edition of Spann's work in 1930
attests. The tragedy of this kind of sociology is not that it provided
support for the Nazi credo, but simply that sociology will always be
misused if it fails in critical scope and courage vis-à-vis its own
national society.

A much more sensible and important thinker is the sociologist
Hans Freyer. He is actually a latter-day German Lester Ward, with a
thoroughgoing Enlightenment understanding (if overly nationalistic) of what sociology should be. All the themes we are familiar with
that have since largely dropped out of sociology, are present in

Freyer's work. He sees sociology as a historical creation, as a platform for social change and a continuing critique of the present. For Freyer, sociology is value-based because it takes its departure from human volition. It should properly be oriented to chosen social ends. Like Comte, he sees that wide, scientific agreement over values is possible precisely when an appeal is made to empirical data. Perhaps most important for the history I am tracing here, Freyer is an acute, modern thinker who sees that the great nineteenth-century systems are not merely advanced phases of social theory; but rather, they represent *an entirely new perspective* on the problem of man in society, a problem that was born after the French Revolution. Consequently, he understands that sociology alone has the proper historical perspective to provide a criticism of liberalism. In the Saint-Simonian and Comtean spirit, he is prepared to argue the problem of parliamentary liberalism from the vantage point of a historically sophisticated superordinate science of sociology (see Ernest Manheim, 1948). Like Ward in the United States and Hobhouse in England, Freyer represents the attempt to keep alive the Enlightenment hope of the superordinacy of science and morals over politics. He is an important figure who—again, significantly—has been translated into Spanish, but not into English. The English-speaking countries are not now on the reconstructionist frontier.

The Failure of the Systems

So much, then, for a brief sketch of some of the major urges to systemic, superordinate sociology in the nineteenth and early twentieth centuries. The question now must be answered—why did they *all* fail, even though they were quite popular and influential for a time? Why did the younger generation in Germany criticize Freyer? (Karl Mannheim, 1953, p. 218.) Why was Ward so soon forgotten, even by Ross, and why is Hobhouse today an antiquity?

When we answer this question we will have disclosed the major reason why sociology is still today fragmented into sometimes bitterly opposing schools: into "value" sociologists such as Myrdal, Gouldner, Mills, and McClung Lee; "grand theory" sociologists such as Parsons; "empirical" sociologists such as Lazarsfeld; "formal" sociologists such as Leopold von Wiese in Germany; and the "historical-critical" sociology of his opponent Franz Oppenheimer. And how the disputes rage over minutiae, over whether sociology is really only the "geometry" of social relationships, or whether social facts are really unique historical events, and so on (cf. Oppenheimer, 1932, p. 259; Heberle, 1948, p. 266; Abel, 1959, p. 477). And there are other "styles" of sociology which seem to some critics truly "individual" and idiosyncratic, for example, the "phenomenological" sociology of Vierkandt.

The great historical dilemma of sociology was never better stated than by Albion Small in 1905, and I would like to quote him at length as the answer to why superordinate sociology has so far always failed:

> How did it come about that sociology is in the world at all? This is something more than a mere matter of historical curiosity. The answer to the question goes far toward explaining very prevalent confusions about sociology itself. The subject sometimes seems to be utterly abstract speculative philosophy. As it is represented by other men, it knows nothing whatever of logic or philosophy, and is simply a scheme of sentimentally benevolent experiment. How does it come about that such different things can pass under the same name?
>
> The answer is, in a word, that in all probability the sentimental philanthropic impulse has done more than the scientific impulse to bring sociology into existence . . . certain types of philanthropists, in this country, so industriously advocated *the improvement of social conditions* that presently attempts to develop a scientific sociology became inevitable. The various agitations for social reform or improvement worked in this way: People of philanthropic temper decided that something was wrong and ought to be righted. It might be the existence of paupers; or of competent workmen out of work, or of long hours, low pay, and bad sanitary conditions for those who did work; or of private ownership of what might have been owned by the public; or a hundred other things. Earnest people declared that these things ought not so to be. Then obstinate conservatives were roused to opposition. They said: "Nonsense! These people are crazy. Sentimentalism has gone mad in them. They mean well, but they are trying to do the impossible. . . . There is no scientific ground for these visionaries to stand on." There was some truth on both sides. Evils were being allowed to take their course which the proper amount of attention could have mitigated, if not wholly remedied. On the other hand, schemes of reform were being promoted without serious attempt to find out what their conse-

quences would be, outside of a very narrow circle. . . . All
this tended to educate people of a different type; people
who could see the evils, on the one hand, but on the
other hand, could see that our knowledge of social
relations is too meager to be a safe guide in attempts to
reorganize society. These men said: "Yes, the sentimentalists are right that we ought to do better but the conservatives are also right that we ought to look before we leap.
We must be sure we are right before we go ahead; or, at
least, if we cannot be sure, we must study society deeply
enough to justify our beliefs that courses of action are
reasonable, and in the direction of progress."

It followed that a few people accepted the logic of
the situation and marked out a course of study accordingly. . . . The shortest and surest route to better doing
in the end is more thorough knowing. There is work for
a few students who will devote themselves to patient
study of human society as a whole, without impatience
about the length of time which will be required to reach
practical results. There is work for men who will consent
to be sneered at as dreamers, who will be patient while
people revile and ridicule them as impractical transcendental philosophers. There is work for men who will
run large surveys of life in its ultimate meanings, and will
discover general principles that are always valid in
society. This will in the end prove the most practical sort
of work, for it will furnish the only possible rational basis
for intelligent programs of social action. . . .

After what has been said, it is to be hoped that two
things have been made clear: First: The program of
sociology aims finally at the most thorough, intense,
persistent, and systematic effort to make human life all
that it is capable of becoming. Second: This thoroughly
social and constructive impulse is held in restraint by
scientific sociology until a philosophy and a theory of
action can be justified. . . . The impulse is humanitarian.
The method is that of completely objective science and
philosophy (1905, pp. 36–37).

Sociology, in a word, was caught in the ambivalence between
scientists and sentimentalists, students and social reformers. Small
did not see the ultimate bind in which sociology as a discipline would
be caught—namely, the one we sketched earlier in discussing Giddings: Giddings started out to put reformist measures on a sound,

scientific basis; but, a *superordinate* social science having been lost, there was no way for the *discipline* of sociology to put results into practical action. But this was a lesson of later history that we are only today disclosing. During Small's day, his program seemed eminently reasonable and realistic. The disciplines had to be freed for objective study. But this led to another limitation that was to have an equally serious effect and that we mentioned earlier, namely, that when the researchers were freed of the need for hasty reforms, they also became forgetful of the need for a conceptual system: as a result, the study of facts and of empirical regularities tended to become an end in itself. Now we can understand the revolt against the systems, and their ultimate failure. To the new emerging empiricist, the systems seemed both personally sentimental and intangibly philosophic, and he felt he had to eschew both.

The sciences had to find out what they were all about and they did not want to be hampered by commitment to either a super-ordinate social science—such as Ward's sociology—or an immediate action imperative, like social reconstruction. Small cited Ward's program approvingly, but he did not foresee Ward's fate. A. G. Keller, in a review (1903) of Ward's *Pure Sociology*, put the case of the nascent human sciences quite well. He said that there was a need to hold "systems" back pending investigation; there was a need for facts, labor, and not largely a priori systems, such as Ward offered. Other thinkers were also urging a careful analytic period, to succeed the hasty, synthetic one. Durkheim, making a scientific case against both laissez-faire economy and socialist Utopian systems, also pleaded for facts over premature conceptions: "Those aware of what social science must be . . . cannot be fond of these premature solutions, these vast systems so summarily sketched out" (1959, p. 7). Durkheim wanted the disciplinary division of labor to be pushed to its furthest point, and only thus, he thought, would unity come about naturally, as the various disciplines ultimately became conscious of their organic solidarity (1947, pp. 370–371). Another critic of the systemic approach in the early stages of a science was Eugenio Rignano, who pointed out that all the sciences had started in this primitive manner, from the Greek synthetic philosophers on. He deplored the attempt to grasp the innermost laws of things, and all their reciprocal relationships, by one "master-stroke" of systemic synthesis (1928–1929). In the face of this view of science, Ward suffered the fate of Comte.

Hans Freyer was later to suffer his eclipse for the same reasons. Ward's disciples had acknowledged the importance of his system, and launched themselves on a factual quest in order to fill it in empirically—only to chafe against the system and finally to forget it. Freyer's disciples acknowledged that he gave to sociology "the securest foundation," but reproached him that he did not "fill in with empirical matter the framework he constructed" (Mannheim, 1953, p. 218).

The systems failed, then, partly because they were premature, because they had to find out what their subject matter really was like. The hope, at that early time, was well expressed by William Strong in 1870, who saw the need for the disciplinary quest, but who firmly believed, like Durkheim, that future students would be able to integrate a fully mature science of society out of the seemingly unrelated disciplines (Bernard, 1943, p. 581). Only when the disciplines would one day be "fully developed" could a synthetic social science be formed. Strong's position seemed logical and it was fully supported by the primitive stage of knowledge at that time. For example, when the American Social Science Association broke apart as a unified, social-welfare science, one of the organizations that split off was The Association for the Protection of the Insane and the Prevention of Insanity. What good was a superordinate social science, guiding the practical work of helping the insane, if there was no theory of insanity? Some narrow, specialized research seemed very necessary *in order to find out what it was that they had to prevent*. The case for fragmentation before future synthesis thus rested partly on the enormous complexity of the human subject matter, and seemed the only path to take. The grand systems died, in sum, for many valid reasons, not the least of which was the complexity of the human subject matter; the much-coveted unity of science in the service of man was hopefully deferred to some future date.

THE DISCIPLINARY CLARIFICATION: THE EXAMPLE OF THE "SOCIAL FORCES"

The new hopes, then, were attached to the disciplinary quest. Sociology had to find out more about the nature of the human subject matter before it could hope to become a mature science and only then would a unification of the disciplines be meaningful. Our next important question must be, what was accomplished by the disciplinary quest? To answer this, it is fortunately not necessary to treat the history of all the disciplines over the last half century. I think the benefits and the disadvantages of the disciplinary quest can be strikingly

conveyed in a shorthand manner, by focusing on the discipline of
sociology itself, and tracing the fate of one of its early guiding
ideas—the social forces. American sociology began as an attempt to
clarify the social forces, the forces that animate individual action and
govern social phenomena. The idea of social forces was gradually
clarified and then abandoned. The story of this brief venture is
extremely instructive. If we hark back for a moment to Fourier's
ambition to establish a fully deductive science of the human passions,
we will be able to understand what this venture represented: it was
an attempt to derive an understanding of the "passions" by descriptive, empirical study, *in place of an experimental, hypothetico-deductive approach.* If this is true, it then becomes supremely important
to see what was accomplished by the objective, disciplinary approach. This new understanding should then help us frame the
problem of unity and the problem of a hypothetico-deductive science
in much more sophisticated terms than would otherwise be possible.
We should be able to draw on fifty years of effort and accumulated
experience.

I noted earlier the close resemblance between Ward's social
forces and Fourier's passions. I also noted that some of Ward's
observations on the social forces could have been expressed in almost
identical language by Fourier. Ward saw the social forces as the
central key to understanding social phenomena and, like Fourier, he
felt that once we understand these forces in their "pure state" we
could go on to build a civilization that would harness all the best
energies of nature.

> The sociologist who has a proper conception of his
> science as similar in all essential respects to these other
> sciences, and as having, like them, a practical purpose and
> use for man, looks upon the social forces as everybody
> looks upon the physical and vital forces, and sees in them
> powers of nature now doing injury, or at least running to
> waste, and perceives that, as in the other case, they may,
> by being first studied and understood, be rendered harm-
> less and ultimately converted into servants of man, and
> harnessed . . . to the on-going chariot of civilization
> (1909, pp. 101 and 110, *passim*).[1]

Ward seems to have realized that the problem of the social forces
was an extremely knotty one, and that the thoroughgoing study of
them lay well in the future. In other words, like Fourier, he knew

that his framework was correct—the Enlightenment framework—but immature and scientifically inadequate as it stood.

Ross wanted to see Ward write more on the social forces, and sent him Spinoza's analysis of the passions for possible suggestions (Stern, 1938, p. 365). Ross volunteered in another letter that "Jealousy, it seems to me, is a very important social force" (Stern, 1938, p. 367). Decidedly, the notion of social forces was in a very primitive state of analysis, but it was on a supremely right track: it was to take a full fifty years to develop a clear and usable understanding of the phenomenon of jealousy—uniting the insights of sociology, psychiatry, and existential phenomenology (cf. E. Becker, 1964a).

Many people were talking about social forces at the turn of the century, and their notions were equally primitive. The economist S. N. Patten used social forces in a Fourierian sense, urging man to get back to a pleasure-seeking economy rather than a pain-avoiding one (see House, 1936, pp. 236–237). The sociologist Stuckenberg spoke of the social forces in reductionist terms, as "those ultimate social atoms, or energies, which are found in the mind. . . . A mental energy is a focus of power, the elemental factor by means of which society is constituted" (1903, p. 189). Stuckenberg listed ten forces—"economic, political, egotic, appetitive, affectional, recreative, esthetic, ethical, religious, intellectual" (p. 207). These were words that represented only a minimum of systematic, contextual understanding of the phenomena they represented—again, the primitive state of analysis at that time.

Ratzenhofer, who made some early innovations in sociology, had his own crude notions of what constituted the "inside" of social action, and listed five organismic "interests." Small took over Ratzenhofer's notion of "interests" and expanded his classification into six elements: health, wealth, sociability, knowledge, beauty, rightness. All this promised to give a centralized and systematic grasp of the human subject matter, which would serve as the basis for a complete sociology of man in society. In 1905 Small could say, "The latest word of sociology is that human experience yields the most and deepest meaning when read from first to last in terms of the evolution, expression and accommodation of interests" (Barnes, 1948a, p. 378). Small hoped that by observing and classifying these social forces, laws of social interaction might be organized (House, 1925–1926, p. 171).

The reaction to these early and fumbling sociological analyses of human motivation was not long in coming. In 1911 E. C. Hayes wrote a sharp critique of "The Social Forces Error." He said that it was extremely superficial to refer human actions to motives or causes which were essentially biological—like the passions—and hence antecedent to social activities. Thus, the same critique that we have made of Freud was very early leveled at Ward. He felt that Ward placed too much emphasis on the biological organism. Science, said Hayes, must proceed by abandoning discussion of forces, as biology had abandoned the discussion of vitalism. Science accounts for reality in terms of relationships, and the job of sociology as a discipline, Hayes thought, was merely impeded by trying to find causes antecedent to social activity. Somewhat later, the philosopher Morris Cohen made a similar attack on the physical nature of the social forces, accusing Ward of confusing social and natural causation (1959, p. 360).

What was happening? Sociology was trying to systematize its notions about what makes people act the way they do, and not having much success at it. It wanted to be a precise science, and, since its subject matter was man, it sought to put man under scientific wraps in the most exact ways. There was a fervent movement to dissect, classify, tabulate, simplify. Sociologists were reaching out for some uniform principle by means of which to explain all the manifestations of social phenomena. Everyone had his own favorite. Ross looked to Tarde and fastened on fear, hate, gregariousness, and suggestibility as the social forces which account for social groupings (cf. F. H. Allport, 1927). Giddings looked to Adam Smith and revived the simplistic single principle of "consciousness of kind" to organize his sociology. Many sociologists, apparently appalled by the problem of explaining human motivation and the nature of the social bond, fastened on the notion of instinct. Besides, "prestigious" sister disciplines such as psychology showed the way: no less a thinker than William James dazzled the scientific world with a list of thirty human instincts.

All in all, the period from 1883 to 1918 was one in which the concepts of social forces and instincts were dominant in sociology. They seemed to offer the only hope for a scientific grasp of human action. Sociologists saw social forces everywhere: as feeling, desire, geographic factors, instincts, interests, institutions, groups, persons, wishes, attitudes (cf. House, 1925–1926). For a time, Watson's hopeful and incredibly narrow behavioristic psychology exerted intense influence. So too did McDougall, and his many variations of human instincts. The easy reductionist way out was not to last. L. L. Bernard ultimately laid the instinct concept to rest for sociology in a series of brilliant writings in the early 1920's; his essay destroying Freud's libido theory is an early classic. And Hayes, finally, summed up the vagaries of the whole period by coming back to the attack on the social forces in 1925, with a matured version of his earlier criticism (1925–1926).

Conclusion

So much, then, for the briefest possible history of the fate of early sociological attempts to clarify the nature of human motivation. It contains the basic lessons we are seeking. The descriptive, disciplinary quest, which was launched as an alternative to an experimental hypothetico-deductive science of man in society, ran its course as might have been expected. The social forces did not show themselves to be amenable to neat labeling, precise definition, or exact classification. This was a major lesson of the history of the quest for the social forces. *The understanding of the dimensions of the passions or desires of man could not come from sociology alone.* How could it have been otherwise? When we undertake specialized, segmented inquiry, without any central, synthetic control, we disperse our subject matter even further. Thus, sociology as a discipline could not get at the nature of human nature; only a superordinate social science could. The result was that sociology gradually abandoned this ambition, even while it tried to remain a scientific discipline. It staked out new and sharply delimited areas of research interest that are familiar to us today: small group analysis, the study of organizations and mass communications, the analysis of class and social structure, mobility and social change. It elaborated sophisticated empirical techniques to focus on public opinion, the effects of mass media, the behavior of consumers, laborers, voters, migrant farmers, etc. No one would dare argue that this was not a great achievement, this vast accretion of empirical data and this tremendous refinement of technique. All future theorists will be indebted to it, just as one of the harshest critics of narrow empiricism was indebted to it, in his own daring theoretical work—I mean, of course, C. Wright Mills.

But the point of our discussion is that in this process of scientific disciplinary gain, something serious happened. Sociology shifted its focus. The scientific gains were offset by a loss in scope and human relevance (and the minor tradition of fine community studies only highlighted this loss). The Wardian emphasis was completely lost: the centering of sociology on the individual—that great achievement of Enlightenment science. When Albion Small founded American sociology, he did so in the face of the older disciplines, by defiantly insisting that, unlike them, sociology had a concrete human subject matter, and not mere abstractions. By the time of Small's death in the mid-1920's, sociology had joined these other disciplines, with a completely objectified subject matter. Perhaps the only attempt to keep the earlier focus on the living, acting person was the tradition of "action theory"—but even this was half-hearted. In sum, then, sociology found itself as a distinct science, only to lose man. By the 1930's Floyd H. Allport was moved to write his *Institutional Behavior* as an attempt to put the individual back into the picture of social life, from which he had been pushed by sociological abstractions.

In one way, this development was forced, and logical. The problem of explaining the nature of human nature belonged to all the disciplines, working together. As each of them broke apart and fastened on a segment of man, they each found that they had only a limited amount of insights to offer. And as a result they felt free to pursue *the specialized problems* that grew out of these limited insights. It was a vicious circle, a self-feeding process that gradually dispersed any meaningful grasp of the problem of man. But, as we said above, the whole experience did finally yield up a positive result from its unsuccessful quest. Sociology, by striking out after a full-field theory of human motivation from within the confines of a single, empirical discipline, proved that this was impossible. As many of its explanations were proved to be patently primitive and inadequate, the vigorous and optimistic early focus on the social forces quietly lapsed. When the confusion cleared, we could see a remarkable and coherent vista before us: fifty years of experience had been accumulated by sociology as a separate discipline, to prove that sociology was inadequate to a comprehensive understanding of man. In coming up against many dead ends while pursuing partial approaches to the human subject matter, sociology also came up against other disciplines, especially social psychology, psychology, and anthropology—and, to a lesser extent, philosophy. The disciplines gradually came to see that they overlapped on their subject matter, that there was a real but ill-defined point at which separate investigation was not fruitful, but was even hindering to the understanding. This was to provide a primary stimulus to new attempts at unity, as Luther Bernard so well understood (1943, p. 582). Undoubtedly it was potentially the greatest gain for science in this whole fifty-year interlude. It was the adumbration of organic unity that Durkheim had foreseen.

It is not surprising, then, that the *actual* and *really epoch-making* contribution of American sociology to world science was the one it shared with anthropology and philosophy, and which was fed by thinkers such as Cassirer, Max Weber, and Georg Simmel. And it is precisely the one that has gone practically unnoticed, and is a sort of unintended by-product of the American experience: I mean the discovery of the fictional nature of the social self—and consequently of social rules, conventions, and "cultural games." This discovery of the fictional nature of human social meanings emerged incidentally, so to speak, apart from the main scientific aspirations of the discipline —aspirations toward method, rigor, quantification. The self-theory of Royce, Baldwin, James, Cooley, and Mead was continued principally by the Chicago school, and issued in the penetrating social psychology of Erving Goffman (cf. Berger, 1961, esp. chap. 3; E. Becker, 1962). Needless to add, this seemingly minor and highly individualized current of thought has been neglected by the majority of the discipline, partly because its propositions are not "rigorously testable" and do not lead to "good" research designs. Yet we can already say that, like all really powerful and revolutionary scientific discoveries, this one is more portentous and will be more broadly influential than those discoveries which fit the institutionalized fads of any particular epoch. Habits of investigation are outlived—great ideas are not. There will one day be an immense harvest of liberating self-awareness for all mankind, when the fictional nature of social meanings becomes our common and explicit property. Certainly Berger's work (1961) already shows the far-reaching implications of such knowledge: it may do nothing less than bring together two thousand years of secular and radical religious striving for true freedom and dignity.

As for the more orthodox quest of the discipline, it also of course accomplished some "negative" work: it tried on and discarded some of the very attractive simple approaches to explaining human motivation—inner instinct, narrow behaviorism. This is a laborious weeding-out process, but it advances science—man learns by painfully discarding. We have thus been able to outlive or sidestep many of the problems that were posed. It was this negative work, as I noted above, that contributed to broadening the problem of the nature of human motivation; whenever the separate disciplines tried to get at the "essence" of motivation, they only showed the inadequacy of this kind of attack. One of the best sociological efforts helped only to draw the full circle. W. I. Thomas, who elaborated the notions of "attitudes" and the four basic human "wishes," later offered a contextual theory of attitudes; he saw that attitudes were relative to the situation in which tradition had placed the individual (cf. House, 1936, p. 237). The *discipline* of sociology, in other words, succeeded in clarifying the problem of human nature, by showing how contemporary was Fourier's basic theory of personality formation. Much later, when Talcott Parsons made a sociological restatement of Freud's personality theory, he too succeeded in confirming how contemporary was the Enlightenment view of human nature: despite the greater relative sophistication of Thomas over Fourier, and of Parsons over Freud, their work was more a matter of undoing an overgrowth of false knowledge than of contributing a new basic view—the basic ideas of the contextual nature of human striving, and man's essential modifiability, had long ago been achieved.

Thus we might say that the "action theory" that Ward introduced into American sociology finally justified him in two ways—even though the development of action theory represented only a fraction of the activity of the discipline, and that was sporadic, half-hearted, and usually too objectified: in the first place, it showed how correct Ward was to approach sociology from within man-centered evaluations and strivings; in the second, it showed how correct he was to understand sociology as a thoroughgoing and superordinate theory of human action in society and in history.

Sociology, having enjoyed fifty years of coveted integrity as a discipline, found itself face to face with the earlier problem now posed more strongly than ever: the need for a unified, man-centered science of society. When the disciplines had cut themselves off from the constraint of the earlier systems, they could not foresee the anarchy into which they would one day be plunged. Man was buried under the new mountains of data, and there was nowhere to go but back. Small showed how well he understood the problem of social science versus disciplinary sociology, by describing the shape of the new disciplinary science, in 1910:

> Specialized science, whether physical or social, inevitably passes into a stage of uncorrelated scientific piece-work. In this stage of dismemberment, science is as inconclusive through its lack of coherence as it was in an earlier period from its superficiality. That is, it then had breadth without depth, it now has depth without breadth (1910, p. 38).

Small also foresaw, with almost uncanny accuracy, that the nature of the social forces would have to be fathomed by many disciplines and that sociology itself would then have to take a subordinate place in a new, unified, man-centered science:

> [Sociology] may be wholly absorbed and distributed among the different parts of the science which . . . 100 years from now [1910] . . . may be unified around the discovered center of gravity of human experience (1910, p. 31).

Thus we can record with deep satisfaction that Albion Small, who did so much to father the disciplinary quest, was also to be the prophet of its outcome. We will see, as our history progresses, how the nature of the social forces was gradually revealed by the various disciplines and how this new understanding dictates the unmistakable character of the science of man. But it took only fifty years— and not a hundred—to affirm the center of gravity upon which to found the new unified science.

The Science of Man as Anthropodicy

The Convergence of the Disciplines in a
Synthetic Theory of Alienation

*A science can be comprehended either as a whole, i.e., including
its central problems, or not at all.*

KARL JASPERS *(Kolle, 1957, p. 446)*

Part II is the story of how the various disciplines taken together solved the problem of the social forces, of the human passions, of what makes people act the way they do. It was a momentous historical achievement, and it took over two hundred years. Although the story is somewhat technical, the result is thrilling enough, I think, to make it interesting even in its details.

And it will be no surprise to us now to discover that what makes the result thrilling is that the solution of the problem of the social forces provided us with exactly what we had been seeking since the Enlightenment: an anthropodicy, a synthetic theory of human alienation in society and history. This is the framework that permits us to understand the results of all the disciplines taken as a whole, to merge all their central problems within one central problem: the liberation of man from the constraints of society. It carries out Rousseau's critique; and at the same time orders Rousseau's passion within a single unified framework as attempted by Comte and Ward; and it fulfills Small's prophecy that this unified framework will rest on a center of gravity within human experience.

The achievement of a theoretical edifice of such elegance must fill us with reverence for the long line of thinkers who have prepared it for the profit of future generations. Here is a structure of thought that mankind might conceivably use for its own liberation, for the creation of a new kind of man in a new society.

CHAPTER FIVE

PERSONALITY AND VALUE:
The Contribution of Psychology

True science recognizes neither materialism nor idealism, for it includes them both.

ADOLPH BASTIAN

Ever since Aristotle defined man as the "social animal" the theoretical problem was set, and we have been working at it since, namely, what made man live in society; what, precisely, is the nature of the social bond? Other animals also live in societies, but the Greek and Roman thinkers already saw that since man was at best meagerly supplied with animal instincts, the explanation for man's social behavior must derive from uniquely human qualities. This was the problem that the nineteenth century set out to solve and—*mirabile dictu*—did solve. As we shall see, no really satisfactory answer could be given about the nature of the social bond until after Darwin because only then could we see it as a true, naturalistic emergent phenomenon in which the *effects* were on a different and higher level than the genetic and environmental *causes*. Yet, before Darwin, many thinkers had insights into the nature of human association: it is a tribute to Polybius, Bodin, Althusius, Spinoza, Berkeley, Adam Smith, and Hume that they saw some natural, sympathetic, and organic bond in human life long before the theory of evolution firmly established that man had arisen out of lower forms.

With Darwin the discourse was lifted onto a more refined plane; we then had to try to find out the precise difference between the *pre-*

99

social and the *social* levels of organismic behavior, how mere animal gregariousness became human sociality. In other words, it was only after Darwin that a scientific psychology of human association was possible. But, while Darwin helped us to narrow the problem by phrasing it in undiluted naturalistic terms, he also helped to obscure it. On the one hand, thinkers such as Le Bon, Tarde, and Giddings picked up earlier insights by Adam Smith and others on the nature of sympathy, and tried to integrate them more firmly with biological principles of explanation. But, on the other hand, this approach had dangers; it tended to reduce man's uniquely symbolic behavior to a few drives and instincts. We saw earlier how this current played itself out in attempting to cope with the "social forces" from within the single discipline of sociology. This was part of the "social Darwinism" that obscured human uniqueness by linking man at every point with the rest of the animal kingdom. Much effort was devoted to proving these facile analogies false—thinkers such as Novicow devoted a whole lifetime to showing that aggressive competition and warlike hostility were not necessarily human drives. We also noted earlier how Darwin's mechanistic principle of natural selection fitted perfectly with the materialism of the mid-century, as it showed up in Spencer's unconscious evolutionism. Comte, who wanted a moral society based on love, also aggravated the problem of defining human uniqueness when he reduced psychology to biology, and when he insisted that sociology had the same facts as the physical sciences. And Marx did nothing to help matters when he settled on a mechanical historicism that played down the ideal factors in social life.

It would thus be wrong to blame Darwinism for giving any more than a temporary boost to facile biological and physical reductionism. This current of thinking antedated him, beginning, in modern times, with Hobbes, and it was given its strongest recent support with Freud. In fact, it seems never to want to be laid to rest. Freud's instinct theory infected almost all the other disciplines in the human sciences; and, unhappily for the progress of science, there never was any real and decisive theoretical confrontation or amalgamation between the Freudians and the anti-Freudians. The Freudians, absorbed in their medical education, long psychoanalytic training, and clinical work, never had much inclination or time to read and digest Luther Bernard's writings on libido and instinct theory, cited earlier; much less did they read similar trenchant writings by philosopher-theologians such as W. E. Hocking. Also, the Novicow current of thinking was continued into modern anthropology, and was reflected in a work like Margaret Mead's *Cooperation and Competition Among Primitive Peoples,* a work which showed how competitive and aggressive attitudes were things very much learned in society. But these currents moved side by side; where they did interpenetrate, the ascendancy went to the Freudians, who exercised their influence over the broader and more critical thinking of the social sciences, and not vice versa.[1] The historical ascendancy of the physical sciences thus combined with the discovery of man's emergence in evolution, and it saddled the human sciences with a real labor of Penelope: each age seems to have to come to grips anew with erroneous forms of reductionism and with naïve instinct theory.

THE EMPIRICIST CONTRIBUTION TO THE SCIENCE OF MAN

When we look back from our present vantage point on the nineteenth century, we can see very clearly what its central theoretical problem was and why it was so difficult. It had to unite in one single framework two seemingly incompatible approaches to human nature: on the one hand, the approach called empiricist, individualist, reductionist, or materialist; and, on the other hand, the idealist, collectivist, or organicist approach. It was clear to most people that each had unique and necessary insights and correctives, but they seemed hopelessly antagonistic. The great achievement of the century, then, was nothing less than the uniting of the empiricist and the idealist approaches into one synthetic whole. The line of development of this synthesis is very interesting: atomistic empiricism was gradually discredited, and so too was metaphysical idealism; as a result of this double disillusionment, by the end of the century mature thinkers were ready to look at the heritage of idealism in a new way—with new clarity and with fewer expectations. The science of man matured at that time. Let us see how this happened.

In the first place, we noted that the empiricist approach to human nature, on the Newtonian model, never had much of a chance. The atomistic, association psychology simply did not describe nature: man's ideas were superordinate and organizing, they did not build up by the accretion of discrete atomistic sensations: mental facts did not have a one-to-one connection with sensory facts. But this was not apparent at the beginning of the century.

In the second place, and even worse, the Newtonian model not only did not help to father a science of man—it actively hindered it.

This is nowhere more clear than in Bentham's failure. Like his descendants today, Bentham thought that only by using the model of the exact sciences—measurement, geometry, mechanics—could he make a respectable science of human nature. But he wanted to keep, at the center of this science, an active, willing human subject; and so he used individual strivings as a point of reference, and a simple motive like "egotism" as an animating principle. This would make a peculiar hybrid that would still be respectable according to the then current mechanical model. But we can see that Bentham tried to create a freak, to graft a mechanistic science onto a man-centered ontology.

The difficulties of this scheme were obvious to many. It was already clear that the idea of "egotism" could cause more trouble theoretically than it was worth; for example when one sacrificed his life to save his fellows, he had to be put into the category of unusual forms of "self-interest." Today we would attack this same theoretical problem from the point of view of the social nature of the self, as we shall see further on. Bentham could have worked his way out of this kind of dilemma by moving in this direction and by focusing on the motive of "sympathy" to which Adam Smith had given such prominence. But he did not do so for two very good reasons—and here is where our lesson on Newtonian models comes in. The first reason was his simplistic conception of social science as explanation by reduction, by decomposition into simple elements. And simple elements could only be found in individual qualities like egotism, *and not in group qualities* like social sympathy. Halévy has some excellent things to say about Bentham's failure to use broader concepts, and points out that the Benthamite jurists and economists had to organize their knowledge around concepts of *individual responsibility*—simply because this is the only thing a modern jurist can work with: "Supposing the sympathetic feelings were stronger than the egotistic feeling, the social group in which the feelings in question prevailed, would, in a way, assume more social reality than the individuals which comprised it" (Halévy, 1960, p. 467). Not only would this dissipate hard and fast notions of responsibility, but it would also foul the exact science that was sought; as Halévy says: "This group would, moreover, be essentially variable . . . the really irreducible element of society . . . would be impossible to determine rigorously . . . . The result would be that social science would be condemned never to possess the character of an exact science, with which the Benthamites tried to endow it" (p. 467).

Again, the Enlightenment lesson is demonstrated acutely: social science cannot develop in the service of ideology (in this case, laissez-faire jurisprudence and economics), and cannot be subordinated to Newtonian mechanism. The Benthamites willfully missed major insights into the social basis of individual action. On the Continent too this lesson had to be learned. As an example, if we had to choose one thinker who summed up in his own career the major movement of the century, it would be Wilhelm Wundt. Wundt began working during the reaction to Hegelian idealism. As a youth he picked up the psycho-physical problem and rigorously pursued his studies along these lines. But he was a serious scientist who gradually saw that this approach to human cognition and striving was sorely limited. He found that psychic facts differed markedly from physical facts, and elaborated his idea of "psychic inequivalence." This means, simply, that physical causality is always a matter of energy equivalences, whereas psychic causality, being governed by ideas, is never a mechanistic one-to-one type of scientific problem. For example, we may be more responsive to a faint odor of smoke than to continued loud nagging. (As we saw in Chapter Four, in the twentieth century, Giddings had to rediscover this nonmechanical nature of social phenomena, and consequently one of his students, Douglas Haring, rediscovered the notion of the "dynamic inequivalence" of social facts [1956].)

Wundt followed this lead into historical and cultural studies of the development of human ideas. He came to see the mind as an "apperceptive mass," functioning on levels of superordinate ideas rather than atomistic sensations, thus converging with William James's "stream of consciousness," and Gestaltist psychology. More important for sociology, perhaps, he turned to studies of folk psychology and saw that individual perceptions are part of the social formation of concepts—that the individual is born into totalistic world views. Wundt was thus one of the first, along with Durkheim, to begin the link between an individual and a social psychology (see Goldenweiser, 1948), paralleling the development of Baldwin's, Royce's, Cooley's, and George Mead's ideas on the social genesis of the self. In Wundt's work the problem was in its primitive state: just *how* was the self formed out of the cultural matrix? (The controversies on the nature of the folk soul, between Wundt and Lazarus and Steinthal, show how necessary was the kind of transactional, genetic approach that Baldwin and Mead worked out—as we will see in the next chapter.) Wundt remained at the stage of formulation of the problem that was roughly the same as Durkheim's: he knew that the self was a social creation, but he could not explain satisfactorily how (see Mead, 1956, pp. 168–177). On one important point Wundt as psychologist kept an emphasis that Durkheim the sociologist slighted: the approach to action from the inside, the subjective and voluntarist nature of human striving. This is the best part of the idealist tradition because it shows the merger of social facts and individual valuations. The fruitful meeting between these two approaches could not be made at that time—which explains the recriminations between the Durkheim school and Wundt (see Goldenweiser, 1948, footnotes 9 and 11).

At first, Wundt had been championed by the materialists, and when his new studies took unavoidably idealist lines, the anti-metaphysicians jeered at him. Merz, who noted this turnabout, concluded that it was the materialists who were wrong, who did not accurately read the drift of the times. Wundt's development was representative of the change of thought which took place, not only in Germany, but in other countries as well, during the nineteenth century. It was a preparation for what Merz so aptly called "the new Idealism of the future" (Merz, 1914, vol. 4, p. 758). In the nineteenth century, as today, the narrow-gauge psychologist or philosopher with vested epistemological interests simply did not understand the mainstream of development of a science of man. By abandoning a simplistic empiricism, Wundt reflected this development beautifully.

The empiricist attack on idealism was not, of course, without some clear gains for a science of man. We had to understand the human spirit in a social and cultural sense, and not in an other-worldly one. Otherwise we could not advance man's knowledge of himself. Empiricism brought man under focus as an object of scientific analysis, and this was a lasting gain. It accentuated the naturalistic nature of human striving, saw humans as material, organismic individuals, each integral in his own right, and not as part of some great organic oversoul. But the soberness and down-to-earthness of empiricism, let it be said, could not rid the science of man of its basic idealist orientation. At most, it put its discoveries into naturalistic form, and declared it a venture within human hands.

Nineteenth-century materialism and empiricism were really a continuation of Lockean psychology and the spirit of the French Enlightenment thinkers who expanded it. But something happened in the nineteenth century that reaffirmed and intensified scientific materialism, and that was the brief flourishing of German transcendental idealism. For a brief time, it looked as though the promise of secular science of the eighteenth century was going to be defeated, and man was again going to be taken out of his own hands. In the materialist reaction against Hegel, all spiritualism came under fire. Had it not been for the idealist interlude the science of man could perhaps better have picked up from where the less materialistic thinkers of the French Enlightenment had left it—Diderot specifically said that mature science must deal with qualities as well as matter. Empiricism, in other words, seemed justified in its one-sided emphasis in order to bring idealism back to earth; but idealism itself was a protest against the ascendancy of Newtonian materialism! This recurrent dialectic in philosophical thought is the price we pay when the dialogue is held on abstract levels, divorced from real knowledge about man *in society* and *in history*. We are still paying it.

The whole idealist interlude, we saw earlier, was partly an attempt to find man within the Newtonian world picture—an attempt that at that time was necessarily limited largely to philosophy. How else put the accent on quality over quantity? Idealism, in other words, can be understood in one way as a recurrent attempt to account for peculiarly human nature in a world of things. But what a great achievement it would be if science itself could deal with the dimension of quality—philosophy would be given an even sounder footing. And this is precisely what happened when we were able to connect, theoretically, the organismic with the symbolic levels of existence. We could begin to talk about the human spirit partly in social and cultural terms. So that today we can take an immense step forward into the "new Idealism of the future" as Merz so well termed it. That is to say, we can put idealism partly on a sound scientific footing, which is truly an unprecedented achievement. Let us then look at the idealist current of the nineteenth century, which we highlighted in our discussion of Wundt, in somewhat closer focus.

THE IDEALIST CURRENT IN THE DEVELOPMENT OF A MATURE SCIENCE OF MAN

The German approach to a science of man had a distinctive cast. The Germans, like the English, consented to live with their institutions, and with theology as well. In this they differed from the French. But, unlike the English, the Germans for the most part thought along grand lines, were comfortable with large organic categories. Their approach to man was almost an Oriental one: he tended to be dwarfed by society, nature, history, the vast movement of the cosmos. And, in the philosophy of Hegel, he actually was.

Leibnitz very early set the tone for German thinking about

science and man. In Chapter One we noted that he wanted both the new Newtonian science and the old medieval order and universality, and that he proposed academies which would group religion and science. Kant inherited the problem and his whole system was a genial attempt to keep radical science and Christian morality—as we noted earlier. We also noted that in his time the empirical program of the development of social morality was at its very beginning. Consequently, the philosophers who followed Kant had nothing to go on but their own intuitions, and the regnant moral code of their society. "What is our duty?" echoed Goethe; and he could only answer: "The call of the day." It was of course no answer at all. Kant's critics saw that he had left a system which was wide open at the breach: Dewey accused him of splitting the world of scientific fact and human value, of setting man to look to external nature for causal laws, and inside for moral intuitions (1915, pp. 121–122). Herder very early made a similar accusation of his former teacher (cf. Wells, 1959, p. 142). In spite of his proposed answers to his anguished questions "What can I know?" "What should I do?," Kant's followers still wondered what they could know, and especially what they should do. German transcendentalism was a search for a secure morality. Had Kant opened up the inner world, had he insisted above all on the primacy of man's subjectivity? Well, then, let us find absolute value there, in the unfolding of the inner spirit in cosmos and history—so said the idealists. The earth was the theater of accident, of the decay of civilizations. And since the science of man was not yet born, a science that would get some kind of conceptual grip on this accident and decay, the only place to look for order was in the depths of nature.

Unlike their materialist critics, the idealists were very clear that the science of man was a moral science—about morals, and for morality. And one thing they stressed above all: that if the Newtonian world had its principle of gravity that would reveal all the mysteries of the physical world, then the science of man had its principle of consciousness which permits us to understand all the mysteries of the human world (cf. Ellwood, 1938, p. 283). Here was the great new orientation that idealism offered to nineteenth-century science. But what could be done with this new orientation, scientifically, at the beginning of the century? Practically nothing. Consequently, Hegel included the idea within a grand philosophy of history, in which history was understood as the growth of consciousness and thus of freedom from within the depths of man's psyche and of nature. It was a three-stage theory which surveyed all of human history, and recorded its ineluctable progress: in the first or Oriental stage, only the despot was free; in the second or Greco-Roman stage, only the citizen was free; in the modern Western stage, all were free.

Now this was an affirmation of human potential that has a close resemblance to Comte's central idea: that human history is the record of the development of the human intelligence toward greater freedom and control. It was Hegel's bid for a new "secular" theodicy, which is why he could insist that "philosophy is theodicy." Like Comte, he felt that his system was compelling enough to oblige an option for the simple historical law. But Hegel's views, and especially Fichte's, differed from the Comtean approach in one crucial respect, which as we shall see had important consequences. Hegel's approach, as he set it forth in the *Phenomenology of the Spirit*, was precisely that—it was a phenomenology that was always potentially psychological; it was not condemned to remain merely an "objective" historicism, as was Comte's law. The German idealists, in other words, had kept a version of the Kantian interplay of organism and objects, and used it to describe the growth of the inner spirit, of human consciousness. This eventually did lead, as we shall see, to a mature social psychology in the hands of a thinker like James Mark Baldwin. But this is getting somewhat ahead of the story.

Furthermore, whatever versions of idealism were put forth, they all tended to one ultimately beneficial result, namely, a man-centered sociology that rests on the psychological dimensions of the personality. Comte had hoped for this, but it was German idealism (which apparently he read only after his life's work) which made it possible. The Germans put the accent on spiritual communalism as an idealist protest against the social fragmentation of individualist, industrial society; and at the same time they were hitting out against reductionism and mechanism. But these protests actually fitted into the science of man because they helped focus on the peculiar nature of the human subject matter. As one example among many, there was the idealist Karl Krause's philosophy of society, which saw society as a spiritual organism and which was adopted in Spain by the Spanish sociologist Adolfo Posada. But Posada naturalized the spirituality by translating it into an emphasis on the psychical nature of social life (Barnes and Becker, 1961, vol. 3, p. 1114).

In France, too, the same thing happened: the conservative protest against the individualism of the new industrial society and the overcocky analytic intelligence of the materialist philosophers was ultimately given scientific form. Joseph de Maistre and de Bonald influenced Comte directly with their strong anti-particularist stand, and in Comte's system the individual was firmly subordinated to the good of the larger organic community. The current of anti-individualism passed through de Roberty, Espinas, Izoulet, and Durkheim, and it was Durkheim who made the most, conceptually, of the communal nature of the individual self. In this whole current of pre- and post-Darwinian organicism and anti-individualism, we see how a largely ideological reaction to materialism, atomism, to the French Revolution and to the new divisive industrialism actually served science with new concepts and metaphors that were later understood to have precise validity.

Thus we can say that after Darwin it was necessary to revive idealism as a protest for human uniqueness, but this protest came at a time when the necessary social psychology of idealism had not yet been worked out, principally by Royce, Baldwin, Cooley, and George Mead. Again, as in Kant's time, the breach had to be filled largely by philosophy, unsupported by a knowledge of the social psychology of human institutions. Thus, the neo-Hegelianism of John and Edward Caird, F. H. Bradley, and T. H. Green was simply a marking time, keeping philosophical idealism while awaiting a science of man that would support scientific idealism. In this sense we might say that the neo-Hegelians were to Darwin what Kant was to the scientific revolution and Hume: a necessarily limited philosophical attempt to keep a high place for the moral nature of man. Only gradually did the body of knowledge build up that would prepare the new science of human uniqueness. Merz has summed up with great insight this achievement of the idealist episode of the nineteenth century:

> Its real meaning and value is only now beginning to be justly appreciated . . . the immediate outcome of Idealistic Thought was not a general acceptance of the higher metaphysical principles, but a reversion to psychological, historical, and anthropological studies. In this direction the second half of the nineteenth century accumulated an enormous mass of material which foremost thinkers of the present day aim at utilizing for the purpose of working out the programme of earlier Idealism (1914, vol. 4, pp. 741–742).

I hope to show as this history progresses how superbly a long succession of thinkers has succeeded in working out this program.

THE IDEALIST CONTRIBUTION TO A MAN-CENTERED VALUE SCIENCE

In their protest against Newtonianism, and in their search for a new social morality, the idealists saw one thing very clearly: that science had been perverted. Like Diderot, they lamented that the beautiful regularity of the universe had no meaning if man was left out. The problem was to get him back in, put the human sciences on a sound footing, give them a properly high place in life. There were two ways of doing this. The first was a half-hearted attempt that neutralized idealism by making it objectively scientific. It was an attempt to make the human sciences viable in their own right, by showing that a science can be non-Newtonian and yet be objective and respectable. The Germans set up a distinction between the natural and human sciences, and those like Dilthey, in his early work, wanted to give the human sciences their own method—the method would not be as rigidly causal as in the natural sciences, but it could be inductive and classificatory all the same. Carlo Antoni calls Dilthey the Bacon of the human sciences for his distinctive new method (1959, p. 19). Others followed in similar attempts to carve out a unique scientific standing for the historical and human sciences—Windelband, Rickert, Max Weber. These people wanted to legitimate a science that would be about values, history, and not about matter—and still be a science. Obviously, this was a side-stepping of the Enlightenment mandate that science should be actively in the service of a new morality. These thinkers were urging a science that would be *about* values, but would stop short of actively promoting new values. This latter was a daring and more difficult venture which idealist thinkers of broader vision had to take.

The idealists at the end of the century were in effect tasked with succeeding where Comte and Hegel had failed. They were tasked with filling out the ideal-type of Diderot's and Rousseau's framework so that a compelling moral science could be built on it. How to go about this? How to bring compelling values into an objective scientific world, values that would be the basis for a new science? What was the principle that would break up *scientific sameness*, that would introduce *a standard of value for judging higher and lower*? Comte and Hegel thought they had found this principle in the idea of historical progress. But we have seen that this was an inadequate anthropodicy: the historical principle of progress could easily be objectivized, precisely because it was not firmly centered on the individual. This is exactly what happened to it, as we saw, with Comte, Hegel—and Marx. The historical principle alone could not break up scientific objectivity and engender an option for value; as an ideal-typology it was thus bound to fail.

There was another way of injecting value into monotonous nature, of combating materialism and mechanism. And this was Diderot's way: by insisting on the superordinacy of *life*—a mechanically undefinable principle, without which the rest of nature has no value (Merz, 1914, vol. 4, pp. 407–408). The idea of life, in other words, allowed the nineteenth century to pick up the problem of the ideal-type where Rousseau (and later Herder and Wilhelm von Humboldt) had left it. It incorporated the romantic vision into mechanistic science, and elevated man over things. Nature could become a moving, purposive drama, directed by the free energies of the highest creature in whom life pulsated. In Germany this idealist affirmation of life proceeded independently of France. It was Herder, more than anyone else, who placed before his age the Idea of Humanity as the quintessence of Life (Merz, 1914, vol. 4, pp. 424–425). He wanted to be the Newton of history, and sketched out what is still the plan for anyone who would claim the title: he offered a daring and in some areas strikingly modern conception of the human race as a historical development, and urged that man educate and elevate himself. The idea lived in his contemporaries Goethe, Kant, Wilhelm von Humboldt, and Schiller, and was locked into a transcendental system by Hegel. But it was precisely this that Herder had not wanted.

With the downfall of Hegelian absolutism the idea of life had to be rehabilitated, so to speak; it had to be made scientifically respectable. This was the daring and difficult venture of the post-Hegelian idealists of the end of the century. It was accomplished in two ways. The first thing was to reach back around Hegel to Herder's basic Idea of Humanity as a historical development, and to reground it on human effort. The second thing was to reach back beyond the Absolute Idealism, and find Kant as he was before Hegel filled his system with transcendental insides. In other words, the end of the century had to reconvert the transcendental soul into the respectably scientific garb of the simple idea of life. This was the task that Lotze accomplished so well. He resolved the Kantian dilemma after the failure of idealism in the only way it could be resolved: he made *personality* central to his formulation. Thus, at one stroke, he was able to reconcile the claims of careful science and the emotional needs and demands of our best natures, which urge us to value life.

With Lotze's personality-centered system, man could have a sort of holiness or distinction, as well as a more mature self-reliance. Lotze cut the ambitions of philosophy down to size, and consented to work within the givens of science (Merz, 1914, vol. 4, pp. 663–666). Thus he continued Feuerbach's great work (1841) of redirecting and naturalizing the idealist metaphysical and spiritual philosophy.

In the first place, by focusing on personality, Lotze—like Feuerbach—could answer the question of how value was realized in the world by accenting individual decision instead of transcendental mystery. The religious attention to the soul was, as Feuerbach so carefully showed, a way of adumbrating the supreme value of the individual personality, "the great heart of nature." The idea of the soul, the fundamental principle of Christianity, was really a "consciousness of human personality, conceived naïvely as substance"—as Emil Lucka explained (1922, p. 240). Lotze performed a shift in focus that was thus always potentially, but not actually possible until after Kant and Wilhelm von Humboldt, and after Hegelian idealism had failed. It had to wait until a new science of man was urging itself upon the scene, a science within the mature Enlightenment vision, but now sophisticated by a knowledge of psychology. Lotze made soul scientific, and at the same time affirmed the peculiar superordinate value nature of the new man-centered science. Merz is lavish in his praise of Lotze's resolution of the problem of the soul, his reconciling, in one secular synthesis, of the various currents of his time:

> To grasp and do justice to the many-sided aspects which it [the problem of the soul] now presented there was required an intellect of the high order . . . [of]. . . Leibnitz. It had to combine the common-sense aspect of Britain with the metaphysical of Germany; the physiological and pathological of the Continental naturalists with the spiritualistic of the religious thinker; and lastly, the mathematical with the poetical spirit. At the same time, it had to rise to a higher form of eclecticism than that which was characteristic of the French school which bore the name (Merz, 1914, vol. 3, p. 264).

Only Lotze, he concludes, had the qualifications for this task, and thus stands at the center of the philosophical and psychological thought of the century.

It was in his *Microcosmus* that Lotze tried to pick up Herder's unfinished task and to show Man, not merely in his historical development, but in all his relationships. Coming a century after Herder, Lotze's attempt was bound to be more mature (cf. Clark, 1955, p. 105;

and see Wells, 1959). By making personality central to his system, he declared with the idealists that man was the locus of all value. By keeping the Kantian perspective, he showed that values are necessarily anthropocentric, since perceptions are relative to the human organism's apparatus. He thus left room for science within the larger frame of human needs and valuations. Other thinkers saw the shape of the new science, but did not systematize it as well as had Lotze. In France Lotze's counterpart, Renouvier, called for a new era of philosophic thought, a "new conception in which the idea of personality will be utilized for the explanation and interpretation, as opposed to the description and construction of the phenomenal world" (Merz, 1914, vol. 3, p. 417).

We can judge the import of these views. They called for a centralization of science in the French Encyclopedic spirit: not centralization by reduction, or by building upon physics—not physical centralization, but a *purposive, value centralization* (cf. Urban, 1949, p. 200). They again opened the way for a science that would serve human meanings and no longer leave man a stranger in a world of physical meanings. Value is injected into nature from a wholly anthropocentric position. Not only the physical world, but life itself becomes a category of personal fulfillment. Lotze, by centering science on the inner world of the personality, was declaring that the poetic, the artistic, the religious formed one of the horizons of nature, on a par with the physical horizons of the external world. We might say that he wanted a science that would be a dialogue between the warm heart of nature and the cold infinite extremities of nature. In this science, human creations and human meanings would occupy the central place, and rightly so: they are emanations from the organismic center of nature, expressed by the highest organism—man.

In this way materialism and idealism were merged, and a distinctive new science proposed that would satisfy the motives of both empiricists and idealists (cf. Burtt, 1932, pp. 323–324). The external world would be manipulated experimentally, but it would be done in the interests of the human spirit. This merger of idealism and materialism would be "true science" as Adolph Bastian understood the term over a hundred years ago, and as we must still understand it today; Bastian's words are worth quoting at length:

> If the so-called materialists have hitherto vainly at-
> tempted to construct new systems, if they have been
> unable to satisfy public expectations and have found
> no surcease for that longing of the human heart which
> has always hovered over the earthly horizon of all races

like the promise of dawn, it was because they neglected
psychology, not knowing how to rescue it from the hands
of dialectic speculation and to claim it as their own
province. They opposed the idealist on party lines, instead
of drawing his objects also within the sphere of scientific
investigation. True science recognizes neither materialism
nor idealism, for it includes them both (quoted in Gumplowicz, 1963, p. 107).

Bastian was one of the founders of that large humanistic discipline, anthropology, who could still talk about the longing of the
human heart in the days before most of the anthropologists also took
their place by the side of the laboratory managerialists: today they are
being urged to study symbolic logic and computer techniques, and
thus to have their own "objective" and narrow brand of "true
science." The voices of a Bastian and a Redfield are all but drowned
out by the hum of new machine noise.

THE NEW PSYCHOLOGY

We have already had a glimpse—in Wundt's development—of the
new psychology which made Lotze's proposal possible. A mature
science that would satisfy the motives of both empiricists and
idealists had to rest on a psychology that would also have roots
in both camps. The noted historian of psychology G. S. Brett argued for
just such a psychology: "The system of Lotze had shown that an
ideal realism is not an impossible conception. For psychology this
might prove the most useful attitude to adopt" (Peters, 1962, pp.
604–605). (From this we can fairly conclude that like anthropology,
psychology too had its giants in its early days, and certainly less in
present times—as the striking exception of a Gordon Allport attests.)
The whole current of the century moved in the direction of a new
ideal-real psychology, away from atomism-sensationalism-physicalism
to the idea of a continuous all-embracing, introspective field of
consciousness. A host of thinkers converged on it: Wundt and his
"apperceptive mass"; Renouvier and his phenomenology; Alfred
Fouillée and his notion of *idées-forces*—guiding, superordinate ideas
which motivate action from above; his disciple, Jean-Marie Guyau;
William James and his "stream of consciousness"; Bergson; Dilthey
in his later period as he gradually became impressed by the super-
ordinancy of humanly created meanings—the list is long, and covers
a span of time reaching well into the twentieth century.

By the end of the nineteenth century, thinkers could see with full clarity why a psychology based on Newtonian physics was simply not adequate as a view of the workings of the mind. Herder had understood this almost a century before, but his penetrating views had come too soon and were themselves mixed with metaphysics (see Clark, 1955, pp. 315–316). As he saw, there are no separate faculties of "reason," "feeling," and "will"; neither is there any way of mechanically ordering the multitude of constant sense perceptions. In the unity of the world of the mind, the whole precedes the part, and a physicalist, atomic approach is simply not possible. In France, Maine de Biran was one of the first really to understand this. Dilthey and the others who pressed for the uniqueness of the human sciences later also saw this very clearly (cf. Ortega, 1963, pp. 178–179). Lotze was thus able to accomplish what Diderot proposed and to champion a new science, precisely because the early atomistic quest of psychology had finally failed and had decisively revealed that man is a distinctive organism in nature and not a mechanism. This was one of the great fruits of the century: psychology had finally fulfilled its promise and come to grips with its unique subject matter. F. C. S. Schiller's lament was really no longer appropriate, but it did sum up a long and fumbling history:

> . . . every science has been held up, at some stage or other of its career, by the lack of conceptions that would give it a real grip of its subject-matter and enable it to analyse it and to deduce consequences which could be verified in fact. In some sciences this condition has been chronic. . . . As a good example of a science hung up for ages, in a manner strongly suggestive of a lack of appropriate conceptions, we may consider the sad case of Psychology. Here we have a science of apparently enormous potentialities and pretensions, of universal interest, of great antiquity. . . . The obvious explanation . . . is that Psychology has not so far succeeded in getting hold of appropriate conceptions. . . (1921, pp. 436–440).

Schiller seems to have overlooked the new psychology of the end of the century. It *had* found its proper subject matter: it was a science of the individual subjectivity in its social dimensions—a science of *"being-in-the-world"* as the modern existentialists would say. The modern existentialists are to late-nineteenth-century psychology as Veblen and C. Wright Mills were to Marx: they are insistently calling our attention to something which we once knew but have consis-

tently chosen to ignore as we have played the narrow game of disciplinary science. It was the nineteenth century that affirmed life,
personality, and value as the proper orientation of science.

But we can hardly accuse Schiller of failing to see this, when
psychologists themselves seem not to have understood it and when
we seem to have forgotten it. I mean that the progression to the new
psychology of the end of the century was extremely halting and
painful, and its full import is only now being realized. As we noted,
it had to combat not only mechanism but also the wholly transcendental idealism. The British, for example, found themselves in the
difficult and even embarrassing position of having to abandon their
own passive, empirical tradition that extended from Locke to Mill,
and rejoin the activism of Leibnitz and Kant. It was Alexander Bain
who was finally led to assert the active nature of the psychological
process, but he did not go any further. There was a reluctance to admit
into scientific psychology the superordinate unifying ego, which had
the aura of discreditable transcendental idealist overtones. Thus, even
the excellent early ego psychology of de Tracy and Maine de Biran
was allowed to lapse. But only by admitting the notion of a unifying
ego could the tradition of bogus accumulative associationism be
left behind. James Ward took the step in Britain, but only *after*
idealism was dead and *after* materialism was seen to be inadequate.
Bain stood too much in the old tradition to make the radical step; he
adopted German activism, but not subjectivism. By the time of
James Ward, psychology could opt for the active ego or self, and
could do so without taint of unscientific romanticizing. Ward actually
fused British and German psychology and provided a real-idealism
(cf. Peters, 1962, pp. 678–679, 681, 683). This was the new psychology
in which the self was seen as a purposive agent and as a locus of
values.

This was considerable—but still not enough. As we shall see
shortly, it was not until later that the self could also be understood
genetically as a social, cultural creation. The new psychology was
still incomplete, which as we shall see partly explains Lotze's failure.

Why did the psychologists themselves fail, in the main, to rally
around and continue to build this new psychology? Largely because
it was a psychology of functional relationships, and this kind of
psychology strikes at the heart of disciplinary integrity. And the
psychologists did so want to be a scientific discipline. With measurement and fractionating atomism, the psychologists could have their
science. But a functional psychology meant that psychology had to

realign itself with the other disciplines. Furthermore, a stream-of-consciousness psychology, which accents the personality as a creator of values, would have to maintain a *qualitative* contact with the other disciplines, and not merely a quantitative one. In the disciplinary understanding, this is science fouled at the base. Small wonder that Kant's, Fichte's, and Hegel's transactional phenomenology has been crowded out by atomism and measurement in psychology, even down to this day, or that Maine de Biran's anti-reductionism was considered a "betrayal of science." Experimental psychology could ignore "mere philosophers" like Lotze, and continue on to champion "real scientists" like Titchener and Watson. It had to remain a discipline at all costs, and this meant, in the naïve understanding, cutting its umbilical cord to philosophy once and for all.

Of all the present-day psychologists, perhaps it was E. G. Boring who scorned philosophy most. In the conclusion of his expert *History of Experimental Psychology* (1950) he takes some pains to justify psychology as a discipline, and to congratulate it proudly on its final divorce from its no-good parent, philosophy. Then Boring proceeds to treat the reader to an exercise in incredible logic. Why is psychology justified as a discipline? Because it is thriving! (p. 741). In other words, if the laboratory managerialists are hard at work, "good science" is automatically assured. Who, at the conclusion of this exhaustive history of experimental psychology, would Boring nominate as the great men in psychology's history?—who are its father figures? Darwin, Helmholtz, James, and Freud. And the two greatest? Darwin and Freud! (p. 743). No comment is really necessary. By his very choice of father figures Boring admits that psychology has no business being separated from philosophy. After all, it was the theory of evolution which conclusively introduced the idea of process into the organic realm, thereby attacking the primacy of static measurement of regularities in the human sciences. Has experimental psychology treated man in an open-ended way, as a creature in a continual process of becoming? As for Freud, we will examine his distinctive contribution later, but it is really difficult to understand how a careful laboratory scientist could be comfortable with the scientific shoddiness of Freud's subjective method, much less with Freud's avowal that psychoanalysis has its own distinctive mythology and rhetoric. Have experimental psychologists really tried Freud's type of science? Even worse, Freud helped to undermine the very disciplinary integrity that Boring so eagerly covets: Freud and a half century of case-history biographies showed once and for all the utter inseparability of the individual psyche from its social context.

But Boring's ambitions notwithstanding, today psychology is beginning to show some signs of emerging from its long scientistic sleep and a willingness to pick up again the current which the discipline abandoned at the end of the nineteenth century. D. O. Hebb, for example, now states that cognitive processes themselves can have immediate drive value, and so draws the full circle back to the later Wundt and Fouillée. It has been a relatively fruitless journey, and has exhausted many talents, this anti-philosophical, disciplinary quest of psychology.

CONCLUSION: THE FAILURE OF LOTZE'S SYSTEM

Merz, in his truly great work on European thought, says that Lotze's *Microcosmus* was the first attempt to take a comprehensive view of the world and of life from an introspective and man-based standpoint (1914, vol. 4, p. 767). But, like Herder before him, Lotze failed to advance a compelling world picture. Today only a few hardy and independent souls—confined mostly to Germany—will maintain that "philosophy ended with Lotze"; for the most part he has been forgotten. Lotze's failure, as Comte's and Hegel's, led to a dissipation of efforts and energies: in science we came into the extreme specialization of the twentieth century; in philosophy we came into an equally specialized and largely sterile discussion of separate logical, metaphysical, and ethical problems (Merz, 1914, vol. 4, p. 768). Neither science nor philosophy now aspires to give us wisdom. And wisdom, for man, must be a comprehensive picture of evil.

We have seen how all the great systems failed, both because they were not historically and socially compelling and because more knowledge had to be sought by the disciplinary quest. Lotze's failure was the last one of the nineteenth century, in a sense the most unfortunate one, and certainly a most instructive one. It was the last simply because no one else at that time tried this kind of man-centered synthesis of knowledge, although two of Lotze's former pupils—Borden Bowne and Josiah Royce—introduced the problem into America, made their own distinctive synthetic statements of it, and passed it on to the twentieth century. Lotze's failure was the most unfortunate because it came at a time when idealism had been naturalized, and was beginning to offer up its ripe psychological fruit; but Lotze was still too soon upon the scene. It was a most instructive failure, precisely because it showed conclusively that a compelling system had to be based on two things:

1. *A thoroughgoing theory of the nature of the social bond.* This would have to include a precise knowledge of the genetic formation of individual character that Stuart Mill urged: how are individual traits molded by the social heritage? It would have to show how social groups functioned and what effect the various social institutions had on the groups and individuals (cf. Randall, 1940, p. 520). In other words, it would have to be based on a full theory of human nature, of man in society and in history, *which would be at the same time a compelling anthropodicy.* Lotze's synthesis simply did not do what he wanted, it did not show man "in all his relationships." It was too philosophical: it came too soon to draw on the sophisticated findings of a mature sociology, as represented by the tradition of Marx, Veblen, Weber, Mills, *et al.* It also came too soon— as I have noted several times—to draw on the mature social psychology that would be elaborated by Baldwin, Royce, Cooley, and George Mead. Only this could give a thoroughgoing explanation of the nature of evil in society, which would compel an active option for a new morality. Furthermore, by showing how the self develops genetically through the use of language, a major defect of Lotze's system could be corrected, namely, the separation of subject and object, of thought and things. In this sense, Lotze's own former pupil, Royce, began what had to be done to complete Lotze's system; and Dewey, with his *Logic: The Theory of Inquiry,* finished the task. Royce adumbrated the social dimensions of each individual personality; and Dewey showed fully the transactional, pragmatic nature of thought (cf. Schneider, 1946, pp. 488, 538). Thus, Lotze could not present a comprehensive picture of human ills on a concrete individual and social level. He tried for a cosmology before we had a rich and detailed philosophy of mind—of the human psyche in its transactional social dimensions (cf. Burtt, 1932, pp. 323–324). He proposed, in sum, a new world view to go beyond the Newtonian before the rich texture of this world view had been articulated and elaborated.

2. In the second place, he did not discover any *new scientific principle*; he offered a synthesis without any unifying principle. Hegel, Spencer, and Comte had used a historical principle as the basis for unity, but we saw how inadequate such a principle is. Lotze saw the problems much more clearly than they; he understood that *unity must be in the living presence,* it must be a principle *which exists in the individual organisms* (Merz, 1914, vol. 1, p. 48). But he himself did not discover such a principle. A system based on human nature cannot be synthetic without it, simply because we need a

unifying principle as a basis for adjusting all the various factors of the analytic theory of human ills. A complete synthetic system, then, would contain a single principle based in the individual that would be connected with the thoroughgoing theory of man's fate in society. In this way, the long development of a mature psychology in the nineteenth century would offer up its full fruit to a science of man as anthropodicy: we would see how the irreducible individual mind was a function of the social world.

This is the problem that Lotze passed on to us. Let us see what his successors did with it. Merz wrote his splendid history on the fundamental assumption that a philosophical unification of thought was both necessary and possible; I hope to be able to show that he was correct, that he did not write in vain. Only, the *philosophical* unification was to be made possible by a long tradition of *scientific* analysis, and ultimately, synthesis. In the next chapters I want to show how the nineteenth century developed a thoroughgoing theory of the nature of the social bond, which was the first lesson of the failure of Lotze's system. In Part IV I want to take up the second lesson and show how the new scientific principle was finally made clear.

CHAPTER SIX

NATURE AND THE SELF:
The Contribution of Social Psychology

> We are now swinging into a scientific era in which we shall
> give ourselves fewer airs about the type of knowledge which
> becomes impressive by arbitrarily limiting its outlook.
>
> ALBION SMALL (*1910, pp. 122-123*)

One way in which the nineteenth century contrasts with ours is that
it was very clear about its major theoretical problems. The two great
ones that preoccupied it were commonly known as *Die Seelenfrage*—
the problem of the soul in relation to the body, of the mind in relation
to nature—and *Die Soziale Frage*—the problem of the individual in
relation to the social system, the problem that had to be solved in order
for intelligent social reconstruction to begin (see Merz, 1914, vol. 4,
p. 162). With the solution of these two great problems, the nineteenth
century provided the basis for a synthetic theory of alienation. Let
us then take a closer look at this central chapter in the history of
human freedom.

DIE SEELENFRAGE

In the last chapter we sketched how psychology began the solution
of the problem of the soul, or psyche, or self; but we also noted that the
solution was unfinished. James Ward was prepared to see the self as
a purposive agent and as a locus of values, but we still did not understand the self genetically as a social and cultural creation. The

century discovered how man's mind functions on a level of symbolic meanings, and is not to be broken down into materialistic components. This was a great step forward, but we had to go further and see exactly how these meanings *were built into* the human organism; only then would our theory of alienation be able to show how social meanings controlled the individual. This is one of the major points on which Spencer's vast evolutionary system foundered; as he himself realized, he could not account satisfactorily for the origin of mind. This is crucial too for understanding the prematurity of Lotze's synthesis, because only with a thoroughgoing theory of personal development is a system based on personality possible. Stuart Mill understood this problem on a logical level, as we will see further on, and someone like Théodule Ribot understood it from a point of view of the problem of psychopathology.

As we would expect from our earlier discussion, it was the idealists who solved this problem, and they solved it precisely because they were not reluctant to talk about the category of spirit or self; and also because they liked to think in terms of dualistic categories like "spirit" and "matter." For a long time, under the spell of the prestige of materialist physics and Darwinian naturalism, many shuddered to think in terms of closely knit dualisms. Behaviorists like Watson assured us that all was reducible to material components while the Russians championed Pavlov and accused anyone who talked about "spirit" of bourgeois reactionism. Today we are finding again that we have to talk about the dualism of the self and the body, and even the Russians are no longer ignoring their equivalent of George Mead—the psychologist Lev Vygotsky.

This self-body dualism is essentially the same language the idealists used, but of course they did not stick to any clear-cut naturalistic usage. Kant started this line of thinking when he performed his Copernican shift and placed man within nature as a limited cognizer of objects. This "solved" the problem of man in nature, but it did not solve the psychological problem, the problem of reconciling the phenomenal self and the noumenal self, the body and the spirit—to show naturalistically how they were part of one developmental system. From Kant onward, the psychological problem remained. The idealists who followed Kant began to work this out in a brilliant precursory way. What they did was actually to lay the basis for understanding how the spiritual self is built into the organismic body. Schelling, Fichte, Schleiermacher—all did rich theoretical work in this area. Fichte understood that the individual self was formed of social content, and spoke about a Selfhood (*Ichheit*) in which subject and object are identical; and he understood the development of consciousness as a dialectic between the subject and the object (Merz, 1914, vol. 4, p. 161 note). Schleiermacher, intent on getting at the value of religion from the inside of experience, could likewise talk about the self in both subjective and social terms (Merz, 1914, vol. 4, pp. 314–315 note)—a line of thought that Feuerbach was later to develop richly. In this tradition Schelling's dialectical method was also central, and the whole movement of thought was to be crowned with great originality and power by Hegel (see Royce, 1919).

But between Kant and the later idealists who filled in his system something important was lost. Kant's introspective ego was a psychological construct. By the time we get to Fichte and Hegel, the Kantian psychology gives way to pure logic, and the self or ego of Fichte become descriptive not of a living unity but of metaphysical concepts, concepts portraying the development of the universal conceptual self (cf. Schelling, 1942, p. 233). When we take stock of this whole current of thought, we can see that the development from Kant, Fichte, and Hegel was the fashioning of an active, transactional phenomenology. But the idealists who came after Kant put the emphasis on metaphysics instead of on an organismically based psychology, as Kant had done. It was only in the work of the later Schelling and especially Schopenhauer that Kant's beginnings were carried forward into a truly volitional and subjective psychology. It was for this reason that Royce saw Hegel's greatness in his *Phenomenology,* and not in his transcendental logic.

The result was that when idealism fell this very fruitful beginning in the development of an active introspective psychology almost fell with it. There was a great yearning for scientific respectability and a craze for precision and measurement according to the model of exact science (see Peters, 1962, chap. 13). As we saw in the last chapter, it was only after the materialist, mechanist approach was itself discredited that thinkers like Wundt in Germany and James Ward in Britain were ready to use the language and concepts of idealism, but in a new naturalistic way. So too were Husserl, Lipps, Meinong—but especially Baldwin.

There was, however, one great and well-known figure who kept the introspective approach, even while he himself did most to bring down and naturalize idealism—Feuerbach, of course. Unfortunately, as a philosopher of religion, he was hardly in the mainstream of respectable scientific psychology. As a result, the real flowering of this hundred-year development had to await the American philos-opher-psychologist James Mark Baldwin, who carefully worked out a genetic psychology along the same lines that Feuerbach marked out. Baldwin offered a wholly naturalistic theory of the genesis of the self in the development of the child. He traced the creation and resolution of the self-body dualism in the human animal. Little wonder that he was showered with international honors—he had done nothing less than complete Feuerbach's beginning and bring idealism down to earth, providing a carefully worked-out realist-idealism. Better than anyone else he united the concepts of philosophy with a pragmatic, functional psychology. In his crowning work, *The Genetic Theory of Reality* (1915), he could rejoin the aspiration of the early ideal-ists, but now from a wholly naturalistic position. He provided what Lotze's system had needed: a scientific theory of the social genesis of the self, which fully substantiated the personality as the creator of values and thus accorded the highest place to the artistic creations of the mind.

In order to do this, Baldwin had to reverse what Fichte and Hegel did to Kant, but—like Schelling—he kept their develop-mental activism. He offered an introspective psychology that traced the active development of the individual consciousness in the child. He did what had to be done after Darwin: he showed how the *purely symbolic* level of human activity *grows out of the purely organic* level of animal activity.[1]

Thus he could account for the individual consciousness, as well as for the dualism of spirit and matter, in a purely naturalistic way, exactly as had his predecessor Feuerbach (see 1841, esp. pp. 13, 82–83). And Baldwin's work, coming as it did after Darwin, was more scientifically compelling than was Feuerbach's. The idealists had seen that the self needs objects in order to come into being. Baldwin, along with Meinong and Husserl, understood that man was the only animal who possessed two kinds of objects: not only thing-objects—like the other animals—but uniquely symbol-objects. Human consciousness came into contact with the world, and two different kinds of power were brought into being—active organismic powers and more passive cognitive powers.

What would an animal be like who could relate to symbols as well as to things? Baldwin saw that it would be an animal who would possess a strong sense of the dualism of itself, as well as of animate and inanimate nature. He postulated that the sense of the dualism of mind and body is something that develops as the child learns that

he has an inside—a thought process—that is separate from the outer
world of things. For example, there is something the child wants to
control. He puts together a few memory images of how he controlled
this object in the near past, and then reaches out for the object. But
suppose he finds that the object acts differently than he expected on
the basis of the memory images he had put together: say, it turns
out to be an unfriendly dog instead of the expected tame rabbit. In
this way the child is forced to build and alter conceptual categories,
refashion generalizations, and clarify specific details, to make them
accord with the outer world of things. This teaches him that his
memory images and thoughts are *not* the same as the world of hard
and unpredictable things—that his "insides" (thought) have an
existence "all their own," which may or may not permit easy control of
the outer world. In other words, the individual gradually develops
a symbolic inner realm, a self, which comes to be governed by the
sense of "I." It is this self which he opposes to the outer world and continually reshapes, and to which he attaches his strongest feelings and
emotions. It becomes his unique means of being in the world, navigating in it, deriving satisfaction and safety from it. For the symbolic
animal it thus achieves the highest value, and even the body which
opposes it as an object can be sacrificed for the sake of the values it
has learned.

    Several of Baldwin's contemporaries also mined this self-other
approach and came out with rich, related insights—James, Royce,
Dewey, George Mead, Charles Cooley. They showed how the self
was a social development, how it mirrors the outside world with which
it comes into contact. Josiah Royce acknowledged his debt to Baldwin,
but he arrived independently at some of his results on how the self
develops out of early social relations, and how we build up the idea
of our body (cf. 1919, pp. 127–128). Particularly significant, I think,
for the history we are tracing, is that Royce studied under Lotze,
and in turn taught George Mead. It was thus left to American philosophy and social psychology to keep alive the Herder-Humboldt-
Feuerbach-Lotze tradition of a man-centered synthesis of knowledge,
that would approach action from within experience. Mead elaborated further the idea that the self was a precipitate of reflected appraisals from society, that the individual mind develops by the echoing
of social symbols, and then learning to respond to them. He too
offered what, in effect, Herder had begun: a "social-vocal" theory of
mind. (In France, de Tracy and Maine de Biran had adumbrated a
similar theory.) All these thinkers found, in sum, that man gets his

insides from society—that he is the only "empty" organism in nature, who consequently has to fill himself with the stuff of culture. They gave an objective, scientific account of the process by which the individual gradually constitutes his "insides" or his "social self."

This was truly a superbly rich and fruitful current of thought, by means of which man came to understand exactly what kind of animal he is, and how he got that way. And again, it was a purely naturalistic explanation, the final conversion of the early idealist adumbrations and insights into scientific, broadly behavioral, empiricist language. The Kantian dichotomy of the phenomenal versus the noumenal self was finally bridged by showing the true transactional genesis of values that form the heart of the self. This was the beginning of an almost complete theory of individual development.

THE CONTRIBUTION OF NINETEENTH-CENTURY SOCIAL PSYCHOLOGY TO THE THEORY OF PSYCHOPATHOLOGY

It should not be surprising that when social psychology gave us an almost complete theory of individual development we could use this theory for what we had so long been seeking: an empirical critical basis for analyzing human ills. In fact, as we have learned, we cannot study one without getting insights into the other. When we discover how the peculiarly human arises, it also shows us how the peculiarly human puts a special burden on man—a burden of which other animals are free. When we saw how thought develops out of the substratum of organismic behavior, we could also understand how this dualism of body and mind would cause trouble for man. Thus, it was on this basis that Théodule Ribot (1903) put forth what is actually a very modern view of mental disorder, by postulating that it results from an "in-coordination" between the biological and ideational elements of the total individual. Ribot saw that there is a natural dichotomy between consciousness and the organismic substratum out of which it develops—a dichotomy which, when uncoordinated, will lead to mental illness.

This was a brilliant precursory insight into what we now postulate about the phenomenology of schizophrenia, but little could be done with it theoretically at that time. Like Rousseau's similar great statement of the problem earlier, it had to lie fallow. Ribot was aware of the primitive state of personality theory, and lamented in 1884 that we still did not have the science of ethology, a genetic theory of character formation, that Stuart Mill had projected "more than forty years" ago (Ribot, 1903, p. 23). But very shortly afterward, it was Baldwin again who worked out what was actually an early theory of diverse character types. Let us look at this in some detail, for it is a most important accomplishment of a mature social psychology, of the relation of self to body.

Theorizing on the self-body dualism, Baldwin saw that it could not be "uniform" in everyone. That is to say, man is the only animal who reacts uniquely to two kinds of objects in order to bring his self into being—thing-objects and symbol-objects. Since this is the case, we would expect some of us to pay more attention to the external world, act in it more, test ourselves with the outside of our bodies. Others among us act less in the external world, shrink up more within ourselves, feed ourselves on thought and fantasy, take refuge from the demands of the outside, expand our inner life and nourish ourselves on it. Our "self," in this case, our "sense of being," takes root more in what we feel inside, in what we think and imagine, than in what we actually *do*. In addressing ourselves to a different kind of opposing object, in order to come into being, *we become different kinds of organisms*. This is already a characterology that Ribot wanted.

Having broached the basic dualism, Baldwin went on to build up the following view of the development of the individual. The self-body dualism, he saw, is not primarily a liability for man. Far from it. By means of memory, reflection, and judgment, the individual uses the process of thought to control the external world. As an animal man alone could dependably stop the flow of experience, recombine its salient elements in his imagination, and propose new solutions to external problems. With the rise of thought as a means of control of the outer world, man established his dominion over nature. The matter only becomes a liability when thought turns in upon itself, when the individual uses thought and fantasy to seek justification from within, rather than by testing himself in action. Baldwin concluded then that *one becomes an individual* by overcoming problems, by making successful decisions in trial-and-error action. One gains experience as he successfully combines the inner modes of thought with the outer mode of action.

Again we see the importance of the legacy of the early idealists, as well as of Rousseau. This was actually a modern statement of a thesis adumbrated by Schiller in 1795, in his *Esthetic Education of Man*. Schiller had understood the diverse modes of experience— symbolic and organismic, and had urged that in the esthetic experience they are harmoniously fused. He also saw that some individuals are more symbolically passive, others more organismically active. And it was Rousseau who was perhaps the very first in this whole tradition: he had talked frankly and at great length about the basic and crucial importance of the organic substratum as a repository of lived experience (1762). By the time of Darwin this thesis could find its full scientific legitimation. The Austrian psychologists of the end of the nineteenth century, attempting to describe this deposit of experience in the living organism, used the apt word "funded." Baldwin, along with Dewey and W. M. Urban, borrowed this term, and used "funded" to describe the early idealist prescription: the synthesis of inner and outer, the unity that is forged in successful, adaptational action. As the inner thoughts meet the outer problem and help the individual to overcome it, the organism forms a coherent link with its object, and closes the gap between itself and the world. Every gap successfully closed is an experience satisfactorily had. Hence, in Baldwin's view, the organism "funds" experience by overcoming the inner-outer dualism, by using the mind and body in one active, outer-directed unity. The organism then possesses a fund of experience, deposited in its very structure.

Baldwin (1915) succeeded in giving a view of individual development that confirmed the idealist program in a post-Darwinian world; he put forth an equation that was at the same time an argument for the totality of physical and spiritual experience, the same argument that Schiller had urged: individual development = the synthesis of inner thoughts and outer acts = unity = satisfactory experience for the uniquely symbolic animal = individuation of the most complete kind in nature.

This same current of thought continued in Bergson, Dewey, and more recently, in Merleau-Ponty and Sartre. Dewey put forth a provocative phenomenology of organisms versus objects in his *Experience and Nature*. Crowning the work of Schiller and Baldwin in his *Art as Experience*, he offered the most forceful argument for the primacy and the totality of the esthetic experience—the esthetic experience understood here as the unity of organismic and spiritual powers. It was a position which closed the circle of over 130 years, and added to idealism the full achievement of the naturalistic post-Darwinian epoch as well as the ripest work of the symbolic-interactionist theorists. It established the highest place for the cultural symbolic mode, by which man—as Schiller had suggested—tries himself to become a god who creates values and meaning. But it did not neglect the naturalism of Darwin; it consigned man to his full fate as an organism within nature, doomed to transact experience with the basic coin of biology.

On the basis of all this work it became possible to theorize in a comprehensive way not only about esthetics, but also about what we now recognize as the problem of schizophrenia. It is becoming increasingly clear that there *are* marked differences in mind-body unity; that organisms that are poorly "funded" tend to lack the secure unity that is forged in active experience. As a result, mind and body, spirit and matter, "drift apart," so to speak. This is the basic phenomenology of schizophrenia as we now understand it (cf. E. Becker, 1964a). In other words, the philosophical-functional, social-psychological theory of human development also revealed the heart of typical human pathology, exactly as Ribot had wanted. It also did another surprising thing, as we hinted earlier: it confirmed scientifically the correctness of Rousseau's basic prescriptions for raising children. Rousseau's thesis was that moral learning and the learning that the child accomplishes in freely exercising his organismic powers are two very different things. Rousseau urged that moral, abstract rule-learning be delayed as much as possible until the twelfth year; that the child be allowed fully to develop his own manipulatory powers until that time (1762, esp. pp. 82–83). Today we know that schizophrenia (including its massive, crippling sense of guilt) is the typical result of not following Rousseau's advice: it results from an overburdening of the child with abstract prohibitions and rules, while stifling the free development of his organismic powers. Rousseau voiced the basic pragmatist thesis—that thought should follow action, and that it depends on action; he also described beautifully the surrender of command over one's own organismic energies, the behavioral stupidity (almost his words), that we see today in schizophrenia (1762, esp. pp. 118–119, 127–128). Thus we can understand finally that Rousseau's genius provided not only an argument for social reconstruction, but also the beginning of *the proper psychology* for that argument. (Cf. also the somewhat similar ideas of Herder, on the need for action over abstract speculation—and the superiority of the primitive in this regard [Clark, 1955, pp. 228–230.]) In our time, Wilhelm Reich was one of the very few to understand schizophrenia as Rousseau had: as a problem of crippling the free, total organismic experience. He also relentlessly condemned society for this crippling effect—and, needless to add, was hardly more popular than Rousseau had been in his time.

DIE SOZIALE FRAGE

This is a large part of the long-coveted theory of human alienation. Providing rich filler for Rousseau's ideal-typology, it shows one aspect of human ills and poverty of personality in empirical, scientific terms. An immense theoretical achievement, it took the cumulative work of many minds. Its debt to the early idealists is nowhere better apparent than in the fact that Marx began a similar theory of alienation, drawing directly on Hegel.

In his early work Marx used a Hegelian phenomenology of organisms versus objects, and likewise understood that the organism needs objects in order to come into being. As he put it, in order *to be,* in order to have a nature, it is necessary that there be an object outside oneself (1844, p. 182): each organism must relate to some kind of object in order to substantiate itself in the world. For Marx this was the basic phenomenology of alienation: the failure to develop self-powers by transacting with the world of things. Marx understood that one cannot come into being, literally, unless one develops active powers. For him, alienation meant, first and foremost, the overshadowing of the organism by the object. Again, this is another way of phrasing the modern problem of schizophrenic alienation (cf. E. Becker, 1964b; H. L. Parsons, 1964).

Marx used this early phenomenology of alienation for several purposes. One of them was to criticize idealist philosophy itself, for trying to come to grips with the world's problems on a purely abstract level instead of in an active way. He singled out for criticism the traditional philosopher as a form of alienated man who produces only abstractive, logical, speculative thought. Marx insisted that to divorce oneself from action, to shun total individual involvement, is to condemn oneself to alienation. From our present vantage point, we can see that Marx's insights actually join those of Baldwin, to highlight the phenomenology of schizophrenia. Marx held that alienation exists when man objectifies himself vis-à-vis abstract thought, or symbols. Now this is exactly what Baldwin was later to find, that the individual who transacts only with thought and not with the hard world of things develops an organism that is poorly funded. The schizophrenic, we now know, is precisely one who strives to develop a sense of self largely by basing his development on an opposition to symbol-objects, rather than to real thing-objects.

Marx also wanted his views on alienation to be used as a criticism of wage labor in the new industrial society. He saw how important it was for man to have an active control and personal emotional investment in the products of his labor. In industrial production, on the other hand, the objects man produces are not his own—he produces them merely for a wage; they are a means and not an end. Furthermore, he can fit them into no larger scheme; they are standardized parts, of whose meaning and purpose he is usually ignorant. Marx saw what this did to man: it estranged him from a world in which he should be creatively involved. The world of personal creation is not the world of the industrial worker. Consequently, estranged from his own products, the wage worker is also estranged from the world. Estranged from his own life activity, he is also estranged from others. In other words, when the worker loses self-powers by automatically producing products alien to his own designs, he also loses something equally precious: he loses community with his fellow man. The abrogation of self is ineluctable: as soon as the individual is freed of responsibility for the products he shapes, he is also freed of responsibility for the sum total of human products. When he loses the involvement of his responsible self-powers, *all* objects in his field become alien objects for which he is not morally responsible. This is the phenomenology of immorality in contemporary society that covers such things as political corruption and juvenile-delinquent window smashing. Thus, Marx naturalized the Hegelian dialectic into a criticism of both abstract thought and alienated labor in industrial society.

This turned idealist philosophy into social criticism in a most direct way, which is exactly what Marx wanted—he wanted philosophers to change the world, and not merely theorize about it. Other thinkers who, like Marx, were also steeped in idealist philosophy and in history came up with insights similar to his. They too managed to combine an understanding of the phenomenology of individual development with a criticism of the new industrial society. Georg Simmel, for example, spoke of the dispersal of self-identity, attendant upon the role fragmentation in complex, urban society. In his essay on *The Metropolis and Mental Life,* Simmel also joined in describing what we now understand as the schizophrenic confusion in a world over which one has little or no control, and in which one is not involved. Simmel showed how confused the new city dweller had to be in the face of images, objects, sensations which could not be controlled, ordered, or rendered meaningful. In fact, Simmel's view of alienation as the individual powerless in the face of a world of alien objects is almost identical to Marx's.

Influenced by idealistic philosophy, and with a profound understanding of esthetics, Simmel also offered a view of individuation that is identical with Baldwin's and Dewey's conception. Simmel saw that the subject integrates himself into the world by successfully transacting with its objects, and so accumulates the *contents* of his culture, both within and outside his personality, in the process. This is another way of describing "funding"—in which the individual fills himself with experiences, and creates a meaningful world of objects outside himself, with which he is intimately involved (cf. Weingartner, 1962, pp. 78, 82–84). It is this inner and outer cultural world that the city dweller, in Simmel's essay, usually lacks.

Perhaps the most original effort to combine a phenomenology of alienation with a criticism of the new society was the work of another Frenchman, Fourier. Earlier we had mentioned the prominent place he gave to the "passions" in his work; now we are ready to look at them in somewhat more detail. Fourier might be said to have combined, in a most ingenious way, the esthetic emphasis of the German idealists, the hedonism of Bentham, and the post-Revolutionary social criticism of the new society. But his was an original, not an eclectic synthesis, which makes it all the more remarkable.

Fourier's analysis of the passions has been the target of considerable derision, partly because the cogency of his insights has rarely been understood, and partly because of the quaint words he used to describe them. Fourier gave major importance to three passions which he called the "Distributive" passions. When these passions were combined they gave an impulse to "Series." For Fourier this represented "a social method of which the secret has been lost since the age of primitive mankind." Instead of using this infinitely precious method, mankind has totally misunderstood it, and instead of promoting man's pure orientation to experience, society has condemned the passions as vices (Fourier, 1901, pp. 56 ff.).

Fourier wanted to build his new society on a correct and prejudice-free approach to these basic human passions. What were they? The first Fourier called the "Cabalist" passion. It was simply the inducement to secret, mystery—man's need for conviction and intricate involvement in rich experience. Fourier called the cabalistic spirit "the true destination of man." Later on I want to show how close Fourier was to other thinkers, such as Stendhal, and to the modern theorizing of Scheler and Buber. Here I think it is enough to cite Simmel's later work on the nature of the secret, and the function that it serves in society. Simmel showed more detailedly and comprehensively what Fourier had glimpsed just as profoundly, namely, man's need for involvement in a pattern of humanly created meanings—man's need to believe that life has a deep and underlying meaningfulness (cf. E. Becker, 1962, chap. 8; 1964a, chap. 8). Why was this "the true destination of man?" Simply because man is a symbolic animal, and it is only a symbolic animal who has to impart his own veneer of meanings to a neutral and strange, material and organic world.

Fourier held that man misunderstood the cabalistic passion because up until then civilized mankind had not had the proper social background in which to play it out creatively. Thus, the conniving, scheming, plotting which characterized modern society was bound to appear harmful and evil simply because this society was individualistic and divided into competing families and classes. In his ideal and true communities of sixteen hundred persons, Fourier thought that this passion would work in its original, pristine, and cohesive sense. In today's language, we would talk about the indispensable interpersonal and social basis for human conviction. And the anthropologist would cite the total social creativity, the interpersonal solidarity, and artistic meaningfulness of primitive myth and ritual, over and against, say, stock-market manipulations, Ku Klux Klan activities, and atomic war "games."[2] In other words, as we noted above, Fourier enunciated a thesis that was given modern, scholarly form only very recently: in Scheler's work, and especially in Buber's writings on the interpersonal nature of human conviction, in Simmel's writings on sociality as a "play-form," in the whole tradition of thinkers who developed a naturalistic psychology of religious experience, and later in Johan Huizinga's work on *Homo ludens*. (We will return to Huizinga later, and also show how well Comte too understood this problem.)

The next passion Fourier called the "Composite." It was the passion that derived from the unity of "senses and the soul" (1901, p. 59). This was Fourier's insight into the basic nature of esthetic satisfaction, the same insight put forth earlier by Schiller, and later by Baldwin and Dewey—it declared the high value of a mind-body synthesis in creative activity. In his own language, and using the background of social criticism, Fourier gave a very modern statement of esthetic theory—the need for a unifying, uplifting grasp on experience:

> In the civilised order, where labour is repugnant, where the people are too poor to participate in the consumption of choice foods, and where the epicure is not a cultivator, his epicurism lacks a *direct* bond with cultivation; it is nothing but sensuality, *simple* and ignoble, as is all else which does not attain to *composite* mechanism, or the influence of production and consumption acting upon the same individual (1901, p. 65).

One has only to consult Dewey's *Art as Experience* for the identical view of the need to unify sense experience and cultural experience; of the need to enjoy the richness of complex relationships and only thus to rise above mere sensuality; and of the implicit indictment of modern societies which this entails. And the following recalls Schiller's *Esthetic Education of Man*:

> The point is to determine what influence may be exerted over the physical constitution of children and the developments of the human body by *an integral play of the faculties and attractions of the soul combined with the integral exercise of the faculties of the body by means of proportional gymnastics* (1901, pp. 73–74, his emphasis).

The final passion of the "Series" Fourier calls the *"Papillone"* (Butterfly), or "Alternating." It is the one which links the other two. This is simply the passion which abhors monotony, the twelve-hour drudge day of labor. It is the passion for periodicity, for variety in human occupations and in daily routine. Fourier urged simply that "human reason ought to strive to discover a social condition which shall be in affinity with these passions" (1901, p. 61).

Dewey later urged the identical thing. In Fourier's day, as the failure of his Utopian communities attests, his urgings were premature. In our day, with automation pressing itself upon us, we are finally face-to-face with Fourier's challenge: Shall we make a rational society that will give full play to the basic needs of man's nature: to his need for *conviction*, to his enjoyment of *complex harmonies* of physical and symbolic experience, to his constant search for *rich variety*? Shall we do it under conditions of peace and plenty, or in the old vicious patterns of war and hate? As Fourier knew, the passions function anyway, even if the social context "perverts" them; they can be twisted and satisfied in many ways: war gives mystery and secrecy aplenty; hate gives conviction in all its intensity; the alternation between peace and war, between prosperity and depression, gives variety. Modern corporation man uncritically draws his conviction from the tight-lipped, deeply pensive "executive-type"—as C. Wright Mills very acutely remarked (1959). He also draws it from a philosophy of competition, which seems like a law of nature; from an opulent way of life amidst abject poverty, which gives him a sense of superior achievement; and from the exclusion of other races, which gives him a sense of deserved specialness. The growing race rioting in our cities, where whites try to keep blacks out of their neighborhoods, is not only a threat to real-estate values: it is a threat to one's deepest sense of self, based on a false philosophy of human achievement. Veblen, too, dug beneath this mask, and showed how modern man draws his cheap everyday esthetics from the frills of conspicuous consumption. He merges his self and body into the effortless maneuvers of power steering, alternately lulled and charmed by the new Detroit glitter. He leaves his eight-hour day to "knock out a few golf balls"—and this is some variety. Man is a flexible animal, and he can meet his need for conviction, esthetics, and variety in any number of ways. The call to war and the creative competition to design a new peace monument serve equally well to give the individual rich and challenging experience.

The question that our civilization is now asked to face is whether we are ready to make man the master of his social games, rather than their unwitting servant. In a post-alienated society it would be man himself who would create his own rich and playful and variegated meanings. These meanings would not be left to the automatic functioning of his social institutions, in which man is sacrificed to the blind forces of commercial-industrial economics with its high vision of the eight-hour day, the two-week vacation, the unhoped-for bliss of "full employment."

Thus, in sum, Fourier very early spelled out a social psychology that would reveal to man the social sources of his alienation. It was hardly complete—in fact it was mostly suggestive, like Rousseau's critique of alienation which inspired it; but, as Baldwin's and Dewey's later work attests, it was nevertheless ingenious in conveying the basic levels of human striving. Today we may be more sophisticated, but from a practical point of view the problem remains what it was in Fourier's day: do we place human nature at the disposal of capricious social forces, or do we try to give man control of these forces, for his own happiness and fullest development?

CHAPTER SEVEN

THE SOCIAL DIMENSIONS OF EVIL:
The Contribution of Sociology

The earlier achievements of science were made without the conscious observance of any scientific method, and we should never have known by what process truth is to be ascertained if we had not previously ascertained many truths.

JOHN STUART MILL *(1950, pp. 307–308)*

The contribution of sociology to the theory of alienation is so well known that our present sketch can be very brief. Here the name of Marx, instead of being peripheral, is central, for no one showed better than he how much man is a puppet of the automatic functioning of his economic institutions. We also know how Veblen, Max Weber, and C. Wright Mills filled out Marx's framework and brought his analyses up to date. Weber and Veblen showed how the institutions of society operate in a complex and interrelated way; how economics becomes submerged in a pattern of interlocking ideologies and social fictions. Mills' analysis, which is the latest and the most vital concern to us, gave us a detailed and thorough view of how society fails when man does not put his economic life under rational control. Like Veblen and Weber, Mills had no illusions about historical inevitability: he knew that society can function as a huge drama of the creation of meaning, which continues on under its own complex momentum. The burden of Mills' work is not to demonstrate the possible, but to preach for the desirable. He held up before us a warning of how commercial-industrial society must probably plunge

135

the world into war and death by the simple and logical functioning
of its uncriticized economic and social institutions. When a country
is run on the principle of a blind and wishful national lottery, held
daily in Wall Street, the stakes for the lottery may be nothing less
than the end of the world—and this, whether the people who are
playing know it or not.

Die Soziale Frage

A critique of irrational economic institutions is already the most
vital part—perhaps the only vital part—of a theory of alienation for
our time. And it is expounded with brilliance in several well-known
books so that my meager resources in this area may be spared. What
I would like to do is to show how the nineteenth century led into this
problem, and show some of the currents which prepared the idea of
the alienation of man under the form of the uncritically functioning
economic state.

In order to solve the burning question of social reconstruction,
we have to know what are the proper and possible relationships between the two basic components of society: the individuals in it and
the structure which holds them together—the new national state.
In order to know these relationships, we have to know what individuals
are and what the state is. And this is what the nineteenth century
sought to be clear about. As we have just seen, it took a whole tradition of social psychology to fathom the problem of what individuals
are, how they come to be social. It was Marx's great merit that, although he could not answer that question in detail, he insisted on
phrasing it in the broadest possible terms. So he quickly moved on
from the problem of the individual to the problem of the state. From a
strictly scientific point of view, as we suggested in Chapter Three, it
would have been desirable to work out a complete theory of individual development, but since this was not possible at the time,
Marx must be given credit for the basic good sense of genius, instead
of being accused of shirking a difficult job. Besides, Marx phrased the
problem of man in the spirit of the time: like Rousseau, he saw that
in order really to understand man, he would have to be seen over and
against the particular social conditions to which he was subjected.
As an Enlightenment thinker, Marx shared the views of his time on
human nature: that man is not a fixed but an open creature, capable of becoming anything which society allows. As Robert Owen
so well put the Enlightenment belief: "Human nature, its capacities

and powers, is yet to be learned by the world." To these people there seemed little sense in continuing a minute analysis of the problems of individual development, if the individual would change entirely when provided with the right social context. They already knew the basic lesson that has emerged from modern science, namely, that if you treat behavior on an open-system level you can and must sacrifice analytical detail (cf. von Bertalanffy, 1960, p. 155). All the more so if the behavior is the chaos of a new industrial society that threatens to crush man completely if he does not hasten to act.

But there was another spirit of the time in the nineteenth century that did not understand man in these terms. This was the great mythology of the laissez-faire economists, which Marx had to attack in order to set history and human possibility straight. These were the "individualists"—Adam Smith, Ricardo, Malthus—who held that every man has a different endowment, a natural difference in talent which no amount of social manipulation can change. With this view, the problem of the individual versus the state was resolved in favor of the status quo of the new parliamentary spoils system. It also fitted in perfectly with the doctrine of "natural rights," which served to justify and explain the new commercial state. How did the state come into being? In the most natural and freely evolving way— these people answered. In the darkness of prehistory everyone was equal, and whatever goods there were, were the property of the group. Gradually, differences in natural individual endowment began to make themselves felt, and there came to be lopsided accumulations of wealth. And so it happened that out of differences in skill, thrift, sobriety there developed the present system of political representation of unequal social classes. It was the job of the new parliament to protect the natural gains of a long historical process.

The "scientific" statement of this view of history was Adam Smith's "law of previous accumulation"—and, as we noted in Chapter Three, this was the "nursery myth" that Marx set out to demolish. And this demolition was accomplished in two ways, the first of which we have already seen: when the old faculty psychology was undermined, first by Herder and then by the later psychology, we could see the self as a social creation; this undermined the thesis that each person is differently endowed mentally, by heredity, and that society is merely the stage for the enactment of natural individual differences. Marx also contributed to this debate when he very early took issue with Max Stirner's notions about individual "interest"—an idea which appeared very Benthamite to Marx. The issue was clear: it was a fallacy to see man as the English economists did, and to talk of individual "interests," when these interests were always socially and historically conditioned (cf. Hook, 1962, pp. 184–185).

This took the problem to its second stage, namely, what had *actually happened historically* to give rise to the present chaos of social inequality and exploitation? What was this structure called "the state" that had given itself the mandate to protect the present status quo? If this question could be answered, it would provide the complement to the demolition of the individualist psychology: we would understand historically and socially how false Smith's "nursery myth" was. Putting the problem in these terms opened up a line of thought that was to occupy the whole nineteenth century, and extend all the way up to the present. As we might expect, the great father of this line of criticism was Rousseau, who first posed the hypothesis of primitive equality and communism, and who saw history and private property as the "Origin of Inequality." The task of the nineteenth century was to try to find out exactly what had happened in history and prehistory, to trace the drama of the exploitation of man by man.

The French Revolution was, of course, pivotal in setting this problem before everyone's mind: it was a frank display of the functions of power in rearranging social classes. On the basis of it, Saint-Simon was led to make a historical analysis of the development of classes in France that resulted from conquest and subjugation. And so the old idea of "the robber state," phrased by Augustine, was revived as a modern critical concept. The idea had passed through the Arab scholar Ibn Khaldun, who had understood the historical genesis of the state in conquest and power; through others such as Jean Bodin, and later Hume, Adam Ferguson, John Millar, and through Saint-Simon into the nineteenth century. Marx and Engels seized upon the idea, and it was Engels who gave it modern "scientific" form in his brilliant work on *The Origin of the Family, Private Property and the State.* Here, basing himself on the ethnography and evolutionism of the American anthropologist Lewis Henry Morgan, Engels presented his argument for the origin of the state as the origin of inequality. It was the fulfillment of the challenge that Rousseau had laid down: to show scientifically how inequality had arisen, and by doing this to hold up to men's minds a model of how things ought to be, of how wrong they were in the present. The state, said Engels, was the modern *structure of domination* par excellence; only, people have forgotten how it was in the beginning. They no longer know that they were despoiled in the deeps of prehistory, and that they have been systematically dispossessed by each new generation. Thus, what began as injustice has become institutionalized with everyone's sheepish consent; and the state now uses everyone for the good of the few.

Such was the great anti-statist argument whereby the Marxists sought to induce modern dispossessed man to end his *historical* alienation. The use of the state, and of power relations, as a way of explaining the present condition of man became a primary tool of social analysis, and passed via the Saint-Simonians into German sociology—Rodbertus, Lorenz von Stein, Gumplowicz, Ratzenhofer, up to Oppenheimer, Max Weber, and a host of less-known thinkers in the twentieth century. Philosophers, too, used the idea: Nietzsche, with the incisiveness of genius, saw that the state had simply taken over from the defunct Church, to command the unquestioning loyalty of men. It wants the same worship! said Nietzsche, incredulous and alarmed.

It was possible to call Rousseau's "state of nature" fanciful, or to shrug at Kant's and Herder's suggestion that the division of labor in civilized society can produce insanity (Clark, 1955, p. 229), but it was not possible to dismiss lightly the penetrating and brilliant nineteenth-century accusation of the historical state as a new structure of domination. Here was a really powerful argument in the sociological attack on alienation: it was the state, and not individuals, which had to be changed. (In a concluding chapter we will see why this argument failed to be conclusive.) It was on this basis that Marx enunciated his supreme sociological law—the "great law of class struggle" (cf. Rignano, 1928–1929, p. 619); it was on this basis too that the anarchists attacked central power of any kind. The hope of all these thinkers was to do away with the state; and the prediction of Marx was based on the hope that in the truly new communistic society of the future, the state, the historical structure of domination, would wither away. The class struggle was given its primary justification by the fact that classes had a historical, and not a natural origin, as we saw; modern man was called upon to right centuries of injustice.

And so we can draw the circle on our discussion of the sociological dimension of alienation. By the time this whole current of thought was brought up to date by Weber, Veblen, and Mills, we had the sociological critique that we wanted. We could see exactly how the state functions as a power aggregate. We could understand the state as a vast centralized bureaucracy that takes on its own life, has its own ideology. We could see how intimately it allies itself with the functioning of the corporations, the military—as C. Wright Mills especially showed; how offhandedly it operates a national draft, and grinds up personal liberties for its own abstract power purposes; we could see, in a word, what Nietzsche already bemoaned: how the citizens are sheepishly led to do the bidding of the state structure, by giving their uncritical worship and allegiance. And we have learned that the bidding of the state is not necessarily in the interests of the people or even responsive to them: we have been able to see a whole population vote overwhelmingly for a peace candidate, only to have that candidate follow the thrust of the state structure and push ahead for war.

And so, even after such a hurried sketch, we can see how the social-psychological and sociological contributions to a synthetic theory of alienation merge and complement each other. We can understand that man is only truly man when he is actively exercising his own powers, only when he has some kind of control over the events that shape his life. We are brought back, in a word, to the democratic ideal of Jefferson and Emerson, who wanted a state composed of independent, critically thinking individuals who would exercise rational control over its functions. The nineteenth century understood this ideal very well and hoped to achieve it; the twentieth century only pays it lip service. The aim of the whole nineteenth century was to achieve a unitary, critical world view, without which there was no hope of mastering the chaos of the new industrial world. It was painfully apparent that, with the demise of traditional society, the individual gradually and increasingly lost his previously unified world view. At least he had known right from wrong, good from bad, and had felt himself a part of a coherent, meaningful world scheme—even if he personally was disinherited and exploited. In its place, the world became increasingly profuse, full of often unrelated experiences: it was a panorama over which he could no longer exercise any firm conceptual control, from which not only was he excluded, but in which good and evil became blurred. Furthermore, the new industrialism, by fragmenting his work contribution, seemed to insist that modern man would only be allowed to see things in their piecemeal nature, in sometimes total unrelatedness to any larger design. The world he lived in was always in some disarray; he could not get above it to some firm, self-centered, commanding height. This had been Auguste Comte's complaint—man's need for a "vue d'ensemble," which he had lost. The pre-Revolutionary Enlightenment thinkers had performed well their "divisive" work, and the Revolution itself finished the job. The whole modern industrial world was fragmented—"gone mad" in Dewey's later accusation, with a preoccupation with the specific, the unconnected, the minute.

Durkheim had picked up this important insight from Comte, and substantiated it in his study of primitive societies with their striking unity. It led him to coin the term "anomie," which was another way of describing alienation in a world of unconnected and uncontrolled profuseness. Durkheim too saw how important a firm centering of self-power is, and he espoused the democratic view of what a real person is—"an autonomous source of action." But this kind of creature was rarely seen in the new mass society. Philosophers too joined the chorus—not only Nietzsche, but also Josiah Royce, who lamented the modern loss of selfhood amid vast social forces, and like Marx he referred back to Hegel's idea about the "self-estrangement of the spirit" (Cotton, 1954, p. 258). In recent times it was C. Wright Mills who almost alone in sociology strongly echoed the call to a new, critical command of experience.

With the distinctive contribution of sociology to this critique, the problem of the individual in society was made clear. Kant had given the Enlightenment ideal its perfect phrasing: man had to try to achieve maximum *individuality* within maximum *community*. It was an unattainable paradox, like all worthwhile ideals, yet only by aiming for it could we overcome alienation. Now we knew what had happened to it in the new society: the centralized bureaucratic national state gave the lie to both poles of the paradox: it allowed neither individuality nor community. No wonder we have needed thinkers like Veblen and Mills and Harry Elmer Barnes, C. A. Beard, Graham Wallas, John Dewey, and countless others, to bring home again and again Fourier's lesson, and Comte's, Durkheim's, Rousseau's, and Marx's: *it simply is not enough to play well the game of the new society.* Man must confront the underlying alienation that exists in every age, and alienation exists *whenever the individual does not have a commanding view, a unitary critical perspective* by which to take in hand and react to the determinants of his social existence.

Having failed to do this, the twentieth century gathered all the evils that could seem possible to befall man: genocide of millions, recurrent world war, race and hate riots, famine and world-wide misery for the vast masses of men. And the outlook for the future is more of the same: atomic war, violent revolutions, mass starvation. In our time we have seen the *demonic* emerge in all its starkness, and we have learned why it emerges: the demonic comes into being for man whenever he is manipulated by large impersonal forces beyond his control; forces that *he* is actively and uncritically *contributing to.* Thus, when modern man sets in motion vast social institutions but does not take critical control of them, the institutions assume their own momentum; the people who man the institutions become like ants mechanically doing their duty, and no one dares to question the routine to which the institutions conform. The result is that there is no way of breaking through the uncritical fictions that control society and that are embodied in vast and powerful, faceless organizations. Responsibility is nowhere; grinding power everywhere. Where are the "centered" persons—as Tillich called them—who should guide and shape this impersonal machinery, according to an ideal vision of man? Where is the responsible dissent, the continued review of the *ends* of action? Without these the world of ineluctable movement assumes its own laws, and, like a black widow spider of science-fiction proportions, it turns on and consumes the very people who give it life.

This is the demonic nature of social evil in our time. It is a fitting culmination of the failure to heed the Enlightenment lesson: if man fails to introduce critical reason into the realm of human affairs, he must be prepared to suffer evils which he could have prevented. To function without a central, guiding brain equals death for the only animal in nature who is characterized by the need for such a brain. And the greatest and most crucial lesson of the Enlightenment and the nineteenth century, for our society, is that we must take critical control over the automatic functioning of our economic institutions. This is the contribution of sociology to our synthetic theory of alienation, and the reason that the ghost of Marx refuses to be banished from our national life. The commercial-industrial nations are once again keeping their economies boosted with a vast international flow of arms and munitions—exactly as they did before World War I. Once again, the specter of War Capitalism is descending upon the world. And the tradition of Saint-Pierre, Rousseau, and Marx is a small flame indeed compared to this holocaust. But it should be very clear that it is the only light we have in a world of almost complete madness; and that is why we take the pains to put down the words of the historical record.

CHAPTER EIGHT

THE LAW OF PERSONALITY DEVELOPMENT:
The Contribution of Psychiatry

> *The truer the theory, the more reasonable and simple. The lesson is to distrust all . . . profound and far-fetched theories. . . . The truth . . . must . . . be . . . nude to be effective.*
> LESTER WARD *(in Chugerman, 1939, p. 494)*

We have seen how much solid psychological and sociological knowledge the nineteenth century accumulated. Now we are ready to take the problem one step further and see just what Freud did and did not contribute to our understanding of man. The intriguing question that we will want to answer is this: If the nineteenth century contributed so much to a synthetic theory of alienation, what was left for Freud to do?

As everyone knows who has lived through the age of Freud, this is a question of far-reaching significance. Freudian psychology has occupied a high place in the preoccupations of thinkers in all the disciplines and vigorous disputes have raged around it. Only today, in the 1960's, is the air beginning to clear: as Freud's basic contribution to the history of thought is finally emerging, it is becoming possible for us to speak of Freud as a historical figure rather than as a continuing contemporary.

FREUD'S CONTRIBUTION

The student of the history of ideas learns one thing about its great figures: they tend to sum up in their contribution the central problems of a whole epoch so that the storm of discussion and controversy that rages around them really represents the intellectual stirrings of a whole historical period. This is clear about Darwin, who summed up the evolutionary thought that had long been in the air. This is also very clear about Marx, who forcefully brought together the critical insights of many thinkers and focused them on the problem of social reconstruction of his time (cf. Barzun, 1958). The same is true of Freud. Freud summed up the whole movement of thought of the Enlightenment and the nineteenth century. He clarified the problem of alienation by showing exactly how society cripples its members by means of their early indoctrination. As we have seen all through these pages, others had understood and spoken of this—Rousseau, Fourier, Marx, not to mention Nietzsche, Robert Owen, and even Stendhal. In an undated writing sometime between 1816 and 1837, Stendhal put into almost exact words the later Freudian psychology:

> . . . a man's character is derived from his mother; it begins to form in the second year of life and is established at four or five years of age. . . . These individuals have from childhood a definite way of seeking their happiness, a way, that later adjusts itself to changing conditions, yet always remains the same (quoted in Rank, 1932, p. 3).

Stendhal attributes this insight to psychologists of the time, and indeed it was one of the great discoveries of the Enlightenment inquiry into the nature of man. It began with Montaigne, went through Pascal and on to Helvétius—whom Stendhal so much admired. It is in Rousseau (cf. 1762, pp. 21, 82), and it was also phrased pointedly by the Marquis de Sade (cf. Crocker, 1963, p. 416, note 75). It went on into the nineteenth century in the work of Cabanis, de Tracy, and Maine de Biran, all of whom stressed the power of early habit in the formation of personality. Thus, we see how deeply into the past the problem extended, which Freud was later to sum up.

But it is not enough merely to sum up the preoccupations of an epoch in order to rank as a great man. Each of these thinkers, Darwin, Marx, and Freud, also added some particularly sharp conceptualization; it is this very sharp focus of a broad, historical current of thought which permits posterity to refer to each thinker by name. Actually this is merely a shorthand for the more general historical problem they summed up in their work, albeit their own genius has given it an original and peculiar stamp. Marx, for example gave the problem of social reconstruction the law of class struggle; Freud gave the problem of individual development and the nature of conscience the law of the Oedipus complex; Darwin took many things already known, including the law of natural selection, and wove them into a beautifully tight scheme, which summed up clearly the problem of evolution for all later thinkers. Someone once bemoaned the fact that whenever posterity mentions evolution it will have to refer to "Charlie" Darwin; we could say the same thing about social reconstruction and Marx and about individual development and Freud. Today no one mentions Baldwin or Royce—much less Bernard Pérez.

Now, as a final remark, we can see one thing further about the historical innovator who sums up the thought of his time. He derives his recognition from posterity because he sums up this thought sharply, comprehensively, and usually in a very neat law or striking metaphor. But he himself, as a thinker, then becomes an obstacle to a fuller and more mature development of the historical current *because of the very sharp conceptualization he offered*. That is to say, the abbreviation of the problem is usually a two-sided coin: it permits a ready conceptual grasp but at the same time prohibits the necessary broader understanding of the problem. The innovator's conceptualization becomes itself a dogma against which later thinkers must struggle in order to get back to the complex historical current which he summed up. This is nowhere more clear than in the fifty-year struggle against the "Oedipus complex." We have had to denude Freudian theory, strip it of easy dogma as well as mystery, in order to get back to the Enlightenment problem which he summed up—the problem of the social formation of the individual consciousness.

The nineteenth century brought this problem to a head, as we saw. Marx summed it up on a social institutional level, Baldwin on the level of individual development: it was abundantly clear that the self takes root in society. At the end of the century many diverse thinkers were converging on this problem and attacking it from a precise, genetic point of view. John Fiske, for example, was one of the first post-Darwinians to insist on the outstanding characteristic of the higher primates, which turns them into social animals par excellence, namely, the prolonged helplessness of the young and their need of continual protection and training. And Georg Simmel, as we noted, saw that the individual is formed by building into himself the contents of his culture, by transacting with its objects. With these kinds of insights, it was no difficult matter to conclude that each culture will inhibit a certain range of perceptions, and encourage others. This is exactly what Simmel did in 1911 when he spoke of the skewing of the ego, of the cultural constrictions on perception (Cassirer, 1961b, pp. 186, 192). A year later the great Max Scheler wrote his work on *The Nature of Sympathy*, which was a full-scale attempt to solve the problem of the nature of the social bond (1954, cf. esp. pp. 103, 232). Scheler wanted to know exactly why the self was social, what it derived from its rooting in society.

I mention Scheler, along with these other thinkers, because it helps us to focus more sharply on Freud's contribution. Scheler was looking for a comprehensive theory of the nature of the self and of the social bond; he wanted a coherent, genetic theory of personality. Now this is just what Freud offered: a theory of individual development which was in effect a very economical theory of the genetic development of the self and of the social bond. But he called it a theory of *sex*—and this is just where Scheler was critical of Freud. Freud reduced the problem of the social bond to the child's need to work out a few primitive erotic and aggressive instincts. He offered, in effect, a theory of animality; but what Scheler wanted was a theory of human sociality. It was only in the later ego psychology that Freud's system came clearly to be understood as a broader theory of sympathy in Scheler's sense: a theory of the formation of the symbolic identity, and of the dependence of that identity on society. Scheler would later have been able to find Freud's contribution through, say, Erik Erikson, but he could not accept its formulation by the early Freud. Nor, for that matter, could other notable thinkers such as Luther Bernard and William Ernest Hocking, whom we mentioned earlier, nor John Dewey. Dewey denounced Freudian sexual instinct theory about the same time as Bernard, in his 1922 book *Human Nature and Conduct*. In almost the exact thought and language of Rousseau earlier (1762, p. 280), he accused Freud of the error of confounding physical causes and artifact results. Like Scheler, Dewey needed an economical and flexible theory of personality—a theory that was "concealed", we might say, in Freud's system; but also like Scheler, Dewey had to forgo this theory because of the cynical disguise Freud erected over it—the arbitrary reduction of the richness of human aspiration to a few mechanisms of instinct and sexuality.

If this is the case, we are entitled to ask, as we may ask of any great figure in the history of ideas: would we have arrived at his ideas without him? If so, how long would it have taken and what would be the shape of the ideas without his distinctive contribution? This is not an easy question to answer, and this is hardly the place to attempt any kind of comprehensive reply; but the question is worth posing, and I think that we can risk a suggestion or two, if only to help us put Freud into the perspective of our history.

In the first place, Baldwin and related thinkers had given us a fairly precise picture of the origin of the self out of the organic substratum. I think it is fair to say that we did not need Freud in order to fix the social nature of the self, and its early genesis in the child. In the second place, as we saw, thinkers as diverse and far apart as Rousseau, Stendhal, and Simmel, had spoken in some way of the social formation of the individual character in its early years, and its consequent rigidity and comparative poverty. We noted that Simmel spoke *precisely* of the skewing of the ego and its perceptions before the large, professional societies of psychoanalysts declared this their own esoteric and lucrative cant. Also, there were many thinkers who contrasted the purposive, controlled aspects of behavior with the more diffuse, receptive aspects. Bergson was important here: he spoke of the polarity "intensity of feeling" versus "intensity of effort"; William James too used this dichotomy—he contrasted the "sensitive" type with the "motor" type; and Baldwin, as we noted earlier, used a similar designation, as did Dewey when he spoke of the difference between "doing" and "undergoing," and the different kinds of organisms these behaviors bring into being. These contrasts are found too in the writing of Schiller, for example, who stresses the difference between the "receptive" and the "determining" faculties (cf. E. Becker, 1964a, chap. 1); and Rousseau made very creative use of these contrasts.

In other words, we can say that these ego-psychological conceptions were bound to emerge in the post-Kantian, post-Darwinian world, in one form or other. Even without Freud, we would be in firm possession of the *general* ideas on the social genesis of the individual consciousness, on the elaboration of the self, just as, for example, we would be in possession of the ideas of Saint-Simon, Sismondi, Hegel, Feuerbach, and the other thinkers upon whom Marx drew, even without Marx's powerful synthesis and subtle sharpening.

But Freud's contribution was to take these general ideas and give them precise and indelible form in the human consciousness. For one thing, fifty years of psychoanalytic practice put the decisive keystone on our understanding of the ego, and showed fully the nature of the ego as the central cortical control of behavior; we now had abundant clinical evidence, in great wealth of detail, on how the ego grows and functions, how it exercises its central, unifying control over the organism, how it delays gratification and permits distinctively human perceptions and choices to come into being. This put the perfect crown on the study of individual development begun a century before by Destutt de Tracy and his school.

But more than this, Freud took these ideas and forged them into a daring and imaginative law of early ego development, the law of the Oedipus complex. It was this law that offered us a very precise theory of character formation, the very thing that Stuart Mill, Ribot, and so many others had sought in vain. With it, Freud, and the fifty years of psychoanalytic biographies which his school produced, gave the clearest possible picture of how early training skews the child's world view. He showed us how early training can completely cripple the child; how it can prevent him from coping with the adult world, or train him to cope so well and so automatically and unquestioningly that he never becomes his own person in the process; he showed how the mass of men never get to be persons, but rather remain cultural artifacts. This is what the idea of Oedipus complex boils down to, and what neurosis itself means: the rigid, unthinking life style into which the individual is shaped by his early training. And so we can see the import of Freud's contribution: *the scientific theory of ego development was itself a critical anthropodicy*, a theory of the alienation of man in society. Whereas Marx had crystallized an economic criticism of the new laissez-faire society, Freud had distilled a penetrating psychological critique of early family training and social indoctrination.

This was the crucial superiority of Freud's theory over the earlier tradition we have sketched. His whole work confronted society with its harmful effects on man. Baldwin and his tradition could not muster this degree of critical clarification for several reasons. For one thing, their explanation of social behavior was sketchy. They reduced the problem of the genesis of the self to some simple principle such as "imitation" or "consciousness of kind"—which, as we saw, did not take the problem theoretically much further than where Adam Smith had left it. Baldwin, Giddings, and Tarde made "imitation" the fundamental explanatory principle of their theory, and had little else to fill it out with (cf. Ellwood, 1936–1937). Now Freud also used the notion of "identification"—which is similar to "imitation"—but he did not leave the matter there. He supported it with a very subtle and excellent theory of anxiety, which allowed him to describe the growth of the personality by means of "identification,"

"mechanisms of defense," and the final confrontation with the "Oedipus complex."

With these interlocking concepts, Freud provided a compelling
theory that solved one of the outstanding questions that had plagued
the best thinkers in history, namely, where does the sense of moral
obligation come from, and why does it continue throughout life? In
modern times, Kant had wondered about this in his famous lines
about "the moral law within"; Bain and Spencer tried to solve the
problem in the nineteenth century, and Dewey in the twentieth—but
to little avail. The most that these thinkers could do was to talk about
"habit," just as Cabanis and Destutt de Tracy did earlier. Bain, for
example, developed a theory of obligation which, like the Enlightenment views earlier, stressed the early training of the child and the
ingrained habit and dispositions it leaves behind. But Dewey was
not satisfied with this theory, precisely because it did not explain the
critical problem of a theory of obligation, namely, why does the individual *continue to feel* obligation even after the early figures of
authority cease to put on pressure. Why does the child carry over his
early training so religiously? (See Dewey, 1891, pp. 140–141.) But
Dewey couldn't take this problem any further than Bain, and was also
obliged to talk about the tenacity of "habit." It was, of course, no
explanation at all, but merely a begging of the question.

Here is where Freud's precise and powerful theory of anxiety
and ego development showed its historical importance and its superiority over previous theories. We could understand that the superego,
or sense of moral obligation, is the very life style that the child follows
in order to avoid anxiety and minimize censure by the adults. The
child actually shapes himself into a certain pattern of perception and
action in order to keep the forward momentum of his conduct in
relation to the adults around him. In this way, the child becomes
a reflex of the parents, and performs as they wish even when they are
gone. He has learned to be his own overseer, to call the tune to his
own moral obligation. The whole of Freud's achievement is summed
up in the lines uttered by the responsible child: "You needn't punish
me any more, father—I will punish myself now." These words of
Freud show better than anything else what his theory accomplished
as an explanation of the depth and obstinacy of the moral sense in
man, that other thinkers could not get.

Furthermore, Freud's theory explained social discord and friction
in a way that George Mead, for example, could not. In Mead's
social-behavioral theory of the self, it seemed as though each person

should have the identical social contents, if he learned the same vocabulary as those around him. In fact, Mead, carrying forward Royce's ideas, seems to have wanted to prove that brotherhood is natural to man since the self grows out of the whole social community (cf. Pfeutze, 1961, p. 334). But then if everyone shared a world view in complete harmony, how could we explain the rupture of human relations? Freud could, simply because he showed us that *each individual learns to avoid anxiety in his own way, in a distinctive family context.* In other words, Freud focused on the process of social disruption in microcosm, just as Marx had focused on it at the level of large-scale social institutions. Freud's theory of ego development showed that each individual used different techniques to ward off anxiety and to maintain his sense of self-esteem, depending on the unique history of his early identifications. As a result, with all these different "defense mechanisms," there is bound to be social friction.

Furthermore, like Marx, and unlike Baldwin and Mead, Freud developed a theory that embodied in itself a stinging valuational critique of social conditioning. The Oedipus complex, as Talcott Parsons recently showed, is best considered not a complex as such, but actually as a synonym for the whole period of early training. Thus it is a synonym for the early world view into which the child is fashioned. In discovering the constrictions of early experience, symbolized in the Oedipus complex, Freud could pinpoint his critique by talking frankly about neurosis. More than ever, we are today concluding that there is nothing mysterious about this term—it means simply that the child is burdened by his early learning. By "burdened" is meant that the child learns to conduct himself, and to execute choices, in a manner which will avoid anxiety, and which will be pleasing to his parents. He learns to gain his feeling of self-value by performing according to codes that are thrust upon him by his parents. By neurosis, then, Freud meant to indicate that the early learning remains inadequate to meet the demands of varied adult experience, that it constricts the choices and action of the adult in some ways. When the child made sacrifices in learning in order to please his parents, he necessarily sacrificed the possibilities of broader perception and action in the interests of his own survival, security, and equanimity. It is a sacrifice forced upon him by his early mammalian dependence, a dependence intensified in the higher primates.

Neurosis, in sum, signifies simply that there is a *basic dichotomy in human experience,* an incompatibility between early training and the demands of adult action. Thus, neurosis is itself a synonym for Oedipus complex, for the automatic early world view inculcated into the child. This is the major discovery of Freud, the basic dichotomy of human experience—and it is one that the self psychologists had not been able to bring out with such force. And even if they had, they were not clinicians, and thus could not have brought to bear the enormous volume of intimate and detailed personal biographies which drive home the lesson of neurosis, which themselves serve as a massive documentary indictment of the early "brainwashing" that takes place in each society. This, then, is the distinctive achievement of Freud and his school, which gives him a unique place in the history of man's discovery of his own social nature. When we look at it in this light, we can see that Freud was a true Enlightenment figure who developed and crowned the critical tradition begun by Rousseau. The whole development of modern clinical psychology has served to give full scientific legitimation to the basic thesis of Rousseau's *Emile*.

But, as we noted earlier, this clear-cut view of Freud has not always been possible, largely because of Freud's reliance on instinct as the mainspring of behavior. It is this, as we saw, that repelled many thinkers from his theory—Scheler, Dewey, and others. Something great was at stake here, namely, was Freud's theory one that crowned the Enlightenment, or one that negated it? By using instincts and implying a more or less fixed basic human nature, Freud actually did the Enlightenment a disservice. He objectivized man, placed him over and against society, seemed to make him somewhat determinate and helpless. What would the Enlightenment do with a view of human nature that was anything less than malleable? How would we fashion the new man, discover the new creative depths in the human spirit? Freud gave us a theory of man that was complete in its explanation of the social conditioning that man undergoes in society—and this is just what the Enlightenment wanted. But at the same time he gave us a monster: an image of man which despaired of any real and fundamental changes in his basic animal nature. Thus, Freudian psychology developed two contrasting views of man: man as an object of society and of science; and man as a free, developing subject in society and nature. Herbert Fingarette calls this alternation between a subjective and an objective view of man "the seminal ambiguity" of Freud's psychology (1963): it permitted us to understand man as a developing source of value and also to scrutinize him as an object of scientific study. But I think the ambiguity has been somewhat less than seminal, if we look at Freud in the whole historical movement he repre-

sented. The subjective view of man, as we saw, was already championed by Diderot and was elaborated by Wundt, Lotze, Fouillée and
other late-nineteenth-century thinkers. The objective view of man
was used to good effect by Baldwin and the self psychologists. But
Baldwin's objectivity was in the idealist tradition, and always took
man as a center of value. Freud, despite his historically important
clarifications, actually interrupted the smooth flow of the social
psychology of the nineteenth century by again subordinating the
free creation of value to the mechanism and determinism of instincts.
And we cannot overlook that it was Freud who thought that even
his psychology would one day be ousted by a precise reductionist
physiochemistry of character development. As Emmanuel Mounier
aptly put it, Freud began by humanizing psychology, and ended by
dehumanizing it (Minkowski, 1962, p. 347).

For these reasons, Alfred Adler today serves much better than
Freud to convey the continuity of the nineteenth century to the
present: he played down the instinct theory approach to human
motivation, and frankly talked about neurosis as a "life style" formed
during the early conditioning. He always saw the individual as an
open creator of value, and never as mechanistically determined; he
saw that the "Oedipus complex" could not be conceived narrowly as
a sexual constellation, that when it occurred in this form it was rare.
He allowed us instead to understand the "Oedipus complex" as a
synonym for the many varieties of the "life style." And one thing
above all Adler helped us to know was that the basic situation of the
child is one of natural inferiority in the face of an overwhelming and
superordinate world. In order to overcome this inferiority, the child
plunges ahead trying to fashion his own distinctive powers. But since
the child has no cognitive grasp of what his "life style" is, what he is
actually doing is deriving his sense of power uncritically. Or, put
another way, he is deriving his sense of power vicariously, from a way
of being in the world that is not his own since it is not under his control. The result is tragic, and puts the stamp on man's fate: the adult
finds himself rooted in a source of power that literally controls him;
he is determined by his unconscious choice of a model of power. The
tragic paradox, then, is that instead of overcoming his early inferiority, the child merely exchanges it for a semblance of power, a power
that is not his own but that is delegated to him by the models that he
uncritically follows. The struggle of man against man and the terrible
evil that men will unleash on their fellows stem from this unconscious
rooting of their own felt powers: they will fight to the death to pro-

tect the models of power on which their lives are predicated. To lose
the ground of their delegated powers is to lose what they feel to be the
right to their own lives. And so we see how Adler got to the heart of the
human tragedy; in a word, how he is seminal without being ambiguous.

Freud's ambiguity is very reminiscent of Alexander Bain's: it
is really the self-created bind of the thinker who is not able to step
fully out of one tradition into another. Neither Bain nor Freud could
fully envisage the possibility of a science that would place the distinctive, human subjectivity firmly at its center. But this science, as
we have said many times, was the nineteenth-century vision which
was given to the twentieth as a mandate to be worked out, and not to
be obscured by a metaphysics of pan-reductionism or by an instinctual determinism over which man has little control.

We have had, in sum, to go back around Freud and rejoin the
Enlightenment view of man as a malleable, plastic creature, shaped
in all that we call human nature by the society in which he is immersed. Freud, while contributing greatly to the Enlightenment
tradition, at the same time obscured it. He made a biological problem
out of what had to be primarily a social and historical one. Rousseau
had been very clear about the danger of confounding social motivations and physical needs, of imagining that inflexible physical urges
were at the foundation of human society (1762, p. 280). It is perhaps
for this reason above any that Dewey never took Freud seriously:
Dewey understood that the science of man had an Enlightenment
mandate, and not one derived from Hobbes and Schopenhauer,
which took man out of his own hands.

In modern times this thesis was given explicit phrasing in the
psychology of Karl Jaspers, who perfectly combined the empirical
and the subjective approaches. Jaspers held that the whole man cannot
be known by any partial approaches; in this respect man is like any
other object of science—he can never be completely known. But,
since man is a human agent, we must give first place to his free agency,
to his open possibility. Jaspers had his own version of the Enlightenment thesis: since science can only know things by establishing
wider and wider relationships, then psychology itself—as a single
discipline—can never know man, and must consequently take its
place with the other disciplines; it must join its empirical knowledge
with theirs, in the service of man as a free agent. The partial is always
the provisional, and can acquire meaning only by serving human purpose (Lefebre, 1957). We recognize this as the familiar thesis of
centering science on man, using empirical knowledge as a means,

and not as an end. Again, it fell to modern existentialism, partly in the form of Jaspers' philosophy and psychology, to continue the nineteenth-century subjectivity without the Freudian ambiguity.

A Post-Freudian View of the Human Personality

If we add Freud's contribution to that of the nineteenth century, we can proceed to a fairly complete theory of personality. But for a long time Freudian dogma itself kept us from unifying the nineteenth- and the twentieth-century social psychology. In order to continue the Enlightenment view of man, Freud's instinct theory had to be overthrown, which is exactly what was accomplished: we know now that the child has no innate aggressive and sexual drives—he has only a need for closeness and continuing affection and protection. Freud had spoken about man's "unconscious," which he thought was a reservoir of primitive drives and antisocial urges. But when the instinct theory was abandoned, this led to a radically different view of the mysterious "dynamic unconscious." What is the dynamic unconscious if man is free of instincts? It can no longer be the "seat of instinctual life," as Freud understood it. The unconscious now refers simply to the fact that in his early training each child is formed into a particular world view; this kind of exclusive training leads him to distort or obliterate certain perceptions—perceptions not pleasing to the parents, or taboo in the particular society in which he is brought up. Today we speak of the unconscious in quite matter-of-fact terms: it has lost its mystery. Instead of being a fatal subterranean core which we inherited from Paleozoic times, it refers to the particular skewing of our world view and of our capacity to act, which occurred during our early training or mistraining. Man is not saddled with a phylogenetic fate, but rather with his own early choices, which themselves are designed by his parents—by their tyranny, impatience, or simply their own limited world view. In other words, with the overthrow of instinct theory, Freud's biological problem has again been reconverted to a social and historical one.

For one thing, when we take out the heavy deterministic weighting of instincts, human action again becomes neutral. By this I mean that we can look at it in terms of a full field of interdependent relationships rather than in terms of one or two drives or determinants. Thus we broaden the theory of personality in the same way that the Continental thinkers broadened the British individualistic psychology of the nineteenth century. This was done in the early part of this

century by thinkers such as W. I. Thomas who spoke of attitudes instead of drives, and saw that any action tendency on the part of the
human organism was ultimately conditioned by values. Thus, values,
not drives, became the stimuli. The human personality, from this
standpoint, would be regarded as an organization of attitudes, ready
to respond to values. Personalities would be distinguished among themselves by the range and kinds of values to which they would respond,
in the kind of roles in which they would be most comfortable, and
so on (Barnes, 1948a, p. 803). Again, this is actually a refined, modern
statement of Fourier's view of the passions: typical human desires
are basically neutral; the particular quality they assume depends on
the social context, and takes the forms it imposes: there is no "evil"
in man that is not caused by civilization.

These simplifications perhaps sound axiomatic, but actually it
was a long, tortuous development to rejoin this simple Enlightenment view. Schopenhauer and the whole emphasis on faculty psychology had to be abandoned. Only when this was done could we see that
"will" was not an entity that moved the human actor, and that played
itself out (usually) for worse on the human scene. Rather, "will" was
inseparable from the full field of values in which the individual
was at all times immersed. Thus, in modern jargon we would say that
the individual "will" is the social role stimulus. "Will" is the internalized social values. But Freud did not help this clarification in his
early work. He continued, with his instinctual drive theory, the
Schopenhauerian view of volition as causal. That is to say, he saw
the unconscious as a reservoir of latent antisocial emotions that sought
outlet in society. Only when this view was abandoned could we see
clearly that emotion is merely a synonym for the tendencies of the organism in action; it is a way of describing an investment in action
and does not represent underground reservoirs or a separate faculty.

Now in all of this we must remember that Freud's intent was
"historically proper," so to speak. The thing Freud wanted to do was
to show that human reason is an epiphenomenon on organismic
striving—he wanted a post-Darwinian view of man that would correct
the facile rationalism of an earlier time. This was the same thing that
the later Scotch school of psychology, represented by Shand and
McDougall, also wanted to show. The problem was to show this in
the same way that first Rousseau and then Fourier had sketched it,
namely, to show that passion was supreme, that the strivings of the
organism and its overall desires took a priority over any particular
kind of rationalistic "civilized" world view in which it was immersed.

But the great challenge and difficulty of the problem was that one also had to show that the passions could only be understood socially and not biologically. The organism had to be given primacy, but a "scientifically neutral" one.

Phrased another way, the problem was to combine the proper romantic emphasis on the primacy of will and desire with the Enlightenment emphasis on reason and human malleability. Freud kept the romantic emphasis on desire, but by holding to the idea of deterministic, specific instincts he obscured the view of the necessary malleability of the desires. There was only one way of keeping the primary emphasis on organismic desires and at the same time to accent human malleability, and that was to trace the genetic development of the ego without any determinist, pan-reductionist dogma. In this way we could see how the whole organism was shaped by values, even in its very desires. Emotions could then be understood as inseparable from the perceptual world view. But at the same time we did not lose the organism: we could see that the particular world view into which the organism was conditioned was bound to skew its perceptions in some ways. That is, culture fouled the total organism itself: the social destiny extended into one's very nerves and blood cells. We could see, in sum, what the romantics as well as Freud wanted to show, but in a new way—without any trace of fatality: it was now clear that reason conditions desires and directs them into socially approved channels, that reason even brings desires into being, but that, nevertheless, reason does not cover all the organism's activities; reason forms only a part of the total stirring of the organism toward satisfaction.

This picture gives us a complete view of human striving, one in which we can keep both rationalism and irrationalism. But in this way we gained an unprecedented clarification of the nature of irrationalism: it was now clear that each organism is hampered in its freedom by the particular world view into which it has been indoctrinated. Irrationalism, in other words, comes potentially under human control, no matter how "deep" it goes. It has indeed been a long progression from the poles of Locke and Leibnitz, which began the shifting Enlightenment history. It has been a difficult task to unite the neutral environmentalist and the subjective voluntarist traditions. We have had to go through Kant and Schopenhauer and Freud, to the modern "attitude psychology" of Alfred Adler, W. I. Thomas, and Gordon Allport.

All this, then, by way of introducing the modern view of the human personality in its total field that we are now ready to sketch. Simply stated, we can consider the personality as composed of three interdependent elements: the organism's own *feeling* about itself, the *objects* in its field, and the *values* it has learned to give to itself and to the objects; these values take the form of *rules* for navigating in a particular social world; the rules are embodied in the *behavior* that we learn for deriving satisfaction from this world.

As for the first element, all we need say is simply that all organisms—as far as we know—experience self-feeling. We can call this feeling neutral because it derives its quality from the transactions of the organism with other objects. The nineteenth-century social psychology had shown that organisms need objects in order to come into being, in order to develop their peculiar capacities and identity. And Freudian psychology had shown how helpless and anxiety-prone the human organism is as he learns the specific cultural rules for gaining satisfaction in his object world. Self-feeling comes to be dependent on and inseparable from the objects in one's field, and the rules one learns for dealing with these objects in an acceptable, anxiety-free way. Thus, instead of using the neutral term "self-feeling" to refer to object transactions which are satisfying, we use "self-esteem" or "self-value." Then we can talk about high self-esteem or low self-esteem, according to someone's ability to navigate satisfactorily in his cultural object world. Man tends to feel good about himself when he can address himself to a dependable range of objects for his satisfactions, and when he has firm command of the rules or behaviors for negotiating with these objects. His very personality can then be said to be a firm amalgam of self-feeling, objects, and rules (or behaviors). He is partly composed of the very objects with which he transacts, because they elicit the rules or behaviors which are literally built into his organism (cf. E. Becker, 1964a, chap. 5 and 6).

This neutral and full-field approach to the human personality has one great advantage over the early Freudian approach: it allows us to talk about human needs in a new way. Whereas Freud could talk about *absolute factors* such as the satisfaction of aggressive or sexual drives, we can talk about *limiting factors* which are very relative, but still do not entirely disappear into a total relativity. For example, we know that man needs self-esteem and that it is the primary function of each culture to provide for the continuing possibility of self-esteem for a symbolic animal. But, on the other hand, we also know that people can run on very low levels of self-esteem and still function in society. The schizophrenic is the most handy example. Thus, we can talk about the relativity of the need for self-esteem. Yet the relativity has a limit, and when the self-esteem is completely undermined the result is usually a schizophrenic or depressive withdrawal from society.

In the second place, we know that man needs objects in order to come into being as an organism, and subsequently in order to provide for continuing action and experience. The organism needs objects in order to feel its own powers and presence. Yet we know that after the early socialization some people can do without others; instead, they feed themselves on the early world view which they have internalized and consequently draw almost all their satisfaction from it. This would apply to religious recluses, as well as to certain isolated but creative personalities. However, this relativity too is limited; there is a danger that this kind of self-feeding in fantasy may cut the individual off from the social world entirely. He may withdraw into systems that become increasingly unreal because they are not interpersonally validated and verified.

Finally, with this view of the personality, we can talk, with Fourier, about man's need for rich, variegated experience and a deep sense of conviction. We see that man draws his conviction from his transactions with objects, and from the satisfactions this gives. But we also know that man can cut himself off from the object world and draw his conviction and variety from within, from the fanciful preoccupations of his imagination. Yet we can see the limitation on this relativity: one's hold on the object world can become so narrow, one's behavior become so impoverished, that one's action tends to assume the form that we call "fetishistic" or "paranoid" (see below for a full discussion of the "perversions").

As we will see in a later section, to talk about human needs not as absolute, but as limiting factors, allows us to project a scientific ideal-typology for man; but at the same time it permits each individual the freedom to choose his own life style and be his own moral agency. It stresses that the individual subjectivity, as the creator of values, must occupy the center of the new science. It uses at the same time a certain objectivization of human regularities, but only to design greater freedom and not in order to determine man's conduct. In the old understanding of a science of man, a complete determinism was the fondest hope, and someone like E. C. Tolman could look forward to the possibility of completely manipulating the correlates of the individual's life. But now we see that such an aim is wholly unrelated to a broad, human science.

When we look at the human personality in terms of the broad relations which comprise it, we can understand how experience derives its peculiar qualities. And we can understand this, again, without falling back on absolute, predetermined qualities, such as hate or aggression. For example, another way of looking at human action is to conceive it as a triad of *feelings, a repertory of symbols, and a range of behavior patterns.* The feelings are part of the organism's tendency toward objects: they are neutral in themselves, and cannot be conceived as a feeling of, say, love or hate *apart from the specific object* toward which they are directed. The second part of the triad, the repertory of symbols, is a complex cultural amalgam of words and word sounds which are meaningful in that they conform to some logically coherent patterns. At a minimum, they would have to be grammatically logical. But these symbols are not all meaningfully linked with the third aspect of the triad: the *dependable behavior patterns*; and certainly words are not all linked to behaviors with the same degree of meaningfulness.

Self-feeling, as we said, can be considered to be neutral in quality; but as we come into contact with objects we find that they can either enhance it or diminish it, according to whether they allow us satisfaction or not. Thus, the neutral self-feeling, when it is enhanced and when it finds a proper object, is positive in tone; when it is diminished, or can find no proper object, it seems negative. Using this scheme, what would determine whether one would love or hate a new object? Assuming that the need for the object would be uniform, the kind of *symbol* one attaches to his *feelings* would depend on the kind of *behavior* he can dependably undertake toward the object.

Our striving, as we learn it in every society, comes to be dressed in words, and to assume definite learned forms. But, on very simple levels of operation, whether we choose the words "love" or "hate" toward a particular object depends upon whether we can behave satisfactorily toward it, whether it enhances or diminishes our self-feeling. For example, a male who tried to make a satisfying contact of some kind with another male, but who lacked the behavioral aptitude or who was consistently rebuffed, would have to resort to a "hate" definition of the situation in order to maintain some kind of positive self-feeling. Lacking appropriate behavior, he would have to contrive a symbolic mode of generating self-feeling. Hate is a rallying of feeling in the absence of satisfying behavior, which we define as "paranoid" conduct or fantasy. A female, in the same situation, lacking practiced behaviors, could always use her sex as the ultimate way of making contact with the male object. She would then be able to define this situation as a "love" relationship, which is exactly what many schizophrenic females do: their range of behavior is so narrow that they must fall back on their genital apparatus as a means of approach, and thus they may define every encounter as a "love" situation. In other words, the availability of satisfying behaviors usually determines the type of symbolic self-reference which an individual will use. Love and hate, then, are always relative to a field of possibilities, and do not stand for absolute, essential inner emotions. The problem, of course, becomes complex in the individual case, according to how the word "satisfying" is defined.

As a final, graphic example, we can cite the case of a female schizophrenic patient who found that the hospital defined her situation symbolically as one of potential suicide. In order to bring herself into the picture as a person, she invented a new appropriate range of behavior, a way of relating to the doctor in charge, by offering him weapons that she might possibly be able to use against herself—her glasses, sharp jewelry, and so on. From these examples we see clearly etched the basic need of the human animal for satisfying self-feeling; and we see that he is the only animal who can juggle words and behaviors to arrange for this. Hence he is the only animal in whose life love and hate can become major guiding themes: he has no instincts that automatically provide for satisfying self-feeling.

Why do we dwell on these conceptualizations of the personality in terms of the basic organismic self-feeling? Simply because this is the task that the Enlightenment itself passed on to us: to show in detail how man is a malleable creature, a creature whose "human nature" is inextricably part of the total contextual situation in which he finds himself. Historically, it is a task of the highest importance. And let us make no mistakes, it is a *historical* task: the first statement attempting to phrase all the passions in terms of self-feeling was Jouffroy's essay on "Self-Love" (1823, see esp. p. 205). Jouffroy wanted to explain love and hate as expansions and contractions of the basic self-feeling of the organism so that we could understand man's motives in all their purity, and in their shaping by society. If we fulfilled the Enlightenment program and developed Jouffroy's analysis in all its complexity, it would allow us to explain human conflict without falling back—as did Freud—on a phylogenetic fate beyond man's control. And Enlightenment science, as Helvétius argued and as we have repeatedly stressed, must be a science in which human control is possible. Otherwise it is simply not science. And human control is only possible where man's fate is not organically predetermined, where his destiny is something amenable to change via education. This is why Helvétius struck out against Montesquieu's *Spirit of the Laws*: if human institutions are shaped by diet, climate, and geography, then education can do nothing, and the growth of scientific reason can never promote human well-being. In this sense, Freud is our adversary, as Montesquieu was Helvétius'.

Today, 150 years after the early phase of Enlightenment science, I believe we have fulfilled the program laid out by Helvétius and Jouffroy: we have a more-or-less complete social psychology which can explain human passions in an unmysterious way. It conceives of individual action in terms of three distinct but interdependent dimensions of striving. We might call them "dialectics of striving" or "strains" within which human action takes place.

The first was elaborated, as we saw, in the nineteenth century. It is the *dimension of individual action of disparate phenomenal kinds*. This is the strain between the symbolic self and the organismic body; it conveys experience of two disparate kinds—spiritual and physical, or self and body—which must be unified in action. The problem that it poses is the one we sketched above, that of unifying behaviors with appropriate symbolic vocabularies. This is, as we noted, the phenomenological problem of the behavior disorder we term schizophrenia.

It was not until Freud that we obtained a clear understanding of the second dialectic of human striving: *the dimension of individual action in time*. Without Freud we would not have been able to gain such a sharp and conclusive conceptualization of the strain between early training and later adult experiences. This is a crucial dialectic of human action. The individual carries over old learning which is not appropriate to new challenges; he develops a life style which may be inflexible in the face of new opportunities.

The third dialectic of individual striving is an inextricable aspect of the second: it is *the dimension of individual action in space*. This reflects the problem of moving about in a world of things which must be labeled verbally in order to be controlled, and toward which dependable behavior patterns must be learned. It is just this definite learning that occurs during the early conditioning. The dilemma it poses arises when words are not available, or when behavior is not dependable, in new situations that are problematic. If we do not have the words, we do not adequately frame the problem; on the other hand, if we have the words, but do not have the dependable behaviors, we may manufacture problems where they need not exist; for example, by creating paranoid situations.

In each of these three ways the individual develops a world view and a capacity to react to experience, which forms his personality in a unique set. The problem, for the individual, is always one of developing greater unity and flexibility of the personality in the face of new challenges and experiences. But this, as Freud showed so well, is supremely difficult, precisely because the personality is formed as a way of assuring anxiety-free action; and new conduct is usually anxiety-provoking.

When we conceive the personality on the dimensions of these three dialectics, we can understand not only schizophrenia, but the more common behavioral disorder known as "depression." Depression occurs when the individual's action, operating uncritically and in a narrow range of objects, bogs down. For some reason or other, the self-satisfying performance to which he is accustomed is no longer possible. But the individual is unable to frame the problem in an appropriate critical vocabulary and he gives up in defeat. Depression, as I explained in detail elsewhere (1964a, chap. 4), is basically a problem in behavioral stupidity—as is also schizophrenia in another way. People vary in behavioral range and prowess, they vary in explicit cognitive command over their problems, they vary in ranges of objects. In other words, people vary in the richness of the worlds which they experience, and they vary in the amount of keen, adaptive intelligence they can bring to bear in the face of new problems. Théodule Ribot was prophetic when he urged that mental illness was not a problem of entities, but a problem of coordination, of the relationship of many elements. Modern personality theory has merely spelled out the peculiar adaptive problems of the most complex creature in evolution, which is exactly what remained to be done after Darwin.

Finally, having understood this, we can understand one last thing about the human personality. We can see clearly that the so-called "unconscious" is not a problem in "depth." Rather, it is a problem in range of behaviors and in richness and flexibility of cognitive grasp. Understood in this way, the unconscious is seen as a result of the early conditioning, which puts some curbs on the child's awareness. As a result of this curbing, the natural ability to learn by trial and error is paralyzed in certain areas. Furthermore, it is in these areas that the individual will experience anxiety, and will distrust his own powers of independent judgment. This paralysis of learning and self-distrust is what we mean, basically, by the unconscious. Why then do some people have "more" of an unconscious than others—schizophrenics, for instance? Simply because they have suffered a longer and more oppressive moratorium on the exercise of their own initiatory powers. Today we can give full theoretical support to Rousseau's early insight (1762, p. 19) that the cruelest child training of all is the one that frustrates natural trial-and-error action. In our society, perhaps even more than in Freud's Vienna, there is a great period of delay between the early childhood training and the assumption of responsible adult action. This means that for years the child and youth is forced to abrogate trial-and-error action, and the assumption of his own responsibility. He is simply not allowed to be an uninhibited agent in many areas of experience. The effect of this abrogation is precisely one that will *reinforce* the limited perceptions of the early learning period. If the youth cannot broaden his awareness by his own responsible coping action, then he must operate completely and unthinkingly under the constrictions of the early parental training, and the continual guidance of the parents, even up to late adolescence. We can see, then, how the society in which one is immersed actually creates neurosis by ushering the child into a limited world view, and then preventing him from broadening this view by his own self-critical and independent action. This is, in effect, a form of forced alienation, which creates the human unconscious. We can say that the unconscious is relative to the particular society in which the child grows up. And we would expect that the greater the period of delay between early training and the assumption of responsible adult action, the greater the unconscious which inhibits free and broad-ranging choices.

Thus, we can now finally see with great clarity that Freud did not clarify "mental illness" or neurosis in any medical sense: he did not discover an entity that could be cured in a physician's office. Rather, he helped to pinpoint the microcosm of alienation, as Marx had pinpointed the macrocosm. Mental illness is really a synonym for constrictions on self-powers. The typical psychiatric syndromes are simply failures to carry through self-satisfying action in the face of new, problematic situations. The basis of this failure is—in every nonorganic case—a kind of stupidity, a behavioral stupidity, as we noted, a blockage in the face of challenge and choice. The schizophrenic simply cannot cope with the pluralistic world of uncontrolled situations and objects; the depressed person simply cannot or will not understand the elements that make up his failure; the hysteric cannot formulate an essential cognitive grasp of the frustrating situation. In other words, people break down when they are not "doing"—when the world about them does not reflect the active involvement of their own creative powers.

And so, at the conclusion of our discussion of psychiatry and its contributions to the synthetic theory of alienation, we can see how it, too, merges with the psychological and sociological dimensions. We have the fullest possible support for the nineteenth-century accusation that alienation is present wherever man does not have an effective grasp of a total situation, where he does not command a unit of prime of decision, to use C. Wright Mills' phrase (cf. E. Becker, 1964b). We saw earlier how well the nineteenth century understood the importance of a *"vue d'ensemble,"* a "synoptic" view; now we can judge how well the twentieth century has shown how human failure results when such a view, combined with possibilities of action, is absent.

Understood in this way, we can also see that the modern theory of personality brings closure on a long-standing ideological problem— the problem of whether man is a rational animal or a basically irrational one. The problem crystallized after the French Revolution, because at that time it was apparent that the hopeful promise of unbridled reason had not been fulfilled: reason seemed to have only added to the misery in human affairs. Herder, Fichte, Schelling, Hegel, de Bonald and de Maistre—all of them attacked the idea that mere rational deliberation and conscious choice could change society. They opposed the rationalism of the *philosophes* as a naïve, "surface" factor in social life: they held that, instead, the real moving forces and motives of society were not to be touched by mere reason, that these forces had a logic all their own; furthermore, the moving power of these forces accumulated over time so as to dwarf the bright ideas of any one epoch. The romantic protest was directed not only against the violent upheaval of the French Revolution, but also against the new rationalism of the ugly and antihuman industrial society. It wanted to come to grips with the whole elusive man, and not with the new, trim, consumer puppets, who were all on the surface, all stamped out of the same mold. In one sense, of course, the very helplessness of sensitive individuals in the face of the new disorganization and industrialization was responsible for the romantic protest. The external world was so mean and miserable that the logical thing to do was to stress the vitality of the inner life—as the modern Zen Buddhists are doing again today. When the world is disintegrating, where can one meaningfully relate his active powers? He is forced to dig within, in order to find a new source of ultimate values (cf. K. Mannheim, 1953, pp. 292–297).

But this new intuitionism did not sit well with rationalists like Stuart Mill, who saw the danger of the devaluation of reason. The romantics, by stressing some inner nature prior to social and empirical reality, were actually creating a form of mystical conservatism that could be used to frustrate wise efforts at social reconstruction. The problem was thus one of reconciling the utilitarian and the romantic currents of thought in a synthesis that would take into its scope the whole man, but would be progressive at the same time. And this reconciliation is precisely the one that we have achieved, by reinterpreting the problem of neurosis as a problem of cognition, of the restriction of one's active powers. We have been able to understand that human self-contradiction is not a medical or a narrowly biological problem, but is always and at heart a social problem—a problem of what society will allow people *to know* and *to do*.

The effect of this reinterpretation of Freud was to rejoin the full Enlightenment current which he had temporarily sidetracked. It provided for a synthesis of the rationalist and romantic views of man, but without bowing to the irrationalists. We are able to reconcile these two positions, and keep the full cogency of both. When we talk about the bind in which early training places the individual all through his life, how anxiety-based learning obscures broader, more spontaneous perceptions, we are actually keeping the romantic intuition of the primacy of the total, striving organism over any partial, rational world view. But at the same time, we leave open the possibility for man to continually broaden and change his world view, to permit broader and freer action. We thus keep the high place for the rationalist position. We have, in sum, lifted the problem onto a plane of higher scientific cogitation. The romantic position is given scientific footing, but is deprived of any obscurantism. We are ready to speak of the *whole* man in terms intelligible to the scientific reason.

With this merger of psychiatry with the other dimensions of a full-field theory of alienation, we can understand one thing further, namely, that the problems of psychiatry itself are dissolved in a general criticism of society. We can understand that mental illness is fundamentally a problem of the social facilitation of individual action and meaning. No one has better put this merger of psychiatry and social criticism than William Ernest Hocking. Hocking saw that *basic human optimism* is simply not possible unless man can grasp the character of the world as a unity and can survey the flow of history from some kind of single, commanding perspective (1912, pp. 167 ff.). And, more recently, expanding the same thesis, Hocking saw that what we call mental illness is really a problem in human meaning, and he stated the credo on which our present understanding of mental illness is fashioned:

> . . .the problem of psychiatry reaches into the realm of meanings. If one dreads the world he lives in and cannot change it, and cannot accept the silly advice to think of something near at hand and forget the frame of things, the psychiatrist instead of tampering with his emotions as such ought to advise suicide. There is no cure for mental diseases without consulting the total meaning of the world (Hocking, 1944, p. 42).

Thus, a whole long tradition of personality theory leaves little doubt about the basic character of alienation, of man's inability to act meaningfully in a "frame of things."

The nineteenth century obscured this problem with its laissez-faire promise of bringing peace and happiness to man, by turning him into an "owning" animal. The twentieth century has redoubled efforts to make everyone a satisfied consumer, who will live in an effortless world. Today we see that this basic premise is utterly false, that man is a "doing" animal, and not an "owning" one—and that he must "do" within the largest possible framework of meaning. All in all, then, we have the most powerful scientific evidence of the basic antihumanism of our present consumer, profit-oriented industrial system. Little wonder that both politicians and academic social scientists have turned their backs on the authentic nature of social theory and its urgent message to our times: to recognize it, they would have to become antagonists to some of the basic features of the social system which sustains them. The problem of the relationship of human knowledge to society remains exactly where it was when Plato first lamented it twenty-five hundred years ago: political and social leaders must scorn those who would radically change their habitual world.

CHAPTER NINE

ESTHETICS AS ETHICS:
The Contribution of Descriptive Ontology

> *What if language closely related to poetic diction were in-*
> *dispensable for a natural science of man. . . ?*
> MÉDARD BOSS (*1954, p. 54*)

When the nineteenth century discovered that human behavior could not be reduced atomistically, all our thinking about the nature of human action had to be reoriented. It was obvious that what characterizes human action could not be lodged in the physiochemistry of the brain. And so, many of the best thinkers of that century, who began as psycho-physicists, had to grope their way back to a new kind of tempered idealism: Wundt, Lotze, and Dilthey especially come to mind. We have already sketched the highlights of Wundt's career; Dilthey's was similar: he began with strong leanings toward psycho-physics, and a belief in the possibilty of a psychology of the mental structure (Antoni, 1959, pp. 18–19). But, as his ideas developed, Dilthey saw that human events are not mere physical events, that they have meanings added to them. This made necessary a wholly new kind of science, a science that would be able to approach action from within, from the way it appeared to man. Renouvier also heralded this new science, a science that would approach the world of personality from within human perceptions. The only problem was that in the nineteenth century this kind of science did not seem like science at all; materialism, mechanism, reductionism—these were great triumphant words of the day. Whereas in our time Dilthey's and

Renouvier's vision of a new science is a forgotten fruit, in the nineteenth century it was a forbidden one. Little wonder that Dilthey struggled his whole life to clarify his insights, and that it was not until his last writings that he seemed to begin a complete revision of his thought, with the aim of fully championing the new point of view. And the new point of view was that the characteristic category of human life and human science is the concept of *meaning* (Dilthey, 1962, pp. 21–22, 99–100).

Lotze had offered the century a vision of science in which its prime task would be to promote Life and Being; Dilthey offered the superordinate datum for such a science, human meanings. Here was the complete structure that would "embrace pragmatic science and idealist philosophy in a common, unified system"—as Croce later understood the task (Antoni, 1959, p. xxvii). It was a structure in which poetic, artistic, and religious meanings would be the prime reality of science. The nineteenth century casually brushed past this vision, with its own Olympian structure based on Newton and Darwin: here were rigor, success, and unlimited promise; how could anyone imagine detouring this mighty force, in order to build a science that would occupy itself principally with mental meanings? Yet, today we are very clear that if the nineteenth century has any significance for us now it is that it fashioned precisely this kind of vision.

No one has summed up better than Merz the logical steps which led to the new view of the ultimate subject matter of science. In the first place, the nineteenth century was characterized by what Merz calls the "synoptic" tendency of thought; it was reflected in Comte's continued urgings that man needed to recapture the *"vue d'ensemble"* that he had lost, or, in Dilthey's word, a *Gesamtanschauung*. This tendency joined with the revolution in psychology, as it changed from atomism-sensationalism-physicalism to a psychology of a continuous field of consciousness. This in turn led naturally to an approach to the world of consciousness from within, a comprehensive, introspective approach to the all-embracing field of consciousness. Scholars began to study the growth of the self and the formation of the cultural world view. Finally, it had to be concluded that—for man—it was precisely this larger circumference, this world as seen, understood, and interpreted, that formed the greater reality. In other words, human meaning is the superordinate datum for science, even though this meaning defies the traditional image of acceptable scientific subject matter. Merz concludes his superb summing up of the distinctive nineteenth-century legacy in these words: "The main advance in philosophical thought in the . . . nineteenth century and beyond has lain in the direction of psychologically understanding that this region of artistic creation and religious thought has an independent existence . . ." (1914, vol. 4, pp. 787–788).

The nineteenth century hesitated to acclaim its own revolutionary scientific offspring. The problem since that time has been what to do with this unwanted legacy. It has been ripe ever since 1914 (Merz, 1914, vol. 4, p. 787), and yet we have still not come to grips with it. Perhaps the principal reason is that we have not been able to get clear on exactly what kind of program the new scientific idealism would be occupied with. I mean that although the nineteenth century discovered the need for a science that would promote Life and Being, and although it offered us "meaning" as the proper superordinate datum for such a science, we have not known how to translate this structure into a critical ideal. Simply stated, the problem we have been saddled with for the past three-quarters of a century is: exactly how does man maximize his Being? If we answer—as we must—that man maximizes his Being by creating rich, deep, and original human meanings, this leaves the further question: how exactly do we talk scientifically about maximizing human meaning?

The answer to this question would give us a critical ideal that we need to make the nineteenth-century structure viable. If we could understand how man maximizes meaning, it would at the same time carry implications for the problem of the good life. In other words, it would be the central contribution to our synthetic theory of alienation. And it is precisely this contribution that is offered to us by descriptive ontology. Let us explore then, in some detail, this rich and central dimension to the problem of alienation. We will see how it leads, in the next chapter, to the intimate union of Marx and Freud, and thus provides a unified vision for all future research on the problem of alienation.

HOMO POETA: MAN THE CREATOR OF MEANING

The nineteenth century introduced *Homo poeta* from any number of suggestive and rich perspectives, but the idea was kept alive by only a few isolated thinkers, quite on the borders of the central development of scientific research and theory. I am thinking of Cassirer, Ortega y Gasset, Max Scheler, and Georg Simmel—to mention only a few of those who are of immediate interest to us here. Fourier's central insights on the fundamental human need for conviction died out without leaving any identifiable offspring. And the rich theories of idealist esthetics—Hegel, Schelling, Schiller—have been lying dormant in Simmel, Baldwin, and Dewey, and have not been made a central concern for the science of man.

But if man is truly *Homo poeta*, then this whole legacy needs to be forcefully revived by growing numbers of thinkers. If the science of man is the science of human personality approached from within, then we must elaborate a thoroughgoing ontology of human striving, which is exactly what the nineteenth century began. We must know what man is *trying to do*, what he is trying to get out of his world, and what he is trying to put into it. No theory of action will be adequate unless we have clear ideas about this; and so far in the history of science the clearest ideas have come from the idealist estheticians: from Fourier and Comte in the early part of the century; and from Baldwin, Scheler, Dewey, Sartre, and Merleau-Ponty at the end of the century and reaching up to the present time.

In previous writings (1962; 1964a, chap. 8; 1965), I developed one or another aspect of this esthetic theory as it applied to some of the central problems of a theory of action. Here I would like to place some of these ideas in historical perspective, and develop them somewhat further. For this it will be necessary to restate briefly some of the central contentions of a theory of esthetics, and to recall some of our discussion of Schiller, Fourier, and Baldwin. An ontology of esthetic striving has to answer two basic and related questions: what does the esthetic do for *Homo poeta*, and why does he want and need to have it done? As we shall see, today we can answer these questions; and the fact that we can testifies to how much we have achieved in the science of man by building on the nineteenth-century legacy.

Today we know that Freud was never more wrong than when he opined, in his *New Introductory Lectures to Psychoanalysis*, that "Dark, unfeeling and unloving powers determine human destiny." Freud missed the full appreciation of *Homo poeta*, which is why psychoanalysis could never be more than a tool of the science of man; Freud did not understand man's basic striving. Psychoanalytic theory pretended *to be* an integral science of man, but the epitaph for these imperialistic pretentions can be written in one brief sentence: Freud thought that man strives primarily for basic biological satisfaction, but *Homo poeta* strives above all for firm meaning. From this point of view, Fourier was ahead of Freud in acumen as well as in time.

The problem for a science of man has thus been twofold: in the first place, we forgot the legacy of Fourier's beginnings in esthetic theory; in the second place, and more seriously, we have had to develop what might be called "a full-field theory of human conviction" that would give more mature form to Fourier's insights—as Simmel and Buber have done. In other words, Fourier stated the truth that man strives relentlessly for conviction. The problem has been to show *what* makes the conviction convincing for man everywhere, and *why* he wants and needs conviction—since other animals seem not to have this problem.

We can only speculate on why man needs conviction and why other animals seem to have bypassed this problem, but the speculation is well-grounded and compelling. Man is the only animal who is not "built into" his world instinctually. An animal with an instinctive set of responses suffers limitations because its world is already "ready-made" for it. Evolution has built up the proper response patterns and sealed the animal firmly into its adaptational mold. Man alone among the animals gradually develops his own perceptual response world by means of imaginative guiding concepts. He is actually, in this way, continually creating his own reality. The advantages and disadvantages here are obvious. The potential world at man's disposal is enormous; other animals seem to be condemned to experience the same world for all time. In the present discussion we will not be concerned with the *advantages* of this potential openness to new perceptions and experience, but rather with its marked *disadvantage*. It is this disadvantage that gives us a major clue to the nature of human striving in general and to the problem of esthetics in particular.

The fact is that an animal who is already pre-equipped with instinctual response patterns is served up, so to speak, with a world that is rich with intrinsic meaning. A portion of nature is eternally alive for a bird and a cat, calling on their instinctive capacities, challenging their energies. The world that has been already prepared for instinctual response is, in other words, a world that carries its own inherent meaningfulness and conviction. But what does an animal do who comes into the world instinctually almost nude? In what particular ways is he to direct his own energies, how is he to seal himself into the life process around him? Furthermore, the matter is complicated if he is equipped with a large, highly convoluted brain and restless, emotional primate energy. The everyday food quest alone cannot answer to his restlessness; the cycle of eat, fight, procreate, and sleep—

that absorbs the adult members of other species—has only the barest meaning for man. He has learned to use language and dwells in dreams and concepts, in a past-present-future, a space-time largely of his own creation. The result is that he *brings more to* the world than it is prepared to give to an animal equipped with instincts alone.

And here is where the problem seems to lie. For an animal who lives in a world of symbolic creations and who is relatively devoid of firm instinctual response patterns, the everyday reality that galvanizes all other animals tends to lack conviction for him. In order to render reality meaningful, in order to stimulate his own productive energies, man must bring his own meanings to the world, impart his own sense of conviction. This is the tragic burden, as well as the unrivaled creative opportunity, of *Homo poeta*. Man creates his own meaning, and the penalty for failure is what we would expect: if man creates his own life process, his own reactive world, then when he fails to do this sufficiently or well he edges back from life; this is what we see in the deculturation of certain tribes and peoples and in the psychiatric syndromes known as schizophrenia and depression. Evolution has thus left man with the greatest burden and challenge: he is born, not into a world, but into a "backdrop," that contains the raw materials for his manipulation and for the creation of his own world. By the time the infant-training period is over, almost all animal reactivity has been recast into symbolic modes. Hence, *Homo poeta* seems indeed the most apt title for the human animal.

If we accept this speculation as an accurate insight into the human condition, we can see clearly that meaning must be the superordinate category for the science of man and that esthetics and the problems it involves must be its central concern. This means that the largely *fictional* nature of human meaning and conviction is the *real fact* that must concern the science of man. So far only philosophers and historians have dared adumbrate this crucial thesis—the modern social scientist would probably scoff at it. But we have seen that the reason for this is that the modern social scientist has largely turned his back on the Enlightenment heritage and its significance for his science, and he has almost completely ignored the historically important nineteenth-century legacy. By default, then, this legacy has gone to others, and they have built the most fruitful work on it.

The historian Johan Huizinga worked for a lifetime until history urged this fact overwhelmingly on his attention: that throughout the ages man has been absorbed in creating his own conviction and meaning. Man has done this rather playfully, in large part, which led

Huizinga to title his brilliant work *Homo ludens*. For Huizinga it seemed obvious that the sphere of humanly created meanings was a make-believe, but it was a serious make-believe which brought the world to life for man, as only it could be brought to life. Huizinga says: "In play as we conceive it the distinction between belief and make-believe breaks down. The concept of play merges quite naturally with that of holiness" (1955, p. 21). What is the sense of holiness that emerges from play? From our discussion above we can now guess that it is the sense of awe that results when the world suddenly comes alive and calls upon all our potential creative energies—luring us and dwarfing us at the same time. Play creates for man a world and holiness at the same time; for other animals it is instinct that must give rise to holiness, to the rapt absorption and inner expansion that a cat seems to experience as it watches a bird glide down into a clearing, just outside its immediate reach. Play, in other words, is the creation of meaning for an animal who can experience it richly and convincingly in no pre-set way. It is "the cutting edge of the mind," as Collingwood put it, in an argument akin to Huizinga's: "The spirit of play, the spirit of eternal youth, is the foundation and beginning of all real life" (1924, p. 107).

The creation of meaning, then, while it is done with great pomp and often evident playfulness on the so-called primitive level is not really a playful matter. It is an artificiality that is deadly earnest, because without this artificiality man has no distinctive world: it is this playful imbibing of meaning that gives him the deep sense of conviction that comes naturally to the other animals. Georg Simmel— that superbly original thinker—was one of the very first to realize that man *lives in* and *through* his social *performance*. Simmel saw that the "social game" is not a social game because it takes place "in" society; but rather that the social game is actually to "play society" (see Wolff, 1959, p. 50). Society may be a play-form, but it is a deadly serious business, as behavior in any Italian firm or British Club will soon make obvious. The point is again that man needs the conviction of his own reality, and without it he is deprived of his life space. Thus, he must be grim about the play-form of everyday performance and even be ready to kill to safeguard the niceties—as when one bungles the sacred words in ritual activities, for example. When man loses the conviction of his everyday social performance, his basic and elemental life meaning grinds to a halt (see E. Becker, 1962, chap. 8). In this kind of play, in sum, and for this kind of animal, the stakes are life itself.

This thesis, then, about the distinctiveness of *Homo poeta* and the urge to create meaning is already a basic ontology of human striving. It answers the fundamental question about what man is up to in his world, the activity that differentiates him from other animals in the most characteristic way. Let us develop this ontology further by turning to the related question to which we promised to address our inquiry, namely, what makes conviction convincing? And the answer, as we suggested, has come from the basics of idealist esthetic theory.

CONVICTION AS AN ESTHETIC PROBLEM

From a theoretical point of view the salient insights of idealist esthetic theory are still very much alive. We have not been able to improve very much on idealist esthetics except to strip it of transcendental overtones and bring it down to earth, after Darwin, as Baldwin first and Dewey later did. In Chapter Six we touched upon the self-body problem and noted how this problem provided some of the central concepts for Schiller's, Baldwin's, and Dewey's esthetic theory. I merely mentioned, at that time, that the esthetic experience occurs when the physical or organismic body, and the culturally constituted symbolic self, are harmoniously merged in action. This is the baldest possible statement of a theory that began with Kant, Hegel, Schelling, and Schiller, and we must now go on to see exactly what it means for man to merge the organismic or the physical, and the self or the symbolic, into one active and integral unity.

The notorious mind-body problem that has plagued and titillated thinkers down to the present day was actually solved *for all practical* purposes by the idealist estheticians. For all practical purposes of a unified science of man, that is. If, as Dewey said, intellectual progress usually consists not in solving questions but in abandoning them (1910, p. 19), then it is high time we abandoned the mind-body problem by including it into a larger active framework.

The idealists already saw that man's productive concern with the mind-body problem was not how the mind could be found in the body, or why it seemed to enjoy a separate phenomenal existence. Rather, they were more concerned with the problems posed by the difference between the experience of self and of culturally created meanings, and the experience of organisms and things. Seen in this light, the problem for man as an active being in the world was not to look into his body to find mind, but rather it was *to make mind and the creations of mind secure in the universe.* This reflected man's peculiar history and condition. Instinct-free man adapted to life and found his world by creating it, by becoming *Homo poeta*. And, as happens with each new level of emergent adaptation, new problems are posed. The highest level of adaptation would, expectedly, pose the most intricate and unusual problem. This means that *Homo poeta* has to resolve the problem of the apparent separateness and fragility of his own created meanings, against the hard backdrop of organisms and objects provided by brute nature. It means that the creations of culture, in order to carry their maximum conviction, must be woven inextricably into the hard world of things that man uses as a playground. It is this that gives art work its esthetic quality: it represents the firm fusion of playful fiction and disturbingly neutral nature, a union whereby man takes possession of the world and makes it his own by infusing it with his meanings. Thus, the esthetic is always characterized by integral unity, lively movement, extreme diversity, and yet overall naturalness and simplicity. All these attest to one superordinate fact that gives conviction at its maximum: they declare that fabricated human meanings and natural, nonhuman, neutral objects belong inseparably together; and that consequently man's tentative symbolic striving is right for all time. Thus, we see that art is the distinctively human mode because man is the only animal who must fabricate his own conviction, and the esthetic object is the most convincing possible object.

Small wonder, then, that the esthetic object gives the highest joy. When man weaves together human symbolic design and earthly material, he achieves something unprecedented: by embodying the cultural fiction he gives himself immortality, as only it can be had in a world of death and decay. For this reason Goethe, with his supreme artistic intuition, ends his *Faust* with the familiar and memorable appeal:

> Then dared I hail the Moment fleeing:
> *"Ah, still delay—thou art so fair!"*
> The traces cannot, of mine earthy being,
> In aeons perish—they are there!—
> In proud forefeeling of such lofty bliss,
> I now enjoy the highest Moment—this!

Faust finally bid the passing moment linger, when it had become fair, and so lost his wager with Mephistopheles. What made it finally so fair, and worthy of lingering on? Only when Faust contemplated his work of building the great dike, and reclaiming land from the sea.

When, in other words, he conceived the beauty of the organism making its human, creative energies felt in the neutral universe. With man's works thus solidly embedded in the world of earth and sea, man achieves immortality through his own design. The esthetic, as Goethe understood so well, is the superordinate category by which man merges himself into the world, achieves the highest conviction, and defeats the meaninglessness of dumb desire and brute nature.

It was Kant who began the idealist esthetic tradition, by first showing how man can achieve reconciliation even though immersed in a universe which he cannot hope to understand fully, a universe which transcends him. Herbert Marcuse (1956, p. 161) credits Heidegger with first seeing the central place of the esthetic reconciliation in Kant's system and Marcuse also insists on the importance of Schiller's work in this tradition. But Heidegger's work was as late as 1929, and we have noted that Baldwin wrote his *Genetic Theory of Reality* in 1915, building directly on the work of Schelling, Schiller, and Lotze. Baldwin delineates the whole tradition beginning with Kant (1915, p. 209), and caps it himself superbly. The problem of an esthetics that would build on Kant and Schiller, and yet be post-Darwinian, was very much in the air in the latter part of the nineteenth century.

Baldwin's work also came long before Huizinga's, and in it he states explicitly that his theory—which he calls Pancalism—is a theory of the play-form creation of human meanings; by which he means the interweaving of human design into the world of things, a resolution of the dualities of the human condition. In play and art the "semblant" becomes the Real, and the dualism which we discussed in Chapter Six is overcome. The philosopher Bradley could see nothing very original in Baldwin's work, remarking, in a letter to Baldwin, that Schelling had had the same thesis (cf. Baldwin, 1926, Vol. 2, p. 170). But Baldwin's work was, in any event, very important for science, since it was—as we saw—a post-Darwinian theory of the development of mind out of interpersonal interaction; it was not a transcendental theory of mind.

Finally, some of the outstanding isolated essays in this tradition were written independently of Baldwin, by Georg Simmel. Simmel too saw the importance of incarnating the cultural design, and of conveying maximum conviction thereby. In his superb essay (1959) on the esthetic significance of the face, he made breath-taking observations on the face as the characteristic esthetic locus of mind-body unity. As we shall see further in our discussion of Buber's work, it is into the face above all that man looks for his conviction of the real.

A BRIEF ONTOLOGY OF LOVE

No ontology of human striving can be complete without discussing what is most peculiar to man—the urge to love. When we understand that man is the only animal who must *create* meaning, who must open a wedge into neutral nature, we already understand the essence of love. Love is the problem of an animal who must *find* life, *create* a dialogue with nature in order to experience his own being. It is another dimension of the need to be brought into the world, by being brought into contact with life at its quickest and most striking. As Spinoza saw, love is the increase of self by means of the object. Love is the sentiment of a peculiarly alienated animal, one who is separate from the natural, instinctive life process, and must be urged back into the world (E. Becker, 1964a, chap. 8).

Beauty and love are all of a piece because it requires the unique and singularly striking to open a convincing wedge into reality. Love fuses the total organism with the world by offering an overwhelmingly compelling object for one's attention and action. Again, for the lower animals, built-in response patterns have already provided for a world that will be quickening, compelling, exciting, awesome; nature has thus taken care of the matter of love. But for man, the predominantly symbolic animal, the problem is precisely this: to find a world that will be compelling in a total, organismic sense; a world that will be not only symbolic, but also organic, and not only organic, but also symbolic. A world, in a word, of maximum esthetic conviction. Auguste Comte summed up the human lament in a letter to Clotilde de Vaux, when he said that he experienced great sentiments of universal love through his work, and that these were indeed delicious to experience. But he went on to add that the "vague philosophical energy" of these abstract sentiments was very far from sufficient for his real needs for affection (quoted in Gouhier, 1933, p. 27). Again, we see that man must seek the maximum of uplift in his relationship to another *concrete* organism.

This is, simply stated, a basic ontology of love, an ontology of a peculiar kind of separation, of a distinctive kind of need for fusion with a convincing life process. In this century many thinkers have converged on this ontology, and offered their contributions to it— Paul Tillich, Martin Buber, Max Scheler, James Mark Baldwin, Jean-Paul Sartre, Simone de Beauvoir, to cite most of the major ones. Max Weber also had some excellent things to say about the historical aspects of eroticism as a "drawing into the world" (Gerth and Mills,

1946, p. 345 ff.). Another brilliant theoretical treatment of historical and ontological aspects of love is Emil Lucka's largely neglected work (1922) to which we shall refer in the following pages.

An ontology of love, if it is worth anything, should throw considerable light on the "problem" of love; that is to say, it should clarify the various kinds of love, the constricting as well as the liberating, the usual as well as the unusual or the "perverse." And this is precisely what the contemporary ontology of love, elaborated in one or another of its aspects chiefly by the above thinkers, does. Love is a problem in idealist esthetics, in a post-Darwinian world of organisms and culture; and only when understood in this way does it open most of its secrets to us. The "problem" of love is the problem of the complex and unique esthetic needs of a peculiar animal.

In the last section we saw that conviction was a problem in esthetics as the idealists understood it, a problem of weaving the maximum amount of spirit into the world of concrete matter in a way that is at the same time complex and inextricable, harmonious and integral, yet simple in its overall unity. What is man trying to do with this design? He is trying, as we said, to weave the culturally created meanings of the human personality into the neutral world of nature. Now we can only understand the love object as the locus, par excellence, where this esthetic drama of spirit and body unfolds, The love object localizes the problem of what man wants in the world, and what he is trying to do to it. Thus, an ontology of love should reveal in encapsulated form the whole problem of the relationship of man to others.

THE "PERVERSIONS"

Emil Lucka understood that eroticism has two roots, and that man seeks a rich and perfectly synthetic blend of spirit and body in his loves. He observed that man rarely achieves a perfectly balanced and synthetic blend of spirit and body in his loves, and that this failure is precisely what explains the so-called "sexual perversions" (1922, p. 273). Since he wrote, the best elaboration of a theory of the perversions has been made in these terms, in terms of the problem of the apparent separateness and the desired integration of spirit and body. Sartre and de Beauvoir have approached it from a phenomenological point of view, and Médard Boss has written some excellent things from an existential psychiatric approach (1949).

The problem of the esthetic integration of spirit (personality) and body, presents itself to each one of us in terms of the following two questions:

1. *The kinds of objects one wants to see in the world* (cf. Ortega y Gasset, 1957).

2. *The kinds of objects one can handle,* in one way or another.

The basic problem of esthetics in love is to achieve a union of these two, a union of the kind of object one wants with a drawing upon the kinds of powers one can exert. When this union is achieved between desired kind of object and congruence with the powers one is prepared to put forth, the *maximum* of conviction is obtained. Thus we see that the esthetics of love answers to the two kinds of human action: the symbolic and the organismic. The kind of objects one wants to see in the world reflects predominantly the world view into which one has been indoctrinated; the kind of objects one can handle reflects predominantly the particular type of total organismic training one has undergone. The conclusion, then, is logical and ineluctable: the *kind* of maximum conviction that each individual needs *will vary* with the individual. And it is precisely this that explains the curiously wholehearted devotion to the most incomprehensible esthetics, which we then call "perversions."

For example, the simplest perversion, fetishism, actually sums up the whole problem of reality and meaning that we have been discussing. The fetish object is precisely the one which presents itself to our eyes in the most striking and compelling way; it is our overpowering point of contact with reality. The thing that makes it so ludicrous for a man to fawn over a boot or a corset is that they seem so narrow in meaning and hence belittlingly limited to be so overpowering; they monopolize the attentions, feelings, and behavior of an entire human organism—and this is what seems disproportionately ludicrous. Contrast the boot or corset, say, with a crucifix, which would also represent a very narrow physical entrée into the world, but an infinitely broader one in terms of acceptable meanings.

What is the fetishist doing as he so yearningly covets the smallest possible segment of the reality of his object? The answer is surprisingly simple: he is trying to find an entrée into the world as only he knows how, as only his very narrow and limited range of behaviors will permit (cf. E. Becker, 1965). Fetishism, in other words, represents a relatively desperate attempt by a limited organism to come to grips in some satisfying way with a portion of reality. And, of course, the more limited the reality is, the more striking and overpowering—as when a cat singles out a robin on a lawn. Whitehead permits us to understand the fetish object as the locus of union of the ontological and the behavioral, when he says that "the sense of reality is the sense of effectiveness" (1958, p. 167). This epigraph sums up the whole theory of fetishism.

Fetishism, then, merely encapsulates the general problem of making reality come alive for an organism with limited powers, who must yet make contact with the world. It represents an esthetic integration that is so confining that it seems unworthy of such a complex creature as man. And yet we know very well that we are all fetishists, by the very nature of the problem. We must all pick out some cues in our sex partners, by means of which to identify them—much as birds find their mates by coloring. For man, who is highly flexible, who could mate with anything, the culture teaches him what kind of cues to look for in order that his object be an acceptable one. But the wide-spread obsession with breast size in many cultures is already a fetishism of a low grade; it attests to a singularly narrow appreciation of what a total woman is. In the West, the medieval knights were the original fetishists of love, as Lucka observed (p. 272). To carry parts of the clothing of one's lady love near the heart seems already to reduce man to an ignoble game. But this is just what fetishism reflects, a poverty of behavior, a narrow range of games that one can play. The medieval knight, without tournaments, trials, and challenges for his lady love, or crusades, would have led a poor existence indeed—he would have had practically nothing for which to unfold his energies in the world.

Why is it so often the male who seems to suffer from such a limited range of action, and not the female? This difference is partly responsible for leading many writers to call the woman more "unified" or more "integrated" than the male (cf. Ortega y Gasset and Lucka). The woman seems to react to the world in a more integral way; she seems to be less prone to split experience into small segments. But to talk about better "unification" in the woman is merely to beg the question, and to shift the matter back into phylogenetic time. Actually, the problem is one of meanings, of the kind of meanings that a particular type of organism is prepared and trained to find. Woman is in one sense more fortunate than man, in the quest to find the real world, since she has it, so to speak, right at her door: she can find meaning in her own body, as a locus of reproduction, of the creation of life; she can and does actually create her own flesh-and-blood objects, then proceeds to weave into them—by child training—the cultural design. She is thus equipped by nature to create esthetic objects of maximum conviction. Man, on the other hand, has to seek meaning continually outside himself, away from his own body and into the more fictional symbolic realm of pure culture. The relative fantasy and helplessness of the male's condition seems to have been appreciated by a primitive tribe like the Chagga (E. Becker, 1962, chap. 6), and in the West as far back as *Lysistrata*.

The second reason why woman in her approach to experience seems more solidly "unified" than the male is a cultural one, and not a biological one. Woman is less fetishistic in our society because she is culturally exempt from having to look for fetishistic clues by which to identify the sexual desirability of her partner. The male is trained to look for exciting and identifying body protuberances in our society; the female is not. Hence, she tends to react to the male as a whole rather than in terms of any specific body part. Thus, the female tends to react to heterosexual experience in a more integral way, whereas the male tends to separate the female, detach her personality from her body, as well as areas of the body from one another.

But the fact is that the problem of fetishistic perversions cannot be sexually distinct if it is fundamentally a problem in limited range of behaviors; consequently, the female can be subject to them as well as the male. This is nowhere better apparent than in a related type of action, kleptomania. Médard Boss says that men are more prone to fetishism, and women to kleptomania, and he very correctly observes that the reason is that women suffer more from the "barriers of official morality and of the social prohibitions" (1949, p. 66). In other words, where woman must exist in a man's world and be limited by it in the number of behaviors she can undertake, she will also be limited in the number of the fruits that reality will offer her. Kleptomania in some women is just like kleptomania in children and in American college youth: it is a stolen entrée into a forbidden world, by someone who is limited in behavioral powers. It is a breaking into the adult world by children and by those whom the culture has condemned to remain childish and without effect (cf. Boss, 1949, p. 77).

Finally, the best way to understand fetishism is to realize that it is not restricted to sexual behavior—it extends over the whole of our action and we all make use of it. For example, at any time when we have difficulty in making our energies felt, in making our environmental field come alive for our responses, we tend to resort to fetishism. We pick out some object within the field and address a dialogue to it, whether the limitation is appropriate or not. One tends to fix on some object as a locus of meaning, where all other meanings are shaky. Thus, married couples tend to find fault with each other precisely at those times when they are traveling in strange surroundings, or those times in which troubles are mounting up at home. One seizes upon the object as a hold upon reality, as something upon which to vent one's energies; one seeks to experience the fact that one *has* an adaptive capacity and the strength to cope, the strength to manipulate *something* in the total field. This is a technique that we might call *"fetishizing the field"*—creating a locus of meaning in a very narrow area, in order to be able to have *some* reality that calls upon one's adaptive energies. We see it most commonly where behaviors are most constricted—in schizophrenia and depression, for example. Fetishism, in sum, like all words applying to human behavior, is not absolutely valuational: it is and must be a clue to the ideal-typical.

Fetishism is usually found together with masochism, and the reason is obvious: masochism is another word for poverty of behavior, as is also sadism. Fetishism-sadism-masochism describe the same kind of ineptitude; they sum up action constriction in the human animal. They reflect clumsy ways of getting into the world of objects and reality, by organisms that are relatively weak and limited. From a behavioral point of view, there is really little more that needs to be said about the perversions. Masochism and sadism are interesting and instructive, however, in another way: they sum up the *kinds* of esthetic integrations that people undertake precisely when they are weak in behavioral range and powers. Let us consider this briefly, since we will not be able adequately to treat the problem of historical psychology—in the next chapter—unless we have roughly familiarized ourselves with the problem of the perversions (but for a fuller treatment see E. Becker, 1965).

The sado-masochist is someone who has trouble believing in the validity and sanctity of people's insides—their spirit, personality, or self. These insides could be his own or others'; if they are his own he tends to be masochistic, if they are others' he tends to be called a sadist. In other words, the sado-masochist undervalues the culturally created personality and tends to act in the world of the body—it is here that he achieves his maximum conviction. Of course, to undervalue one's own insides can lead one to overvalue those of certain others. As a result, when the masochist surrenders to his partner, he annihilates himself in favor of some stronger reality. In terms of esthetic theory, we would say that his body comes into convincing contact with the world, but that thereby he loses his personality. This is a poor kind of love and a poor kind of esthetics, precisely because the spirit is effaced in the merger. Tillich, concerned with this problem, describes the weak self, who is precisely the one that resorts to masochistic love: "The surrender of such an emaciated self is not genuine love because it extinguishes and does not unite what is estranged. The love of this kind is the desire to annihilate one's responsible and creative self. . . ." For Tillich, beings without such a personal center, such an inner self which has its own validity, are without genuine *eros* (1960, pp. 69, 31).

The sadist is delighted with the masochist precisely because he allows the sadist to get at his insides, to efface his personality. As Sartre and de Beauvoir have so well argued, the sadist comes to grips with the insides of his partner by bringing them out into the world, and grounding them in the suffering flesh. Why does he do this, why does he feel the need to efface the inside of another's personality? The reason is twofold. In the first place, by virtue of a singular upbringing, the sadist is one who sees a sharp distinction between the public and the private, the outsides and the insides of organisms. This may be due, as some of Boss's (1949) patients testify, to the singularly harsh and foreboding nature of their parental objects, to a very rigorous early training. As a result, the individual has been deprived of open, free and spontaneous inter-action with another of his kind; thus, he does not see people as open to warmth, tractable to reason—in a word, "responsibly" responsive. Rather, these objects will seem difficult to approach, difficult to deal with, objects which harbor potentially dangerous insides. These objects may be yawningly aloof, dangerously explosive; or perhaps they may even be organisms that—for all their pretensions—seem pitifully empty—and flesh without valid inner spirit is already degraded. Thus, these are all objects which seem to reflect a sharp distinction between inner and outer, objects which are not unified. As one of Boss's patients put it:

> There is an isolating sheath around me. I cannot pene-trate into anything. . . . I want to break down the walls, because they divide and isolate. . . . I have always been much impressed by the story about Till Eulenspiegel who said, when his father died: "Drill a hole, his soul wants to come out." . . . When I insult the women and humiliate them, when I rob them of their dignity and call them dirty names, then I tear down their proud personality-casing (Boss, 1949, p. 86).

The second thing that characterizes the sadist is something he shares with everyone: namely, the esthetic desire to fuse the world into a unity that is convincing, and that is amenable to his powers. But since he has already overly separated the insides and outsides of things, and since he has never developed adequate powers for relating to people as integral wholes, his means for achieving his desired esthetic of unity will be clumsy, violent and effacing. Again, Boss's patient sums this up beautifully.

> Each time I really crave something, I must force it, break it open. I live among alien opposing clods, and I am a clod myself. My reason for forcing a woman into physical submission is that *I myself never had any direct relationship to the human body,* neither to my own body nor to the body of a woman (p. 87, emphasis added).

It is only when the harshly divided world melts into a whole that he can achieve satisfaction, feel at one with life. The sadist reveals the essence both of his clumsiness and his cosmology, with these superbly instructive words:

> Only physical pain can pierce the body to the marrow. I have experienced that myself when a dentist hurt me badly. This pain was accompanied by such delight that I had an erection. The pain penetrated to the very center, to the inner core, where my true "self" is located. It reaches through all outer layers, even through the hardest tooth enamel. This is the sensation, when the real nerve of life is touched. Then the nerve is exposed. Reality is opened. There is no more dividing wall, there is "the very thing" (p. 88).

Here we see beautifully how and why the sadist cannot stand the separation of the public and the private; nor can he grant to others the mystery of their personality, the validity of their inner self, because it is this that threatens his powers. Consequently, one way to achieve esthetic satisfaction, to assert one's powers on the kind of reality one is comfortable with, is to *actively* treat the insides of others, their culturally constituted personality, as a fraud, an ethereal thing which enjoys undue and unseemly immunity from the tests of reality. The esthetics of the sadist is thus partly due to the deficiencies of his own self: in order for reality to be convincing, in order for him to feel his maximum powers, he wants the world to be peopled with concrete manipulatable objects, with objects that do not have any elusive insides. This is the reason that he expends all his effort on manipulating the flesh: either he cannot deal with the insides of others or he will not recognize these insides as valid.

Here we can understand the interchangeability of the sadistic and masochistic postures. These are terms which describe one and the same thing: weakness and felt limitation in oneself; sharp duality of spirit and matter in people. When one does not believe in the validity of one's own inner being and powers, and when one cannot relate to others as integral and unified persons, then the private self, the inner mystery, becomes a threat. Therefore, the mystery that others conceal in their inner selves must be brought to light by whatever means at one's disposal: in this way it can be rendered safe, or it can be justly exposed as the fraud that it is. And so one can be comfortable in the peculiar world one needs. It is only when the sadist is unquestionably in face of a stronger superior inner reality that he gives in and becomes the masochist. With the weak person there is no question of a relationship of equals. But it is important to stress that most people tend to devalue one or another aspect of the human reality. In our feeling for the real, in our world views, some of us would grant existential priority to the natural organic aspects of things, whereas others would grant this priority to the cultural-symbolic aspects of things. In sum, we all tend to invest human objects with meaning in a lopsided way, at one time or other. Hence, as we shall see further below, our idea of a "properly esthetic blend" of spirit and matter will vary in each individual case. As we said at the beginning of this section, the problem of esthetic integration depends on *what* we value, and what we can do *to bring about* this value. Max Stirner— another of the first social psychologists—also pointed out long ago that what we value varies according to the ages of life: we tend to value things over thoughts in childhood, thoughts over things in adolescence (in our culture, at any rate); in maturity, ideally, we proceed to some kind of balance (1844, pp. 15–16). And of course, in the history of an individual life, the powers and wisdom one gains will deepen and broaden the esthetics one needs and can handle.

"GOOD" VERSUS "BAD" ESTHETICS

In all of this the sadist is trying for the maximum esthetic effect; but, as we said, what one tries for, in his search for conviction, depends on the range of the equipment one brings to bear. All limited individuals must achieve their esthetic effects at the expense of a much wider range of artistic canvas. It is like the difference between what a lobster and a fox can organize and integrate in their respective worlds. Ideally, as we said earlier, the maximum esthetic effect is created when the maximum amount of spirit is inextricably woven into the hard world of things. Now spirit is personality, and personality is spontaneity, and hence privacy. Thus, theoretically, we should want as much privacy to enter the world as possible. As Scheler has understood, the love object is essentially a privacy that enriches our world. This is the most tangible way we have of imparting to life the abundance of meaning that we seek. The esthetic effect seems to be derived somewhat like this: the manifold private selves which people the world add another dimension to nature; they become a true reservoir of creative energy. Consequently, we seem to be immersed in a world of larger meaning that is greater than ourselves, more valid than the best we can put forth. If one is strong, one transcends the limitations of his single existence by accepting this very multiplicity, by subordinating himself to the rich life process.

But again, it takes strength to allow the world to be overrun with privacies. How does the person *bring his energies to bear* in this kind of world and fit into it? The best way is to *bring one's own valid privacy* and join it with the others. As Buber understands, this gives the maximum interpersonal meaningfulness. But if one does not believe in the inner self, he cannot do this. He is not sure that he or others have any privacy that is worth anything. His recourse is to fall back on the organism itself, which always carries strong conviction. And he can take command of a small segment of the organismic world, play out the drama of public and private within the fleshy confines of two bodies. We might conceive of this as a sort of hothouse excursion into esthetics, a safe way of bringing private spirit into the world, and at the same time of feeling one's own energies.

But we can see that in its very limitation it is self-defeating. To be obliged to take command over private spirit is already to efface it. To use one's own powers only in the interests of maximum control does not bring the real liberation one desires—it brings only momentary surcease. Real liberation comes only in a community of privacy, in the respect of being for being, in the release from one's narrowness and separateness, into a richer, more dramatic world. The sadist is thus a poor artist: his restricted manipulation of materials, in order to produce something convincing, defeats the true aim of art, which is to liberate and not to confine. The sadist, of course, shows tremendous ingenuity in his scramble for some kind of dependable meaning. He proves how clever man can be, even with poverty of powers, weakness in the face of the multiplicity of experience, in a world that is over-whelming with objects, and with private meanings. He uses whatever range of behaviors and aptitudes he has, in order to connect up with other objects, build himself into the world, overcome the threatening separation, and harvest the meaning that comes with commitment to the life process.

So much, then, for the esthetics of "perversions." The formidable-ness of objects, the discrepancies between one's felt powers and the behaviors that are demanded of one, the puzzling twofold nature of reality—spirit and matter—which confronts us with double meanings—all these, in sum, put a continuing burden on our coping powers; they require a range of mastery that few of us can dependably possess.

Thus, our ontology of esthetic striving when applied to the problem of love explains why we have so many kinds of love—liber-ating and expanding kinds, and constricting and belittling kinds. The kind of world one wants depends on the kind of world one is trained to want, and equipped by training to get. Most people, creatures of habit, will seek their esthetics within a mold that is deter-ministic: it cuts the world out for them, seeks to deprive it of threaten-ing novelty and too much surprise. But liberating love is precisely a matter of novelty and surprise, of the richness of the spontaneous, the private, the unexpected (cf. E. Becker, 1964a, chap. 8). Again, the difference between good art and bad art: the one opens out the world to new experience and carries one beyond the deterministic con-strictions of his past. The other merely relieves built-in anxieties, calms and assures one that the accustomed world view, the usual perceptions, are right, that the world is an expected place into which one's accustomed energies are sure to fit. Bad art, in sum, gives one conviction merely by building one more firmly into the world. Bad art, then, performs for man what nature has already performed for the lower animals. Bad art imprisons, whereas man should instead seek to open out his world, to bring freedom and spontaneity into the universe. But for this, as we said, man needs strength.

The difference between good esthetics and bad is another way of saying that man, like any animal in nature, *can be defeated by the very needs which characterize his organism.* Just as the lower animals survive *because* of their instincts, they also lose a larger world because of them. Man needs the reliance on habit in order to make his world safe and alleviate the anxiety of the unfamiliar and the unknown; but at the same time this deprives him of a potentially larger world. In other words, for the lower animals, evolution stops with the firmness of the built-in instinctive adaptive mechanisms. For man, development and freedom stop with the groping for conviction that stems from weakness and cowardice, from failure to respect the life process. This kind of conviction seals him irrevocably into a confined world. His need for narrow satisfaction defeats his possibilities of becoming something different. Thus we might say that man is the only animal who can *defeat* the evolving life process, the continued groping of nature, because he is the only one who has the *possibility* of continuing this groping.

The problem of good esthetics versus bad is an immense and complex one, and I realize that I do not do it justice with these kinds of sharply dichotomous conceptions. They are an aid, merely; they are not a guide. Man needs to see that his cultural design is right for all time, by seeing it woven into the world. But what standard can we use for the thin line between conviction-and-liberation and conviction-and-bondage? It is impossible to prescribe the margin by which man should edge himself into higher esthetics. This is the function of the artist: the liberating is always the spontaneous and the unknown, and he prescribes by demonstrating. He who is not an artist can only clarify up to a certain point. Perhaps it is highly appropriate that it was an artist of the stature of Stendhal who saw the problem of love, art, and the good life, and did not hesitate to make a straightforward prescription.

STENDHAL'S ONTOLOGY OF ESTHETICS AND LOVE

For Stendhal, love, art, and the good life were the three great themes of human life, and they all sprang from a common source—from spontaneity and freedom. Taken together, these three themes and their common source were for him the final cause of man (Barzun, 1956, pp. 108–110; cf. also Roy, 1962, pp. 15–59). This places the highest premium on free activity, and consequently it follows that the worst vice is hypocrisy. Here is a simple and straightforward ontology that at first reading might seem the typical romantic dream, the option for offhand and carefree joy. Furthermore, it seems like an option that would have no relation to the real world, and could not have. But Barzun sums up beautifully the true penetration of Stendhal's prescriptive ontology, and cautions against seeing in these few strokes a merely casual Utopia.

The proof that Stendhal saw the problem of good esthetics versus bad—of the good life versus the everyday one—lies in his hierarchy of love types. In top place Stendhal put "passion-love" and, following in order, "love ruled by good taste within a confined social circle," "physical love," and, finally, "love that springs from vanity." He sums up the meaning of his option in these words, words which Barzun well understands as the clue to his whole penetrating ontology:

> In my opinion a man ought to be a passionate lover and at the same time should carry life and animation into every company where he happens to be. This universal gaiety, moreover, this art of pleasing everybody, ought not to rest on the art of flattering everybody's tastes and weaknesses. . . . The amenity I desired [as a youth] was the pure joy of Shakespeare in his comedies, the charm that reigned at the court of the exiled duke in the forest of Arden (quoted in Barzun, 1956, p. 108).

What is Stendhal proposing here? In terms of the ontology of esthetics and love that we have been reviewing, the answer is already self-evident. Stendhal's trilogy of man's higher destiny is nothing less than a recognition that man's greatest need and deepest joy stem from the free creation of meanings. Stendhal realized from within the intimate intuition of the creative artist the same thing that Huizinga had so plainly read in history, namely, that man *plays* life, and only thus does he create it. Stendhal realized that for man the illusory is the real, the imagined invests reality with truth. And in this way man draws himself into a world that he helps create, by infusing its objects with his freedom. Thus he put in last place, in his hierarchy of love types, that love which is *self*-conscious rather than *object*-conscious. If the main function of love is to draw the organism into the world, then love that springs from vanity defeats that purpose. It only draws the organism back into itself. The love that Stendhal placed second—the one that is ruled by good taste within a confined social circle, still has one great merit: it is imaginative, and it is part of an interhuman discourse. Simple physical love, finally, merits third place, because at least it has the quality of spontaneity.

Stendhal had to condemn hypocrisy as the foremost vice for the same reason that he placed vanity love in last place. Hypocrisy, along with pedantry, defeats that very thing which the good life seeks, namely, a spontaneous link with an ever-richer object world. Hypocrisy is the interposition of self-consciousness, of second thoughts about *commitment to* life. Pedantry is nearly as unforgivable for much the same reason: it kills social spontaneity, breaks creative communication, dampens wit. If the "real" is free, developing contact with the object world, then pedantry breaks this very thing: it makes its own "real"—makes of it an inverted, *internal, symbolic* affair. In other words, on the problem of good versus bad art and life, Stendhal knew what to condemn: all meanings that did not genuinely spring from the free creative energies of the organism—the organism that incessantly seeks contact with a rich object world precisely in order to bring to bear its free creative energies. The hypocrite lives in a world of second thoughts; the pedant in one of foregone conclusions.

We should have no remaining doubts about the depth of Stendhal's ontology, or the appositeness of his prescription for the meaningful human life, even though they are simple and clear. Someone who could uphold such a program for the good life could not delude himself, could not believe that people would find it easy to realize that life. Consequently, Stendhal held firmly to the belief on which the whole vision must be based—a belief which Rousseau had already put forth (1762, p. 48), and which was to Nietzsche a revelation, namely, that the prime condition of virtue is strength (Barzun, 1956, p. 110). In terms of our previous discussion of sadism and masochism, we can now see fully how sober Stendhal's Utopian vision is: it takes strength to allow free creative energies to come into the world, and to dazzle us with their unaccustomed and imaginative performances; it takes strength to break ground in a continually new world.

THE SPECIAL PROBLEM OF THE AUTONOMOUS CREATION OF MEANING

All this is another way of saying that, for man, the liberating is a dialectic that is played out on two poles: the pole of imagination and the pole of belief in one's inner powers. The problem is divided into two parts. In the first place, one must be able to fabricate the daring innovation, the symbolically new that breaks through the accustomed cultural forms. In order to do this, one must already have separated oneself from the generally shared version of meaning. But the second part of the problem really begins here, and it is much more difficult than being able merely to call up ingenuity. The innovator must believe that the symbolic is the real, that his creation has validity.

Art takes care of the problem, as we saw, by providing the esthetic object, or the esthetic event and experience, the interweaving of symbol and material or organismic thing that carries its own conviction. In other words, art gives the innovator a vehicle by which he can fabricate the conviction that the symbolic is the real. But art, having taken care of the art work itself, does not take care of the artist, as it did not take care of Vincent van Gogh. By this I mean that the esthetic object alone cannot support the strength needed to be an innovator. The artist stands precariously alone, still prey to unbelief in his powers, even in the face of the esthetic object. Stendhal saw only part of the problem, that strength must precede virtue for an animal who must create its own precarious meanings. But we know that there is more, that even so there can never be security in human meanings.

It is only in our time that we can really begin to see the complexity of the dialectic of human liberation. Only an ontology of human striving, coupled with a comprehensive theory of personality, could enable us really to appreciate the sheer complexity of the problem of creating meaning. Let us explore some of the unusual and fascinating dimensions of this problem.

How can we best convey the nature of man's disbelief in his own meanings? Psychoanalysis has offered us a word which conveys some of the problem—the technical word "transference." A lot has been written about the idea of transference, some of it very meaningful, much of it merely designed to serve the closed interests of psychoanalytic therapeutic theory (cf. Szasz, 1963b). I think that the word can be understood very directly and simply: it refers to man's tendency to seek stable meanings in others, instead of in himself. In one sense, transference is very necessary and natural, since we need support for our meanings. But at the extreme, when man must seek meanings in others because he cannot offer any of his own, or feel any inner validity, transference becomes self-defeating. Thus, the word "transference," like "liberty" and "democracy," helps us to clarify our strivings. Transference, in other words, helps us to affirm the ideal, while we see very clearly the real: the ideal—as we shall see in Part III—is Feuerbach's and Buber's vision of a true dialogue of equals, sharing their mystery, working together in the joint creation of meaning.

The real, on the other hand, is usually much less than this. It sees man looking to another man, because he believes that the other's existence transcends his own in meaningfulness. It includes the best of men, who need and want to find their betters. Listen to the following poetic ruminations of Gorky, watching the aged Tolstoy sitting by the sea:

> He seemed like an ancient stone come alive, that knew and pondered the beginning and end of all things. . . . In the old man's musing I felt something portentous, magic. . . . In my heart were rejoicing and fear, then all melted together in one blissful feeling: "I am not bereft on this earth, so long as this old man is living on it" (quoted in Thomas Mann, 1932, pp. 74–75).

What could be better than an ancient stone, upon which to lean for solid support, for dependable, eternal meaning?—an ancient stone with piercing gray eyes. Gorky, we may remember, was the one who honestly revealed that his life task was to "squeeze the slave out of my soul." Thomas Mann takes the above scene as an indication of Tolstoy's powerful personality, but we could better say that it shows the whole human condition through Gorky's search.

Now Gorky was an artist—and this is the point of my discussion. He fabricated his own esthetic meanings, but he could not lean on them alone. When we look at the lives of the greatest, the most daring innovators, one fact shines out: that no matter how compelling is the edifice he creates, man simply cannot feel that *he has the authority* to offer up *his own* meanings. Perhaps this is in the very nature of the way the human animal is shaped. All our meanings are infused into us from our transactions with others, which means that most of our existential authority is borrowed. We are literally "empty" until filled by the forms of culture, and once we are full we cannot ever wholly claim the insides as ours. The cultural insides that fill the human personality are ours by location, and never completely by inner creation. Some of us, of course, fashion ourselves through struggle and responsible choice, more than others; as a result we are more centered on our own firmly possessed meanings—but there is always a margin left over that eludes us. Some humans are so thoroughly created by others, have so forfeited their own responsible powers, that culture takes possession of their entire organism, and they lose the authority that even lower animals enjoy—what we might call the "right of organism." They have to learn that their organism has the right to its own life space. Thus, man is uniquely the animal that has to learn that he has the authority to be "his own" animal, so to speak. We know that the best way to learn this is by behaving the part.

With the innovator the problem is further complicated. He is offering up a fresh reworking of meanings, and cannot lean on the outside for support. He is actually transgressing the meanings that he was filled with in the first place, and breaking his links with his every-day fellow man. But, once the links are broken, where can he find the authority for meanings that come from the *inside* out—rather than from the *outside* in? This is the problem in essence, the problem of an animal who is built on outside authority, and then finds the need to proclaim an authority from within. As we can well see, by definition this is almost equivalent to negating *the very nature* of this kind of animal. Little wonder that it was Goethe himself who somewhere observed that the sense of individuality becomes "almost unbearable for the exceptional man." Emerson recognized the overriding import-ance of this problem, and for him it was a major life theme. Certainly his essay on "Self-Reliance" (1904) is the historical classic on the problem of autonomy. For Emerson the ability to believe in one's own meanings was so rare that it was itself tantamount to genius. In his words: "To believe in your own thought, to believe that what is true for you in your private heart is true for all men—that is genius. . . Trust thyself: every heart vibrates to that iron string." But it is the rarest heart that has the courage. Poets such as Goethe and Emerson would be peculiarly sensitive to this question because it is precisely the poet who offers up his own meanings. This explains why artists often experience despair, fear, and guilt after fashioning a unique work of art. Psychoanalysts might say that the unique work of art is an "aggressive act," and that the despair and fear are due precisely to the guilt that results from the aggression. But this is clumsy and obfuscat-ing reduction, even if it does crudely sum up the matter. We should better say that the work of art is a unique creation of meaning, for which the singular person afterward feels helpless and unsupported. When Freud adduced case histories on this problem, he aptly termed them examples of people "wrecked by success" (cf. 1936). But the artist—Wordsworth and especially Melville—understood this problem long before Freud, and in much the same way. They saw that the creative person dealt in new meanings, which created a kind of megalomaniac's world that he could not easily substantiate from with-in himself. Hence the poet easily passes from "gladness" due to his creation, to "madness" (Chase, 1949, pp. 163 ff.).[1]

This problem of authority for human meanings is so important to understanding human behavior that it would truly be impossible to overstress it. Only thus can we understand some of the peculiar torments of the innovator who has really dared openly to flout the standard meanings of his time—a Luther, for instance. Luther's defiance of traditional authority was a problem that tormented him all his life. He had to face up to spells of acute anxiety when he was flooded from within with an obsessive command that seemed to shake him to the very soul. Luther was in a terrible bind, verging on madness all his life, partly, I think, because of the peculiar nature of the new meanings he offered up. How was he to validate new meanings which in effect attacked God through the Church? He tried to do this by believing that God himself wanted him to offer up the new meaning, but to someone brought up within the Church this was evidently not wholly convincing. One can imagine Luther's bind somewhat like this: "If I have the right to impugn the Pope, and therefore God's authority vested in him, am I sure that *God* gave me this right?"

When Luther was not sure, when he felt the terrible undermining from within, he blamed the devil. Here was a convenient scapegoat: the problem of explaining the undermining from within was historically facilitated by the belief in the devil. Today we know that there is no such easy way out. The anxiety that floods the daring innovator is not the command of God or the devil—although it could very well be mistaken for such. It is simply an acute sensation *that one has no authority* for his own meanings. The only way to describe it is to say that it is a kind of total organismic helplessness, an overall behavioral consciousness of loss of support; it often takes the form of a seizure or a gripping in the pit of the stomach. It is as though someone outside oneself were reaching in, and blocking one's forward momentum from within. Both John Bunyan and William James felt this sharp inner subversion, apparently at times of crisis over their own meanings (cf. James, 1902, pp. 135–136, and footnote 18). It seems to be the characteristic mode of undermining that accords with the characteristic human condition: the fact that one's insides, which permit action to go forward, are never wholly one's own.

It is easy to ascribe the undermining to a purely religious crisis—a separation from God, and a need to lean on Him again. But it is becoming increasingly difficult to do this in modern times, since we are developing new vocabularies to replace the religious ones. Today, when one feels that he is losing his inner world, that he cannot assert the identity or the self that he is straining to justify, he usually resorts to the psychiatrist. It was surely much easier and much more life-enhancing to bed down for a few weeks or a month, have a feverish hallucinatory bout with the devil, and be nursed back to a sense of solidity by reaching anew and more fervently for God, aided by some warm grog. The back wards of our mental hospitals are crowded with degenerated schizophrenics, many of whom would have been re-habilitated by this kind of rationale and treatment. Of course, when we use the word innovator in this context, we mean anyone who strikes out for meanings and a life of his own, away from the grip of the early world view and the early objects which shaped one's first, auto-matic meanings.

What is the innovator to do when he no longer has the easy rationale of God as a support for his new meanings, or the devil as a ready scapegoat? He can no longer say, with the ease of a Descartes or a Luther, that God wanted the elaboration of a new system. He is obliged to rely on other forms of "the courage to be," to borrow Tillich's well-known and apt expression. And when we scan the face of history, we see that such forms are limited. Man must use his great-est ingenuities and his most honest effort to come to grips with this problem anew in each historical epoch. Sometimes the innovator tries to draw all his strength from his own creation, from the esthetic creation itself—which we will recognize as a form of fetishism. The esthetic creation becomes as monopolizing as possible; and with this fetishistic investment of all one's meaning and strength in the object of his work, we would expect to find what we might call the "concep-tual sadism" of the true visionary. Having created meaning in one range, he must extend it into all ranges; otherwise the esthetics is frag-mentary, unconvincing, and the old meanings remain jarring, threaten-ing the veridity of the new vision. The secret aim of the innovator who has only his esthetic work to fall back on must be to take command of as broad an esthetic canvas as possible, to weave his new meanings into the broadest possible segment of the world. The problem is, how convincing will this performance seem to him if he does not reorder everything in accord with it? He is caught up by the urge to maximum conviction—he has to see his vision embodied in all the objects of the real world in order to feel more secure. Hence, his conceptual sadism follows logically: once he creates a symbolic new world picture, every-thing must pale beside it; he is here precisely to reshape the world so that all present meanings must suffer. He comes naturally, there-fore, to disrespect anything "private" that opposes itself to his design. It is this very conceptual sadism that we might call the "occupational hazard" of the unique systematizer. Having offered up a new, idea-tional pattern of intended meaning, he must see it woven as broadly and thoroughly into the world as possible; otherwise, he cannot make esthetic sense out of the environment. If the environment contains a plurality of meanings, his own are threatened. Historically, of course, most innovators combined conceptual sadism with divine justification: they leaned on otherworldly authority and sought also to change the entire face of the earth; the toll has been frightening as a result of these kinds of efforts.

But we know that not all systematizers show this obsessive conceptual sadism, this all-or-nothing thirst to achieve total conviction from the dominance of their world view alone. Some of them realize that the reordering of the world cannot be wholly in their command. In other words, some innovators have the ability to believe in their vision without fully reordering the world esthetically, without demanding a complete reflection, everywhere, of their newly intended meanings. They stop short at imposing their categories on everyone and everything; they do not dictate the private insides of others. While cutting rather mercilessly through all previous esthetic conceptualizations, they still tolerate a great amount of inaccessibility to their own reordering; they accept that there will remain powers outside their control. They supply a new world view, and yet allow the old panorama of private individualities to continue, and to risk showing up their vision.

We think of a Dante or a Goethe in this regard; and no sooner have we uttered their names than we know their strength: they have called upon new sources of self-transcendence. Lucka has some very thought-provoking things to say about Dante and Goethe, whom he calls "metaphysical lovers" (1922), but for our purposes here we can sum up the problem he addresses himself to in a few of his words:

> Not only the great thinker's thirst for knowledge, the mystic's religious yearning, the aesthetic of the rare artist, but also the love and longing of the passionate lover must reach beyond the attainable to the infinite. This earth is the kingdom of "mean" actions, "mean" emotions and "mean" men. And the lover, unable to bear its limits, creates for himself a new world—the world of metaphysical love (p. 303).

This is another way of saying that the world that has not been reordered according to one's vision is also "mean": the everyday version of the cultural drama seems too limiting, stupid, ignoble, or just shallow and lifeless. Remember that the especially gifted person is striving for truly self-created meanings, he wants those meanings that transcend all others, and yet that are still valid in their isolated uniqueness. Thus he must logically seek support for his powers from outside the ongoing cultural fiction. We might even say that the genius of this type cannot permit himself any objects in the real world with meanings greater than his own, else he would defeat his own project: the object would reflect a superordinacy on the innovator's own private meanings. The metaphysical love is one recourse, and has the unique quality that he seeks: it will support autonomously fabricated meanings, without nullifying them by any higher ones. It gives added impetus to the uniqueness of the innovator's meanings, by imparting approval "from nature itself," so to speak.

Lucka talks about Dante and Goethe as the type of innovators who reach for support in the perfect metaphysical love, in order to sustain their visions (pp. 291–292). One could also cite others like John Stuart Mill and Comte. Mill found and idealized Harriet Taylor at the very time in his life when he had pulled away from his father, that overpowering transference object who had given Mill all his internal meanings. At the time of his depression the young Mill felt like a wholly determinate creation of the older man. He reached for Harriet Taylor when he planted his option for autonomy. Little wonder that he dared flout openly the conventions of the time: his relationship to an idealized Harriet was literally a matter of life or death for his own self. As for Comte, critics read "dementia" and its tragedy into his consuming love for Clotilde de Vaux, who died after Comte had known her for only a year. But this is narrow and errone-ous; the death may have been tragic, but not the love. Comte was alone with his meanings in every sense, and his vision of the new society was powerful, radical, and highly unusual. He reached logically and naturally for support in a validating, transcending love. Little did it matter that he fed it with his imagination. When he in-cluded copious references to the place of his beloved Clotilde in the new Religion of Humanity, he was stating a truth: his con-suming love for this departed spirit was the only thing which now gave support to his whole vision. He literally had nowhere else to turn. It was not Clotilde who led Comte to "water down" the earlier *Cours de philosophie positive* into the *Politique positive,* as some critics erroneously were quick to imagine. Rather, it was the utter disparity between Comte's vision and the world of his time which led him to reach for some unusually life-enhancing support for his *whole* system. When Saint-Simon found himself wholly out of tune with the "mean" reality of his time, he tried suicide; Comte remained in this "mean" world, but reached beyond it to the vision of a perfect, all-sustaining love.

Where could Goethe get support, or Michelangelo, if not in

"the Mothers," the "eternally feminine" that beckons from above? Hence, the extreme longing of this type of man for the perfect woman, for the perfect esthetic synthesis of transcendent spirit and organismic beauty. This is the love that gives the utmost strength, because it presents the support *of nature* to man, it gives courage in the only way it can be had (cf. Lucka, 1922, pp. 291–292). If his esthetic objects do not fill the world with the proper and omnipresent combination of spirit and matter for all time, then at least the perfect woman will. She will radiate out for all to see the unique blend of profound spirit and perfect matter that holds up the lesson for man, and for all time: that human powers are not brought to bear on the world in vain, that there is a transcendental significance to life, a meaningfulness that shines through the life process itself, and that will sustain man.

But man's attempt to be Olympian by reaching for support to the perfect woman as the all-sustaining metaphysical love is doomed to failure. As Lucka has so well understood, this kind of love is impossible. Hence the ultimately and deeply tragic nature of life: man cannot consummate himself or still his strivings "once and for all." One attempts to transcend "mean" present meanings by finding the ideal love object, as did Wagner, Michelangelo, Dante, Goethe, Comte, Mill; one wants to be spared the frustrations of this world, its meanness, its imperfection, its clash with one's own unique visions. But to find the ideal in this real world is, of course, impossible; there is no perfect spirit in flawless earthly bodies that will fully support man in all his strivings; there is no "absolute freedom" in nature that can take determined form and still remain unconditioned. Even if the perfectly free spirit could exist, how could she support man at every point and still remain independent, spontaneous, private, and free? The earthly woman as a metaphysical love is thus an impossible contradiction. The most one can hope for is to be sustained by the fantasy, and in this way gain courage for the everyday struggle.

Here is the ultimate tragedy for the man who would be truly free, but who still limits his striving to determinate objects. One may avoid constricting transference objects, one may shun conceptual sadism, but there is no possibility of freedom in a determinate world. Its objects can never be perfect; nor can they support all our wishes and desires and still remain free and aloof—as we would want them to in order for them to retain their aura of maximum conviction. The simplest organism can never be wholly affirmed in its striving; and the rarest genius cannot banish the burden of his creation. Nature has passed its sentence on all organisms alike, and whether one reaches with a

pseudopod or an aching heart, he can never find perfect peace or un-
shakable support. Sometimes the lover is fortunate enough not to
discover that his ideal love is not perfect—as Somerset Maugham
observed in his trenchant story "Red"—but this itself is very rare.

Through all his twistings and turnings, there seems no better
way for man to gain the courage of his existence than to trust and
hope in divine support. If, historically, we can no longer have the
assurance of a Newton, a Luther, or a Descartes, then our ingenuity
and effort must be all the greater: we must make full and creative use of
our symbolic, imaginative equipment. The problem, at any rate,
remains constant, and it seems that the only truly victorious way of
supporting human meanings is to focus one's trust on a truly divine
object. When Dante and the aged Goethe finally made their perfect
woman into the "love from on high," they reflected their inner growth.

The great question for a synthetic theory of alienation begins
precisely here: what is the most liberating way of achieving support
for human meanings? Or, put in other terms: what is the ideal type
of God-consciousness proper to free men in a united society? As
Feuerbach saw, to make God the object of love carries one great
danger: it risks taking one out of this world and its *human associations.*
This was the basic reason for the atheism that was embodied in Marxism, and that grew out of the Enlightenment: the passive trust in God
obscured the need to actively fashion a new equalitarian community.
The problem is a tremendously involved and complex one, and it
runs through the thinking of all the religious geniuses of history. I
don't pretend to do more than approach it from the side of a science
of man, by arguing that man's passionate search for supernatural
support is best accomplished via the intermediary of the human
community as a unit. This we will do in Part III. In the present section
I have wanted to give the background for that discussion, by showing
how deeply rooted in the anxieties of each individual is the problem
of where he gets support for his existence. The contribution of
descriptive ontology to a synthetic theory of alienation is precisely
that it permits us to talk about this central problem of social theory in
descriptive, scientific terms. And in this way we can design a dependable higher moral ideal.

SOME OBSERVATIONS ON GOETHE

Once we understand that this problem, like all the rest we are discussing, is not only descriptive, but also ideal-typical, we will want to find

as many cues as we can to help us design an ideal of conduct. What
are the complete resources of man as we know him so far? What does
a particular context or historical epoch do with these resources? Let us
close our discussion by looking at the puzzling peculiarities of a few of
the great innovators who throw great light on our questions and prepare us for the further discussion in the next chapter.

When we talk about puzzling peculiarities of great innovators,
Goethe again comes to mind. As with all great figures, he has been
dissected from all sides. Biography, literary criticism, psychoanalytic
characterology, existential biography—each has sought to reveal some
of the workings of Goethe the man. I want to add only a tiny bit to
the store of speculation, by looking at Goethe solely, from the point of
view of this chapter, as someone who tried constantly to create his
own meanings. When he is seen in this light, many of his most irk-
some peculiarities seem explainable. If the problem of meaning is
truly a superordinate approach to human conduct, then even some
brief suggestions should reveal important things about Goethe, and
through him about man everywhere.

Goethe seems to have had to face the major problem of the innovator who seeks to create autonomous meanings, and his major source
of self-transcending validation was, as we noted, the urge to the
perfect, metaphysical love. Goethe grasped at it all through his
life, trying, even in his sixties and seventies, to find the perfect, all-
sustaining, all-validating love. When the old man threw his heart to
a girl in her teens he of course looked ludicrous—and, if the perfect
love on earth is impossible, perhaps he was ludicrous from a pragmatic point of view. It is simply not the best way to be sustained in
one's creation of meaning.

Yet for Goethe it remained a major life theme, and this particular life option seems to sum up much of the strengths and weaknesses
of his character. I do not pretend to do more than highlight these
strengths and weaknesses with this approach to Goethe; the problem
of a characterology cannot be reduced deterministically, no matter
how broad a theme one fixes on. Yet we have already seen the strengths
of this kind of attempt at self-validation. It relieves one from
dependence on his fellow man, and as a result one has no need to
manipulate others in the interests of his own well-being. Since most
people live precisely in this manipulative way, we can see how rare a
strength is this by-product of the option for a metaphysical love.
Goethe was hardly a conceptual sadist; he delighted to live in a world
of plural meanings, was content to let the future bear out his vision

of the good life and the good society. He was in the world on its terms, but he kept his own meanings intact. In this sense Goethe had the dignity and aloofness as well as the practical stoicism of some of the Plains Indians. His investment in a metaphysical love, in the divine woman, in order to validate his meanings, permitted him to be a thoroughly decent man among men.

But the option for the impossible had its weaknesses, and they are the weaknesses which are usually attributed to Goethe's character, even though the reasons for these weaknesses have never been clearly made out. In the first place, the innovator who reaches for a meta-physical love is attempting to draw all his support directly from it—in other words, from a source beyond the everyday social world. This tends to throw him back upon himself, draw him out of the social world. As Lucka understood so well, the unreal thirst for a metaphysical love leads to the fallacy that *the single person comes to stand for all mankind.* If he thinks that woman gives to man all that is highest and purest, satisfaction of the senses and the spirit, as well as friendship, then we can well understand that the true seeker for a metaphysical love would have little to spare for friendship (Lucka, 1922, p. 250). The relationship of Goethe and Schiller is instructive here. Goethe simply could not allow himself to need Schiller as much as Schiller needed and wanted him; Schiller often reproached him for his coldness, his reserve. It is obvious that Goethe had made another option, was drawing upon another source of sustenance. When I say that Goethe "could not allow himself to need Schiller," I mean it in two senses: in the first place, he actually did not need an intimate male friend as much as the friend needed him, because of his option for a metaphysical love. Schiller made no such option. In the second place, Goethe did not want to *share* in the creation of meanings, as Schiller seems to have wanted to do—Goethe wanted his own. If he allowed himself an equal relationship with Schiller, it would probably have threatened the autonomy of his own meanings.

On the face of it, this seems like an unjustified speculation: yet there is evidence from Goethe's whole life style that he was often protecting himself. Sometimes, indeed, it seems as though he was desperately trying to contain himself as a source of meaning, integral against the undermining of the world around him. And this would follow from his option: if a perfect metaphysical love on earth is an impossible thing, then one has to trim in other areas to keep one's creation of meaning intact. How else to explain the change in Goethe's personality after his return from Italy? Why did he become more stiff, more aloof, capable of remaining silent in a corner an entire evening, while Schiller bore the brunt of conversation with a group? The point is, I think, that before his departure for Italy Goethe's life was still brimming with meaning. He could still live the illusion of any young man, even at thirty-seven, that he could be and do anything he wanted—he could even create meaning as an artist, studying in Rome. But after two years in Italy the escapade was over and he returned to Weimar. No more innumerable life paths available, no more boundless horizon, no more protean promise. This must have meant a serious curtailing of the possibilities he felt of being a free and autonomous source of meaning. The number of life paths—which before the trip to Italy were boundless in fantasy— were now reduced to the earlier one of living and working as a poet and *Geheimrath* in Weimar. In other words, I think we can say that since Goethe could no longer *be* a free source of boundless meaning, then he had to fall back on studied dramatic talents: he had to *perform* more carefully as a deep and unique genius. One way of doing this is by long silences; another by being an intellectual inquisitor of travelers, probing each one about what they have seen and what they know; a still more forceful way is by obliging people to be punctiliously clear and subtle in their thought, and to dismiss them sharply when they are confused and cannot clarify one thing or another. Studied aloofness is the basic note in this kind of performance, projecting an aura of heavy meanings and interiority that do not condescend to be drawn out into the everyday world. Hence the cold chill that he threw over admirers who came to behold him from afar. One must not communicate his deep wisdom, said Goethe, but must let it radiate out from his person. After returning from Italy, a changed Goethe had emerged—and the change was very noticeable in its unreal stiffness and reserve.

What was Goethe to do when life itself had shown that perfect freedom was impossible, and the metaphysical love object would still not reveal itself? The only possibility was to retrench on oneself, *try* to be an autonomous source of meaning. But one cannot feel himself to be such a source without the very validation that Goethe sought: the fantasy of freedom, the fantasy of support by the perfectly incarnated sublime spirit. The lesson became more clear at thirty-nine, and it was presumably at that time that Goethe must have had to rely on stage props, as it were, to support his self-conviction.

Yet we know that, for the symbolic animal, to perform is a considerable part of to be. As Simmel, and more recently Burke (1945; 1950), Duncan (1953; 1962), and Erving Goffman (1953; 1961), have intricately shown, man *plays* at society, plays at being man. To perform the part in the social role is almost equivalent to being the very thing one plays. It is only in this sense that we can understand the megalomania of the courageous innovator, or the unnatural stiffness of the later Goethe. The performance itself lends credulity and conviction to what one would like to be. It is an effort to create some kind of esthetic continuity in the surrounding world. If one creates a total performance in which all the elements are esthetically congruent, then the conviction will follow. If one plays at being a great man, and others perform the correspondingly obsequious roles, then one is very close to the kind of esthetic monopoly of one's own meanings that the conceptual sadist seeks. One demands, by one's very performance style, that all surrounding objects recognize one's claim. One obliges them to bear the burden of the very conviction one is seeking. If one believes that one's artistic vision is the most important thing in the world, then one must believe that what one is doing is the most important thing in the world; ergo, *what one is* is the most important thing in the world, and all surrounding objects must esthetically support this option. For man, integral role playing is a symbolic structure that can, by itself, carry an enormous brunt of meaning, provided it is integral. Hence, when Saint-Simon decided that he was the most important figure in post-Revolutionary Europe, he made an overture to Madame de Staël to become his mate and partner, since it was fitting, he said, for the most illustrious of each sex to belong to each other. But we miss the point totally when we ascribe this kind of conduct to some global and vague motive such as "egotism." On the contrary, the performance strivings often called megalomania are an attempt to lend credulity to one's world, and indirectly to one's whole being. But since it is, as I said, a kind of forced ordering of the performance of others, it is related to sadism. In this sense we can call Goethe somewhat sadistic, which is just what the sensitive and outgoing Schiller seems himself to have felt at times. Schiller, we can now see, was much the truer and freer person in Stendhal's sense: he was prepared to offer up to the world the spontaneous meanings that emerged from his action, whereas Goethe had to hold tight to what he already believed himself to be, or rather, hoped that he truly was.

The pull of the staging, on a purely symbolic level, easily becomes the grain of habit. The general performance style that Goethe developed, in order to create a world which reflected his own image of himself, seems partly to have degenerated, with age, into the merest symbolic tricks by means of which to assert his superiority over others. Thus, he could affirm that his life was more meaningful than another's by priding himself on longevity—as any Vermont Yankee might do. When one distinguished acquaintance died in his sixties, Goethe alluded to his weakness. He said that he admired Hume, among other things, for being eighty years old like himself. On another occasion, when someone remarked that Goethe's face bore the marks of life's vicissitudes, Goethe was quick to point out that his face bore the mark of hard work. The implication is that suffering vicissitudes is a passive task and basically without meaning; hard work is purposive. Goethe wanted his face, like Faust's final bid to the passing moment, to attest to the same thing: that human life becomes meaningful only when man's purpose is interwoven in the world of organisms and nature.

Goethe, then, was creating meaning as only the human organism can, by imposing his own categories on the world. The greatness of his life and the almost mythical model that he became for many of the youth of succeeding generations prove two things, it seems to me: in the first place, the tremendous richness of his poetic and literary work carried its own proof that man can indeed create his own meanings; in the second place, he affirmed that the man who performs in his interpersonal life as a locus of superordinate meaning becomes a source of conviction—a transference object—that others who are hungry for meaning need. Goethe's life, in other words, proves the strength of creativity, as well as the weakness of even the most gifted human animal: the inability to be personally secure in one's own meanings. Recent Goethe criticism, such as that of Ortega y Gasset (1956), reproaches Goethe with not having had the courage to make certain existential life choices, specifically, with having chosen to stay in the comfortable court at Weimar instead of engaging in the literary life of the young country, and leading a distinctive literary movement. This reproach is an echo of Emerson's earlier quip: "who ever heard of a poet living in a palace?"

What does Ortega's critical essay show, in the light of our suggestions about Goethe? Two things, I think: the first is that it is unfair to impose Ortega's categories on Goethe's life—this is a conceptual sadism of a sort. Yet Ortega's criticisms reveal a truth, or rather a true urge which we all have a right to feel, namely, the urge to use the great historical figure to permit succeeding generations of men to define and deepen their ideals. Thus Ortega's essay allows us to consider what we might call a middle line of approach to the historical genius, an approach that intelligent criticism might use: we can ask, of any innovator, what were the typical sources of sustenance upon which he leaned for his right to create meanings; and what was the life style that he built upon it? This does not allow us to say what he should have done, or should have become, for the simple reason that there is no *one* right choice; it is the unique organism in its own peculiar context that determines what shape a particular existence will take. The matter is complex beyond any possibility of outside prescription. But it does allow us to see where and why his personality failed to additionally enrich the world around him. By recognizing many of the aspects of man's urge to meaning and his ways of sustaining it, we give ourselves a clearer idea of the ideal. This is, then, a sort of character analysis on a superordinate level, that aims not to reduce its subject to our design, or to any particular striving "mechanism," but rather to help us further define our own ideals—as we will see in some detail in Part III.

In sum, then, we can say that Goethe resorted to ingenuity from within a certain kind of desperation, the desperation of an animal who must be sustained by the belief in his own overriding value. I would like to close this discussion with an example of ingenuity from a much more desperate personal situation—the famous controversy of Rousseau and Hume.

SOME OBSERVATIONS ON THE HUME-ROUSSEAU CONTROVERSY

Generations brought up in the habit of aborting the human understanding by forcing it into spurious psychiatric categories have called the aged Rousseau "paranoid." But this explains nothing. It only masks the complex human situation, conceals what man is really striving for, and what is at stake in each human life. The Hume-Rousseau controversy shows beautifully how necessary is the esthetic integrity of one's world in order to sustain the meaning that one projects. Rousseau, we may remember, was invited to England by Hume, as a respite from his harassment on the Continent. Hume found Rousseau a place to live, tried to get him pensions from the Crown and favors from his friends, and so on. For a while everything went nicely, but Rousseau's attitude changed unexplainably. Instead of seeking friendship and help, he began to suspect plotting and foul play; where Hume showed extreme kindness, Rousseau saw duplicity. He accused Hume's friends of plotting against him, and named Hume the arch plotter.

Of course, this completely abashed Hume and everyone else. It was utterly unsupported by facts, obviously unreal to the true situation; it was a bizarre figment of Rousseau's imagination, a "paranoid" delusion as we might want to call it. There is no way to explain this strange turnabout of Rousseau, this odd behavior in the face of such hospitality; no way, that is, unless we try to get at what Rousseau saw as *the proper esthetics* for his life meaning. When we read the documents of the case, which Hume was obliged to publish (1766) to give his side of what he considered a fantastic matter, we can see what was really troubling Jean-Jacques.

The most touching and revealing document in the whole case is Rousseau's letter to Hume (July 10, 1766), in which he lays bare his accusations. It is obvious from this letter that Rousseau began to feel cheapened by the obvious attempts to extend charity to him. Coupled with this, and much more to the heart of the matter, is that Rousseau felt himself being tolerated, even ignored. Hume was his only real patron in England; others ignored him, including the press. Rousseau's whole being-in-the-world at that time is summed up in a few lines in his letter ". . . dans le pays où vous m'avez conduit, & où, sans amis, je suis presque à votre merci" (pp. 109–110). Rousseau, after all, was one of the outstanding intellectual figures in Europe, not only in his own mind but also considered objectively. He had put forth, as we saw in the early chapters of this book, the basis for a theory of human alienation, and had offered the crucial conception for an ideal-typical science of man in society.

In other words, the esthetics that should have sustained such a creative innovation were utterly absent in Hume's England. No press, no attention, *not even* the persecution which would be a proper esthetic for one of the first men in modern history who declared war on society as a whole. Instead, Hume, although warm, seemed stoic and self-contained with his strange Anglo-Saxon manner; his long stares took the place of conversation. It is not difficult for us to explain Hume's manner, or Rousseau's isolation. How could two such original innovators, with such dissimilar orientations to the intellectual enterprise—how could they really exchange ideas? Besides, Rousseau's work was done; there was no way of translating it into action on the Continent, and certainly not in England. Rousseau was a curiosity, perhaps already an antiquity. It is easy to imagine that Hume's long stares and silences were probably meant to convey warmth and good fellowship, in the place of aimless conversation. The most Hume could do was to be "nice" to Rousseau, show him he respected his work. And this is precisely what Rousseau resented. It was thoroughly unesthetic, incongruous for the meanings that he needed to have sustained.

For example, Rousseau used to find a copy of *Héloise* on Hume's table every time he visited; it was obvious that Hume placed the book there, probably out of consideration. But Rousseau knew Hume could not have liked it, or certainly could not have been reading it continually. Consequently, the gesture seemed utterly condescending. It was all of a piece, however, with the frightfully unesthetic backdrop that England provided to such a great man. What to do? With ingenuity one could take the frightfully unesthetic backdrop, and, since it was already all of a piece, one could convert it into one, whole, esthetically integral panorama that would sustain one's accustomed image of himself and his coveted life meaning.

This is what Rousseau did: he reversed the significance of all the neutral events in his field and created once more a rich drama in which he was the center of significance. His whole world came alive, and it all pointed to him, and sustained the meaning of his work and life. In Hume's long stares he read secret plotting: this converted imagined bemusement and condescension into real consideration. Hume became someone who thought Rousseau worthy enough to machinate against, and not merely to be obsequious to (cf. pp. 63–66). Not only was Hume converted into a respectful enemy, but so were all his friends. The result was that Rousseau created a full range of objects, all performing in a new way: they were sustaining the esthetic vision he had of himself and his work; he was now an important personage in England. Thus Rousseau, like Goethe in another way, created a performance world that answered to his needs. The difference is that Rousseau's attempt was made *in his imagination* only, whereas Goethe's was carried through in the flesh of a full performance cast. And this is the whole difference that makes one performance "paranoid" and the other real. Goethe elicited the proper response from objects in his field for an esthetic ideal with which he was comfortable; Rousseau could only conjure up the response in his mind. Paranoia, then, refers to an asocial esthetics, simply because it conjures up a game that no one else is playing, or wants to play. In this sense we are correct to consider the paranoid vision as out of harmony with the everyday world. But my point is that it is an esthetic, and hardly a medical, problem. And the matter is even more complex than this.

Saint-Simon, for example, once wrote to his nephew Victor that he had attempted to make Victor mad because only madmen can do great things. Certainly only madmen can have their own peculiar visions and in this sense Saint-Simon saw truly; it is the visions that lead the rest on to new lives. But we must understand that when one is "mad" one is not exempt from the esthetic problem that all others share: the problem of making satisfied contact with a world that sustains our image of the real. Even worse, the true innovator has an aggravated problem. Since his vision is so daring and is unique, his esthetic needs are heightened, peculiarized. He needs to see a world around him which singles out his person and his vision as *things to be reckoned with,* truly extraordinary things. It is in this sense that we are justified in speaking of a normal megalomania, a justified paranoia, *a queerness that is esthetically integral and necessary.* In other words, if the truly radical innovator brings into the world a vision that cuts through cultural forms, and we grant the validity of that vision, then we must also grant the validity of a performance style that sustains that vision, an esthetics of the convincing which permits the innovator's life to be rounded and whole. We cannot fragment *Homo poeta.* This is how man must live.

In everyday life the same process is at work, but since the visions of the mass of men are thoroughly orthodox, their performance styles and the esthetics they demand are not strikingly apparent. Usually the demands follow the cultural prescriptions for the "right" thing to say or do, and if everyone hugs to the standard version of social performance, the tableau is convincing. The problem then becomes one of rigor for details, like delivering the lines properly and convincingly (cf. Goffman, 1953, 1961; Becker, 1962, chap. 8). This, of course, leads to a sadism of its own, even more pernicious than the conceptual sadism of the megalomanic innovator. It is the sadism of conformity, in which the marvelous human organism, in all its complexity and potential promise, is sacrificed to the plodding everyday drama of conviction. It is not even a sadism with the promise of liberation that the innovator offers. The categories for esthetic fitness are almost as arbitrary as the figments of fantasy of the wildest innovators; they vary from society to society in a great range of relativity—at least they have always done so in the past. Each culture dictates its own life-enchancing form, its own style for "living the ethnic dream." One can judge the inappropriate and unesthetic only from within the culture, because one knows what he will be comfortable with and the finest details to be alert for.

The value of foreign travel, of a "cross-cultural experience" lies precisely here. It defeats the sadism of conformity by showing that the forms of esthetics vary, while the human organism is always more or less the same. The result is that the observer then tends to value the human organism over the particular esthetic performance that is demanded; he sees the primary place of the organism, and the relative place of the proper lines that it delivers. Thus, he might come to be less willing to sacrifice the person to the particular style of training. This is the same kind of liberation from the artificial and constricting that should come with love: one comes to value the organism, the total personality of one's partner, rather than mere conformity to some one kind of performance style. One values the "thingness" of the marvelous organism over the artificial conventions. This is why foreigners often find couples well-mated, when the couples themselves find their own interpersonal lives unesthetic, unconvincing. The foreigner tends to see two well-assorted organisms. He does not see—as one or the other spouse may—that the proper performance is not being upheld. The point is that the foreigner doesn't need *that* particular esthetic in order to feel sustained, so that he can be less sadistic than those who grew up in the culture itself. In a recent film story, for example, an American mother with a somewhat mentally slow but attractive and childishly spontaneous daughter goes to live in Italy for a while. When the daughter and an upper-class Italian fall in love and want to marry, the mother is thrown into great moral perplexity. Should she be honest, and signal the daughter's lifelong lack of responsible maturity? She decides to remain mum, and allows the wedding to take place. She has opted, in other words, for the good of her daughter's organism over the performance categories which her culture imposed on it. And her decision proves correct: when the daughter stoops to eat the thrown wedding rice, the groom's family laughs and applauds; when the daughter talks jazz music and clothes, the groom's friends approve. The point is that, with all her childishness, she fit roughly into the young Italian version of a proper American esthetic, and since they didn't know what was appropriate in her own culture on the finer points of her performance, they could not be disappointed or undermined. In this sense the cross-cultural union was an exercise in Stendhalian freedom: the human organism came to be valued almost in its culture-free uniqueness; it came to be prized for what it could spontaneously offer of its own free energies. The task of love and of artistic liberation was freakishly fulfilled.[2]

In his plodding everyday life man is not so lucky: he stays usually within the strict confines of his world view. But it is important to stress, as I am attempting to do here, that much human misery, even—or especially—on the everyday level, is a problem in basic esthetics, in conviction. One can suspect that many cases of impotence or frigidity in marriage are fed by the fact that one's partner does not project enough meaning to sustain the plot. The partner may lack the depth of inner mystery, as well as the external command of cultural niceties. If one's partner is not worthy, one's world does not seem worthy—and this is the same as feeling that one is not oneself worthy, not fully alive, not fully human and dignified. In a word, not meaningful. The same problem covers other acts; for example, often suicide may be a way of simply ending an unconvincing drama; we can look at it as the salvage of a bad work of art, an unconvincing esthetic. Terms like "paranoia" and "hypochondria" refer to every-day tricks that man everywhere uses to make details of his life come alive; they are like splashes of red added to a pale canvas, to lend it significance. Elsewhere (1964a), I have called them "meaning-games" in order to show that they are not psychiatric categories, but rather esthetic or artistic ones. The meanest man must have his canvas, and it must be one that reflects, somehow, his own sense of signifi-cance in a world that is significant. Above all, it must be integral, unified, even if it should suffer from being pale. It may be that this is one reason that many college professors are so self-effacing: they live, after all, in a society that has always declared it can get along without them and has rewarded them proportionately to this sentiment. The intellectual has to play down his work, if only in order to make it esthetically integral with his life. If he thought that his intellectual contributions were great, but that the world consistently refused to recognize this, he would be in great artistic trouble. He might have to declare war on society, like Rousseau, or attempt suicide, like Saint-Simon. Perhaps the best solution, for the peaceful continuation of life, is to disclaim real merit.

We can conclude that in the world of *Homo poeta* every man must be his own artist, his own creator of convincing meaning, or at least a contributor of convincing meaning in the everyday plot that others have fashioned. We have sketched in this chapter many of the dif-ferent ways in which this can be done by resourceful individuals. Let us now go on and explore how societies have handled this prob-lem. If we have been able to give a theoretically rich picture of what man is after and why, we will want to know how society helps or hinders him in this striving. If we can put both parts of this picture together with sufficient depth and breadth, it will give us a theory of alienation of the scope that we have so long been searching for, a scope that is summed up in the promise of a "union of Marx and Freud."

CHAPTER TEN

HISTORICAL PSYCHOLOGY:
The Union of Marx and Freud

For, try as we may, we cannot get behind the appearance of things to reality. And the terrible reason may be that there is no reality in things apart from their experiences. . . . The true mystery of the world is the visible, not the invisible.

OSCAR WILDE

The union of Marx and Freud! Here is a promise that has been outstanding for almost half a century. And this is precisely what a mature historical psychology would be. It would answer the question of what makes man act differently in different historical epochs; and it would do this by calling into account the range of choices people have in a particular social context. It would accuse society of limiting human development, by showing the constrictions of the whole range of social institutions—from early child training to the workings of economics and jurisprudence. In this way, it would give the most comprehensive possible answer to the question "What makes people act the way they do?" It would do this by showing how the regularities of human psychology are affected by the accidental situations of history. It would show how man tries to be man in the social and historical conditions into which he is born. By using history to highlight psychological regularities, historical psychology would show why human conduct assumes particular forms in each epoch. Finally, but not least, it would be the consummate union of Marx and Freud because from the picture of the effects of historical accident on natural regularities we would draw the weightiest possible evidence for designing an ideal-typical image of man.

Let us then consider the problem of historical psychology from the point of view of some of the individuals who, in my opinion, have made outstanding contributions to it. We can then bring to bear upon their work some of the knowledge and insights that we detailed in the previous chapter. Although this will hardly give us anything near the comprehensiveness that a mature historical psychology would need, I believe that it goes a long way toward outlining the shape that such a psychology would assume. In view of the importance of a historical psychology, every possible contribution must be seized and exploited. The reason is that a mature, comprehensive historical psychology would be a full-field theory of human alienation.

THE HISTORICAL CREATION OF MEANING

We mentioned in the last chapter, briefly, that Johan Huizinga's *Homo ludens: A Study of the Play-Element in Culture* (1955) is a very important work. Perhaps now we are in a position to see that to call the work *Homo ludens* was really to do it an injustice because the title did not quite convey the deadly earnestness of man's symbolic "play-forms." (Parenthetically, this may account for some of the neglect and criticism the work has suffered.) What Huizinga was really talking about was *Homo poeta*, Man the Creator of Meaning; and "meaning-games" would be a much more apposite term than "play-forms" for the activity that characterizes the human animal. It conveys the utter necessity of this kind of action, and eliminates any tendency that the reader might have to consider meaning-games as incidental, casually playful, or even superfluous.

In the last chapter we talked about *Homo poeta* from an individual point of view; what I want to do now is to talk about the problem of creating meaning on the part of historical societies taken *as a whole*. And it is in this kind of discussion that Huizinga's work assumes its fullest importance. What he actually did was to show how man has created meaning in the various epochs of history; he presented what we might call "a panorama of the differential creation of meaning." He began with so-called primitive society, because there the process of the creation of meaning shines through so clearly in myth, art and ritual. He found the Middle Ages "extraordinarily great" in the play spirit; and finally he traced the decline of the play spirit after the eighteenth century. Huizinga lamented the fact that

in modern society man has lost the talent of genuine play, and has consequently lost the style and flavor as well as the true dignity of human
life. As Plato had seen long ago, with his superb insight into the true
nature of man—the gods are happiest when man plays (Huizinga, 1955,
p. 212). Huizinga saw that modern man, having lost genuine play,
has somehow estranged himself from his characteristic human activity. In his words:

> . . . if our modern puerilism were genuine play we ought to
> see civilization returning to the great archaic forms of
> recreation where ritual, style and dignity are in perfect
> unison. . . . More and more the sad conclusion forces
> itself upon us that the play element in culture has been
> on the wane ever since the 18th century, when it was in
> full flower (p. 206).

Huizinga's own favored epoch for the unison of the play-form
into a rich tapestry of life is archaic times. What did man actually *do*
with ritual that made archaic times and medieval chivalry so laud-
able? What do ritual, style, and dignity bring into the world? At this
point we need not trouble to answer the question—we already know
it. When man creates his own meaning he takes possession of the
world; when he does it recreatively, with style and dignity, he "stages
the dream" of human life as only it can be staged. He makes an
esthetically significant panorama out of a gray, neutral world. In ritual
the weighty sounds resonate through the head, music pierces the still
air; with his measured body movements, in the ritual dance or pro-
cession, man takes command of space, makes a humanly meaningful
unity out of it—claims it for man; banners, colors, flames flood the
world, and add to nature what she only sparingly gives: symbolic
significance. Ritual creates a dream world that raises life to the
highest pitch and intensity, and we have seen why this is so: because
shared dramatic meaning is man's perception and enactment of the
holy. To the natural mystery of quiet nature, with its strange neutrality, man adds his own mystery, which stems from his unique
abilities to manipulate symbols and things.

Furthermore, the individual who is performing the ritual builds
his whole organism solidly into the world, uniting it entirely with the
socially agreed cultural form. All the separate and fragmentary aspects of everyday experiences are fused into one esthetic whole, as
body and symbols partake together of an integral life. The effect is to
intensify individuality, rather than disperse it in part meanings. Man's

existence is quickened both organismically and symbolically, as it can be in no other way. The feelings of the pulsating organism carry their own conviction that symbols alone cannot give. In ritual man converts flesh and blood into symbols, and grounds airy symbols in flesh and blood. This is the total organismic character of the esthetic merger, which pulls the disparate aspects of experience together. It allows man to be consummately individual and fully social at the very same time. It is not enough for man to transact with symbols alone, and if he transacts with flesh alone he is not man. The esthetic merger of ritual puts man into the world on his terms: he changes from a passive plaything of fate to someone who creates a world of meaning. Thus we see how ritual, even though it builds man into the world, also liberates him: when he actively creates his own meanings he rises above both the animal condition and the passive condition of an everyday role participant in culture. Pavlov, in a farewell address to his students, wished them the highest joy that he had found in science: getting his hands dirty while doing cerebral work. In other words, a total organismic integration that is at the same time creative and liberating.

As the epigraph to this chapter so well puts it, what fascinates man is the awesome mystery of life as he lives it and experiences it. To "stage the dream," then, is to *create life* because one creates more visible nature; to "live the dream" is to partake of the richer life that one has staged. Man's life is composed of the trivia of appearances, but archaic and medieval man knew how to turn this to account, namely, by maximizing appearances, and so expanding life. If words, colors, and forms mingle with human effort and emotion, and offer man his peculiar world, then so be it: the task is to revel in it. Let us recall Stendhal's words, "The amenity I desired was the pure joy of Shakespeare in his comedies, the charm that reigned at the court of the exiled duke in the forest of Arden." Modern man, already in Shakespeare's as well as in Stendhal's time, thus had to yearn hopelessly for the pure joy and the amenities which every primitive claims as his daily bread, and which medieval knights took as a matter of course. In the Middle Ages, for example, mealtime too was a great ritual, with trumpets, music—a celebration of food, a celebration of "man eating." The white-powdered wig that went out of style after the eighteenth century was not an "idle custom." It was a pure play-form that allowed man to give to his person an added dignified and dramatic attention, as British law courts still do today; and to give to the world a continual drama of personages on stage. All of life was a theatre, a theatre for which a free soul like Stendhal's could pine.

Huizinga, like Simmel earlier, saw that all of society is a game which man *plays*. But again, it must be stressed that we miss something in his lament over the wane of the play-form if we treat the matter lightly. We miss the whole spirit and the terrible criticism it implies if we say merely that ritual and style have left the world. Huizinga himself was very clear about the significance of his thesis, and did not intend to treat the matter as a mere loss of "fun," "good times," or childish delight. The wig was a serious affair. It must be emphasized that the game of society "is the living principle of all civilization," and that "in the absence of the play-spirit civilization is impossible" (Huizinga, 1955, pp. 100–101).

What, then, has gone out of Western culture if ritual is such a serious business? We can see that the answer is even more serious and portentous: *modern man has lost the possibility of the intensive social creation of life meaning.* Unless we understand this, we will not be able to come to grips with historical psychology, and with the heavy and urgent intelligence it holds for a science of man. Huizinga came to grips with it, but he somehow failed sufficiently to communicate the gravity of his discovery. It is up to present-day scientists to underscore this, to give it its fullest possible weight. Man is the meaning-creating animal, and when he is not this he is not much more than an animal; simply because the world is not his unless he stages it. But surely man has been creating meaning since the decline of the rich play-forms of the eighteenth century? Of course he has—in one way or another—and the central problem of a historical psychology is precisely here. In the absence of a strong tradition of socially created meaning, of rich forms that bind people together in the celebration of life, in the absence of such a unity of life and ritual, what does man fall back on? Where does he find his world and his own sense of significance and dignity? What happens to the human spirit, in sum, when society fails to provide for and promote a rich esthetic of life meaning? This is the question that we shall want to examine in these pages. Let us then come to grips with the historical problem.

What was there about the Middle Ages, specifically about chivalry, that Huizinga thought "extraordinarily great"? It was, simply, that chivalry embodied the perfect play-form, the perfect "meaning-game," by which man creates a world of the real in his image.

In other words, what chivalry did was to carry over into the growingly diffuse medieval society the pure meaning creation of primitive culture. Even though the birth of knighthood as a class arose from the development of the feudal system, the origins of knighthood lay in the sacral customs of primitive culture. The knights as a class still lived the rich and esthetic life of the integral and spontaneous primitive man. As Huizinga says:

> The three most momentous elements of chivalric life—consecration as a knight, the tournament, and the vow—stem directly from age-old sacral rites. . . . Even in its first development as an actual way of life, in the twelfth century, chivalry displayed the characteristics of a renascence, a conscious revival of a romantic past (1959, pp. 86–87).

And the romantic, as always, was an attempt to recenter action on the free, creative springs of the human personality. Furthermore, chivalry shared one basic thing with primitive life almost everywhere: it had a social conscience, it was altruistic—it stressed the duty of man to other men, the virtue of selflessness, the strong bonds of brotherhood. Thus, the dream that chivalry created was not a private holiness, it was always potentially a communal one. The ritual of chivalry was religious in the broadest sense, which is why the chivalric conception of life, its devotion and altruism, was always closely related to religion (Huizinga, 1959, p. 87). Chivalry carried over the best of primitive society: it was, so to speak, partly an attempt at a planned world view that tried to embrace men in a meaningful community, in which rights and duties were balanced.

In rapidly changing, growingly anarchic medieval society, chivalry could obviously be little more than a holding action, utterly unrealistic to the currents of the time. Cervantes could caricature chivalry because it was fair game—it was doomed to fail. It was a mere form that, as Huizinga so well said, constantly ran empty. It tried to realize itself in the world, and succeeded only in showing how utterly false it was. "An unheard-of amount of dissimulation was needed to maintain the fiction of the chivalric ideal in actual life" (1959, p. 89). Huizinga goes so far as to say that those who upheld the chivalric ideal were aware of its falsity. But falsity is relative to reality, and not to the dream. The recurrent renascence of ideals like the bucolic and the chivalric, attest to man's groping for a better vision, an attempt to deprive life of its meanness. If the medieval synthesis was absent, if its fabled collectivism is an exaggeration, the social vision was not. With the decline of chivalry even the dream of the Middle Ages came to an end. Socially, it was succeeded by an epoch of decline, which we call the Renaissance.

The problem of the nature of the Renaissance is a complex and continuing one, and I am hardly qualified to add anything to the outstanding scholarship on it. But, from the point of view of a science of man, I think it is important to stress the negative as well as the positive side of the Renaissance. Burckhardt, more than anyone else, provided an argument for those who would see the Renaissance as the epoch of the true liberation of the human personality, out of the constrictions, collectivism, and superstitions of an earlier time. But the other side of the picture is quite different, and it is precisely the one that a science of man in society should be interested in. In the social realm there was a great difference between the Renaissance and the earlier time, a difference equally as important as the individualism which the new epoch threw to the fore. I mean of course the attempt at social altruism, the ideal of mutual support, the very idea of the "fabric" of a society—all these declined seriously. Whereas the Middle Ages knew "true service and true fealty of man to man" (Huizinga, 1959, p. 285), the Renaissance really represented a stagnation of these sentiments. The Middle Ages had a religiously based social awareness that the Renaissance lost.

Looked at in one way, in Burckhardt's way, the Renaissance represents a brilliant flourishing of the individualistic current that was only nascent in the earlier epoch. In this sense the Renaissance seems to represent a true "revival" of the human spirit, an "awakening" of man. Looked at in another way, the Renaissance represents precisely the further development of those forces which had already made the chivalric ideal impossible and unreal in the Middle Ages. The Renaissance was less a "revival" than it was a "heightening" of currents already well under way—the development of uncontrolled forces: individualism, the complete undermining of any possibility of altruism and community, the fragmentation of art from a social into a personal joy, from a public into a private commodity.

For these reasons, scholars have contrasted the Reformation and the Renaissance, and have seen in the Reformation an intensification of the medieval spirit, a mass movement with roots in the old society, and with puritan intent (Huizinga, 1959, p. 270). The Renaissance, on the other hand, sought its beauty and purity in the ideals of Antiquity. As we would expect, the best minds of the time, a Petrarch, an Erasmus, saw the Renaissance and the new Humanism as an opportunity to go beyond the old, while keeping the best that traditional society had to offer. They saw, in other words, the possibility of a Christian society that would be a true community, that would unite Antiquity and the Christian spirit (Huizinga, 1957, p. 103). But these were the visionaries whom history, as always, swamped.

With this contrast of the Renaissance and the Reformation, it was possible for scholars to criticize even the much-lauded Humanism of the time: it would be little more than literary snobbism, preciosity, an alienation from the full current of the Middle Ages flowering (Huizinga, 1959, p. 266). Someone like the art historian Carl Neumann, for example, could criticize Humanism for reaching back to Antiquity, and could see this reaching back as the reason why the Renaissance failed to develop its own unified and distinctive civilization. He saw the main upsurge of the human spirit in the development of the Middle Ages: it was there that the feeling for the human personality, for nature and for the world, was already perfectly enshrined in the vision of Dante. Compared to this, who were these new Humanists after all? For the most part, organization men, climbing uncritically in the everyday business of life, using their world to further their own tastes and ambitions. They were the minority culture, to use sociological jargon, developing what meaning they could, in default of the rest of the society. They were hardly revolutionaries inspired by a guiding higher ideal, and intent on helping everyone approximate it. A skeptic like Montaigne could see through the spurious blend of culture that the Humanists had fashioned.

In sum, then, it was this great failure that is the "other side" of the problem of the Renaissance, and the one that troubles the social scientist interested in a critical vision of society. There was no new and broader, integral culture, such as Petrarch and Erasmus envisioned, a culture with its own ideal-types, its own poetic expression, its sense of social solidarity; in a word, a unitary culture that would celebrate itself on the broadest possible basis, generate its own authentic life meaning, develop its own unique forms. Instead, the Renaissance was already celebrating private gain—something the Middle Ages had fought against. The great cities of Renaissance Italy were merchant cities, and the public statuary feted the power in the service of capital, as Verrocchio's Condottiere equestrian so eloquently testifies. The Church could be revived as a central social institution in form, but not in the spirit that characterized the previous age. And the public life that grew out of all this was very much like the ancient Rome that the Renaissance tried to ape: it was a public life offered *to* the people, and not created with them.

THE SOCIAL CREATION OF MEANING: THE ESSENTIAL THESIS OF POSITIVISM

We are now in a position to understand why the problem of the Middle Ages has troubled the social scientist right from the beginning of social science. We are also in a position to understand that if the problem of the Middle Ages has ceased to trouble present-day sociology it is because that sociology has lost contact with its own vital tradition. We should not be surprised, then, that scholarship in the science of man for over a half century has failed to come to grips with what is most central and lasting in the work of Auguste Comte. I mean, of course, his historical psychology, and the social criticism and social prescriptions based on it. Not only has the essential Comte been missed, but he has been vilified for precisely that which is best in his system, and which needs to be revived.

Comte was very clear in his own mind about the central problem of *Homo ludens* or *Homo poeta* a full century before Huizinga. Vico had begun the tradition by taking a historical view of culture, but it was Comte who elevated this view to the level of Enlightenment science, and instrumented it by using it as a basis for social criticism. Since modern scholarship has missed what is central in Comte, it naturally had to misinterpret some of Comte's preferences and prescriptions. For example, for Comte, as for Huizinga, the Middle Ages were extraordinarily great in the social creation of esthetic meaning. Comte criticized the Enlightenment rationalists for wholly overlooking the importance of the attempted medieval synthesis; thus he could appreciate the opinions on this matter of reactionaries such as de Maistre and de Bonald. Now, Comte's option for a reassessment of the Middle Ages did not stem from his alliance with the more narrow reactionism of these post-Revolutionary nostalgists. Rather, it stemmed from his unique and peculiar understanding of the fundamental characteristic of *Homo poeta*—the need for rich, variegated, unitary esthetic meaning. Thus, Comte devoted an important place to art in his system, and he even shocked some of his narrow positivist disciples and admirers by saying that scientific discovery should be held in check if it interferes with social harmony. To them it was obvious that Comte had gone mad. But, in terms of Comte's own insights, scientific discovery is only a fragment of esthetic meaning; if it damages the whole social fabric of meaningfulness, then it is useless and even dangerous. I do not mean to play down the conservative aspects of Comte's system—they are real enough; but I do think that much of Comte's devaluation of individualism and dislike of anarchy have been misinterpreted as conservatism and timidity, when actually they stem logically, in part at least, from his recognition of what is most important for *Homo poeta*.

For instance, when Comte made the statement, over a century before C. Wright Mills, that private troubles depend on public issues, he was declaring that, for man, personal needs can be undermined by the lack of social attention to man's characteristic strivings. And when he said, long before Alfred Adler, that social interest should precede personal interest, he was not aiming to sacrifice individual liberty to the dogmatic perpetuation of conservative social forms and imposed order. Instead, very much like Adler, he was sketching an ideal of human character, a model on which man seems to thrive best, and to contribute most. Social interest, for Comte as for Adler, draws on love and knowledge, and not on blind self-abnegation. Social interest describes the free, whole man striving to make a distinctive contribution by joining his meanings to the larger fund of social meanings. It does not describe modern grab-bag man, who imagines that he is free because he can hoard, or twist shallow meanings to suit his caprice. Much of Comte that resembles conservatism, then, and that echoes the conservative complaint, was based on an ideal of man which drew on a rather sophisticated historical psychology. It did not draw on a mere nostalgia for order and for the *Ancien Régime*. If history reveals one thing it is that the poetic has primacy over the scientific—something which Comte repeated again and again; it is just another way of saying that total, unitary meanings have primacy over partial, fragmented meanings. And this is what Comte saw—a thesis that later thinkers like Royce and Hocking developed with keen psychological insight.

Thus, I have paused on the problem of the Renaissance, as seen by recent scholarship, in order to give support to the clarity of Comte's insight, and to affirm his realism. By now it is widely agreed that one reads history for what one wants to find, and the "correctness" of one's reading depends at least partly on one's "purpose," and must therefore be fairly judged on that basis. The perception of historical fact, like the perception of sense data in the external world, is partly a matter of what the organism can organize and wants to organize. Judged by Comte's purpose, then, his reading of the Renaissance as a loss of medieval integrity, as a decline, is eminently defensible.

Like Huizinga, Comte's reading of history was an attempt to trace the "differential creation of meanings." Specifically, Comte wanted to show that social life had steadily become impoverished since the Middle Ages, and he too used medieval chivalry as one strong argument. And, like Neumann, Comte would not accept the Renaissance as a historical-psychological model for the good social life. For Comte, the Renaissance represented a *degenerated* Middle Ages, and not the true flowering of the human personality. Thus, he was not in error to use art as a clue to some kind of medieval synthesis, and to lament its fragmentation from public life at the Renaissance. And he was hardly wrong about the change in the over-all spirit of the time, and the fact that art no longer reflected any central ideals which might bind the whole society together. It was the same thing that Herder had seen earlier, when he urged the Germans to keep the primitive unity of art and culture (Clark, 1955, p. 253). Since the Renaissance, of course, the process of the divorce of art and life has accelerated, until today we have precious little public or private plastic art, worthy of the name. Collingwood very nicely summed up this problem in its historical context (1924, pp. 15–38). Comte could have forecast the complete *reductio ad absurdum* of visual art in our time. He already saw that Renaissance art, although techni-cally superior to that of the Middle Ages, was in fact inferior from a social point of view, simply because it was less socially relevant. It became gradually an art of private acquisition, in which the artist performed talented feats for isolated individuals. Fortunately, in our time, the artist has nowhere to turn but to the celebration of social meanings. The personalization of art has combined with the deperson-alization of taste, to utterly deprive him of any meaningful public. He now paints for himself or for money, and this is a condition which he cannot tolerate for long.

Comte anticipated Neumann, then, by making a sharp criticism of the Renaissance, and of its reaching back for classical ideals, and he made this criticism for much the same reasons as Neumann. Besides, Comte gave Antiquity very short shrift largely because it looked backward to a lost Golden Age rather than forward to the perfection of man and human progress. As we saw in Chapter Three, Comte wanted a new society, a society that would worship humanity and would be predicated on love. It would be a rational society, guided by the findings of science. But science would not lead the society—much to the displeasure of Comte's narrow positivist disciples. Rather, art would lead it. What did Comte mean by this? Again, it would be impossible to overstress the clarity of Comte's insight, and the realism on which it is based.

For Comte, the fundamental motivating idea of a science of man in society is the idea of progress, a relatively new idea that came again late in human history; its birth really marked the beginning of the Enlightenment, and it was the Enlightenment that began, as we stressed earlier, the true modern Athenian Celebration of Man. Thus, if there are lines to be drawn between the Middle Ages, the Renaissance, and the Enlightenment, they must be drawn between the latter two. Comte appreciated this, but he appreciated one thing more, that only became clear *after* the French Revolution, namely, that the idea of progress *is a total social problem* and not merely a matter of "doing" more science, or investing in narrow coteries of brains that would bring the rationalist millennium. In other words, Comte's narrow positivist disciples had already in the nineteenth century forgotten the lesson of the Revolution, and reverted back naïvely to a trusting rationalism, somehow divorced from the problem of total social reconstruction. When Comte talked about "art," "Religion of Humanity," and "love," they imagined that he had abandoned science. But, as we saw in Chapter Three, Comte never gave his whole allegiance to the leadership of science. In this he was the true disciple of Saint-Simon. Science was merely an aid to the new society and had its crucial place—but it was only a place. Science had not shown either that it was prepared to solve the problem of social reconstruction or that it could solve it. Comte knew that it could not.

The point was that the idea of progress was not a narrowly scientific problem—we still make this fundamental error today, imagining that it is. This is of course why we cannot understand that even with atomic physics and relativity theory we do not have the good life. We pour literally billions of dollars into scientific research and cannot understand that no laboratory team has come up with the formula for the good life. Yet we continue to hope. Part of the reason for the continued naïve hope is that we *want* science to take on the burden, and thus as citizens we can postpone coming to grips with the real issue of total social reconstruction.

The idea of progress, as we saw early in this book, does not and cannot stand alone. It is part of an inseparable triad composed of progress, liberty, and the ideal-type. Now liberty and the ideal-type are social and political problems, and not narrowly scientific ones—at least science has always refrained from pronouncing on them, except perhaps on liberty, when there was a question as to freedom to do research. Comte saw that the idea of progress was inseparable from an ideal-typology. He also saw that science would have to help design an ideal-typology, by showing the dependence of private troubles on public issues. Again, the same task as that begun by Rousseau, as we saw in detail in the earlier chapters. But Comte also saw that the ideal designed by man would and should be an ideal for the whole society. Thus, it would have to be a design for the continually better life, for more and more improvement, in a word, for Utopias. Comte understood further that the task of designing an ideal-type could never be finished because progress could never be finished—there would always be something greater and better to do and to strive for. Science, therefore, could never design once and for all an ideal-type; it could only give continuous and cumulative information on the constrictions on human happiness, and so help man gradually to liberate himself on the road to an ever-renewed ideal. Comte wanted the continued proposal of Utopias, but proposals guided and corrected at all times by scientific knowledge.

Comte's understanding of the problem of progress and the ideal-type is so clear and dispassionate that one cannot read it today without a thrill. The thrill, I think, is that we see the correctness of his vision, and are capable of bringing over a century of knowledge to its support, and thus substantiating it as could never have been done in Comte's time. In other words, as we have seen throughout these pages, we are at last bringing a full-field theory of alienation to bear on the problem of the ideal-type. And we also have gained the immense clarification of the nineteenth century on the subordination of science to the furtherance of life, of human spontaneity and being. Comte obviously knew these things, as his writings witness, and so he offered a system in advance of the kind of knowledge that alone can make it convincing. It has taken us a long time, and will undoubtedly take still longer, to accept the union of the idea of progress with the ideal-type. It will take us a long time to realize that the task of science is subsidiary to man's main job of opting for progress and ideals. We very early seized upon Comte as the champion of positivism, and then spent over a hundred years finding out that positivism, as we have understood it, is a narrow, restricting doctrine that does not even reflect the true tentative nature of scientific activity. If we had *read* Comte, instead of following our own hopeful interpretations of him, we would have known that he understood Positivism with a capital "P"—as a system of social reconstruction aiming to promote the worship of humanity, based on love, dedicated to ideals and progress. This cannot be repeated too often. Positivist science, as he understood it, was a branch of Positivism. It took care to outline the *main adaptational problems,* the problems that would have to be delineated in order for mankind to move ahead under its own guiding power. Also, Comte knew that these problems could *never* be sharply delineated even by science; science was relative to human perception and purpose; it could never pursue the "true" in the absence of some kind of concentration on the well-being of humanity. Science, in sum, would have to be kept relative, if the truth was relative; and it would have to be kept relative to larger concerns like the Good and the Beautiful. These, under Positivism, would be the main concerns of man in society.

Thus there is no mystery as to why Comte placed art over science in his system. The generating impulse for society would be the projections of Utopias, of ideal-types, toward which to direct progress. If science only helps this process, by delineating adaptational problems, then art has the main job of *idealizing* the projected ideal-type. Art serves the fully synthetic function, which science must forfeit by default, since it is not and cannot be a total synthetic activity. Art rallies feeling, and enjoins the option *to the ideal-typical Utopia* that leads the whole society on. Art leads, science helps. Art rallies the whole man in the service of human advancement; science merely helps adjust the progress.

Comte's vision was actually an adumbrated synthesis of idealistic esthetic theory, and a social-critical science of man in society. He understood that what the individual needed was a unitary, synthetic, superordinate meaning; and he harnessed the findings of science to help design that meaning by offering the controlling knowledge for a rational ideal-typology. Thus each individual could achieve the esthetic integration that he needed—he could find a real world to answer to his powers; but he could do this on a public, instead of a narrow private basis: he could share in the ideal vision that animated the whole society. Comte, by recognizing the need for a fabric of meaning as the primary need, rather than the urge to "scientific truth" as narrowly understood, offered what we have always been seeking, namely, the union of science and art, of philosophy and poetry (cf. Collingwood, 1924). But he was realistic about this union; he saw that it could come only from *within* a framework of an ideal-typical science of man in society. It was not to be had, as we naïvely imagine today, by "better communication" between scientists and artists— whatever that may mean. We suddenly have "discovered" that there is a problem of "two cultures"—in other words, we have discovered the problem that has been with us for several centuries. But we phrase it from within our limited social and historical perspective, and so, as usual, we propose feeble solutions like "better communication" and "more college courses"—measures that do not begin to envisage the problem.

Today we can recognize that Comte probed into historical psychology with a profound understanding. He saw clearly what each epoch had accomplished, where it had failed, and what remained to be done. He could appreciate the subordination of the empirical to the Good and the Beautiful in medieval times, without carping about the superstition and the backwardness of science. He could signal the failure of the Renaissance to elevate a social vision of the Good and the Beautiful, even though that epoch had begun the march of modern science. He could criticize Antiquity for looking backward in time for the Good and the Beautiful, instead of using them as guides for building a new future. Finally, he could bitterly condemn the early Enlightenment for investing everything in science and erroneously supposing that science subsumed or contained in itself the Good and the Beautiful. Comte could thus judge every epoch by whether it catered to what man needed most. Did society celebrate man, nature; did it give to its members a unitary, critical world view; did it include the individual as part of the momentous panorama of forward-moving mankind; did it use rational knowledge to dispel self-defeating beliefs; did it, in sum, use all of these or any of these means of giving man a full and rich, dignified life?

If we had to sum up what Comte was aiming for, we could say that he wanted nothing less than the "institutionalization of meaning creativity." But he wanted it, not as primitive tribes or the Middle Ages had it, but rather on as much of a scientific basis as possible. Thus, in pleading for a high place for art, he did not want to "live the dream" on the model of the Middle Ages. He saw that chivalry—the striking embodiment of man's creation of earthly meaning—stood by itself over and against Catholicism. Medieval theology looked to the other world, which is another way of saying that it looked to self-interested rewards for abnegation in this world, whereas chivalry looked to this world, exercised its ritual and its altruism as part of a life code, and not an afterlife one (Comte, 1848, pp. 284, 286). Social sympathy, fealty, the creation of rich present meaning, did not need the Catholic apologia. In fact, it was actually hindered by it, by splitting man's meanings between two worlds, two different systems of rewards.

Comte, then, wanted the new society to have the worship of love, and women, and social fealty, but without the theological superstructure; for not only did this superstructure undermine them by splitting them between two worlds, but in the case of fealty it actually rewarded the selfishness of seeking personal salvation. Feuerbach put forth a similar argument in Germany at the very same time as Comte wrote (1841). The humanistic society that both Positivism and Feuerbach envisaged did not want or need otherworldly support because it offered its own distinctive ideal-type, an ideal-type partly designed by science, not superstition; one facing into this world and not turned toward the other. Thus it would be an ideal-type that *liberated* man, even as it gave him rich meanings, and not one that shackled him *in exchange for* these meanings, as did the medieval ideal-type. In this sense, Comte (and Feuerbach) sought something similar to what Erasmus sought, a union of the humanism of Antiquity with the altruism of Christianity, a union that would proceed on clear knowledge and not superstition. The ritual of the new Religion of Humanity, like the Christianity of Erasmus, would be devoid of ignorance, of hollow automatism; because it rested on reason and on this-worldly cares, it would be infused with a dignity greater than anything that the Church had been able to offer. The critics of Positivism at the time—such as Spencer and Huxley—could not have been more right when they called it Catholicism minus Christianity (Simon, 1963, p. 202). Only in their animus toward Catholicism they missed Positivism's whole content and spirit.

Finally, then, we can do no better than sum up in Comte's own words his vision of Positivism and his understanding of historical psychology:

> The regeneration of society will be incomplete until Art has been fully incorporated into the modern order. And to this result all our antecedents have been tending. To renew the esthetic movement so admirably begun in the Middle Ages . . . will form part of the great work which Positivism has undertaken, the completion and re-establishment of the Medieval structure upon a firmer intellectual basis (1848, p. 332).

With the help of intellect the full current of this esthetic movement can be released. With the help of science man can broaden the range and types of activities for the creation of meaning: we might say that he can stage a less compulsive dream. He need not be limited to death duels over the fetish handkerchiefs of ladies in the castle.

THE CREATION OF MEANING IN HISTORICAL PERSPECTIVE

Comte's great legacy to the modern world, then, was to teach us that we must look to history to trace the evolution of the human spirit: history is the record of the flowering of the human personality. It is also the legacy of other great figures—Vico, Herder, and Hegel. But the problem since their time has been, simply, how do we put such an ambition into scientific terms? How do we know when the human personality is flowering; how do we know the conditions of that flowering? If we accept the teaching of Comte, our aim becomes that of accusing society for the failure to provide for the rich social creation of life significance. But just what form does this accusation take? What kind of institutions or attitudes do we want society to develop?

These are the great questions that these thinkers did not solve, but only left us. Comte gave us many clues, as did Newman, Hegel, Carlyle, Ruskin, Arnold—a host of the best thinkers of the nineteenth century. And the rich source of their understanding was, as we said earlier, that they were able to focus specifically on the problem of a unified world view—the problem that was uppermost in the thought of the nineteenth century. They understood that one of the basic conditions for the development of the human spirit was that it possess a rich and unified structure of meaning. Hegel's work is especially suggestive here because he understood the matter so well in modern phenomenological terms. His analysis of *Oedipus Rex,* for example, is well worth studying today, especially after the psychoanalysts tried to make this tragedy their special preserve and so trivialized it almost completely. Hegel saw the matter far more clearly than they because he knew that what urges man on is the unity of meaning and the need to maximize that meaning. Thus, he could understand what Oedipus did that made his fate so tragic and noble. It was not that he punished himself for his guilt, as the psychoanalysts would have it. Rather, he created a unity out of his personality by assuming responsibility for acts that he was not really responsible for; in this way, his personal existence attained a grandeur and a supreme and willful meaningfulness (Hegel, 1920, vol. 1, pp. 252–253). He laid hold of the diverse fragments of his accidental fate and forged them into a whole—a fictional whole, it must be said—by assuming responsibility for them. Only thus does man rise above nature—by making its neutral and accidental panorama *meaningful in his own design.* It must be said again and again, for it shows how crucial the esthetic is to an understanding of man's striving. The Oedipus tragedy does not sum up the human condition as relentlessly determined by the fate of one's first five years—as the psychoanalysts have been wearily insisting for over a half century. Rather, it sums up the human condition as the *esthetic transcendence* of natural accident, of *indifferent* fate.

Hegel's whole philosophy of art is a philosophy of the ideal, by which we can understand that it is a philosophy of the counter-fiction, of the human creation of substantive meaning in a neutral world. It allowed Hegel to see that for man the creation of meaning is primary. Furthermore, it allowed him to offer some unique insights for a historical psychology. He saw that the important thing in the ideal (i.e., the creation of meaning) is its organic wholeness, its integrity and richness, the large area of spirit (i.e., personality) that it includes. And with this abstraction he could offer us insights that today we are able to fill out in more scientific terms than was possible then. For example, he could say that the joint family (as we now call it), produced a larger ideal substance than what we now call the nuclear family (1920, pp. 252–254). Simply stated, this means that when we group many individuals under a single ideal of mutual striving and interresponsibility, we thereby create a more dependable and broad reservoir of meaning for each individual in the group. Historically, the joint family was Comte's Religion of Humanity in miniature, especially in China, where God was in the background and the ancestors were worshiped at the ancestral shrine. With the historical change of the family in the modern Western world, we have trouble today understanding the great strengths of this intimacy, and with the breakup of traditional society we have almost completely forgotten the great benefits we have left behind. This is hardly the place to make an extended analysis of the problem of the joint family versus the nuclear one, in Hegelian terms. Nevertheless, we know that with the loss of the intimate communal structures the individual has been confined to ever-narrower segments of life meaning. And this is the problem that Hegel so well understood. In the joint structure, each person shared a responsibility for the acts of all the others. The family was treated as a legal individual, and all were punished for the crimes of one. Today this submersion of the individual into a corporate mass seems to us monstrous—and in a way it is. But it offered a possibility to the individual that most of us no longer have, namely, the obligation to forge an esthetic unity out of his own life, within a context of self-transcending meanings. Each one could be his own Oedipus, as it were, assuming the responsibility for the accidental happenings to all the other individuals in the family. Thus, also like Oedipus, each single existence embraced a broad spectrum of meaningfulness, took its nourishment from a larger interpersonal substance. The most obscure member of the family could draw on this broad canvas, with its many objects, its single ideal, its unity in the face of natural accident. What is the obscure individual to do today? What is the unobscure individual to do today, in his house on Malibu Beach, huddling close to his possessions, his very few objects, his disjointed splinter of the wider world? The Hegelian understanding is still very contemporary, as Josiah Royce tried to teach us in his important work *The Philosophy of Loyalty.* It is already a scientific guide to some of the basic problems of social reconstruction; but not only our legislators do not read it—neither do our social scientists.

And yet, with all our attention to the problems of class and sect, of social stratification, and in-groups and elites of all types, with all this attention, we have largely missed the essential that Hegel and Royce already understood: that the basic stimulus to group exclusiveness is that it signifies a protest against the impoverishment of meaning. The exclusive group stages its own ideal dream, which all members live in unison. It draws on the combined personalities of all its members, including ancestors with whom the group feels intimate ties. After all, why do Greeks seek to marry Greeks, and why do Jews turn up their noses at a Gentile wife? Largely because the outsider represents an immediate impoverishment in a joint drama. A bride from outside the group cannot contribute what one from inside the group could in terms of the value of her personality. If she has a rich personality, full of mystery, the mystery that she brings is a threat; it does not spring intimately from a shared past, from a similar ancestral pool of organismic meanings. Furthermore, her performance part spoils the "ethnic dream" that all would live. The creation of meaning is a staged drama: the right lines must be delivered, the proper conviction must be forthcoming. The outsider to, say, the Jewish in-group cannot quite appreciate the finer tones of good smoked salmon or an unusually good black bread from the new baker. The Greek who marries the Irish girl will simply not get the proper celebration of *feta, ouzo,* and cracked olives. Thus, not only is the ideal substance sapped by intruding a personality with alien allegiances and responsibilities, but also the everyday performance world is sapped. The thousand petty ways in which meaning is created daily are thrown into jeopardy. One does not hear the properly enthusiastic lines over the finer shades of food quality that draw one decisively into the world. Thus, for a Jew to say, "How can you live with a Gentile?" is really to say: "How can you stand forgoing the two things man needs most?" The first of these is, as we just said, a pool of substantive meaning drawing across generations and solidly between individuals, a pool which allows one to assume responsibility for a vast panorama of the human world, over and against meaningless nature; the second one is also indispensable for *Homo poeta*: the daily celebration of life, the trumpeting at the myriad petty aspects of reality that enhance life and make it livable. To marry out of one's group is to add a ghost to a living world. In traditional Japan the wife was formally adopted into the husband's family, a process by which she lost her family and merged with his—ancestors and all.

Western culture, then, has historically been diminishing the reservoir of meaning upon which the individual can draw. While we thought that the increasing individualism should make personal life richer and more meaningful, it has actually done the opposite. Both in range of objects and in richness of shared performance, modern man has been increasingly narrowed down. To stage the dream and live the dream, one must draw on many objects, be able to perform with some kind of supporting cast.

During the Middle Ages, almost the whole society joined in one great performance—the entire class structure was set up for it. Everyone in the society was significant for everyone else in some way. The serf had a place in the lord's drama, land had rights and duties, and so on—the whole picture is too well known to need repetition. We also know that the subjugated place of the lower classes was hardly enviable. Whether the synthesis was complete or not, whether the subjugation was based on power and tyranny, there was a general pool of meaning which spread in an interrelated way across the whole society—or most of it. This is the *"vue d'ensemble"* that Comte saw was lost. As in the caste society of India, it compensated for the exploitation. The generalized sense of responsibility gave to each individual a chance to place himself within the whole and to draw the feeling that his life was a unity comprising many objects and destinies.

Post-medieval society drifted apart into classes that no longer shared in any unitary responsibility. Only the upper classes could still stage a rich drama—even though it was one that was now wholly socially inverted. Modern industrial society weakened the class structure further, and tended to generalize the styles of performance between classes: in nineteenth-century Europe there was less difference between the nobility and the bourgeois; and in highly commercial industrial societies such as in the United States today, there is less difference between the vast white-collar and the upper classes, in terms of general performance styles, than ever before. Added to this is the phenomenon of the breakup of the joint family, and the increasing mobility and out-group marriage. Taken together, this represents a serious diminution in the possibilities of staging the dream, in the esthetic of life significance on which man can draw. Mass man, in one important sense in which this term has significance for a historical psychology, is man *who must contrive to celebrate life all alone.*

In his own very suggestive way Huizinga has traced this problem down through history, and has come to a similar conclusion. He has focused on the universal "agonistic rituals," as he calls them—the particular forms that each society has to provide for the derivation of self-value of each member. This is another way of talking about what we described in the last chapter: that each individual needs to feel that he is a locus of meaning in a meaningful world, and that he must actively create his dialogue with a sector of reality. Each man is his own artist, building himself into the world on the basis of his particular talents, seeing his powers reflected as he brings alive a convincing segment of reality. Each man develops what he needs by pitting himself against the world to prove his excellence; hence, the agonism. After all, the most persuasive way for an individual to carve out his own meaning is to prove that he can; and man can only prove things in contest with his fellows, in the demonstration of superior performance.

Now cultures have always provided for this demonstration of individual excellence in one way or another, and Huizinga has traced in anthropological fashion the various forms of agonistic ritual in societies across the span of history. In this way we could see very clearly the one fundamental process at work—we might call it the basic cultural process: namely, *the agreement by each society on the ways it will allow people to establish their own sense of value.*

In primitive societies one distinguished himself easily from others by excelling in certain skills that the community rewards: hunting, raiding, etc. In ancient Greece it was the athlete above all who had the social mandate to strut about; in Rome, the gladiators and the military leaders swaggered under the admiring popular gaze. At other times, but usually at lower levels of admiration, the artists, poets, scientists, and holy men were the people who distinguished themselves by the agonistic creation of their own special virtue.

All this is well enough known, but it raises a central problem for historical psychology: how can we try to promote what is necessary and good in the agonistic creation of meaning in a particular society without unleashing what is bad? Or, put another way: how can we use the liberating aspects of individual idiosyncrasy without falling prey to the accompanying sadism? To each society this same question

applies. How to promote the *most intense kind of agonistic* performance without allowing the society to become an anarchy or a playground for destructive talents—as the military was in Rome? How,
then, to control agonistic performance *without stifling* it in a broader
sadism of everyday habit? The whole problem of liberating individual
creativity versus ordered culture is summed up in these questions.
Intellectually, the problem is as old as Socrates in the West: to what
extent can society allow the innovator to offer up new meanings
opposed to the ongoing cultural forms?

To mention Socrates is really to sum up the whole problem. We
know that he was sentenced to death because he was disrupting the
uncritical social game being played in the Athens of his time. Or,
put in the terms of our analysis, we would say that when one does not
attempt to derive his meaning by playing according to the culturally
approved game, then one is in effect attacking that particular play-
form of meaning. Socrates was, in this real sense, an enemy of his
city-state, as the individualist almost always is.

To those who hold social order above divisive individualism,
Socrates may seem the archetype of the socially disruptive intellectual
innovator—as he was to Georges Sorel. Sorel was reacting to the
rampant individualism of the nineteenth century, but he knew what
was at stake in society. He understood the basic nature of *Homo
poeta*: it is not truth that man seeks, either in society or in the cor-
ridors of established science; what man really wants is joint ritual for
the creation of meaning. When any individual breaks into this ritual
with his own idiosyncratic preferences, he is upsetting the esthetics
that the group needs in order to declare its own value. Esthetics is
hardly a narrow matter of truth in any abstract sense: it is a matter
of total organismic integration into a segment of reality, upon which
there is common agreement. And groups—we need not remind ourselves—can be just as skewed in their esthetics as any individual:
once they agree that a particular kind of reality is desirable, they
develop the necessary skills and style that permit them to deal only
with that segment of reality. Woe to the individual who has other
ideas.

The only thing the executioners of Socrates did not see, and the
thing that the group will hardly ever allow itself to see, is that, in order
to survive in the world of continual change, it would do well to lend an
ear to the one who dreams up new kinds of adaptations. In fact, as
Bergson has argued in his *Two Sources of Morality*, the radical
innovator may be the very instrument of creative evolution itself.

In our time, as we painfully know, the problem of keeping the best aspects of agonism and discarding the worst has become equally a matter of our own survival. History has taught us that in periods of rapid social change man resorts to the worst forms of agonism—hollow self-display, material acquisitions, envious competition, war and hate. The problem is as old as the breakup of organized tribal societies. The thing that distinguished most tribal societies from historical ones is precisely that the agonism was kept under control and worked in a socially beneficial way. We might say that at the tribal level the creative energies of agonism found their best use. In this sense, primitive society was far more "rational" than historical, civilized ones, as some anthropologists have always argued (cf. Diamond, 1963, 1964). Primitives managed, for the most part, to allow the individual the relative freedom to celebrate his energies in a rich present; and they managed to combine this celebration with a strict code of social mutuality. *This* is an intelligent approach to the problem of agonism that the world has since lost. The Middle Ages tried vainly and half-heartedly to recapture some such formula. When the Middle Ages themselves declined, there was no longer any possibility of controlling man's urge to make himself a locus of primary meaning— even at the expense of society around him.

This is how we can understand Pascal's dilemmas at the time of the passing away of medieval society: how to educate children in a divisive world? Pascal could see that the mainspring of education was the individual's urge to self-value, that children had to be educated to seek glory and to envy, otherwise they *"tombent dans la nonchalance"* (Lovejoy, 1961, p. 245). But alas, in the now divisive society, when they are so educated, they resort to an agonism that is uncontrolled—to mere strutting appearances, to social disruptions based on greed and competitiveness. Pascal could only sigh over the problem, and utter what has come to be our modern existential lament: that man has ceased "to be" in any solid sense and, instead, seeks only to "appear." It was the same lament that was voiced in Lucretius' time, and Seneca's—in all historical periods where an integrated communal life no longer exists to offer a beneficial structure for natural individual strivings.

We get a good glimpse of the historical problem of agonism, by comparing the primitive potlatch with the civilized ones. It was again Huizinga who characterized Roman society as a huge potlatch, one that would surely shame the primitive prototypes in volume. In primitive society the potlatch is still partly embedded in an inte-

grated and reciprocal structure: it is part of the controlled creation
of meaning, which is broadly beneficial to the whole social group.
But at the time of Imperial Rome the Western world had long since
lost the integration that would be able to turn a potlatch into socially
beneficial ways: it could now only be an ostentatious form, without
real social content. Imperial Rome only hoped to institutionalize
firmly what the Republic had already accomplished: a society built
on slavery and private gain, sustained by domination, devoted to individual glory. Romans had to bolster their private potlatch with public
bread and circuses. They outdid themselves to divert the dispossessed
masses and to earn glory by the most conspicuous consumption—
ostensibly for the good of the state. The Colosseum was inaugurated
with the killing of five thousand wild animals in the first month. As one
reads Roman history it almost seems that the endless portrait heads
of favored citizens, which stuff our museums, were paid for in the
blood of proud lions and equally courageous men. It is enough to make
one wince at being oneself a higher primate—this sacrifice of so much
concrete, pulsating life for the vainglory of mostly nondescript primate
heads; heads, furthermore, which have so much trouble trying
themselves to partake of a concrete, pulsating life. It seems like an
ignoble barter, but it allows us to see what these potlatchers were
after—which is precisely what makes it seem ignoble. They were after
what higher primates need most, and what they will sacrifice almost
anything to get, namely, a sense of self-value, one that is constructed
out of symbolic acts, in place of one built in by instinctive neural
circuits that other animals have. What seems "antinatural" is a barter
of tangible flesh bathed in the mystery of blood, to feed a symbolic
self-inflation. It does not seem to be what nature "intended"—if we
can permit ourselves this unpardonable teleological musing. But it
does reflect some truth. Nature takes care of all the animals which
possess instinctive types of reactivity—the proof is that they are still
here in spite of the destructiveness of our peculiar needs. But nature
seems to have left the symbolic animal on his own—and it is precisely
the way *he* construes *his own* needs that wreaks such antinatural
havoc.

The Roman potlatch was followed by the medieval attempt to
inject social responsibility and altruism into a tyrannical feudal
communal society; but there was no real synthesis, and medieval
society was succeeded by the new Renaissance potlatch—and the royal
potlatches of the European monarchies; and finally by the great modern
potlatch of commercial-industrial consumer society (cf. Dorfman,

1934). This latter is close to being a mass potlatch in the original primitive communitarian sense of the idea. Has history proceeded in a cycle? Alas no, the resemblance is only formal and outward, in the pace and spread of the distribution. The modern mass potlatch tries desperately to capture the basic sense of human value that the primitive already enjoyed—and it fails. It fails, as I point out elsewhere (1964a; 1964b), because man's basic sense of self-value can be had only by *doing*, and not merely by *owning*. The modern mass potlatch is mechanical, sterile, unconnected to any integral fabric of transcending values.

But the potlatch shows us what man is after, and how he will use a certain technique to get it. The fact that he will use a similar technique through different historical epochs is itself instructive. Apologists for modern commercial society have been citing this outward historical similarity ever since Hobbes', Mandeville's and Adam Smith's time, to show that man's nature is fundamentally one of boasting and grasping, of owning at others' expense. And that consequently the state exists only to regulate a natural process. But actually the technique shows something much more subtle to students of agonistic rituals, namely, that man needs a feeling of self-value, gained somehow *in concert with his fellow man*. When the social context for the ordered and mutual regulation of self-value breaks down, then man uses *the one owning technique alone*. This is exactly what has been happening since the breakup of primitive society. Self-display has remained one of the major, recurrent devices available for the derivation of self-value. The economic mythology of the nineteenth century, still too alive in the West today, has been effectively punctured, after Marx, by anthropological studies which show that the historical tenacity of self-display in the West, coupled as it is with aggressive social competitiveness, is not a "natural" human trait. Many societies allow man to achieve his necessary sense of value by permitting him to excel in ways that are not destructively competitive. All of this, as we saw in the early part of this book—in noting Novicow's work and that of modern anthropology—is firmly a part of the history of a science of man. We might say that the basic agonistic encounter is Roycean, not Hobbesian: it reflects agreement by the community of man, not the elemental forces of individual egotism.[1]

And so we see that Huizinga's reflections indeed rejoin ours. Like Pascal, today we decry pride because it leads to the self-display of consumer man—perhaps the emptiest agonism of all historical

time, and certainly the loneliest. Need we wonder that modern man is
driven so eagerly to seek some kind of self-assertion in some kind of
community, in the shouting spectatorship of mass sports, the exchange
of batting averages, the daily gossip about national celebrities? And
need we add that this kind of "national unity of the grandstand" is
no unity at all? Modern mass man is like his dispossessed prototype
who watched combats in the Colosseum—but with many great differences: he has to work long hours at wearisome jobs, and does not get
free bread or the leisure to idle away his days playing dice in the shadow
of great public buildings (cf. Dorfman, 1934, pp. 431–432).

And, as we are witnessing today, he can also be drafted and
marched off to fight in wars that he is against, or does not even see the
need for. Society offers him these substitutes for some kind of group,
some kind of community; and, as we are learning, they are the most
dangerous substitutes of all. In addition to the unity of the spectatorship group, and the war group, there is the hate group, with its intense
unity and conviction: the KKK, the "black" and "white" power groups.
These are hardly socially creative agonistic groups, as we are discovering to our woe. When society does finally try to conjure up some
kind of creative unity to offer to its faithful, even-tempered citizen,
the best it seems able to offer is the unity of interconnecting freeways,
which he plies faithfully in the carapace provided by Detroit, in which
he straps his little nuclear family. And this substitute unity costs him
fifty thousand deaths of his loved ones per year; but he himself will
fight to the death to preserve it. Like all other animals, *Homo sapiens*
will defend his small segment of the world because it is the only one
he knows.

THE HISTORICAL CHANGE IN TIME PERSPECTIVE

As we sketch this picture of human need and historical circumstance,
one thing above all, I hope, is clear: that the task of historical psychol-
olgy is to teach man when his social world is crushing his spirit. As one
final perspective on this problem, we might mention the great change
that has come over Western society in its general attitude toward
lived time. There has been a shift in time perspective, a shift from a
focus on present happenings to future ones. It is part of the problem
of agonism and ritual, and the cumulative emptiness and impoverishment of life that we have been tracing. As we have seen in our discussion of ritual, the main thing it does is to intensify the *moment*
and celebrate *it*. Let us stress this one final time, because it is so

strange to our own lives. Ritual is a focus of all human symbolic and organismic energy in an attempt to extract the full, lived significance of the present moment. All time perspectives cross on the present; past and future find their completion in the "now," as ritual celebrates the total organismic-symbolic act. The whole organism is caught up in some kind of self-involving movements, which make of it the temporary center of all reality—whether the movement be a dance, a sacred gesture, a sip from a golden cup. The whole human universe is brought to bear in one moment of time—the universe as it is dreamed, imagined; and the universe as it is felt in the inner processes of the complex human organism. Ritual is a declaration of life in the present, a celebration of the only thing that life can celebrate: its own conscious existence.

Some cultures celebrate the moment more than others, and in different ways. When James Mark Baldwin remarked that French culture was more esthetic than American, he likely meant this, that French culture has traditionally been one that celebrated the present, by celebrating the virtues of good wine, food, and the qualities of female organisms. The expression *"goutez-moi ça"* does not translate very well, but it obviously includes the feeling that a morsel to be tasted is an interpersonal event, the significance of which is to be marked. In tasting a piece of choice lamb or a sip of good wine, one celebrates the moment, performs a rite that heightens life. One Frenchman literally "hangs" on the other's taste buds, waiting for the declaration that the present has been consummated. Americans are for the most part strangers to this play-form, and they are even often annoyed with the politeness ritual that exists in many cultures: it holds up business transactions by overly insisting on formal niceties. Even the "After you, Gaston" courtesy seems to be an unnecessary break in the pragmatic process of moving through doors.

But commercial-industrial man, having lost ritual, naturally misses the point of it, which is precisely to *celebrate* the *distinction* of an organism as it performs the simple business of *moving* through life. In his accent on "business," on getting things done so that other things can then be done and in the end profit can be made, modern man betrays what has happened to Western culture. There has been a shift from present gratification to future gratification. Whereas the Middle Ages tended to nourish life in the present with a number of rituals devoted to celebrating it, modern man for the most part *bypasses* milking the moment of its significance. Instead, he devotes all present moments to the harvest of future rewards. The process was already rooted in the Middle Ages when man turned to otherworldly rewards. And, as Comte saw, it is precisely this that militated against the this-worldly preoccupations of chivalry. Futurism took its full upsurge in the puritan Protestant ethic, whereby man forswore any present enjoyment. Coupled with the decline of social unity and the possibilities of staging a drama in the present, the future perspective literally "ran away" with man.

The whole process was given a strong impetus when the idea of progress came upon the historical scene. One of the major contributing factors to the "living in the present" of ritualistic society was indeed the belief that the future held no promise, that the golden age of mankind lay in the past. This helped man to concentrate as much as possible on milking at least the present of some of the remaining joy which had once been possible. But with the idea of progress not only was the past devalued, but the present as well. The future now had the highest value, and it was for this that the present came to be sacrificed. The idea of progress, infused with the puritan Protestant ethic, had only to be coupled with modern commercial-industrial society and its wage-work day in order for the process to be complete: a whole world view conspired toward future gratification. Man now worked, put in time, lived a dead present, merely in order to barter his wages for the goods of consumer society (cf. E. Becker, 1964a, chap. 7). Weeks of dead time were applied to the anticipated thrill of purchase, which itself was undermined by the new advertising: one could no longer be happy with the new purchase because the new model came out the very next day. One had then to begin to put time in all over again. One was caught in the most vicious of circles.

The result was the complete abolishing of any sense the organism might have that it was making its energies felt in the present, of its own free will and accord, and that life was being enhanced thereby. The change in time perspective to future gratification thus conspired to kill almost entirely the possibility of the esthetic celebration of life. In trusting everything to the future, in exchanging one's energies for the belief that things were getting better and better, man simply lost the present. And we know that even the human animal has only the present; the past and future are abstractions—only the present is real (cf. E. Becker, 1964a, chaps. 1 and 2). To forfeit the present is to forfeit life itself, which is exactly what modern man has done.[2]

Max Weber made his grim prediction about the Leviathan growth of bureaucracy in modern times: that it was a necessary, but a lamentable prospect. He meant that it was necessary to better human adaptation, but lamentable because it sacrifices all the richness and roundness of life to the sheer pragmatic process. "Functional rationalization," as the jargon has it, grinds up everything to utility, to the end result, the time saved, the efficiency gained, the work speeded up, the money earned. Man throws away the present, the only life he has, for a new messianic cult of working-for-saving, of future living that never comes and never can come. When Huizinga lamented the decline of ritual in modern life, and said that civilization has become impossible, this is certainly what he meant. There is no better way to describe the automatic surrender of life that takes place every day in our society. Our lives are bankrupt, hollow, simply because we do not *live* them under the aegis of our own esthetic energies. It is not civilization that has become impossible; it is life itself that is being forfeited. The automobile craze that chokes our lungs and streets is all of a piece with the bankruptcy of modern life: getting behind the wheel and manipulating controls is one of the last places where one can bring his own direct energies to bear on the present; driving, like skiing, makes a unity out of the neutral landscape; as the driver weaves in and out of traffic he claims a segment of the world to his own design. We will only overcome the car craze when it, too, becomes a physical impossibility, or when we undertake to build a way of life in which more dignified and socially relevant esthetic satisfactions are possible. Meanwhile, the automobile industry, happily oblivious of Fourier's thesis on the social distortions of the passions, urges each new generation to give vent to their "natural desires." The whole fiasco was appropriately summed up by the comedian Lenny Bruce, who wanted to know how else to get sexual satisfaction except by driving a sports car? And the owner of one, who recently shot and killed a stranger for sitting down behind the wheel, is the perfect modern "natural man." Where else could he get his feeling of basic worth except in the exclusive domain of his last and only play-form?

The attraction of Oriental cults like Zen Buddhism answers to a real, felt need in a certain dissatisfied and sensitive segment of our population. Zen does for the modern practitioner what it did for the medieval *bushido* knighthood: it is a purely present, ritualistic creation of meaning. The modern devotee of Zen is merely trying to correct the terrible skewing of time perspective that has taken hold of society. He is trying desperately to come into possession of a lived present.

When Huizinga pointed out that the powdered wig and the costumes that went with it were abandoned after the French Revolution, he very correctly saw that this change was not merely a trivial, extraneous affair. "This levelling down and democratization of men's fashions is far from unimportant. The whole transformation of mind and society since the French Revolution is expressed in it" (1955, p. 193, cf. also p. 202). The "standard uniform" of the post-Industrial Revolution is part of the futurism of time perspective. The idea of progress, and the wage-work day, gradually undermined the creation of present meaning that had characterized the old society. This was the profound transformation of mind that made the powdered wig seem idle, effete, debased. Judged from the point of view of the Protestant ethic, the celebration of the present does seem frivolous and unmanly. There is a soberness in renunciation that makes indulgence of the present seem unworthy, but the question we must always ask is: who is renouncing what, and for what significant purpose? The Protestant ethic is one that sacrifices human playfulness to future goals, makes of man a means rather than an end. Wage work and Protestant-ethic futurism were akin to the Stalinist epoch in Russia: they built an industrial world on the renunciation of present life. Perhaps one day man will attempt to right the balance; when he does, it will be not only a question of developing the means of leisure, but of shaking off all the habits that we have developed to create those very means. Today the illness of modern man is very nearly worldwide; the commercial-industrial and the Soviet Communist world share the same problem: the sacrifice of life to the ingrained habit of futurism.

CONCLUSION: THE TASK OF A MATURE HISTORICAL PSYCHOLOGY

This is a very gross sketch of some of the historical processes that have contributed to an impoverishment of human meaning. Crude as it is, it does show how the union of psychology and history can be effected, how we can get—at the same time—the broadest historical picture of the human condition, united with a penetrating psychological one. The task of historical psychology in the future will be to refine further and build on the observations of the men we have mentioned, and so present the broadest possible, coherent, tightly-knit picture of the human condition across time. Even as we glimpse the possibilities of this picture from the present beginnings, it is breathtaking in its scientific importance. It represents a union of Marx and Freud that can accuse society everywhere of constricting the human spirit, by providing the exact critical categories that show up this constriction.

And it is a union of Marx and Freud that points to the true end of life, insisted upon by philosophers since Plato: that man is the unique offspring of nature whose task and purpose is "to live the dream of creation" (cf. Huizinga, 1924, pp. 38, 43 ff.). In the accumulation of this scientific knowledge, of these exact critical categories, Max Weber improved on Marx by analyzing whole civilizations in terms of their interlocking styles of meaning-creativity. Veblen's work is also part of this development, and central to it—perhaps even more than Weber's, because it has a critical cutting edge. But the true scientific flowering of this whole large-scale approach to society had to wait until it could be complemented by a sophisticated individual psychology. We had to be able to talk, as we did in the previous chapter, about the field of meanings of the individual, about the numbers of objects and different types of behavior available to him (cf. also E. Becker, 1964a, chap. 7). We had to understand the problem of investing meaning in a narrow segment of the total environmental field in order to facilitate some kind of control, some kind of self-assertion—a "fetishizing of the field," a clumsy but intense attempt to pinpoint some manageable locus of activity, when one is swimming in a sea of meaninglessness.

When we draw these two poles of analysis together into one picture, the events of history become more logical, lose still more of their randomness. It was no mere accidental coincidence, for example, that the "fetishism of commodities" was offered to the new commercial-industrial man, at a time when traditional society broke up in the West. And it is no mere accident today that this same fetishism is being offered Asian and African man with the breakup of their traditional societies. It is the same story of wage-work man forfeiting his own directive powers for the sake of puppet rewards.

A mature historical psychology would be able to tally all the factors, to weigh the gains against the losses in each particular society and historical epoch. It would show the price we pay in human potential for the creation of a certain kind of man. Today, for example, it is already clear that the "freedom" of modern consumer man is illusory, that though the consumer goods might make his life easier, they were bought at too much of a sacrifice to make it any richer and freer. Gone is the possibility of creating his own meanings because the new society has stripped him of the very means of doing so: the self-transcending social ideals, the joint family, the generative ritual, the sense of tradition, of a place in history, and even of a lived present. Modern individualism is a slogan, an ideology, but not a living body. We might say that modern man has emerged more sharply as a person simply because all his background has been cut away. His sharp form is empty, if you will; it is a sharpness of potential still unrealized. The individual is no longer submerged in the unquestioning obligations of traditional family society; he has a chance to reach for his own meanings, leave a more distinctive stamp on the world. But the gain of greater potential individual meaningfulness is offset by a tremendous burden, a burden which a historical psychology has to define in every epoch, namely, the burden of creating *one's own* meaning.

In our own epoch, with the decline of the traditional family, and of social rituals and self-transcending ideals, man still must reach for the "substance," as Hegel put it. Man must reach for the meaning which transcends him. Actually, today the "organization" seems to be taking over to provide the fund of ideal meaning in the gap left by more traditional forms. The individual, by accepting to work within the role forms of bureaucracy, accrues some larger substance to himself. He acquires the destinies of many other organisms for which he may consider his acts responsible—the head of the company, its past presidents, and so on. The organization, as we know, also provides its own ritual—its executive suite, its hallowed key to the executive toilets, and so on. Modern man, unable to draw meaning out of himself, even with his more sharply outlined form of individuality, actually thus repeats the submersion of the individual into the mass, just as it existed in the worst aspects of traditional society. Just as in the joint family, he gains in security and meaning what he loses in subjective freedom. I do not mean the analogy to be complete. The modern organization is a poor barter for the joint family in many ways, most notably because it defines the individual solely in terms of his role as an economic man devoted to futuristic gratification. It thus not only robs him of his present, but narrows him into a facet, deprives him of the possibility to be many-sided, and thereby to transcend his narrow historical destiny.

Man's self-knowledge follows closely the career of his disenchantment; it was really only after World War II that the emptiness of modern life could be seen in full. We saw the mechanical emptiness of the social forms, over and against the vast toll of human life they took. We saw, in a word, the enormous cost in human organisms of modern man's pitiful attempts to create meaning.

It was the existential dramatists, above all, who brought the matter home, who saw in acute detail that the self-creation of meaning in modern times was a pitiful thing. Samuel Beckett's plays marked the dramatization par excellence of the self-creation of meaning, by words and word sounds. His characters are either blind or alone, narrowly fixated on some segment of reality. With his profound artistic vision, Beckett sums up everything that man is striving for as well as the reason he cannot find what he wants in the modern world. I do not know if Beckett intended the latter, but he certainly has grasped the former. His *Endgame* is an insight of Shakespearian stature into the human condition, but an insight appropriate to our own disillusioned times. There is not the joy here that Stendhal would have sought, for Beckett means to convey the peculiarly modern failure, namely, man's need for generating meaning and the impossibility of doing it oneself. In *Endgame*, the lead character, Hamm, is blind, and during the entire play is immobile in his chair. All his efforts are directed at coming into contact with a segment of reality, of getting into the world in a convincing manner. But, since he cannot do this himself, he must rely on a servant or valet to intercede between himself and the world of everyday events. Thus, the everyday dialogue between oneself and the world is relayed through an intermediary person; the desired effect is to highlight the basic fact of human existence, the fact that action is composed of a myriad of petty events, carried along by words and word sounds; that the whole human organism takes the tiniest foothold into a wedge of the world, and this becomes his reality—whether it is looking out a window for sails at sea, or tracing down a flea with a spray gun. Time, weather, petty events succeed one another, and the organismic life is played out. *Endgame* approaches real tragedy, the tragedy of an animal who must create his own meanings and who sees the futility of it. The play ends as Hamm finally cuts himself off, courageously, from his intermediary, and so from the world.

Another of Beckett's plays, *Krapp's Last Tape*, contains a related aspect of the human tragedy in miniature. Its hero is a single actor— an old man, alone, alcoholic, who plays back tapes made at various stages in his life. The events he prizes most are his love affairs, and it is obvious that these are the high points in a life that has failed. The whole play conveys the nature of love, as it is narrowed down fetishistically to an attempt to get into the world and validate one's existence in the most forceful way. Krapp of course is ludicrous as he portrays an old man who can only seek justification in the memory of his younger loves. Like Goethe in his aging loves, Krapp tries to find all of his meaning in the fantasied love object; the object represents the hoped-for, but now lost, possibility of fully justifying himself in the world. The object becomes a source of all meaning, a direct life contact that is all-consuming, that transcends time and place. Krapp, like many others in our time, attempts to validate an entire life by means of the single, consummate love.

These are the techniques of Beckett's artistic genius that show us what happens to a life when it narrows down. In *Endgame* he uses a simple metaphor to convey the impoverishment of the small nuclear family: he depicts Hamm's two miserable parents in ashcans, off to the side of the stage. How better could one show, with this ashcan parenthood, the final petering out of the meaningful joint family, the loss of mutual engagement in a self-transcending life task? Or take Beckett's depiction of Krapp eating his bananas with relish—a striking typification of the primate condition: eat in order to keep moving, without obvious rhyme or reason; the organism must move forward. But our cynicism over Krapp must be tempered by an important realization: he eats to keep moving in a life that is not moving forward in in any kind of broad, interrelated scheme; this is the crux, the reason that his eating seems as ludicrously primate as his love is fetishizing. The human animal attains dignity only when he subsumes the mechanical processes of nature to some higher, self-transcending ideal, one in which others can join.

This is the great lesson of modern existential criticism for our historical psychology: man fails when he tries to create meaning by words and word sounds alone in the absence of rich, self-involving action. Beckett presents an exposé of man in our time when he is powerless to act significantly on the world; but this is not man in all times, even though it is an excellent comment on the modern condition. Perhaps this is the weakness of Beckett's art: it does not show us, as does *Oedipus Rex*, how man can master the meaninglessness of accidental experience. This helps explain why the viewer of Beckett's plays gets less than a full dramatic catharsis—there is no heroic way out, no resolution of the accidents of history and fate. We get very close to it in *Endgame*, as Hamm performs a truly significant act: he very courageously cuts his ties to the one object he has—his valet Clove—and so opts out of life. He just could not keep life moving convincingly with the lines at his disposal, with the segment of reality within his feeble reach. But opting out of life is no solution for man. Hamm's blindness is an artifact for the purpose of underlining his extreme dependence on the artifices of the interhuman, precisely because he has failed to involve himself significantly in the world. But the real Hamm, everyday man, is not blind. And Krapp fetishizes love because the rest of his life has been a failure. Where is Hamm's life engagement, Krapp's family and friends? The question we must ask, the one that gives the full dramatic resolution is, "What is the heroic way out of the human dilemma of self-created meaning *without dying pointlessly, without fetishizing?*" This is the answer that transcends time and place, and it is the one the artist should also provide.

But we are not asking the artist alone to provide it: it is the great task of historical psychology to help him. If we had a science of man in society worthy of the name, the artist could turn to it as a sure scientific aid to his imaginative labors—just as Stendhal turned to Destutt de Tracy, and hoped thereby to surpass Shakespeare since his work would be based on the most advanced scientific psychology. What we want to know is the same thing that the artist has always wanted to know: what makes man seem particularly empty, confused, impotent, and self-destructive in certain social contexts? We might boil all our questions down to this simple one, and call it the generic question of our science. All inquiries take their inspiration from the human condition, and have as their goal the maximization of human power.

We have traced some of the large historical aspects of this question and we might close our sketch by noting a few remaining problems that a mature historical psychology would want to be very clear about—problems like love, heroism, illness and death. For example, if Beckett gave us such a pathetic picture of the fetishization of love in *Krapp's Last Tape*, we would want to know why this fetishization appears only in certain periods and contexts. We already have many clues for a deep discussion on this matter. Emil Lucka saw that modern man, in his struggle to unify his life into an esthetic whole, turned more and more to woman as the main source of this unification. And the reason was partly that only in modern times has the woman become a full personality in her own right, someone who possesses an inner spirit as well as a reproductive body. Thus it became possible for modern man to seek all of his self-justification in woman (1922, p. 250).

But we are also becoming uncomfortably aware that woman herself can be a fetishization of love in the absence of other sources from which to derive our enhancement of life. It is becoming difficult to live in modern commercial-industrial society without feeling that one is being turned into a sex fetishist, and without fighting against it. Where is the rich and broad-ranging life into which love fits as an added dimension? Where is the sustained dignity of a life well-lived, a life that has a place in a sequence of generations, a life based on duty to others, devotion to a cause? We have mentioned these things already too many times, but we can ask again, is all this to be narrowed down into the search for a single love object?

The question for a mature historical psychology is, what happens in history and society when there are other ways, rather than love alone, of building meaning? What happens when there are rich possibilities of building oneself into the world without having to resort to a total investment in the love object? We know, for example, that a primitive society, such as the Arunta of Central Australia, built a rich world without fetishizing the woman as a love object—although they did fetishize many other magical and religious objects. We also know that Greek society notoriously did without the notion of love for woman. The Greeks, in fact, put a very wide range of permissible love objects at the disposal of man—including young boys and wise men like Socrates, for whom Alcibiades pined. Today we tend to condemn this Greek universalism of love partners, perhaps even erroneously considering it a stage "in the development" of sexual morality. But it may well be that we are condemning the Greeks for their strengths, and priding ourselves on weaknesses. Perhaps Greek society, rich in generative ritual and social idealism, did not need to be as fetishistic about woman as we are today. As Feuerbach saw, among the Greeks the "religion of friendship" could take the place of love (1841, p. 156). There were other places to seek for deep personality, mystery, and the validation of one's life. This is one question which a mature historical psychology will want to be very clear about.

There are other questions as well which, though difficult to be exact about, are nonetheless real. For example, there seems today to be much less personal heroism and dignity in man's attitude toward fate; perhaps this is best focused in mass man's pervasive fear of death and his unwillingness even to dwell on it. Death is usually shocking, incredible, overwhelming in its attack on his meanings. Is this because his meanings are shallow and insecure? Partly, of course, this is due to commercial society itself and to the propaganda it sows in order to maintain its forms: the incessant preaching of security in old age, the desire to sell insurance, sick benefits, and so on. This is inseparable too from our living in a futuristic time perspective. Everything conspires to put off gratification to the future; as a result, modern man, lacking a present, lacks anything solid to marshal in the face of the mystery of death. If all gratification is put off for the future, how can one bear the thought of bartering a whole life merely toward the reward of death? Spinoza framed the insight for this inquiry long ago when he said that a free man thinks of nothing so little as death. And Rousseau saw that man had forgotten how to die because he did not know how to live (1762, p. 31).

What is a free man? Here is the other side of our generic question for historical psychology: What makes man empty, confused and impotent? The opposite of this condition would be to be free, truly free. It is the question that man will be asking as long as his career continues on this planet; and in each age there will be new answers because there will be new shackles on his freedom. At our point in history we already have a workable answer, and it is the one we have been sketching in these pages: man is free when he enjoys a rich participation in a broad panorama of life experiences, when he dwells in an expansive present that responds to his own energies (cf. also E. Becker, 1964a, chaps. 1–3, on the problem of freedom in relation to schizophrenia). When we understand this, it will lead us to redefine our habitual notions of freedom, as many anthropologists have already been redefining it. We will see that in one sense the primitive is the most free, even though he may be subject to the unthinking yoke of tradition. Energetically, as an organism, he is free, because he is free to make his integral powers felt in the world. Also, he is dignified because he senses that the control over life stems in large part from within himself, and that therefore he can and should assume responsibility for it. Again, his participation in a rich esthetic of life has permitted him to unify, within his single personality, a large domain of natural accident. Modern man may live in fear of death or obliviousness of the ways in which death can be given heroic dignity simply because, like the schizophrenic, he has been unable to appropriate a sufficiently broad tableau of cultural meanings. Insufficient participation and reflection of one's powers in the world, in a self-reliant and controlled manner, leads to a feeling that the world is not one's own, that one will lose something one does not securely have, that life is overwhelming, precarious, even unfair. The schizophrenic, like many modern mass men, thinks very often of death simply because he is not free—not free to participate in life under the aegis of his own energies and control. We should contrast the stoic attitude toward death in primitive society and in heroic civilizations such as Greece, Rome, feudal Japan. It may be partly a matter of believing oneself to be in the indestructible care of guardian spirits, of joining one's ancestors, or of being reborn—but it is not only that. It is also all of a piece with the richness of a life lived. One opens one's veins, Roman-style, or one's stomach, samurai-style, when one has already had the experiences of being a locus of control over a rich, meaningful world (cf. also Russell, 1926, pp. 54–55). Life is ended with the dignity with which it has been lived. In modern society, suicide—as I noted earlier—is often the last resort that an individual has, to unify esthetically a life that has failed. In this sense, suicide always offers man a potential for meaningful self-realization, even if only as a saving grace, a desperate artistic resort. In schizophrenia, suicide may be the last "safe" act that the individual feels he can perform (E. Becker, 1964a, chap. 3). The main difference from the samurai, of course, is that the samurai's suicide reflects a network of broad social obligations, a life that has always fit into a transcending scheme of things. It is logically integral to a life lived, as a work of art, and not merely a last-minute ingenuity to salvage a bankrupt existence. It is Socrates, again, who comes to mind as the model for this kind of integral suicide.

These are the questions, in sum, of a mature historical psychology, of an intimate union of Marx and Freud. They all grow out of our basic preoccupation: what kind of person is developed in history, according to the range and types of opportunity that society provides for the creation of life meaning? Huizinga wanted to know why the temper was very labile in the Middle Ages, and one day we shall have at least an approximate answer. We shall also understand mass movements, outbreaks of hysteria, as we are already beginning to understand them. They are not illogical events, but logical ones, events that we can and should explain on the basis of our knowledge. The union of Marx and Freud gives us the basic key to these phenomena because, as we said, it deprives social life of its randomness and of its mystery. We are coming more and more to understand that the real enemy of the human spirit is man's own stupidity in regard to his social arrangements.

Since this is so, let us go on to Part III, and see what better kind of design we can propose for the ordering of social life.

The Ideal-Type:

The Individual and the Community

If there were to be one comprehensive science of human life, character, action, and so on, it could not operate, as do the physical sciences, on terms of "limited liability," or to put it another way, within "a closed circle of Ideas." . . . If there were to be a comprehensive sociology, or science of man under any other name, it would have to include or to be theology . . . . [It would have to answer Aristotle's question:] What is the chief end of man?

ARTHUR D. RITCHIE (*1958, p. 161*)

CHAPTER ELEVEN

A DESIGN FOR ETHICAL MAN

The great advances of the future in ethical understanding are likely to be achieved only by those who are firmly resolved to press ethical inquiry to its logical limit without regard to immediate practical consequences.

MORRIS R. COHEN *(1956, p. 186)*

And so we are ready to draw the lessons from our general theory of alienation. If it is a good theory, it will allow us to design an ideal of man that would defeat historical alienation. It would show us how to achieve the integration and rich creativity of primitive societies, but now on a new basis, with the fullest possible liberation of individual energies and freedom. It would answer to the ideal held up by the Enlightenment itself, and phrased by Kant—we noted it in Chapter Seven, and can now repeat it here since it is *the* ideal for overcoming historical alienation: man must try to achieve maximum individuality *within* maximum community. We also noted that, phrased this way, the ideal is an unattainable paradox—and this too is proper for an ideal. As Royce taught us, the only things worth working toward are those which are unattainable: the ideal is the "un-real" by necessary definition; it leads man ever onward.

We can use Kant's paradoxical ideal as a measure of the failure of many social epochs: either they give too much room to rampant individuality—as in the heroic age of Greece and Northern Europe and in the Renaissance; or they do not give enough room. This is

251

one of the points on which Comte's vision stumbled. He saw the need for a unified society based on the rich creation of meaning, but he allowed little place for the distinctive individual energies that would create that very meaning! Comte wanted art to hold up to man the ideal vision for the new society, toward which it would progress; science would help guide human adaptation toward that vision, and would provide knowledge for modifying the ideal. As for the individual, he would be further developing and perfecting his sentiments toward humanity, and his capacity to love.

But we can see the contradiction in Comte's vision that led many to turn from his system with a shrug: how would the ideal-type be continually remolded by science and art if creative energies had to be confined under the regnant ideal? Comte's vision of society is really an apt picture of Soviet Russia under Stalin, where science served the needs of ideology and artistic energies all dipped into the same socially approved vat, to sketch monotonously the standard ideal of social achievement. The problem is, simply, that we have found no way of controlling scientific and artistic meanings without smothering them.

THE NEED FOR AUTONOMOUS MEANINGS

This is another way of saying that the ideal of the innovator must remain pure; this pole of the paradox must remain undiluted—we cannot compromise on an ideal of maximum individuality. What would happen to the creative, innovative spirit, if it could not counter *all* present meanings, scientific as well as artistic? We noted earlier that Bergson saw the innovator as the instrument of evolution itself, nature working against encrusted social forms. Max Weber too held a similar view, and assigned a very important place in his thought to the charismatic person, the radical innovator who reworks all meanings and cuts through the "routinized" cultural forms. Weber built a whole philosophy of history on the alternation of periods of standardization of meanings and periods of charismatic innovation and shattering of accepted meanings. Like Bergson, he saw charisma as one of the few hopes for mankind.

When the Enlightenment thinkers called for the discovery and promotion of genius, they wanted a similar thing: to release the pure forces of nature embodied in the individual spirit. It is an age-old belief and hope of mankind, this quest to release the forces of nature in their pure state. And where else to look except in the subjectivity of the most flexible animal in evolution? Hence the awe and fear that surround charisma, as well as the hope. Today we are less superstitious about the matter than our ancestors were because we understand a lot of what goes into making a genius.

As we saw earlier, man's groping for meaning stems from the most idiosyncratic individual needs. This is another way of saying that each individual derives his feeling of self-value in a way that is bound to be a little different from that of all others. What he is doing is resolving his own esthetic tensions in a way proper to his own organism and its own unique and accidental history. The genius is the one who has reworked meanings into a product that the whole culture can share: that is to say, he has made a *personal* resolution which can be utilized by others. What is so marvelous about the genius and why are we so taken with him? We are carried forward with him, and so we experience the triumph of the total organism, moving forward, over the conventional systems of culture. The genius has tensions of his whole organism, his whole "life situation," which cannot be resolved by the standard world view. This is another way of saying that the *total organism* can no longer take its sustenance from the *partial symbol systems* offered to it at an accidental historical time and place. Culture, in sum, has failed to do its universal job, to give the organism what it needs most—a sentiment of self-value derived from standardized symbol systems and the action they direct. Therefore, we can say that with the genius nature triumphs over the constraints of culture by "declaring" that it cannot be nourished in its need for satisfying organismic self-feeling by the particular meaning games being played at that time. The genius carries nature forward, renews the common pool of meaning by organismically breaking out of the narrowing constraints of the old meaning. Hence, he embodies the triumph of the organic life process over the stilted symbolisms of culture.

This is the dialectic of human freedom, the tension between an animal who needs a symbolically constituted sense of self-value and a society which—by granting it to him—reduces him to the slavery of habit and a narrow world view. Sartre understands this very well when he says that genius is not a gift, but a creative solution of the problem of meaning, a liberation from cultural automaticity (cf. Hazel Barnes, 1959, p. 341). And so we see why society "needs" the genius, even though it fights him, and will usually not be ready for his vision until after his death: his supremely *private* achievement is always potentially of the highest public good; and it is of the highest good precisely *because* it is made over and against habitual social meanings.

But, in order to have this high public value, the creative privatization of the genius must be convertible into general currency. In other words, there is the broadest possible leeway for private products in human society, but not all of them can be legitimate. This is the test of "paranoia," for example. The paranoiac makes a resolution of meanings that sustains his self-esteem, by a very creative act—we saw this in discussing Rousseau and Hume. But it suffers precisely because it is a privacy that is not generalizable. Hume and his friends could simply not use this private resolution of Rousseau's tensions. The whole thing, then, depends on the degree to which the creative catharsis of meanings is generalizable. Baudelaire's poetic catharsis and his forgiving God were part of a very private affair, but they did make poetry that appealed to others.

We might note in passing that the work of genius is usually not radical in intent, but rather in its effect. The genius is not at first trying to create novelty in the common external world, but only in his own thoughts and behavior: he wants to set *his* world right. Then he confronts the world with his own private product, and asks that it be recognized as a valid new meaning. Luther comes to mind as an example of the reluctant innovator: he was shocked by the explosion he kindled, but, as he himself said, he could not do otherwise.

We should not wonder that the innovator begins timidly; man is not a world beater when it comes to offering up new meanings. Ordered societies, after all, are usually undermined from without, not from within. We saw that the reason for this is intricately tied up with the kind of animal man is. Since all human meanings are imparted to us by others of our kind, we must always lean on others to sustain these meanings. The problem is further complicated by man's need for conviction: he gets this conviction best from concrete organismic presences around him. The monologue of the innovator, as we noted, would go something like this: "If I create my own meanings, who is going to validate them? Where is the *persuasive other* presence who will do so?" Man feels that he must reach outside himself in order to be himself.

We discussed this earlier, and made a point of noting that the problem is complicated in modern times, especially for the truly radical innovator. In the Middle Ages every man could delegate responsibility for choices that were not his accustomed ones. It is not just a coincidence that the existential consciousness of man's inner emptiness arose in history precisely at the time that man was thrown back on his own meanings: Pascal marks the crucial turning point in postmedieval man's consciousness of his aloneness, and his famous wager on the existence of God still haunts us today. The inner emptiness of the existential consciousness reflected a lack of support, a void within, which was a new burden on man, the burden to validate his meanings without the assurance of God. The task is prodigious, and has been a continuing theme of philosophical and religious thought through Kierkegaard into modern existentialism. The heartfelt lament of modern atheistic existentialism represents a full consciousness of this loss of God as an automatic validation for meanings. Sartre's nausea is an honest nausea, and a historically proper one. We should expect that the human animal would find life *utterly meaningless*, when he is thrown back on *his own* meanings. This is the crisis in religion and philosophy today, and it reaches back to the decline of the medieval cosmology. Goethe could scorn Pascal as a pitiful, mournful figure—but we have seen why: Goethe reached elsewhere for his validation, did not need to make a desperate wager on God's help for his own creative meanings. But is it necessary to add that a Pascal, if he had been able to look back at Goethe, would not have found him just as pitiful as an old man doting over a teen-age love?

We mention Luther, Goethe, and Pascal at this time because this is where we must pick up our previous discussion and complete it. Our question now is, what kind of an ideal of individual freedom can we design for an empty animal who cannot believe that he has the right to fabricate his own insides? Put thus baldly, we can see how central this problem is to any social vision.

THE PROBLEM OF AUTONOMOUS MEANINGS

The great fact that we must be clear about before we attempt any kind of solution to this problem is that for the individual it is insoluble. Let us pause and emphasize this one final time. Man simply cannot believe in and accept his own meanings in the face of all the other meanings that existed before him and that transcend him. We might call this one of the fundamental phenomenological facts of human existence. It has its basis, as we saw, in the very nature of man's immersion in a transcendent world; it is rooted in human psychology. To attempt to offer up new meanings is to give birth, to bring the unknown into the world. In the process, the individual gives birth to a new self, and the anxiety that floods him is a reflection of the gravity of what is at stake: the birth or death of a new person, one who has broken away from the old, common world. It is as if the individual were choosing to create himself as a god. How is one to accept this role? How justify the unique act, the unique choice, over and against all other acts and choices? Where, in a word, is the moral standard by which to justify the act that does not conform to any moral standard? Truly, the situation borders on the divine. And the rub is that man does not feel entitled to the arbitrariness of a god. Herbert Fingarette has understood this very well, and has seen that this very arbitrariness is the "profoundest source of all value" (1963, p. 107).

In terms of our previous discussion we would say that society needs these new arbitrary values in order to cut through the old constrictions of habit. But this process of birth, by cutting the individual off from the society as he has always known it, is a choice for potential self-annihilation or nonbeing. Fingarette has some very excellent things to say about this:

> Responsibility is the readiness to face the absence of meaning, the nonbeing of self. It requires that a self *be* formed, a meaning be instated, a policy adopted. The crisis exists precisely because there is no a priori decisive resolution of the situation. Responsibility is the willingness to "leap into nothingness." But it is more than this: it is the willingness to accept . . . the consequences of one's act. We flinch from this leap, this commitment without decisive justification. . . . [T]he heart of responsibility is revealed when we see that, faced with anxiety and the need for choice, precisely what we wish to know is what we *cannot* know (Fingarette, 1963, p. 101).

The upshot of this dilemma is that it raises havoc with traditional ethical systems. We might call it a modern Humean attack on natural law. We may have imagined that there was *one* right choice, *one* pattern of self-realization; but if meanings are autonomous and arbitrary, and if they can be justified only by the act, then ethical choice has no inner standard. It was this argument that Herder had already leveled against Kant (Clark, 1955, p. 313). Let us recall the grandeur and tragedy of Oedipus Rex at this point: it was due to the fact that he made himself responsible for the accidents of nature, even up to the point of self-destruction. But there were other acts which he could have chosen, which would have been "right." There was nothing

"called for" about the decisive personality which Oedipus formed—
it was an invention, a pure creation in the circumstances of the
moment (cf. also Fingarette, 1962, p. 89; 1963, pp. 104–105). What
Oedipus proves, for the problem of morality, is that the meanings one
puts forth depend on the meanings one *can sustain*. And it is just
this proof that shatters any monistic moral code. The Aristotelian
view, for example the belief that there is one best line of development
dictated by nature, implies that one can know a priori what choice and
decision to make because some choices are more in accord with one's
"true nature" than others. But if the context determines the choices,
and if one's own courage determines the decision, then the leeway is
vast. It only *seems* that one is unfolding his "true self"—Aristotelian
fashion—because one accepts responsibility, and the action moves
forward (cf. also Fingarette). In this sense, it is a liberation which
seems to reveal "the proper course" of nature.

We might remind ourselves in passing here that this is just the
error that Ortega made in criticizing Goethe's option to stay in the
sheltered court at Weimar; he imagined that thereby Goethe had
missed his "true vocation." But what if there is no one true vocation?
What if there are almost an infinite number of ways of looking at a
life, at a choice, at a series of choices? Goethe's choice to stay at
Weimar, in other words, cannot be evaluated, as Ortega would want,
against the sole perspective of a literary movement in Germany which
Goethe might have led from Jena. Rather, the question is an overall
one, and consequently a more difficult one to judge: what kind of
life was opened up, and in which ways was it a productive and distinct
one? There is no standard by which to judge whether Goethe was
shirking the one choice which would have liberated "the distinctive
energies" of his "true nature." Ortega doubtless wanted Goethe's life
to have had even more significance, to have enriched the world even
further; and perhaps this is why he lamented that Goethe had missed
his "true vocation." We want the charismatic to release the maximum
amount of charisma; we want our ideal to be a maximum ideal. But
if there is no one right way, if there are no standards for this, how
can we formulate such an ideal? Now that we have been able to
pause on the additional complexities of this problem, we are ready to
proceed to an answer. We have seen that nature steadfastly refuses
to help us out of our dilemma: neither on the level of individual
psychology, nor on that of natural law, will she provide a basis for the
emergence of maximum individuality. Since this is so, let us see what
man himself can contribute to his own liberation.

THE INDIVIDUAL CONTRIBUTION TO THE STRENGTH FOR AUTONOMY

If the meanings that one puts forth depend on what one can sustain, we have one clue to the promotion of human creativity, namely, that we can try to increase the strength and the courage of the individual in the face of the potential rebirth of his self. As Rousseau, Stendhal, and Nietzsche saw, the great fact about morality is that it needs real strength, the strength to assume the responsibility for one's uniqueness. On the level of individual psychology, then, the problem is simply, what does strength mean for the human animal? Immediately as the question is asked we know the answer. The human animal is the only one who can frame a cognitive grasp of the problematic situations he finds himself in; it is this that gives him a potential that is denied to all others. For man, strength means understanding.

The whole problem of neurosis and anxiety is basically a problem of cognition: we cannot be anxious about that which we truly understand. To say that one is "neurotically constricted" is simply to say that one lacks understanding of himself in relation to a situation in which new choices are demanded. Looked at in this way, we can say that there are always two basic things that the individual has to find out about himself in order to earn more freedom of action: (1) Why do I not feel that I have the *right* to my own meanings? (2) Why do I not have the *strength* to sustain that right?

This formula may seem overly simple, but the basic problem of neurosis and individual freedom is contained in it. What the individual wants to know, and needs to know, is what is depriving him of the right to act on his own. Why does he not feel that he has the right, as an organism, to do what he has to do? In terms of self-analysis, one would have to try to find out what has happened in his past, and is happening in his present, that influences the way he sees the world, the way he feels about himself, that prevents him from moving forward under his own power. This is what the Oedipus complex really means, as Adler knew long ago, and as Fromm has repeated more recently: neurosis is a problem of the authority over one's life. Freud may have talked about sexual rivalry as the core of neurosis, but in his own personal drama of self-liberation we see quite different things.[1] The Oedipus complex, as we saw, is better called the oedipal phase of learning. It is here that one builds up a mode of perception that is more or less automatic and habitual: all of one's action potential is influenced by an a priori definition of the situation. Perception, after all, is action, it is the movement of the organism in a situation; thus, to limit perception is to limit action.

On the individual level, then, the problem of courage is clear: man must try to frame problems in ever-more-explicit, cognitive terms, because this alone unblocks action. One can convert a situation in which there was no choice to one in which there are new choices. In this way, man liberates himself by *creating indeterminacy*. On the individual level, the whole of ethics becomes a problem of self-liberating choice possibilities. And the strength *to be* ethical, we can now conclude, is really the strength *to design* alternatives, and to follow them out. Ah yes, to follow them out. How to really believe that one has the strength, how to act on what one knows—here is the lifelong complication. As one of Gide's characters put it, it is so difficult to act on the basis of the truths one has learned.

THE SOCIAL CONTRIBUTION TO THE STRENGTH FOR AUTONOMY

It is this last complication in the problem of the courage to be that draws a full circle on our discussion. As we saw earlier, man simply cannot rely on himself, he cannot believe that he has the right to offer new meanings without some kind of support. Strength can never be an individual problem entirely; it overlaps fully into the social world. In our design for ethical man, we need a program that will support the individual in sustaining the most original meanings; and since it is the individual who needs to be sustained the program will have to be a social one. A good part of the answer to the burden of individual choice, in a word, lies in society.

Perhaps no one in modern times has understood this better than Martin Buber. Buber's work is especially important for us today because it is the fulfillment of a whole current of thought, dating at least from Fourier. Earlier we mentioned how profound Fourier's insight was when he said that the "cabalistic spirit is the true destination of man." We also noted how contemporary this view is, and how it is included in the best work of Simmel, Huizinga, and Buber. Now it is time to discuss Buber's work because it actually brings Fourier up to date and translates his early insight into a critical ideal for our science. Our ideal would have to be one that merges the problems of the individual innovator with those of society: we would have to have a design for man that gave the individual maximum support, but that at the same time gave society the maximum celebration of life. Or, put in Fourier's terms: we would have to give full play to the cabalistic passion in a way that would be maximally satisfying to the individual and maximally beneficial to the community. Buber gave us the key to the solution of this paradox by reminding us that any ideal vision for man must be built upon the basic human encounter. Whatever else man may reach for, in order to celebrate his existence and get support for himself, his basic dialogue is with his fellows. Now Simmel, as we noted briefly, had also done this, when he said that man finds his own life meaning in the face of his fellow man, in the unique locus of the interweaving of spirit and matter. But Buber went on to develop this basic problem of idealist esthetics into a true "esthetics of confrontation," an ontology of interpersonal becoming in society. Thus he offered us a major contribution toward an ideal-type for a theory of alienation.

Using the basic idealist ontology, Buber understood that man can only come into being by relating himself creatively to an external world; the important thing is transaction, without which there can be no knowledge, no testing of powers, no heightening of being. But from everything that the external world offers to man he can find the greatest enhancement of his being in the encounter with his fellows. The reason for this is strikingly simple: man is the only animal in nature who has a self, and the self can be developed only in transacting with other selves. Man exists in a fourfold field of relations, a field unique in all of nature: man relates to the world and to things; he relates to other men; he relates to the mystery of being; and he relates to his own self. Buber concluded that man can know himself, come to feel his own deep powers, heighten his own being, only by establishing a transaction between his own being and that of another (1955, pp. 177–180). In other words, we would say, in terms of our discussion, that since man is an instinct-free animal he has to get back into a segment of reality in a most convincing manner. And Buber has shown that the problem of conviction for man is one of trying to get into contact with the full mystery and vitality of being. Only in this way can the world he discovers seem ultimately real since it is this very vital reality from which *his lack of natural instinctiveness* has cut him off. Furthermore, since man is the only animal who has a self, he is, as we just noted, further "inverted" from a direct natural dialogue—man is the only "self-reflexive" animal. Buber helps us see that the only recourse is to turn this inversion to good account, and to use the self to relate to other selves. Instead of potential poverty, he has the possibility of finding infinite richness. In this way man can experience ultimate reality, or what Buber calls "absolute meaning," or "absoluteness." In his words:

> Human life touches on absoluteness in virtue of its dialogical character, for in spite of his uniqueness man can never find, when he plunges to the depth of his life, a being that is whole in itself and as such touches on the absolute. Man can become whole not in virtue of a relation to himself but only in virtue of a relation to another self. This other self may be just as limited and conditioned as he is; in being together the unlimited and the unconditioned is experienced (1955, pp. 167–168).

Thus Buber allows us to fuse idealist esthetics and self-psychology: man finds the "really real," the supreme real, in the dialogue of selves: personality elicits personality, and gives birth to a greater degree of spirit, interwoven with the world of organisms. Man has to be convinced that human meanings are truly worth something in the world, that the culturally designed plan for living has self-transcending significance; and the only place he can *see* this is in another organismic existence of the same type as himself, one who is literally permeated with shared human striving. Buber uses the apt phrase "imagining the real" to describe this need, and says:

> Applied to intercourse between men, "imagining" the real means that I imagine to myself what another man is at this very moment wishing, feeling, perceiving, thinking, and not as a detached content but in his very reality, that is, as a living process in this man. . . . The human person needs confirmation, because man as man needs it. . . . (1957, pp. 103–104).

Maximum meaning for man, as Buber holds, thus lies in the interpersonal realm, in the realm of the "I and Thou." In this way man best goes beyond the feeling of his own determinacy and isolation, the sense of feebleness of his own meanings.

In briefest possible compass, then, this is Buber's basic view of the interpersonal nature of meaning and human becoming. Man needs man in order to discover and validate his own inner powers, in order to unfold himself; and man needs to *see* and experience man in order to be convinced that there is absolute value, absolute meaning, in nature. It is quite fitting for man to have to address himself to the highest organism in nature in order to achieve the highest consciousness of life—both his own life and that of the world around him.

It is this community of the interpersonal that is thus our best and most natural place to seek for ethical man.

This discovery is important because not only does it fully naturalize idealism in the interpersonal realm, but it also allows us to see what we need to know about agonism: that this competitive motive is basically neutral, essentially innocuous. Historically, agonism has had its vicious forms, but the urge to agonism is merely the urge to find the "really real" in the validating encounter with another self. It would be impossible to overstress the value of this discovery because it answers the question that has troubled our best thinkers, and that has been outstanding since Adam Smith and Malthus: if man's conduct has always assumed such competitive and egotistic form in the West, are we not to assume that this is "natural," and then proceed to build our society on the basis of it, as the economic individualists urged us to do? Today we have a thoroughgoing answer: a large anthropological sample of the world's cultures has shown us that competitive egotism is not "natural"; and an ontology of interpersonal striving has shown us the neutral dynamic that the egotism hid.

Now, the discovery of the utter social neutrality of the motive to agonism has been building for some time. From a point of view of the history of ideas, it is important to note that Buber was not building on the work of Fourier, but rather on the insights of Feuerbach. It was Feuerbach who revived the striking Renaissance phrase *"Homo homini Deus est"* (cf. Haydn, 1950, p. 406), and who first naturalized Hegelian idealism. Merz, who missed nothing of the ineluctable synthetic movement of the nineteenth century, noted the significance of Feuerbach's phrase *"Homo homini Deus est."* It reveals the acute similarity between transcendental idealist systems like Hegel's, and positivist humanity-based systems like Comte's (Merz, 1914, vol. 4, p. 186, note). But we know there is nothing strange in this similarity: hadn't Wilhelm von Humboldt also spoken of the "I and the Thou"; and hadn't he and especially Herder sought to design a naturalistic ideal-type? Hegel, in other words, represented merely a transcendental interlude in the direct line of the French and German Enlightenment: the development from Rousseau and Herder of a naturalistic ideal-type. Feuerbach and Comte simply picked up an interrupted tradition.

Right at the beginning of the stirrings for a science of man, thinkers such as Feuerbach found the neutral interpersonal basis for designing a truly ethical ideal. Thus they could aim for a science of man in society that was idealistic and man-centered, and that promoted ethical action. Here is the great achievement of the union of self-psychology with idealist esthetics. It permits us to aim for full ethical self-development, in an interpersonal community of free men, working *with* rather than opposite or against each other. It was possible right at the beginning of the science of man to provide a scientific framework which united the best of idealism with a man-centered pragmatism. And this is just what Buber urges, the interhuman as the basis of the fusion of both systems in modern times, a fusion which we have been seeking to justify comprehensively ever since it was glimpsed early in the nineteenth century.

Buber brought the tradition right up to our time by a further naturalistic refining of the union of idealist esthetics and self-psychology. Moreover, he could be very explicit about the political implications of this whole tradition; as he says, the discovery of reality as essentially interpersonal can lead us to a science of man that goes beyond narrow individualism and constricting collectivism. Ever since the nineteenth century these two extremes have been hobbling an objective, yet man-centered, general theory of action; we needed a subject matter that was ethically neutral, and a framework for the science of man that permitted all of society to work toward the achievement of a transcending ideal, but one that was rooted *in individuals*. In Buber's words:

> This [interpersonal esthetic] reality provides the starting-point for the philosophical science of man; and from this point an advance may be made on the one hand to a transformed understanding of the person and on the other to a transformed understanding of community. The central subject of this science is neither the individual nor the collective but man with man. That essence of man which is special to him can be directly known only in a living relation (1955, pp. 204–205).

Now, again, from a point of view of the history of ideas, it is important to note that Buber continued the current of Feuerbach and Fourier, but that he was hardly alone in this. Max Scheler was another supremely critical and poetic thinker who, like Buber, saw that the science of man must be a science of developing life; and that, in order to be this, it must re-establish a sense of the deepest respect and awe in the face of being. Scheler was another who kept alive the broad nineteenth-century views on the problem of science and life, and refused to narrow himself to reigning fads. What man needed above all, said Scheler, was a sense of unity and participation in the universe—and it is just this that we have lost. In his study of human sympathy, Scheler could see the effects of this loss: it "cut away the ultimate roots upon which all the 'higher' forms of sympathetic and emotional life depend for their subsistence" (1954, p. 104).

The average social scientist cannot feel comfortable with a proposal that man—in order to be truly man—must have and experience a sense of intimacy with the cosmic process, and that it is the business of the science of man to provide for this. For those who have modeled human science on the physical sciences, this fouls all objectivity, all tangibility, all necessary detachment. It seems to be an anthropomorphization, an imposition of human categories on a supposedly "objective" reality; and supposedly it is this that has always been anathema to science. But we have seen that so-called "objective" reality is already partly a human creation. And Scheler answered the charge of anthropomorphism in his inspired way: the sense of meaningful participation within the larger universe, so necessary to fullest development of human sensitivities, is not anthropomorphism narrowly understood as the "projection" of human qualities into the world around. But rather, man is the only creature in nature who is "cosmomorphic": he is the only one who can imaginatively embody existence in all its forms, and so possesses heightened insight and rapport with the cosmos (1954, p. 105).

Like Buber, Scheler saw that the maximum sense of the vitality and mystery of life is conveyed in the contact of man with man. In his words:

> A decisive factor in cultivating a capacity for identification with the cosmos is that sense of immersion in the total stream of life, which is first aroused and established among *men in respect of their mutual status as individual centres of life* [his emphasis]. For it seems to be more or less a rule (of which we have as yet no further understanding) that the actual realization of the capacity for cosmic identification cannot take place directly in relation to external Nature, but is mediated indirectly, in that sense of unity between man and man. . . (1954, p. 108).

And Scheler's concluding statement could just as well be Buber's: "Man's point of entry into identification with the life of the cosmos lies where that life is nearest and in closest affinity to his own, namely *in another man.*"

At this time we can understand better that even though Scheler's ideas suffered because he failed to find Freud's true later contribution —the notion of ego identity as the core of individual development— still Scheler did go far beyond Freud; he was a much more universal thinker. Freud largely reduced interpersonal cravings to the merest animal satisfactions; Scheler stressed the basic meaning dimensions of the human personality, in their fully interpersonal and esthetic reaches. (For another—but today less-known—thinker in this tradition see Mary Follett, 1924.)

From a point of view of the history of ideas we might call this tradition the one which elaborated the ontological and phenomenological dimensions of the "esthetics of confrontation." There was another line of theoretical development that followed alongside, and merged with it, that we might call the tradition of the "psychology of belonging." It was elaborated principally by Josiah Royce and his followers, as a plea for interpersonal community and for a re-establishment of a sense of intimacy with the cosmic process. Royce's system contained several key ideas that went to the heart of the human condition, and offered clear answers for remedying the great void that the nineteenth century had opened when it completed the fragmentation of the human community. Royce saw that man needed loyalty and community above all, and like Feuerbach earlier (1841, p. 159) and Buber later he urged that "Our fellows . . . furnish us with the constantly needed supplement to our own fragmentary meanings" (1901, vol. 2, p. 174). But Royce did not understand this problem in any abstract sense, even if he did not approach it with the precision of Buber's later phenomenology. He saw that man needed loyalty because only in this way could he unite his life, his own history, and the history of his land and people. In a sense we might say that he brought up to date Spinoza's view that man achieves true dignity only by immersing himself in something of larger significance. Royce used historical and anthropological data; his insights were not based naïvely on the vision of the great community he longed for, but rather on a factual appreciation of how man could get back what he had lost. In effect, Royce offered a *psychology* of loyalty and of community. The loyal man, Royce saw, is never lonely because the cause that he serves unites many lives into the unity of one (Cotton, 1954, p. 241). In terms of modern personality theory, we would say that devotion to a cause gives the individual a broad range of objects; or, to go back to Hegel's views on the joint family, we would say that partaking in some self-transcending ideal shared by others gives the individual a greater reservoir of ideal substance. Royce saw that the lonely, isolated individual is truly a lost soul, and that only in community does he come to himself.

He went on to develop this idea of loyalty into the vision of a Great Community, and stressed the social-transactional nature of knowledge; he understood that no human knowledge had meaning apart from its being shared by a "community of interpretation." He also re-interpreted Christianity as the early Pauline vision of a new community in which the individual unites his life into a meaningful whole by dedicating himself to a transcending purpose involving all mankind. Royce's vision has been kept alive in modern Christian existentialism, especially by Gabriel Marcel (see his *Homo viator*). It was carried on, as we noted earlier, by his pupil George Mead, who also held to the idea of the interpersonal support for individual meanings, and the need for a whole "community of interpretation" (cf. Chambliss' appreciation of the contemporary nature of these views, 1963).[2]

When we tally up the immense amount of work, the generous and penetrating thought of these people, we can see two powerful currents emerging and blending into one: the "esthetics of confrontation" and the "psychology of belonging." With this merger, we have been able to fashion nothing less than a closure on a problem that has been outstanding since the early Enlightenment—one that goes back to Spinoza and Leibnitz: how to reintroduce a cosmic religious consciousness into the world after the decline of the medieval cosmology. Leibnitz knew that fulfillment is possible only in community. His words are really the ancestors of Royce and Buber, and we might quote him here to make the historical linkage more firm:

> The spirit can only be made perfect through knowledge acquired in communion with other spirits; this is the meaning of . . ." universal correspondence." . . . Just so the individual soul can only be aware of God "in a cosmic community". . . i.e., in nature (Meyer, 1952, pp. 166–167).

Leibnitz thought that the best way to achieve this was by the creation of scientific-religious academies, which would group minds together in discovery of the highest and most esoteric truths. He saw that in this kind of community, rational striving, commonly shared and intensified in pitch, would give the awareness of a kind of cosmic community. The Enlightenment thinkers, down to Lester Ward, meant the same thing when they called for the promotion of human potential to its highest reaches, and wanted the full subsidization of genius in all its forms. Thus, when we talk about the holy in man, we are talking about it in "hard" scientific terms—it is almost a sheer matter of common sense when put into the framework fashioned by the people we are discussing. But when science opted out of life and objectivized man, scientists of course lost the possibility of seeing any mystery at all in man, of seeing any heightening of being, even in secular terms. The rich and vital tradition that we are sketching here was forgotten, and life itself was trivialized in the service of mechanistic, managerial science. We have seen this tragic fact crop up again and again in these pages.

From the point of view of this whole tradition, and the work of all of these thinkers, we can see better how much beside the point Spencer was when he criticized Comte's "Religion of Humanity." Spencer thought that man was a "Finite Knowable," and that real religion needed an "Infinite Unknowable" as a subject (1888, p. 129). Partly this is indisputable, and partly it is wrong. If man is born in the dialogue with his fellows, then he is truly an infinite unknowable, which is just what he must be as the center of a science of life. The Enlightenment here rejoins the later thinkers who fashioned philosophies of emergent evolution. We can recall that Spencer was one of those who, in the nineteenth century, dispersed the true Enlightenment heritage by off-centering the idea of progress, but we know that this heritage alone offers us that vision of a union of idealism and scientific naturalism toward which we have been fumbling ever since. Buber, discussing Kant's question "What is Man?," affirms that he can never be known in himself, but only in his essential relationships (1955, p. 199). And it is precisely in the wholeness of his essential relationships that man is infinite—infinite in terms of the possibility of unfolding and becoming.

And so one of the thorniest questions that grew out of the Enlightenment and has been outstanding since Feuerbach can be solved by a science of man in society, if it can be solved at all. By holding up the ideal vision of the freest possible individual, working in the most equalitarian social community and subserving the unfolding of the cosmic process, we have answered a question with which so many thinkers have grappled and argued: can human association take the place of worship of the divine? Humanists have argued that it can, and thinkers such as Leuba and McTaggart have been attacked— for example by Hocking, who maintains that friendship and mutual respect cannot take the place of the divine, that we need the divine as an object of worship. We can see this as a continuation of Spencer's argument with Comte. But now we know that the two positions are not really opposed, but that they are indeed compatible: the best way to gain an intimacy with the cosmic process, the best way to find support for man's efforts in the universe, is to trust to some divine purpose trying to work itself out in nature. But the most effective way of establishing and maintaining this intimacy, support, and trust is by the joint efforts of men in a free society: celebrating human meanings together, in a devotion to higher ideal ends. Hocking, who took issue with McTaggart on this problem, put in his own words how a man-centered and God-conscious religion meet: ". . . wherever the individual is recovered, there is in some degree also a vision of God" (1912, p. 434; also, see esp. p. 522, footnote). A century after Feuerbach, the humanist, the mystical idealist, and the theist are at last able to close their quarrel. That is, if they are prepared to reword the argument: it is not that human association *takes the place* of the divine, but rather that the divine is best approached in a true community of truly free individuals.

At this point in our discussion, we may also be aware that with our ideal-type we have given an answer to the dilemmas we raised in the preceding chapters, the dilemmas of the innovator and the search for support for one's own meaning. We sketched many different ways in which men reached for such support, and now it should be clear that maximum support for one's new self can only come from a community of free men centered in God. This would give support from "all dimensions" from which we seek it: from the interpersonal or "transference" dimension; from the metaphysical dimension; from the dimension of a God as a true Object; from the dimension of one's inner depths, from God as a becoming Subject; and finally, from the dimension of the joint activities of men in community—the support of the cultural "play-form" itself.

Put in this way, our solution may seem overly facile, something to satisfy everyone with a minimum of effort toward demonstration, argument, and proof. Yet the foundation is there, and the "proof," if we need it, is direct and simple. The theoretical basis for our ideal-type is the best work of the leading thinkers of the West over the last several hundred years. If we had to sum it all up, we would say that the one thing they taught us was that man is immersed in transcending nature; and that within this situation he must develop a relationship to the world based on his fear of being alone, his need for conviction, self-assertion, and support. If we had to put it in one phrase, we would base ourselves on Van der Leeuw's brilliant work, and say that each individual must orient himself to a *sustaining source of power*. The thing is so universal that we can ask it of every individual: what is his particular source of power? It unmistakably reveals the man.

The sources of power that each of us rely on in order to sustain our existence are limited, and we have already discussed them. Here we might mention that the most common one is the "transference" relationship: man gets his personal power from the father figure, from other men in positions of authority. As Sartre said, the bully never bullies in his own name. This was Freud's great insight into human nature, and one of the reasons that he considered most people "trash."

The second major orientation toward a source of power is the transcendental one, which can take many forms; the most usual are the reach toward a supernatural personal God, the immersion of self in awesome Nature, or in the development of Humanity.

The third great way in which individuals gain the support of power is simply by immersing themselves wholeheartedly and uncritically in the everyday cultural game being played in their society; they are upheld by the intricate web of performance of the game itself. This is the complete "fetishization" of the problem of power.

Now of course these three general dimensions of power on which the individual draws are not mutually exclusive: usually man leans on all three. He slavishly accepts the authority of the stronger person, uncritically plays the game of the society into which he is born, and mechanically worships the God of his fathers. Little wonder that rebellious youth and aspiringly free men everywhere strike at these shibboleths of power: taken together, they represent a complete enslavement of the human spirit.

But the fact is that no one can get along without some source of self-transcending power, as we have seen all through our discussion. And so we must conclude that our ideal-type has to be designed on this universal human need, but it has to offer the possibilities of a freedom that this very need usually denies. Now we can see how our ideal of a community of free and equal men does just this. It fights the transference dimension of power by insisting on self-critical knowledge. If we have this knowledge, we can begin to relate to others as equals, and can truly begin to revere the mystery of their subjectivity, without being enslaved and controlled by it. We also fight fetishization of the social game by insisting that we be critical of it at all times, and that we constantly introduce new meanings into it. Finally, as Kierkegaard so unmistakably taught us, a man who is truly potentially free must reach for a self-transcendent divine object; and if he is a free man he will develop an intensely personal relationship to such an object—it will not be the God of his fathers, uncritically and mechanically worshiped.

So much, then, for our design for ethical man. If there were any need to be apologetic about Leibnitzian words like "soul," "God," or "cosmic community," we can now see that they have a proper place in our understanding of man. They are naturalistic scientific words that describe the situation and the relationships of man in society. It may take us some time (it has already taken us over a century and a half) to feel comfortable with insights that both poets and scientists share. The contemporary scientist must object—almost reflexively—against the kind of constructs we are proposing here. At most, he might tolerate them as peripheral to the "hard" business of science. But we are not proposing mere toleration—far from it. We are now in a position to see that these kinds of constructs—meaning, conviction, sense of intimacy with the cosmic process—must be *at the very center* of a science of man in society. They are part of the human situation, and a science of man in society cannot permit itself to overlook what is typical of the human situation. As Buber has so well understood: "Neither the world of things, nor his fellow-man and community, nor the mystery which points beyond these, and also beyond himself, can be dismissed from a man's situation" (1955, p. 180). Only in this way can we have the science of man that the Enlightenment promised, and that Lester Ward wanted: the fullest possible statement of the nature and dimensions of human valuings; the social forces at their broadest reach and in their most complex interrelationship; the complete exploration of the nature of the social bond.

The Contemporary Subversion of Ethical Man

As we said earlier, an ideal-type, if it is worth anything, should point directly to clear social criticisms; and we have already seen how our vision of man stands in judgment over the emptiness of contemporary society. Let us close this part of our discussion by glancing at some of the specific critical views of some of the thinkers we have been discussing. It will help remind us that not only is modern life impoverished, but that in this impoverishment even the possibility of ethical living is ruled out.

We have known it since the nineteenth century, since the failure of social reconstruction in the new society. Carlyle summed up the new moral undergirding of commercial-industrialism when he smirked about the policemen protecting the merchant shops: the ethical ideal would be one policeman per merchant—and today we are approximating it. Here, in one graphic image, was the new society's answer to the moral dilemma posed by the decline of the medieval community. We would expect that the thinkers we have passed in review would be against commercial-industrialism by the logical necessity of their mature understanding of man, just as the best thinkers of the nineteenth century were against it on intuitive and common-sense grounds. And so they are. Martin Buber, Paul Tillich, Jean-Paul Sartre, Max Scheler, Gabriel Marcel, John Dewey—the list is very long indeed. Max Scheler, for example, held that ". . .the first task of our educational practice must be to revive the capacity for identification with the life of the universe, and awaken it anew from its condition of dormancy in the capitalistic social outlook of Western man" (1954, p. 105). What was there in the capitalistic outlook that made this identification with the universe difficult, if not impossible? Simply that it buried the sense of community, the sense of sharing, of mutual action devoted to shared, self-transcending goals. The characteristic world picture of capitalism, as Scheler saw, was one which understood the world as "an aggregation of movable quantities" (p. 105). In other words, man was seen from the outside, seen as a "thing," disconnected, mechanical, limited, servile, determined. This kind of creature could never transcend himself, could never hope for the larger identifications with the life of the universe.

Today we know that as society sees man, so he is, for the most part. To build a social system on the commercial image of man is indeed to create such a man—and we have created him. His bright and smug consumer face shines benignly through our advertising in his many poses: counting pennies saved, and winking wisely; beaming with pride over shirt sleeves that extend the proper half inch beyond the jacket cuff; transported into heavenly rapture by zippers that do not catch or by a laundry soap that makes just the right amount of foamy bubbles. If anyone doubted that a merely symbolic world view could humble organic nature and fashion such a creature, the doubts are today stilled. He is there for all to see.

Royce, like other nineteenth-century thinkers, had much earlier seen the fallacy of a democracy which merely existed to balance self-interests. He saw that our apparent harmony was illusory, simply because it depersonalized man and deprived him of the truly individual and unique contribution which man must bring to society. A mere balance-of-interests society deprives the individual of the possibility of loyalty and devotion, and so strips him of the sense of belonging; and without this sense he can have no intense interest in the community good. Like Carlyle and Kierkegaard earlier in the century, Royce saw that mass man was being created by the impersonal forces of the economic order (cf. Cotton, 1954, pp. 257 ff.).

But Scheler's criticisms, along with those of Royce and countless others, and their views on the reasons why the interhuman is undermined in our time were not enough from a critical point of view. We needed a scientific critique of the "owning society," and not merely a declaration of what we had lost. We needed a really precise formula for generating interpersonal meaning so that we could use this formula to pinpoint more exactly the reasons and the ways in which we have destroyed the interhuman. Only in this way would a criticism of commercial-industrialism have compelling force for objective students of man. It was Martin Buber who supplied what was needed, in the form of a three-point formula by means of which man helps man unfold and establish contact and unity with the larger life of the universe. Buber sums up the formula in these words:

> For the proper existence of the interhuman it is necessary . . . that the semblance not intervene to spoil the relation of personal being to personal being. It is further necessary . . . that each one means and makes present the other in his personal being. That neither should wish to impose himself on the other is the third basic presupposition of the interhuman (1957, p. 111).

In other words, the threefold formula boils down to this: that one must act spontaneously from his whole being rather than for simple role-staging effect; that one must relate to the other as a whole, indeterminate individual, and not as a determinate, part individual; and, lastly, that one must grant another the right to his own center, his own mystery, without seeking to manipulate or efface him.

These rather abstract enjoinders may seem at first glance to be anything but a precise scientific formula. But when we examine them in terms of our previous discussion of esthetics and in terms of modern role theory, we can see exactly what they imply. Taken together, these three points are a basis for expanding the life process and for re-establishing full contact with it. They permit us to understand how a particular culture can undermine the expansiveness of being. The whole person is always greater than the cultural roles because the living organism always has more potential behaviors than the particular cultural game that society sets up in order unthinkingly to further the business of everyday living. The total individual, in other words, is always greater than the cultural role self. But man does not realize this, except in rare cases, because he must live as society has set up the plot. The result is that mostly people approach each other from the point of view of their roles, rather than as whole beings. The role player stages life; the whole being acts spontaneously. But spontaneous action is a momentous problem for most, precisely because they have learned to keep action going smoothly and satisfyingly by simply and uncritically following out the roles that the culture designed for them. They have, in effect, subverted the possibilities of their total being to the narrow interest of action and uncritical survival. Now this is not a criticism so much as it is a simple observation; man is hardly to be blamed for accepting the ongoing version of the life drama, and drawing the ready satisfactions that this entails. Besides, this gives what man needs most—it gives conviction. When everyone upholds unflinchingly his roles, within the cultural fiction, the joint staging seems right for all time. As we noted several times earlier, Fourier saw that there were any number of ways of twisting "the passions," and that they all worked to give man what he needed, even though they were humanly debasing.

But this view does become a criticism of commercial-industrial society, and as it is rendered more precise by Buber's formula it is an especially damaging one. In the first place, it can be shown that commercial society, instead of promoting the individualism and freedom that it so tirelessly claims to promote, actually is subverting the whole individual by reducing him to a role-playing part. In other words, to further the commercial game of private gain, individuals must relate to each other according to the pre-established role forms, and the spontaneous, potential person is lost. True, the commercial game has its own form of esthetics—we noted earlier how well Veblen and Mills understood its finer points.

But the question posed by any cultural game is the question about higher and lower esthetics—about "good" art and "bad" art, to put the matter simply. The unthinking, everyday role game is simply esthetics at a cheap grade; it is "everyday" esthetics. True, it gives conviction, but at a terrible price—at the price of uncritically building man more firmly into his determinate world (cf. E. Becker, 1964a, chap. 8). In other words, whereas true esthetics should

liberate man, develop his freedom, and further his whole self, "everyday" esthetics sacrifices most of the total man to a mere part, to the part
that must convey the sliver of conviction necessary to sustain the
ongoing cultural game.

After all, even those who doubt their right to their own meanings must try for conviction. We saw this in some detail; it is the core
problem for ethical man. Only the weaker man in striving for conviction, in his attempt to be ethical, must be *less autonomous*. He
derives his sense of rightness from the preordained cultural plot, rather
than from any original reach for freedom. Lack of spontaneity,
façade role playing, rigid and pompous formality—all these describe
people who need conviction and meaning, but cannot bring it out
of themselves. For the most part, it is the rigid, hollow, frightened,
timid people who become the stock bureaucrats and who staff our
administrations. Again, Max Weber's thesis on the ineluctable expansion of bureaucracy into our lives is all of a piece with mass society.
Mass society contributes psychologically to make the process successful. We guarantee the victory of bureaucracy, the choking off of
original and creative innovators, so that the forms of things can continue unimpeded, and we do this by limiting the possibilities of
justifying unique meanings. Man, alone, trembling, hugs to whatever
he has left: the empty role, the façade self, the mere performance
of the everyday part—lines convincingly delivered, the smart salute,
the knowing wink, the sharp decision that furthers the organization.

But "higher" esthetics is precisely that; it calls more of man's
spirit into play, releases more of the inner personality and brings it to
bear upon the world. As we have analyzed the dynamics of this in
terms of Hegelian esthetics, it is this revelation of more inner spirit,
in the hard world of things, that gives the maximum of conviction.
It is this alone that can unite man with feeling for the life of the cosmos
because it already reveals more of that very life in the interhuman
encounter. It is not for nothing that our commercial advertising so
blithely degrades man and arouses so little popular protest: commercial man radiates such a small margin of free spirit that he already seems degraded. The conviction that he supplies is hardly
enough, in other words, to make us respect him. Consequently, the
toll that we pay is truly frightful. Not only do we have less of a feeling
for the great expanse of life, but we also have less for our fellow man,
and consequently *less respect for the whole life process*. Thus the
degradation of commercial advertising is a logical and coherent
part of a particular kind of world view.

Buber has phrased this esthetic problem very powerfully, and has understood how the whole man is being reduced to the part needs of a particular cultural game. Let me quote him at length:

> To be aware of a man, therefore, means in particular to perceive his wholeness as a person determined by the spirit; it means to perceive the dynamic center which stamps his every utterance, action, and attitude with the recognizable sign of uniqueness. Such an awareness is impossible, however, if and so long as the other is the separated object of my contemplation or even observation, for this wholeness and its center do not let themselves be known to contemplation or observation (1957, p. 109).

In other words, man is an infinite unknowable whom we destroy and make finite, by objectifying him in his social roles, by using him as a role-playing source of cues to our own uncritical cultural performance. Buber continues:

> The perception of one's fellow man as a whole, as a unit, and as unique . . . is opposed in our time by almost everything that is commonly understood as specifically modern. In our time there predominates an analytical, reductive, and deriving look between man and man (p. 109).

Buber is here referring specifically to the scientific treatment of man as a determinate object, the same criticism that Scheler, Husserl, Jaspers, and others had made. As many critical thinkers have observed, and are increasingly observing, the development of the Western scientific world view and the development of the commercial society proceeded hand-in-hand. Science took its peculiarly "neutral" form in order that it might survive and be allowed to pursue its research, and the Royal Society was allowed to form in London on the specific condition that it refrain from religious and political matters. Science, in a word, first objectified man tacitly and indirectly; and, when commercial society had objectified him directly, by making of him a determinate and uncritical role player, science found itself face-to-face with an object that seemed truly limited. Hence it seemed a proper thing to reduce and dissect (cf. Paci, 1963, pp. 208–210).

The problem, inescapably, is a social one. We have destroyed the interhuman in our time simply because we have refused to implement social forms which would liberate man. It is not a problem merely of an "analytic cast of mind." Rather, it is this: if we are going to look at the other as Buber urges, as a whole, free spontaneity, then we must help that spontaneity and freedom to unfold. Otherwise, we must relate to the other as a part, as determined; we must oberve him and contemplate him, since he exists to serve *predetermined* purposes, and does not exist to help us frame new ones. We treat our fellow man as the mother of a young schizophrenic girl treated her: as a determinate inner self which is only good to subserve some cultural function. Thus she always asked: "How are your titties coming dear?" (Laing, 1962), much as we ask, "How is your bank balance?"—how, in sum, is that socially determinate part of your identity by which alone I can judge you as a whole person?

It is fundamentally degrading to man to be reduced to his roles. While this is man's "fate" in society, some societies struggle against it rather than reinforce the process. The anthropologist Stanley Diamond brings out this excellent point about some primitive societies when he says that primitive society is generally characterized by a respect for man taken as a whole, and not as a mere mechanical aggregate of roles (cf. 1963). Thus, among the Anaguta, one can say that a man has a "bad character," but one cannot say that he is a "bad *man*." In other words, they seem to be able to say that the role self is disagreeable and bad, but that the total organism is not to be judged on that basis. Probably the reason that they can do this is that they have not objectified man, have not treated him as something "put together" and therefore capable of being taken apart and known (Buber, 1957, p. 109). They still see man as an indeterminate locus of mystery, containing the unfolding powers of cosmos and life.

More directly, of course, they have not reduced man to a commercial puppet, to a tractable consumer, to a transactable bank balance. For the primitive, man is man—just that—a being with whom one joins in the noble quest for survival, a being with whom one adds meaning to life in the many rituals which mark its mystery. We fail to see the whole other man in our time simply because we do not have this basic "primitive" orientation: we do not share in a mutual task, join in some agreed purpose which transcends our personal interest, devote ourselves to some larger promise which allows us to identify our interests with the rest of the community. We cannot look at the other as a spontaneous source of life because there is nothing we can do *with* him—only *to* him, *toward* him, as a co-signer of a contract, a viewer of our status, a role player who mouths the empty words that allow the equally empty forms of daily transactions to go on.

Why, for example, is the social gathering in America, even at a university, as Barzun has so trenchantly noted, one of the most meaningless, lifeless, and generally pathetic experiences to which the sensitive observer can be subject? Simply because there is no real mutuality, no shared purpose, no higher design. It is an agglomerate of splinter individuals, devoted to continuing separately the business of life; these individuals are obliged to shun problems, shun engagement, shun real interhuman exchange, not because they are ethically callous, but simply because there is no mutual design into which to fit the problems, engagement, and exchange. One has only to compare the Western cocktail gathering to a meeting of intellectuals from one of the newly emerging areas to see how the interhuman can become a meaningful pattern of whole persons. Ideals, devotion, purpose, explicit political and social problems—these frame the conditions for the optimum development of the human personality and human life. In America one looks back nostalgically to the few times that such ideals and purposes existed, to the times when man lived for a larger promise, devoted himself in concert with his fellows to a shared problem which transcended immediate selfish interests. Thus, the "old army days" evoke warm memories because a real camaraderie existed. This is just another way of saying that shared purpose and mutual expectations caused men to regard each other as whole, and to value the spontaneity that emerges from wholeness, because it alone can meet the larger challenges of real crises. Today one reads how the members of a jury, which had met for many months at a trial, were sad over breaking up, and continued the personal contacts which the members had built up. We find such conduct amusing and "neighborly," not realizing that it attests to a bankruptcy of our present, individualistic life, to the loneliness of man who lives without larger purpose and problems. These jury groups represent commercial man reaching pathetically for significance, a groping that finds fulfillment only accidentally and sporadically in the perverted version of the "free" life that we have inherited.

But freedom means nothing unless it means championing the fullest play on the powers that each unique organism brings into nature. It can hardly mean freedom to do what everyone else is doing, freedom to follow in the preset cultural design. This is so patent that it is incredible that we consistently refuse to realize it, as a society, in America today. So much so that we consent to sacrifice the energies of each new generation to the going cultural forms. Yet we know that man can never be man unless he is the locus of his powers—we have seen in these pages that this is what alienation means, the forfeiting of responsibility for one's own action. Whether it takes the form of mental illness—of action constricted to the narrowest possible range— or whether it takes the form of mindless collective action, the basic problem is the same: the failure to exercise one's own powers within a unified, critical framework. The phenomena of fascism and collect-ivism in our time are all part of a logical piece with our destruction of the interhuman, with the sacrifice of the whole man to further the empty forms of commercial society.

What is the abject worship of the leader, the willful abrogating of one's own decisions? Why does the mass follow blindly, and hate so firmly? The answer, of course, is again that man needs conviction above all; but that there are a number of ways to draw it. The free man, believing in himself and his fellow man, in the value that springs up from the living organism is more tentative, more willing to fabri-cate conviction daily in the living encounter. His spontaneity draws on that of other free men, and life meaning is constantly enriched with new forms. But the individual who uncritically plays his cultural role, who treats himself and his fellows as transactable objects, cannot, deep down, believe in his own powers: he has none of his own—he is a cultural artifact, nothing more. The circle is vicious and ineluctable. If one does not exercise the spontaneous powers of his being, in free, mutual intercourse with his fellows, he cannot believe he is a locus of value. Thus, his very life lacks conviction. But, since he must have conviction, he must seek it in others. This means that the strong, directive, loud, overpowering object in one's environment will take on a special significance: it becomes a major locus of self-transcendent value. As we noted earlier, this is the undesirable extreme of what we call transference. The individual can feel that the *object* has value, even if he does not—or *especially* if he does not. He then draws all his meaning from the extreme transference object. It is as if the in-dividual says: "I do not experience the free exercise of my own powers; therefore I really feel no value (or meaning); hence life itself has no value (meaning). But if the strong object in my field has value, then meaning is safe in the world." So, in order not to lose the one locus of meaning that gives genuineness to the life plot, in order not to be thrown back on one's exposed and meager resources, one hugs to the extreme transference object. There is only one sensible answer to this problem, and we will examine it in the next chapter.

Collective action and uncritical devotion to unscrupulous leaders have been a problem all through history. But there is no doubt that in modern times it is peculiarly aggravated by the institutions of contemporary society. We have created a quintessential mass man by failing to value concrete living organisms as sacred centers of life. And we have paid the proper toll: The destruction of the human has led logically to the destruction of the interhuman, and ultimately to the unthinking destruction of other humans. Sadism and masochism, as we saw, really testify to the utmost *weakness*, the failure to grant to others the right to their own mystery.

This is the price man pays for allowing the forms of commercial society to take precedence over the vital life process, as it is embodied in the highest organism. The whole thing conceals a terrible and fitting logic: since man is the only animal who, under the influence of certain forms of culture, can be led to deny free and spontaneous life, it follows that he should then lose the consciousness of life as a value. Manipulated by the hollow, external forms of things, modern man in turn manipulates others as hollow, external forms. There is no possibility of indentification with the life process of the cosmos, no hope of ethics, no rich, genuine, variegated meanings. Thus we can see that once we begin to study the superordinate role of meaning in human life, and the psychological, social, and historical bases for it, we can develop the most damaging criticism of contemporary commercial society. There can no longer be any serious question of how and why contemporary man is prevented from being truly free and ethical.

THE ETHICAL SOCIETY

What does it mean, then, to love one's country, and what does it mean to be a patriot? If a poet is busy all his life fighting evil prejudices, removing narrow views, enlightening the mind of his people, purifying their taste and ennobling their opinions and thoughts, how could he do better or be more patriotic?

GOETHE *(in Randall, 1940, p. 379)*

Goethe once exclaimed that he might even consent to support another fifty years of life just to see the Suez and Panama canals built. Wasn't *Faust* the vision of a world that we still want to usher in? Was Goethe right in his poetry, even though he could not be in his own life or times? If we read Erich Heller's superb essays, this is the impression we get (1959, see esp. pp. 48 ff.). The moral of Faust is that man becomes truly man by the esthetic transformation of the world with his free directive energies. But the moral of the nineteenth century was that community was not possible for the truly creative spirit. The only thing that the real innovator could do was to offer Utopias: poetic—like Faust; social reconstructionist—like Saint-Simon, Fourier, Comte, Bellamy; prophetically historicist—like Marx. At times the nineteenth century seems a truly Biblical epoch, in which passionate visions sprang up on a hostile soil, and there was nothing to do but wait. The great difference is that the nineteenth-century soil was not arid; the great wheels of industrial plenty had begun their relentless grind. For the first time in history, grand

280

Utopian human visions were being obtrusively accompanied by the proper means for their realization.

Fortunately, nature does not grant the wishes of men who want to see the promised land. Had Goethe lived another fifty years, he would have seen the curtain open on one of the most grotesque spectacles of history, and he would have been able to sit with Burckhardt and foretell a new age of monsters. Today we have so lost the Faustian promise that we are even afraid to fulfill it. What will happen, we lament, when the wage-work day is abolished, when the automated factories grind out their plenty, and distribute it to all, when annual salaries are guaranteed, regardless of work—what will man do with his leisure; how will he keep from running wild?

The question betrays the whole failure of our time: the failure of the science of man to put forth an agreed, synthetic theory of human nature; the failure of society to see beyond the kind of monster that it has created with its commercial-industrial madness. Of course social welfare dampens public interest in a society in which there is no public interest, no agreed purpose. Why should the individual design larger, self-transcending social ends when the society as a whole frowns on it? Each person is bent on his own security, his own future; as a result, there is no *social* future, no future for men in common.

All of this is commonplace enough, but it explains why mass man is so impotent. He lacks a basic human dimension—control over the future; in a word, he has no "social ego" (cf. Arendt, 1958, p. 245). After all, a society, as a union of free individuals, needs to project a similar kind of control to that projected by the individual ego. "If I (we) do right in the present, by subordinating certain kinds of impulsive satisfactions, then the future will be secure and rewarding." Thus, the individual ego and the social ego design a broad vista for human energy and control, and man achieves a dignity thereby that is denied to other animals.

What happens when the society lacks an ego? The very same thing that happens when the individual has very weak control over his destiny: he fetishizes. He begins to look for control in narrow areas, areas that have nothing really basic to do with his problems. And society does the same: if it cannot handle the principal problem of adaptation by intelligently harnessing the future to its purposes, it tries to exercise firm control over areas where it does have power. This explains why our society is so obsessed with traffic violations, with drug addiction, with the unseemliness of long haircuts. These are social fetishizations of the problem of morality in modern times. It is as though the whole society were to breathe one huge sigh and say: "Ah, if only we could control these, how good life would be." These kinds of fetish controls are harmless enough, of course: a few traffic fines, a few hippies jailed for smoking marijuana—it is all benign. But alas, there are other ways of exercising a fetish social ego, and they are far from harmless: today we are witnessing our society trying to gain some kind of control over the national life and some kind of meaningful national design by forging what we might call a "military social ego." This kind of adaptation is old enough and it has often been necessary for the survival of free communities—e.g., at the time of the Greeks. But the question that is critical today is whether a "military social ego" any longer represents an intelligent adaptation to the problems of morality in the modern world. We know that this kind of ego defeats dictatorships and today our best scientists are warning us that it will defeat commercial-industrial democracy.

Our fetish social ego and our "futuristic living" are all of a piece: they represent a pious wish that everything will turn out well if we feverishly and uncritically play the game of our society. But there is a real difference between this naïve and clumsy attempt to influence the future and the creative design of a new future horizon; and it is the one that Dewey outlined, namely, the difference between mechanical action and real action, the difference between external, coerced means, and individually controlled means (cf. E. Becker, 1964a, chap. 7). It boils down to the question: is the individual a free source of action, does he have aegis over the kinds of means he will use to achieve the desired end? This was the whole basis of Dewey's pragmatism. It summed up his entire social philosophy and justified his theory of education and his vision of a truly sane society. As T. V. Smith urged, "This redemption of the present from some phantom future has been John Dewey's greatest contribution to American thought" (1939, p. 199). Ordinarily man is burdened by designs inherited from tradition that impose means and ends upon him. He barters his free energies in uncritical acceptance of the life the elders impose. Pragmatism sought to overcome this by making means relevant to ever-new problems, changing as the real problem changed. The free man, like the free society, would be one who could continually re-adapt his means to ever-new ends, and would not follow slavishly in the footsteps of tradition and habit. Or, put in terms that are now familiar to us, we would say that the free man is the true genius who creates new meanings and continually cuts through old forms. This is why pragmatism has always insisted on the importance of method. As the noted sociologist E. A. Ross put it:

> A schooling devised primarily to produce good character, or patriotism, or dynastic loyalty, or class sentiment, or religious orthodoxy may lessen friction in society, but it cannot bring genius to bloom. For this the prime essentials are *the communicating of known truths* and *the imparting of method* (1908, p. 360, his emphasis).

We can see how intimately connected are the visions of the Enlightenment on genius, of pragmatism on science, of democracy on freedom, and of all of these on education. Freedom and genius mean education for cultural criticism, education for tentativeness and experiment. Dewey's "progressive education" was Enlightenment philosophy applied to the modern world. And the credo of progressive education was stated by that other Enlightenment man, long before Dewey. In a letter to Du Pont de Nemours, Jefferson said:

> We both consider the people as our children, and love them with parental affection. But you love them as infants whom you are afraid to trust without nurses; and I as adults whom I freely leave to self-government (Padover, 1956, pp. 272–273).

Jefferson, we will remember, believed that each generation should live under a constitution of its own making. He wanted a revision of the Constitution, and a new social contract, at least every nineteenth year—since he calculated that in eighteen years and eight months half of those over twenty-one would have passed away. This was the true Enlightenment man speaking, the critic of culture, of any forms that enslave man. He wanted a pragmatic ethic that stemmed from a full consciousness of the fabricated nature of human arrangements. It is curious that Freud has often been condemned for a hard materialism, a tough-mindedness about man's motives, which he thought stemmed from deep-seated instincts. Actually, this kind of natural law is anything but tough-minded. It prevents us from being truly skeptical about social motives, blinds us to the fictional nature of symbolic striving, even while it pretends to disclose the "true" nature of human striving. In short, it pretends that human choices are *limited*, when in fact, as Jefferson saw, they must be limitless and continually reappraised. Jefferson was thus "tough-minded" in the only way that this word can have sense for man.

The problem for the ethical society can now be stated simply. Granted that we will someday put economic affairs under the control of reason; how do we educate the kind of people who might want to revise the Constitution every nineteen years? What does this kind of progressive education entail? The answer is direct: we saw in the previous chapter how man can be given the strength to be ethical, that he needs critical knowledge and that he needs to work in unison with other free selves. This is exactly what progressive education is, in its original vision. It educates man for the strength to choose, to offer up his own meanings; and it educates him to treat others as sacred ends, rather than as cultural, role-playing means. The function of progressive education is the function of true democratic government, exactly as Emerson envisaged this ideal: namely, to prepare the way for the self-reliant individual. There is thus a clear and direct line of development from Jefferson and Emerson to Dewey and the new science of man in society. Dewey was fully aware of it—which is why he called Emerson the greatest moralist America had produced.

PROGRESSIVE EDUCATION FOR ETHICAL MAN

In our definition of alienation we said that it could only mean exile from the free and responsible aegis over one's own initiatory powers. We also noted that alienation, mental illness, the "unconscious"—are all synonymous. They refer to the results of an early learning process in which the natural ability to learn by trial and error is paralyzed in some ways and in certain areas of awareness. As a result, in the face of new choices the individual will experience great anxiety, and will distrust his powers of independent judgment; he will have a greater or lesser "unconscious," depending on the ways and the length of time in which his self-powers have been crippled. Thus, we said that the "unconscious" was not a problem in "depth," but rather that it was a problem in the range of behaviors and in the richness and flexibility of the cognitive grasp of problematic action situations. Man's alienation, in other words, is not a phylogenetic problem, not a question of man being shackled by instincts. We must repeat this again and again, because it highlights the terrible detour in the continuity of Enlightenment thought that was posed by the Freudian interlude. Man is alienated when he is not "doing," and in order for the symbolic animal to "do" he must command an effective cognitive grasp of a problematic situation. This means that he must not only "know" what is wrong, but he must also feel and believe that he has the powers to act on what he knows.

Psychoanalytic theory helped to clarify immensely the basic dichotomy that exists in human experience between the early training that man is subject to and the adult choices that will later present themselves. It is this dichotomy, as we saw, which deprives man of a belief in his own powers. He does not make new choices—create new meanings—without awakening the anxiety he learned in his early training. By thus discovering this dichotomy, and tracing how it comes into being as an interplay of ego and anxiety, psychoanalysis also outlined the problem of neurosis. We might say, then, that neurosis can be understood *as the avoidance of self-created meaning.* Clarified in this way, Freud's thought rejoins the Enlightenment out of which it sprang, but which it helped obscure.

Progressive education, ethics, and cognition are intimately related, then, and they are an Enlightenment problem; the proof lies right at hand. Rousseau, the first critic of alienation, also proposed that it was a cognitive problem, and that education of the child had to take place away from society—that is, away from the automatic induction into the constricting world view of the culture. Only thus would the child have a chance to offer up his own original meanings. Rousseau very early saw that to be a "normal" member of any society almost automatically spells the doom of true individuality. Nietzsche later echoed the same thesis with great force and stridency; but it had already been said, and the peacefulness of one man's life had already been sacrificed for it. Fourier, Lester Ward, and Robert Owen held similar views.

Long before psychoanalysis, then, culture had been called into question as the cause of neurosis, of rigid early learning patterns that stamp the world with sameness, and drown out flexible behaviors. While Rousseau proposed that the child be educated away from society, psychoanalysis proposed a costly therapy, lasting up to five years and more, that would liberate the individual from the shackles of society, by helping him "see through" his early training. But this is a liberation that can only take place *after* the constrictions have been formed.

My point is simply this, and it seems to me very compelling from a historical point of view, namely, it is quite clear that since the nineteenth century did not act *socially* on the problem of alienation, it was almost an ineluctable historical logic later to devise a system which would attack the problem *individually,* on a post-hoc basis. Today it seems very clear that psychoanalytic therapy is a child of the failure to initiate a true progressive education at the time of the Enlightenment. It is a historical artifact.

Perhaps it was for this very reason that an Enlightenment man like Dewey, seriously concerned with the problem of a liberating education, could not take psychoanalysis seriously—either as theory or therapy. The therapy vaunted itself to undo some of the evils of the human condition, evils which the theory, with its idea of instinct, accepted fatalistically. But a progressive educator had to get at the problem of human bondage *before* it arose; furthermore, as we said earlier, he cannot take this bondage for granted—otherwise, as an Enlightenment man, he would simply have to give up before trying. Dewey, in other words, saw that the educator could never cede his place to the psychoanalyst, that the critical educator antedated him historically, and that the problem of individual maladjustment and liberation really belonged to him. Progressive education itself as Dewey understood it, proposed to overcome neurosis. And the progressive educator's understanding of neurosis is the same as the vaunted "clinical" one; he could rephrase it in terms of two basic and related deficits: (1) *The paralysis of the ability to learn by natural trial and error*; and (2) *The distrust of one's powers of independent judgment, throughout life*. Both of these deficits are a result of the early learning process.

How did progressive education propose to overcome them? By a program of continual engagement of the child in real problematic experiences, in a continuing hierarchy of such experiences. This accomplishes the same result as psychoanalytic therapy hopes to accomplish, but it does this *before* the full burden is formed. The child, by continual engagement of his powers in problematic action, effaces the sharp dichotomy between constricting parental training and broad social challenge. In Dewey's view, as in Rousseau's earlier, the child must be encouraged to make his own adjustment. He overcomes the potential constrictions of the standardized cultural world view, by direct refashioning *of himself and his perceptions* in ongoing problematic situations. Dewey's whole protest, in fact, was against the educational atmosphere of societies like that of Freud's Victorian Vienna where "neurosis" was discovered: the old educational technique simply reinforced the early authoritarian family training; the child was trained to acquiesce in his passivity by browbeating, emotional appeals, sermons, and so on.

Hence, as Dewey saw, true democracy is the only atmosphere in which man can grow because it is against nonreflective action at *all* times. It is geared to meeting with the full force of cognition continually new, problematic situations. The old authoritarian, faculty education, in other words, enforced the early perceptions of the child in their accustomed rut, by not allowing him to exercise and develop his own, spontaneously organizing perceptions. Small wonder that Freud, working in the constrictive atmosphere of authoritarian Vienna, and seeing patients from close-knit families, discovered particularly constricting forms of neurosis. Freud's famous cases on hysteria reflected exactly what we would expect: not people who were "sick" in any medical sense, but confused and purblind children who had been raised as uncritical slaves of their domineering parents and constricting society (cf. Szasz, 1961). In that particular society, the moratorium on original perceptions, and on the exercise of self-powers, came to last from the age of the oedipal transition to late adolescence and beyond. Again, it is little wonder that Freud accented the peculiar force of the "unconscious": he had discovered a very severe socially induced version of it. Today I think we can fairly say that the greater the period of delay between early training and the assumption of responsible adult action, the greater the unconscious which tyrannizes the individual. Since the unconscious is really another way of talking about limited action and cognition that is socially induced and learned, then we can say that the severity of one's neurosis will vary with the *strength and length of the moratorium* that society puts on the child's use of his responsible, executive powers.

Dewey seemed to have realized this even before the mass of evidence from modern anthropology supported it—just as Rousseau realized it before reliable anthropology was born. Anthropologists discovered that in some societies natural bodily functioning is more violently curbed than in others; in some societies childhood lasts longer, adolescence and adulthood are not marked off clearly as growth periods in which the child assumes new responsibilities, and so on; in sum, that some societies more than others train their children to be relatively submissive and powerless in a world that is not of their own making (cf. Benedict, 1938). Perhaps Freud would have understood that his therapy was a historical and social artifact responding to peculiar conditions if he had been less respectful of nineteenth-century reductionist science. It was this that blunted and finally stunted almost completely the full force of cultural criticism that was inherent in Freud's completed answer to the Enlightenment dilemma on the nature of conscience. Psychoanalytic theory even reduced art to the determinism of early psychosexual development, and thus by implication impugned even the contributions of the liberating genius, of the Leonardo and the Michelangelo who lift man to a higher plane of superordinate meanings. In this regard, let us pause to note that Freud's much-lauded *Interpretation of Dreams* is actually his most fallible book. It uses the concrete, physical symbolism of dreams to explain the meaning of man's strivings. Thus, for example, when the person dreams of teeth falling out, psychoanalysts might interpret this symbolism as a fear of castration, of punishment for incestual urges. But the dream symbolism is actually a "fetishistic" language; it is a shorthand for much more superordinate types of experience. The dream of tooth falling, for example, could refer rather to a sense of one's whole inadequacy in life. The dreamer—like the child—seizes on the most narrow and concrete conceptualization to sum up broad ranges of felt experience. It was a simple matter for psychoanalytic theory to use the experiences of childhood to support the symbolism of dreams, and vice versa: the findings in both areas were then mutually reinforcing; but very few thinkers arose to condemn the sterile circularity of the process. It seems fair to say that psychoanalytic symbolism, by building on the shorthand of dreams, and merging this with a sexual theory of infant development, has actually *fetishized the modern consciousness*. It has everywhere made current a symbolism relating to narrow and concrete body meanings, and students of man who use this symbolism gain an easy but false understanding of human striving: they overlook the fact that it is precisely the concretized and fetishized symbols which— in the absence of broader understanding and conscious elaboration— take the place of larger social meanings. We live in a scientific world where the child's fumbling for expression is taken by adults as gospel truth; and where the striking symbolism of dreams is believed almost literally, as it is among primitives.[1]

Because of the default of psychoanalysis, real cultural criticism had to come from other fields than reductionist medicine and medical psychiatry.[2] Thus, the literary and esthetic critic such as I. A. Richards could see very clearly that personal bondage is a problem of the artificial fixation of attitudes, and that this fixation takes place when the child is removed from the free play of experience. And he could say that this kind of exile often makes of the adult a less-aware individual than the child (1925, pp. 202–203). He could understand esthetics as a liberation from what *society* does to man, as a groping for new human meanings, and not as a fixation on animal ones. The esthetician is a natural progressive educator, as Dewey proved with his *Art as Experience*. The medical scientist is not. By missing the superordinacy of meaning in human life, Freud detoured the current of idealism and Enlightenment, both as esthetic theory *and* as progressive education.

I am leading up to this: that when we understand psychoanalytic discoveries as discoveries of the problem of *cognition* alone, we can do something very critical: we can eliminate the aura of mystery that surrounds its use in schools and society. Educators would then have to pay attention, not to the "maladjusted queerness" of children, to the mysteries of their "inner urges," but rather to something much more open, and for this very reason much more difficult to cope with: that is, they would have to ask, *how can the educative process as a whole increase critical cognition?* (Cf. Shoben, 1960.) Here is an open question that would set the problem of psychiatry in the schools right on end. As things stand now, the use of psychoanalysis and psychiatry as an adjunct to the training of "problem children" has really helped obscure the real "problem" (cf. Szasz, 1963a). Is this part of the reason that we have adopted them so eagerly and widely? If cognition is the problem, then educators must approach education in general in the same way we approached the education of ethical man, namely, that ethical action is strong action, and it takes critical knowledge to be strong. The problem, then, for the progressive education of ethical man would simply be: how can we best educate for cognition?

When we answer this question, we will also have answered another one, one that has bothered very many people, namely, why did progressive education fail? If it was on the right track, if it saw the problems of personal growth and freedom so clearly as problems of knowing and doing, why has it almost wholly failed to deliver its early promise?

The answer is that progressive education failed to give real, liberating cognition. As a result, it failed to banish neurosis or alienation. It is important to note that neurosis takes two forms which are two facets of a single problem. In one sense it refers to the long moratorium on the exercise of self-powers, to which society condemns the child. In our society we call this moratorium latency and adolescence. This cripples certain areas of awareness, as we said, and creates a sharp dichotomy between early training and adult experience. In its other aspect, neurosis can be looked at from a more positive angle, but it is just as crippling. That is, it can be seen as the training of the child to act in socially approved ways, even while allowing him a more-or-less free-wheeling disposal of his energies. Whatever powers he does exercise lead him to become a "normal" member of society, only to lose his potential uniqueness in the process. This is the kind of neurosis that exists in primitive societies, where self-powers may not be so curbed or baffled. Thus, looked at from either way, neurosis refers to a curbing of individual potential: either as the active crippling of self-powers, or as the overtraining of powers to function in automatically socially approved ways. Those individuals who end up in psychiatric clinics are not "neurotic" compared to others who are "normal." Rather, they are simply *more* constricted, so that the *general* cultural constriction is broader than they can handle. Mental illness, no matter how we look at it, is simply *relative* constriction of behavior. It has a positive social virtue in that it makes "normal" cultural automatons seem free. "Mental illness" is another term that allows us to clarify a spectrum of ideal-typicality, like the word "transference" or "democracy."

Progressive education, in order to be successful, would have had to aim for an ideal which would diminish both aspects of the problem of neurosis or alienation from self-powers. It would have had to try for the maximum unconstriction of behavior. But what does "maximum unconstriction" mean? We see that it can mean anything, depending upon the ideal that it is measured against. If the ideal is the "normal" of accepted behavior, then education allows the kinds of powers that permit the person to cope in his particular society so that he does not bog down and fail vis-à-vis the accepted routines carried on by his fellows. Progressive education in its original vision sought to shape individuals who could function in a modern industrial democracy. Democracy needed citizens who were capable of independent judgment, free uninhibited cooperation; thus progressive education tried to get them to use their own judgment in the situations and problems of everyday living. One way to resolve the constricting effects of authoritarian training was to teach the child to master his own everyday situations with his peers. But *this is not enough*. It is not enough because the everyday situations themselves dictate their own kind of tyranny: they create the neurosis of "normality" or conformity.

At first glance, this seems like an inevitable stumbling block; it seems that progressive education had to fail, had to fall short of a fantasied "maximum unconstriction" of behavior. In any educational or re-educational program, the individual has to be trained to *live in* the world of his fellows. In order to fashion a social animal, *some* early constriction of perception and behavior is necessary. In order to fashion an independent, self-critical, and fully aware individual, all of the constrictions cannot be undone. No society, for example, can use destructive, irresponsible psychopaths. Progressive education had to meet a broad and total cultural challenge. In other words, it had to create social animals *primarily*, and individuals only *secondarily*. It had to induce compliance and some kind of automatic social behavior, and curb willfulness and caprice. All of this, however, is just another way of bemoaning the fact that progressive education did not create independent and fully aware individuals. It simply created people who would function within the reigning ideology; and it did this because it had no clearly designed ideal-type, and no comprehensive theory of alienation to support it.

And this, as we know so well, was the real tragedy of progressive education. The reigning ideology of democracy was a commercial-industrial one; it was an ideology of the facilitation of business, of merchant and banking transactions. It did not even need classical education, history, philosophy. All it needed was "good fellows" who would join in the various activities, technical and institutional, that would promote the forms of commercial society. Perhaps its only anthropodicy was that it was evil not to vote for free enterprise. We should not wonder that the critics of progressive education have been very angry with it. It became a mass technique for brainwashing the child into automatic obedience to social conventions. Even hard intellectual work can go down the drain when the child does not need it in order to become acceptably social according to the regnant ideology. As in Soviet society under Stalin, in America progressive education simply fashioned its members for frictionless community living under the regnant ideology.

Today we can see that education for social living in a democracy was not an inevitable stumbling block for progressive education. The stumbling block was in our definition of democracy. We have utterly lost the pragmatic, Jeffersonian understanding of it. We have made a wholly false definition of democracy as the freedom to buy and sell goods and to perpetuate the ideology of commerce. We understood democracy as just another *ideology*. Instead, we should have seen that democracy is an *ideal*. As an *ideology* democracy differed little from Stalinism—it treated the individual as a means and not as an end. As an *ideal*, democracy would treat the individual as an end. The ideology is culture-centered and constricting; the ideal is man-centered and liberating (cf. K. Mannheim, 1936). The word "democracy" simply cannot stand for any social system which treats individuals as means. How can we be induced to realize this? When we see the implications of this false definition of democracy, we can understand something very crucial for our whole discussion, namely, that democracy, aiming for the ideal liberation of the individual from constrictions on his powers, would have to aim for what seemed to be a fantasy: it would have to pose, as its ideal, the "maximum unconstriction" of individual capacities. *And it would have to do this despite the fact that this threatens the going cultural belief system.* In other words, democracy, like liberty, normality, progress, cognitive or ethical man, is *an ideal-type.* This implies, furthermore, that in order for the ideal of "maximum unconstriction" not to get immediately bogged down in ongoing cultural forms, the accepted routines of the society must allow for continual change and progress toward the ideal-type. Democracy cannot mean—can *never* mean—institutions which are already formed. Again, this is what Jefferson so perfectly understood when he wanted to allow for a new Constitution every nineteen years. He understood the ideal-typical nature of democracy and human freedom.

Now the next question—and it is an important one—is this: how can we pose democracy as an unfinished ideal-type and still have an orderly society? How can we have a pragmatic and continually changing ethics, and still have basic human decency? Dewey's pragmatist ethics, inseparable from his profound understanding of progressive education, has come under criticism precisely because of this. If ethical precepts are continually changed, the whole world seems to be in danger—there seem to be no standard moral commands that are binding, that keep the world from chaos. This misunderstanding of Dewey stems, I daresay, at least partly from a failure to value man truly; it reflects an unwillingness to treat him as an end, a fear of his creative energies. The answer to the question how we can have an orderly society while posing democracy as an ideal-type is one that Dewey understood; it would mean doing two things we have never done in our "democracy," namely: treating persons as ends, and opening our society to the creative energies of our youth. The one follows from the other. If we treat persons as ends *we trust and look to the unfolding of their unique meanings.* "Maximum unconstriction" would then be an ideal we would not fear simply because everyone would look to it in everyone else, within the setting of a true community.

But this is just what the critic of Dewey fears, that we put true community in jeopardy when we unleash private meanings. The answer again comes from righting our accustomed perverted definition of democracy. As long as democracy was an ideology, and not an

ideal, it used the person as a means, not as an end: it did not permit him
to surpass himself (ethically). It abased man by defining equality as
equal right to consumer goods—equal right to self-seeking within the
national grab bag. This is another way of saying that democracy was
defined as the free pursuit of self-interest. It is only when we define
democracy as an ideal that self-interest can be transcended. *Democracy then becomes a superordinate ideal toward which all members
work.* If this ideal has as an aim the treating of all individuals as
ends, then all members will work toward the ideal of treating all
others as ends. In other words, creative community and altruism
become socially standardized under the ideal-type—which is exactly what Felix Adler aimed for with the Ethical Culture Movement (1918). The most fluid and changeable ethics, then, becomes
morally defensible and desirable because it aims at all times at treating individuals as ends. Pragmatist ethics is thus fully vindicated even
in its most extreme tentativeness, and in its protean morality it is the
most *steadily* moral of all. It carries out the great promise of Kant's
categorical imperative.

Let us then turn to the related aspect of treating persons as ends,
namely, opening our society to the new energies of our youth. It is
obvious both that we must do this if we are to treat persons as ends
and that we need not fear it if we have a superordinate ideal under
which to group young energies. Progressive education would be an
attempt to utilize new creative meanings as soon as feasible in increasing degrees of responsibility, as soon as socialization had
occurred. But the socialization could not be a socialization of adjustment, a process of merely constricting the child's behavior within the
going world view. It would have to be a process of training which took
the form of a partnership as early as possible. That is to say, it would
have to be a training which provided a fund of critical knowledge
and encouraged and allowed the growing individual to bring this
knowledge to bear *on the culture itself*. In other words, progressive
education would seek for a naturalistic resolution of alienation, by
allowing maximum cognition and the unfolding of self-powers before
these became hardened in an authoritarian mold. And it could only
do this by bringing cognition and powers to bear on the forms of the
culture itself. As we said above, it was by failing to allow for this that
progressive education failed to give cognition. If progressive education
has any meaning, if it treats persons as ends, then it must cast its
charges in the role of true individuals who bring their own terms into
the world. It must treat youth as something partly incommensurate

with existing ideas. Otto Rank seems to have had exactly this in mind when he said that "it almost seems in the meaning of our pedagogic ideas of reform that the child itself must be left to construct a new educational ideology, must be forced, so to say, *into the role of the leader*" (1932, p. 147). Each individual, in other words, would bring his own private meanings into the world, and would not fit into any standardized educational plan. Persons, as ends, would contribute in the shaping of education, and would share in the continual reshaping of the world around them. For the society which will value man as an end, this is the only meaningful educational program.

There is hardly anything new in this proposal; in fact, it is Rousseau's. We recognize it as the "reconstructionist education" which has been urged for a long time, but of course society has steadily gone on its accustomed way. We have not shunned the task because it is educationally insurmountable—far from it. We should merely have to concentrate on developing those capacities which place power into the hands of the individuals themselves. In terms of child training, the first thing we would have to do is to abandon the ideology of adjustment; and this could be done by concentrating on furthering a half-dozen related capacities which our present education almost entirely neglects. These are the capacities which, as Rousseau urged (1762, p. 306), would enable the child to meet the world with maximum efficiency and flexibility. In their modern guise, as Robert Lindner proposed them, these qualities are: *awareness, identification, skepticism, responsibility, employment, and tenseness* (1962, pp. 252 ff.). These are the qualities of a model progressive education as we understand it here. To be *aware* means to bring reason continually to bear on problems in real life situations; to be *identified* means to know that one has aegis over his own powers and is someone to reckon with; to be *skeptical* means just that—to be critical of any automatic authority; to be *responsible* means to be able to aim for autonomy—to put forth one's own unique meanings and stand up for the consequences; to be *employed* means simply to be engaged in something meaningful rather than trivial; to be *tense* finally, means that one believes there is something serious and dramatic about life, that it is a cause for real concern and for the best efforts that one can produce. Tenseness, in other words, is the model quality for a philosophy of democracy as an ideal-type, it is the quality that poses self-transcendence as a total social goal, and it does this without swallowing individual freedom. It is the quality opposed to adjustment, selfish security, grabbag individualistic living. Tenseness implies that there is something to which the individual should dedicate himself over and beyond his petty and selfish concerns. Tenseness, in a word, is the quality of personal responsibility in the cosmic community of man and nature. We have wholly overlooked this quality in our ideology of adjustment, precisely because this ideology is all of a piece with our failure to value man, our inability to establish a heightened sense of contact with the cosmos, our terrible overinsistence on creature comfort, and our consequent undermining of basic human dignity.

And all of these things are summed up in our one great reluctance: our refusal to examine the social forms which shape our lives. We know that if we were to educate children into these qualities we would lose the world as we know it and would have to bring *all* our institutions under critical scrutiny. Critical knowledge is remorseless. As Dewey said, we can grant the case of the conservative on this ground: that once we start thinking, there is no telling where we will come out. To be *aware* means to be given all kinds of information that one might need in order to liberate himself. To be *skeptical* means to be encouraged to be critical of any authority or tradition that is no longer serviceable, no matter how closely it is rooted in our habits. To be *employed* means to be given a continuing hierarchy of real problems, problems worthy of adults, responsible social problems (cf. Goodman, 1962, pp. 225 ff.). To be *identified, responsible,* and *tense* means that the youth must be encouraged to actively seek out things that are radically wrong with his society and his world. He may need to offer his own original criticisms and solutions, offer his own powers and be allowed to use them; and, not least, to propose the kind of world *he* might like to live in.

All of this in turn means hard and upsetting things. Children would need to be burdened with racial problems, no matter how anxious these problems are. They would need to take a strong stand on democratic, moral values. The pseudo-neutrality that we now encourage in order to spare the child "emotional upset" can only result—as Karl Mannheim saw—in really crippling restrictions on individual awareness—the one thing we want to unconstrict (1944, pp. 72–73). The children who are going to be their own social engineers need to make their own choices; and in order to do this the child needs sobering cognition. But we saw that he also needs something more: he needs to feel secure in his sense of self-value. This is perhaps the sorest point of all. In order to choose freely, one must be free of unreasonable guilt. Guilt, as I have pointed out elsewhere (1964a, chap. 6), refers basically to a bind on action; it usually refers to the

obtrusion of old training, of old constrictions on new action possibilities. In order to do away with guilt, one needs to scrutinize
clearly the persons and the situations which cause the guilt—and in
our society this is mostly one's own parental objects. It is these that
obtrude their concrete image and presence, and prevent the proper
kind of symbolic abstraction, without which one cannot rise over the
constrictions of guilt.

Durkheim understood the difference between true ethical action
and standardized morality when he suggested that ethical action
is essentially impersonal. Hence he wanted morality to be learned
in the society at large, and not in the family (1960, p. xxvi). It is
only when morality is abstract and impersonal that it is amenable to
manipulation and change. This is the basis for pragmatic ethics.
Guilt-binding family objects perpetuate the old morality because
they reduce the powers of the individual to choose. The implication
of this is that a truly pragmatic ethics is impossible where the often
mythological morality passed on in the family remains unexamined.
In order to make possibilities for self-expansion that are truly unlimited and open-ended, we need to allow individuals to examine
the contents passed on in their early social relationships. This means
focusing critically on the effects of all the institutions of society. We
can no longer accept either the self as a closed unit or the training
provided by the family as an unquestionably good one.

For example, we have to know about the numbers and kinds
of objects which make for relative freedom from crushing guilt;
the optimal sizes and dispersal of living dwellings; the age at which
children should be given over to responsible peer group activity and
no longer sheltered in a tight nuclear family group; and so on. We
would have to have an educational program that would give the
individual an increasing degree of self-awareness, as he becomes
ready to handle it. And by self-awareness, again, we mean overcoming
any unthinking restriction over one's own responsible powers. We
should have to have ways of determining how rich a person's action
world is, how to provide for it, as well as how to provide for a rich
inner world. In other words, the whole educational system would
have to gear itself to the full social and cultural environment, and
attempt to free the individual for full social and cultural development
of his own meanings. Its enemy would be mechanical action—coerced
action—in all its forms. This is precisely what Dewey wanted to overcome with his progressive education, the "externality of means" as he
called it: the sacrifice of the individual to forces over which he has

no control. Today we are getting a truly comprehensive picture of just what these forces may be.

In this sense, progressive, reconstructionist education caps a long historical development dating from Spinoza in modern times. It was he who first offered the program of human liberation through the full exercise of reason, and by this he meant that man had to understand himself in relation to the objects and forces which influence his desires. Knowledge, especially of our own emotions and desires in relation to objects, and a conception of the universe as a whole—these are the keys to human salvation, if human salvation is at all in man's hands. In a way which anticipated Dewey, Spinoza saw that the only way of understanding anything would have to be a way that allowed the individual to *adjust* effectively to it; hence, to know the causes and the complex interrelationships of our desires and their objects was the true and only means to responsible human freedom and dignity. Only today is it possible for the first time to extend our cogitations about ourselves to a range that would make liberation possible—to our early training and implicit beliefs and to the full spectrum of social phenomena which condition them; thus we are at last in measure to realize Spinoza's vision of human liberation through the full use of critical, scientific reason.

Again and again we are thrown back to the realization that choice, freedom, cognition, are a total social problem. The psychoanalytic cure began its work by focusing on the individual; now it is broadening out to the study and "therapy" of the family. But this is all a holding operation for a technique that itself is a historical artifact, as we noted earlier. A pragmatic ethics within a true progressive education would broaden each individual problem to it fullest social, institutional dimensions. This kind of "social psychoanalysis" would give the individual a great advantage that any kind of "therapy," either personal or familial, has to deprive him of. Personal growth in the free social encounter not only changes society—which is the source of human constrictions—it also enables the individual to free himself without putting himself under the tutelage of another authoritarian figure, behind the closed doors of private consultation rooms. It gives the individual a belief in his own powers in the most direct and beneficial way: in open intercourse with his fellow men. He does not need to feel beholden to the esoteric wisdom of one individual, into whose powers he places himself helplessly, for periods as long as five years and more. He can be free, in other words, without undergoing a trial in submission in order to earn it. As a result, he can really believe in his own powers because he has never really forfeited them; he can be free of a life-long constricting transference to the analyst as an authority and father figure. We might call this a truly "naturalistic psychoanalysis"—which is exactly what progressive education set out to be; but, once we had achieved it, we would probably long since have forgotten the word "psychoanalysis" and the historical artifact that it represented. We know today beyond much doubt what cripples people; we have scientific ground to stand on, and can undertake to become the first society in history that aims to overcome alienation naturalistically: that is, not by "therapy" in little closed rooms, or in brainwashing compounds of family clinics and mental health centers. But rather, by using the creative energies of our youth in meeting the real problem, the culturally constituted blindness that forms the core of every uncritical society, from Rousseau's eighteenth-century Paris to our own New York.

A progressive education which provided this kind of critical choice potential could not be accused of puerilism, as progressive education is now being accused. Neither could the school be separated from the community, as is again being proposed. The school must be inseparable from the community and the social life; the child can only learn by doing. But again, we have no alternative but to realize that learning and social living must not aim for total adjustment; they must not cheat the child of real critical awareness wherever *he* has a problem that is binding his own self-development—even if this means calling into question the most delicate areas of social habit.

THE FALLACY OF PHYSICAL HEALTH AS A PRIMARY IDEAL-TYPICAL VALUE

Here we see clearly the fallacy of using "good health" as a primary value to aim for. The point is simply this: if we are to treat individuals as ends, we cannot subjugate them to other kinds of values. The individual, as an end, bringing his own unique meanings into the world, may want to subjugate himself to some larger, self-transcendent identification. Health values are all of a piece again with our philosophy of adjustment, spurious individualism, and unashamed and thoughtless self-seeking. The free, tense individual may want to sacrifice his health to higher symbolic values. We see nothing wrong, for example, when someone assumes the presidency, even in the face of potential self-destruction due to a weak heart, and so on. On the contrary, we applaud it. This is a recognition that health values are not the highest ones—that man's visions of self-transcending striving are the highest; and that these visions are those that treat of all men as ends, taken together in a community of ends. The lesson here is simply that health values invert the human situation; they make the organism passive and acquiescent: they deprive it of the possibility of consummatory activity, achieved under its own power, devoted to transcending its own narrow well-being. In other words, we have a very perverted understanding of what it means to treat persons as ends. We seem to imagine that we treat them as ends by investing in their security, in a fantasied perpetuity of the organism itself. But, as Rousseau realized when he criticized the fad of medicine (1762, pp. 29–31), this is not what treating persons as ends really signifies. It signifies treating persons as inviolable sources of their own unique meanings, as agents of their own energies. This is something quite different. It leads us to talk about control over choices, instead of devotion to health, because that is what characterizes human dignity, as Rousseau knew (cf. Russell, 1926, p. 54). In America today we are finding that health values, in the realm of mental illness, for example, are doing what we might expect, on the basis of our discussion: they are abrogating choice values (Szasz, 1963c).

"Health" has to be defined more broadly and in a more ideal sense: as the striving for more and more complete facilitation of individual choices. In this way, then, health becomes a synonym for human liberation in a wide sense; it also means that this liberation will be a liberation *for values yet unknown, yet to be ushered into the world.* It is an accent on human nature as an inexhaustible source of value; whereas bodily health accepts the determinism of phylogenetic values. To a certain extent, of course, we all want to accept this fatal determinism, and must do so; but we must understand that it is not ennobling in a distinctively human way. We aim for health only to put it behind us as a secure acquisition from which to strive for further flexible choices. This is the ideal to be sought.

One of the reasons that we fall back so predominantly on health values in our society is that they are *at least* a value that we *all* can share; in this sense we might call this a sort of "cheap" community. We all can want the good health of all others, and seek to work out some kind of joint action on that basis: highway safety codes, food laws, and so on. This gives us the impression that we are working in unison on the good life. It also does another important thing, which is to assure that we will all respect one another in one very basic area—health.

And so we may draw our ideal vision of ethical man to a close. We can rest confident in the knowledge that we are not about to attempt to realize it. Is it only the mean and the cowards who fear giving the world over to the potentially rebellious energies of youth, the unknown wellspring of awesome nature? What will guarantee that our youth will handle the elders well, even the most generous and humanistic youth? Will the adult world which has been so laboriously—albeit blunderingly—accumulated over time, will this world be given over to the caprices of children? Will our society become like that of the Comanche Indians, among whom parents had to hope tremblingly that their children—to whom they had given their most generous love and care—would not beat them, but might keep them from starving with an occasional dole in their old age?

We have only to pose the question at this point to realize that it is absurd. We have seen what I hope is a compelling theoretical argument on the whole problem of meaning creativity. At the basis of this argument is the striking realization *that the more choices and freedom are available to one*, the less he will need to impose his narrow meanings on others. The process is circular: the more freedom, the less constriction; the less need to coerce the world, the wider the range of potential new choices, and so on. The individual who has control over his own self-value, who is a locus of his own power, needs to rely less on the habitual. His identity is fed by a realistic appraisal of experience; he draws his sense of value from his rational choices, and from his acceptance of responsibility for them. When we appraise experience rationally, we do not need to agonize in narrow ways. Hollow self-display based on old formulas gives way to more flexibility. Margaret Mead once very aptly called for the "strength of otherdirectedness"—which means much the same thing as I am outlining here: the ability to draw one's self-esteem from the ethics of pragmatism. And Karl Mannheim, in his self-engaged later work, also urged that society give itself over to partnership with its youth; and Mannheim saw no reason to fear the development of a new kind of responsible and directing youth. In his words:

> Our belief is that it is possible to create a pioneering and militant type which is not fanatical, an emotional type whose emotions are more than displaced fears, and that it is possible to train judgment through common-life experience and bring about obedience which is not blind, but a devotion to spontaneously believed ideals (1944, p. 57).

Today we can see better than could Mannheim in his period the social psychology on which we can base such a belief. Still, Mannheim himself was well along on this social psychology. If we banish the conditions for overly binding guilt, if we banish the narrow derivations of pride, we allow for the emergence of a new kind of man. We can educate for true critical awareness, which enables the individual to draw his pride from cultural criticism, a criticism that aims for the well-being of all others as *equal ends*. Furthermore, with the increasing scope and sophistication of our comprehensive theory of alienation, we can plan our society on both the individual psychological and the social institutional levels, so that individual energies will be released while social harmony is furthered. This has never before been possible to the extent that it is today because we can see and understand the interrelatedness of our social institutions at all levels; we know, therefore, how to soften the social disruptions of individual energies that we might release (cf. Mannheim, 1944).

Yet, in spite of Mannheim's well-thought-out assurances, we know we will remain where we are, that our vision is still a fanciful one. And that is proper, as we said, for an ideal. The program of human liberation through progressive education as social criticism is an ideal just as it was when Rousseau first proposed it over two hundred years ago. Yet we must continue to set up the ideal, as Emerson, John Jay Chapman, and Dewey did, in order to hold out the hope for a new kind of man—in order even to support our belief in man. Some of us may find this ideal vision hopelessly abstract and general, and I am purposely keeping it that way. There is hardly any point at this time in designing still another program, in filling in the precise details of how we banish narrow pride, or in calculating optimum degrees of guiltlessness. For one thing, we continue to ignore the proposals that have long existed (cf., e.g., Russell, 1926). Western man is intent on bypassing all planned intelligence in his pluralistic rush to the future. For another thing, even if one day we finally do begin to plan and work from a definite design, it will still have to be tentative and modifiable: the truly free man is something we will always have to work toward; choices can never be as broad as we would like, nor fear and constriction ever banished. Today we have no more idea of what kind of man is possible than did Robert Owen, but we can be just as dedicated and hopeful. For these reasons, at this stage in history, all we can do is to present an argument for ethical man as an ideal-type, and hope that the argument will encourage us *to opt for man* and for a new understanding of the purposes that a science of man is to serve. If it accomplished this, it would be unbelievably successful—and a finely detailed design of the good society is not necessary to enjoin such an option. I think it is possible on the sole basis of a full-field theory of alienation that we have sketched in these chapters; and this theory is not a vision of the future, but rather a striking portrait of the present.

One thing, however, we must and can do; and that is to state the minimum condition for getting started in the present on *making possible the option* for an ideal program of progressive education. How do we take the first step in the fullest possible liberation of human meanings? How can we begin to design a life in which man's basic esthetic needs work toward the creation of ethical man? We have already given the answer several times in these pages, but now we can reiterate it more strongly than ever: the greatest single obstacle to such a program is our present profit-oriented and mythologically based commercial economy. We must say, with Buber, Tillich, Scheler, Dewey, and countless others, that we cannot have human good, ethical man, so long as we have an uncontrolled commercial distributional system of industrial goods.

The main reason, as we have seen, is that in consumer society people simply are not treated as ends; they are used as means to perpetuate unexamined social institutions. How can we even begin to envisage a progressive education when we actively create alienation for every generation of our young? We abrogate their productive energies both psychologically and socially—both at home and in society. As things stand now, we want two things of our adolescents: we want them to buy products, and we want them to stay off the labor market. When they are finally old enough to be blessed with the incomparable boon of wage work, they have already forfeited any possibility of achieving a free identity. Corporate economy feeds upon the energies of each new generation and quietly sucks up their skills and personalities to further its own forms.

Yet history has taught us our lesson. It is not the spontaneity of free human energies that we have to fear—quite the contrary. We have to fear the results of the very restrictions we impose upon our youth. As we subtly bind their wills and constrain their choices we sink them deeper into their fate. We initiate them into powerlessness, and thus we actually encourage a greater explosiveness of release when it does come. We are creating an "unconscious" with our long social and cultural moratorium on the creative energies of youth. We have only to look at the modern Chinese youth and their recent betrayal of their own parents; at the hysterical religious conversions of adolescents in all ages; here we see the possible effects of long exile from responsible exercise of one's own powers. Passive withdrawal from responsibility and violent aggressiveness are, it seems, two poles of the same kind of learning. One lacks sure behaviors for self-expression when he has not been able to learn the feel of his own responsible powers. Aggression is an inept attempt at self-affirmation by someone who has been prevented from learning to cope with life in responsible ways (cf. Parsons, 1954, chap. 14). Rousseau understood this long ago (1762, p. 49). But it is up to us to turn this understanding to good account, by extending critical reason to the realm of social affairs. *This* is the message of a full-field theory of alienation.

PART IV

The New Science of Man:

Retrospect and Conclusion

I do not expect to see in my day a genuine, as distinct from a forced and artificial, integration of thought. But a mind that is not too egotistically impatient can have faith that this unification will issue in its season.
JOHN DEWEY *(in Adams and Montague, 1930, p. 26)*

CHAPTER THIRTEEN

THE VISION OF THE
SCIENCE OF MAN

The natural integration of thought has been a deep hope of thinkers ever since mankind passed out of the stage of mythology. The truly broad thinkers have always aimed for it, but up to now the integration has been forced—it did not proceed from empirical knowledge, from the world as it *was*, but instead from the world as the various thinkers hoped it might be. This led many to turn away from integration as an idle pastime of speculative philosophy; it led others to attempt an integration around mathematical, logical, or physical principles—which is another way of saying that they tried to integrate thought in the same way as speculative philosophers: by forcing it into an artificial mold with which alone they were comfortable. Yet the problem remained. For at least two thousand years Western man has wanted to grasp the world as a whole, as a totality which would give meaning to all experience, no matter from where it was drawn. But except for theological interludes like the Middle Ages this unity has escaped us.

When we see what the Middle Ages attempted, we can also understand one very important thing about the unity of thought, namely, that it is not an idle pastime. It goes to the very heart of the human condition because without a unitary, critical world view human dignity and social order are impossible. This was the great discovery of the nineteenth century, whose thinkers could see what man had lost with the downfall of traditional society. Man no longer had a view of the togetherness of things and of his place in the center of them. It fell to the twentieth century to reap all the bitter fruits of the

307

dispersal of a unitary conception of experience: science in the service of destruction; mankind converted into mindless consumer masses, rocked this way and that by sensational news items and by strong demagogues. What else? Man had no grip on the manifold of experience, could no longer imagine himself at the center, and so he quite naturally had a very poor opinion of himself. The whole phenomenon is summed up in the words "mass culture," words which mean that man has lost the sense of his own significance; he has become a plaything rather than a player.

Yet many thinkers in the nineteenth century did not despair; they saw that something truly new was at hand in the history of thought. They saw that philosophy could only achieve the unity it wanted in one way: it would have to settle for working within questions that were truly soluble, seek answers that man could find; it would have to focus on the human condition as it is lived on this planet—it would have to study man and his works.

The realization of the true task of philosophy reached back to the Enlightenment: Hume, in his *Treatise*, had seen that the true philosophy is the empirical study of man. In the nineteenth century, Stuart Mill continued this tradition and wanted philosophy to mean "the scientific knowledge of man as an intellectual, moral, and social being" (quoted in Dilthey, 1961, p. 23). But the real surge of disillusionment with speculative philosophy came with the bankruptcy of the great Hegelian synthesis. It then became very clear that philosophy would have to come down to earth. Feuerbach, the great naturalizer of Hegel, provided the epigraph for the new philosophy when he said that we now needed an anthropology, not a theology. After Darwin's unification of evolutionary theory, the matter could no longer be in doubt. In Etienne Gilson's words, philosophy means encyclopedia, and encyclopedia means the whole of ordered human knowledge (quoted in Gouhier, 1933, p. 157). Many thinkers had the same insight, and looked to the science of man to succeed where speculative philosophy had failed. Karl Mannheim believed that twentieth-century sociology would supply the guide for action, and show the way toward a better society and a more meaningful life, as philosophy had always hoped to do (Mannheim, 1958, pp. xxvii-xxviii). Collingwood called for a new *Treatise of Human Nature* conceived philosophically (1924, p. 9). And John Dewey, devoting a lifetime to finding a new calling for philosophy, held a similar position. Dewey wanted philosophy to abandon the inverted and mostly sterile problems with which it had been occupied for two

thousand years. He wanted philosophers to study man as an organism
in society, and so offer knowledge that was relevant to actual human
needs. If philosophy was done over from this point of view, he thought,
it would result in a synthesis with science, education, morals, and
religion (in Adams and Montague, 1930, pp. 25–26). This was where
he looked for the natural unification of thought. All of Dewey's work
centered on this problem, and it is safe to say that in this sense he
was a figure of at least Kantian proportions: after him, no one could
do philosophy in the old way; it could no longer by unlimited in
ambition, or divorced from life.

The general change of direction was a revolt against "pure"
intellect, divorced from life and from social problems. It extended
to many branches of thinking, and included even the individual
psychology of Alfred Adler. Adler saw that man needed social interest
above all, and not merely abstract intellectual problems; and that
social interest was just that—an interest in problems of mankind in the
everyday world. But all of these thinkers, of course, are the descendants of Comte, even if not his actual heirs. Comte summed up
perfectly the new anthropology of the nineteenth century:

> If we were pure intellects we should always go from the
> world to man [i.e., objectively]. But in us the intellect
> is only a means. Love is the principle, action is the end;
> and it is to man, finally, that our study of the world must
> be referred (in Lévy-Bruhl, 1903, p. 118).

He saw how speculative philosophy would best be laid to rest,
namely, by extending scientific thought to moral and social phenomena. In other words, if science took under its sway even the most
complex and emotion-laden phenomena, such as morality and social
life, there would be nothing for philosophy to be occupied with in
the real world:

> . . . the metaphysical mode of thought being no longer
> possessed of real objects, *ipso facto* disappears . . . from the
> day when we no longer should seek anything but the laws
> of psychical, moral and social facts, refraining from any
> hypothesis as to causes and essences . . . three results would
> be obtained at a single blow: metaphysical philosophy
> would disappear, social science would be created, and
> positive philosophy would be founded (Lévy-Bruhl, 1903,
> pp. 351–352).

Thus, long before Dewey, Collingwood, and Mannheim, Comte wanted philosophy to be absorbed in the daily effort of social science, and he saw beautifully what would be accomplished by this.

Philosophy and science, if they were united, would liberate man from any unscrutinized and automatic ethical imperatives. Philosophy, as Dilthey said, everywhere arose where the standard religious conviction was no longer able to satisfy the most advanced persons (quoted in Ortega y Gasset, 1963, p. 169). The total unification of philosophy, then, should present a new ethic, and in this sense it coincides with religion. But it presents something more than religion— what Comte wanted, a claim to validity that even religion does not have, because this claim is supported by concrete evidence that many can agree on. This is another way of saying what we said in a previous chapter—that the old medieval theodicy had to be succeeded by a new anthropodicy.

Our whole history of the science of man has been a story of the Enlightenment search for a new "secular" theodicy or "anthropodicy." The idea behind the fervent hope of a science of man was to put the world firmly into the hands of its most advanced creature. The quest for the unity of knowledge, for the merger of science and philosophy, was a quest for an *agreed basis* on which man could act and shape the world into something less unhappy, less evil. When Barnes and Becker wrote their authoritative history of social thought, they said the problem of the unity of science for action—Comte's problem— "still haunts us" (1961, vol. 2, p. 594). Today we can say that it need haunt us no longer; we can trace an agreed history of the achievement of Comte's vision.

It was no mere coincidence, then, that the science of man emerged precisely at the time that the historical problem of a new theodicy arose. The Enlightenment had to face the new problem of determining right and wrong, and fashion a new morality that would replace the declining medieval one. This was the great burden put on the shoulders of Spinoza, Leibnitz, Diderot, Rousseau, and Hume. These people could no longer rely on divine revelations for human action; man now had to look to the natural course of things. The natural order replaced the Scriptures as the source of human hope. One could rest easy in the days of Leibnitz, Jenyns, and Pope by feeling that there was reason in nature and that God had not abandoned the world. The only work published by Leibnitz in his lifetime was his *Theodicy*, in which he urged man to exercise his reason, to penetrate to higher insights, and thereby understand that there was no radical evil in the world, that things had to be the way they were, in order for them to be at all.

On the level of theodicy, we can't surpass this general philosophical conclusion today. Leibnitz had faith in the significance of the world: God could allow no radical evil. It was then up to man to use his reason and try to divine what was going on (Meyer, 1952, p. 161). Spinoza held a similar view when he said in his *Ethics* that the concept of evil is a human invention, that nothing is good or bad in itself. But for Spinoza God was impersonal, above and beyond the matter; things were not necessarily right with man's world. Man's task, therefore, was to overcome evil by analyzing his passions in relation to their objects; in this way he would free himself by placing himself under the governance of reason. Thus, both of these great theorizers on the problem of evil agreed in opening the field to reason; science and intellect were given their mandate: evil was either illusory, or it was in man's power to overcome.

It was Kant who closed the problem to reason, and set about to criticize Leibnitz' work. He wrote "The Failure of All Philosophical Attempts at a Theodicy" in 1791, and his whole system was partly an attempt to show why Leibnitz' rationalism was wrong. By including man within nature, in his "Copernican shift," Kant took care of the problem of a theodicy once and for all: Man "can never know."

"PHILOSOPHY AS THEODICY"

But the idealists who followed Kant still needed a morality; and it was Hegel who reconciled beautifully Leibnitz' faith in reason and Kant's immersion of man in nature. Hegel resolved all contradictions by arguing that the world is the theatre for the development of the Absolute Spirit: there can then be no evil in the world if everything serves the justification of God in history. This was the true theodicy that reconciled every event that happened every day—as Hegel himself put it at the close of his *Philosophy of History*. In this way he took the Enlightenment faith and incarnated it into an airtight system of absolute idealism: he took the problem of theodicy, broached by Leibnitz and abandoned by Kant,[1] and solved it by taking it right out of this world. We might say that the idealists repeated the medieval solution; they gave an otherworldly closure to a problem that the Enlightenment had to secularize. Perhaps the whole idealist tradition was remiss on this very point, of prematurely closing the problem of a theodicy with a supernatural solution.

The nineteenth century rose quickly to the attack, when it sensed this subversion of the Enlightenment mandate to fashion a truly secular theodicy. The mechanistic solution tried to bring things down to this world again; but this had the effect of also violating an important part of the Enlightenment mandate: it left man as powerless to do anything about evil as the idealists had. As in Spencer's system, man had to trust to the mechanical determinism of nature. At any rate, after Darwin, there could no longer be a theodicy that was not naturalistic; the problem was, "What kind of 'naturalism'?" This was the great new historical development. It was now very clear that the Enlightenment was right to look to nature for clues to morality. The thing that had hindered it was that it drew its inspiration from physical-science models, and it placed too much trust on "reading," and not enough on "doing." With Darwin's naturalism, and new sciences like anthropology, a new approach to morality was possible. One could now try to determine its *genesis* and not relegate it to a transcendental Idea. A whole host of thinkers then set themselves to work out a system of morality on an independent basis, trying to reconcile the biological, anthropological and naturalistic points of view. Spencer, Green, Caird, Sidgwick, Lange, Lotze—all attempted to design a new ethic. But they all failed. There was simply no way to define the "Good" or the "Ideal" *philosophically* alone (cf. Merz, 1914, vol. 4, pp. 214, 244). One unfortunate result of this was that philosophy abandoned the holistic quest for a new morality and bogged down into disciplinary trivialities, where largely it still is today.

Nevertheless, there was one significant direction for the search for a new ethics to replace the one lost since the decline of the medieval cosmology. If it could not be done philosophically, then it could be done by a science of man. The solution of the ethical problem was sought in the nature of humanity and society. This was pushed into the foreground, and began to be extensively studied and cogitated (cf. Merz, 1914, vol. 4, p. 445). This represents the nineteenth century carrying on what the Enlightenment had begun, but carrying it on without any transcendental detours. The line of succession from Turgot to Condorcet to Saint-Simon and Comte is clear and direct. The similarities between Rousseau and Marx are striking. They were all concerned with the rational explanation of evil in the world, and saw that society contained the answer. Rousseau vindicated man from the theological attribution of evil: he tried to show that man's "true nature" was hidden under the forms of civilization. Marx set himself directly against the idealists and their theology, and saw his task as bringing the problem of morality back into the world. Hence his famous metaphor about turning Hegel on end. Furthermore, Marx is what I like to call a "late" Enlightenment man, because he saw that *action* was inseparable from any *explanation* of evil in the human world. He could not accept any kind of explanation which did not put power into man's hands, or which deprived man of the right to use power. Thus he could scoff at Adam Smith's "Law of Previous Accumulation," which set out to justify the spoils system once and for all time. In this way, Marx avoided both the German and the English dead ends on the problem of evil, and continued the productive French solution. It could not be an intellectual matter that utterly disregards the social system; nor could it be a utilitarian matter that would give man "relative" power to work within an essentially corrupt social system.

SOCIOLOGY AS A HISTORICAL ANTHROPODICY

The one thing which most clearly distinguishes the "early" from the "late" Enlightenment approach to a theodicy is that the early thinkers did not have enough history in their explanations. This was what the nineteenth century had to discover, and mobilize in its attack on society as the source of evil. Marx, for example, preferred Adam Ferguson to Adam Smith because Ferguson had a better understanding of history: he offered a sophisticated conflict theory of the origin of present inequalities, and not a fanciful nursery tale (cf. Lehmann, 1930). It was only during the "later" Enlightenment that thinkers began to converge on the historical background to social inequality. Of course, there were precursors such as the Arab historian and scholar Ibn Khaldun, the Frenchman Jean Bodin, and the Englishman Gerrard Winstanley, who had shown that the English ruling class was Norman, and that the conquered were Saxons. But it was really Saint-Simon and the French Revolution which gave nineteenth-century sociology its direct historical impetus; Saint-Simon saw that the dominant class in his country was the Frankish and Burgundian conquerors, and that the subject population was descended from the Romanized Celts (Oppenheimer, 1922, pp. viii–ix); the French Revolution left no illusions on how things came to be as they are. Later schools of sociology, such as that of Oppenheimer, thought that once we put together a coherent historical reading of present-day class inequalities, we would have a sufficient picture of why evil exists in the human world. And he hoped that thereby we could muster sufficient indignation to set things right: once we saw the injustice disclosed by the actual facts of history, we would make the requisite moral amends. Thus we might say that Saint-Simon, Marx, Gumplowicz, Oppenheimer—the early conflict theorists—put forth a vision of sociology as a historical anthropodicy.

THE NEED FOR A FULL-FIELD THEORY OF ALIENATION AS THE ANTHROPODICY

But this kind of anthropodicy was bound to fail, as Hume had already understood: he knew that history could never be a direct key to a new anthropodicy, that its chief use is only to help find the "constant and universal principle of human nature" (C. Becker, 1959, p. 95). Hume ferreted out all subjective bias in man's approach to experience, and history, above all, is a highly subjective enterprise. One reconstructs the past largely according to present purposes. How can we base a compelling anthropodicy on a reading of history alone?—nearly everyone would have his own, according to his beliefs and sentiments. We see this very clearly in the nineteenth-century arguments between the socialists and the free enterprisers: they could even agree that history is the saga of the exploitation of man by man, but the believers in free enterprise felt that the benefits of this saga far outweighed the injustices, and that things were getting better all the time anyway.

What we need instead is to find recurrent features of our subject matter, the "laws" of "human nature." The burden of our anthropodicy would rest on these while history would be used to round out and support our vision of human suffering. It would help give us a more compelling and comprehensive picture. Oppenheimer's theory of the origin of the state in conflict could never give the "objective standard of justice" that he sought, no matter how graphic and dependable the facts. And the reason is that men generally do not become outraged, morally, about what happened in the past—especially if the present seems comfortable and promising. Man needs compelling proof that something is wrong in the present, and will continue to be wrong *if present circumstances continue.* After all, an anthropodicy is just that; it has to muster moral indignation; and it can only do this by being based on a full scientific theory of the human condition in and of the present time. When we understand this, we can see that the nineteenth-century venture into history and evolution temporarily sidetracked and delayed the establishment of a mature social science (cf. Randall, 1940). Sociology as a historical anthropodicy seemed capricious.

Perhaps the most direct way of summing up this whole problem is this: that in order to show *the dependence of private troubles on social issues,* one had to develop a thoroughgoing *theory of the nature of the social bond.* And this is exactly what the whole nineteenth century set itself to do. In order to give what Comte wanted, a clear directive for morality by showing the social correlates of private ills, a full-field theory of alienation had to be developed. It could not be enough to show historically that human intelligence was insufficiently developed. What was needed, in other words, was a comprehensive social psychology.

After Darwin, all scientific conceptions had to be naturalistic. And it was just this that posed an enormous conceptual problem for the science of man. An anthropodicy, by definition, had to reveal the source of evil in the world, and provide for directives for overcoming it. In other words, *the naturalistic anthropodicy* had to be scientifically objective; and yet, at the very same time, it had to be suffused with value. There did not seem to be any way over this hurdle within the ordinary conceptualization of science. The nineteenth century then had to find a principle which would break through scientific objectivity and would permit a judgment of higher and lower in a neutral naturalistic world. The answer came from the idea of Life, which would be the high subject matter of science; science would promote life by promoting its progressive development (cf. Merz, 1914, vol. 4, pp. 407–408), and thus objective science and subjective value would naturally merge.

Once this new principle became the focus for science, it could offer a naturalistic anthropodicy that was at the same time inseparable from the central value of furthering life. The next problem was to show how evil and sin arose. And for this it was necessary to show that evil and sin did indeed *arise* in human society—that they were not inherent in man's nature or in his need for social living. Now, we will recognize that this in effect picks up the problem where Leibnitz left it with his theodicy, when he claimed that there was no discernible evil in the world, once reason was given its mandate to understand. This was exactly the task of a social psychology that would offer a full-field theory of human alienation. It had to pick up the problem of a theodicy in a completely neutral frame of reference: life striving in an impersonal world. But, instead of saying, with Leibnitz, that this cosmos was the best possible, it had to say that the social world was not the best possible one. The evil that resulted from human arrangements had to be its concern, and not the rest of nature. This is what Rousseau meant when he attacked Voltaire's pessimism after the Lisbon quake.

Perhaps no one was more explicit about what had to be done than was Max Scheler. And he knew what had to be done partly because of the dilemma in which his generation found itself—that is, the dilemma of being between idealism and materialism, and needing to reconcile the two within one scientific and philosophical synthesis. The only way to meet this problem was to trace in a thoroughgoing manner the nature of the social bond. Thus Scheler says, surveying his book *The Nature of Sympathy*: "We have been seeking to acquire a knowledge of the powers which make up that spirit of participation, intrinsic to all emotional acts and functions of an intentional or evaluative kind" (1954, p. 103). In other words, he wanted to get at action from the inside, to see what the organism was striving for in nature, so that he could have a clear directive for ethical action *within a framework of scientific objectivity*. Scheler was very clear about the import of a study of the sympathetic emotions from this point of view; he says explicitly that it is neither for ethics, nor for esthetics, nor for any single discipline alone, that they must be studied, but rather, for the "whole range of basic disciplines in philosophy and science. . ." (in Werner Stark's penetrating and important introduction, p. xlvii). Nothing could be more eloquent about Scheler's consciousness of his task and its place in the history of science.

Furthermore, he saw that in order to have a social psychology of human commitment to the social process, a psychology that would be ethically useful, he would have to shun both the Kantian and the Benthamite psychologies. He could not hedge, as Kant had done when he considered that man was basically "unsociable," that the desires of the individual are at variance with those of the race. Nor could he use Bentham's view that individual hedonistic desires were *automatically in harmony* with the needs of the race (1954, p. x). Thus, he intended to follow his book on sympathy with one on the "nature of shame," "the nature of apprehension and fear," and the "nature of the sense of honor" (p. xlvi). He wanted to understand these qualities in themselves, and in their order of development in the individual and the species. Once this was accomplished, we would understand how social groups were formed and maintained among men.

Scheler's ambition, then, was to offer up a comprehensive

social psychology of human valuings—the same program that Lester Ward had outlined for sociology. Of course no one man could do it, and Scheler's own life was cut off during his productive prime. Besides, he could have found part of what he was looking for in Freud, but the narrow instinct theory repelled him. A whole school had to focus on the phenomenology of social commitment: Baldwin, Royce, Meinong, Husserl, Cooley, George Mead, Dewey, Freud, Adler, Huizinga, Veblen, Mills, and many, many more. This kind of social psychology avoided Kantian voluntarism as well as Benthamite atomism, and went on to develop a theory of the social self which enabled us to understand the full participation of the individual in society. It explained exactly what Scheler wanted: the nature of shame, of fear, of the sense of honor, and it explained them socially *and* genetically in the individual.

The importance of this complete social psychology of human valuings was that it got at human experience from within, emphasized its utter neutrality with a breadth and subtlety that would have astounded Rousseau, and thus could allow us to see how evil in society arose. It got to the heart of action in its necessary ontological dimensions, where we could see man's search for meaning. Nothing less than this would do. The Benthamites forfeited their chance for a social psychology by having to have recourse to a legalistic principle of individual responsibility. Thus they were embarrassed by the notion of social sympathy, because it was not individualistically reducible. Up to now, most modern social scientists have forfeited the possibility of a social psychology in another—but related—way. They have been embarrassed by the individual subjectivity, and, not being able to deal with it in any objective way, they have overlooked the heart of human action.

Only by getting at human experience from within would we be able to give what the Enlightenment wanted—a science of man in society that was an anthropodicy *and* an ethical design. But, in order to provide substance for the ethical design, a complete social psychology had to be able to answer two basic and related questions, namely, what did man want and how did the feeling of right and wrong and good and bad grow up? And, in order for this answer to be achieved, there had to be a union of three things: phenomenological psychology, a naturalistic ontology of organismic striving in a neutral world of nature, and a complete genetic theory of the development of the sense of self, self-consciousness, or conscience. In other words, we had to have a naturalistic morality that would be under man's control, and not a theological morality under Divine control; neither could we have that curious, grotesque compromise: a naturalistic morality under control of unconscious natural forces. So neither the idealists nor Spencer would do for a mature social-psychological theory of the social bond. This theory had to approach action simultaneously from inside and outside, from science and philosophy, and it had to define where nature transcended human powers and where it did not. It had to place the control of ethical action into human hands, and it had to delineate that control scientifically.

Little wonder that the achievement of naturalistic ontology and phenomenological psychology is such an exciting chapter in human thought: it gave an answer to the first question of a complete social psychology—What does man want? It took a whole tradition of our greatest thinkers to master a problem of such magnitude—and the names are familiar to us: Kant, Fichte, Hegel, Herbart, Beneke, Meinong, Husserl, Baldwin, Lotze, Royce, Dewey, Whitehead, down to people like Merleau-Ponty and Sartre in our time—to list only some of the key figures. They achieved the answer, as we said, by approaching the meaning of things from within human experience. Actually it was Schelling who forecast the development, when he said that the whole of philosophy is nothing but a natural science of the human mind (1797; see 1942, p. 13). Herbart and Beneke also very early proposed to "give a phenomenology of the moral consciousness," and Beneke, like Schelling, saw that when this was done, "the whole of philosophy becomes the natural science of the human mind" (Merz, 1914, vol. 4, p. 244). The inspiration of Schelling was completed in Germany by the development of a psychology which avoided the extremes of objective naturalism and transcendental idealism. It was a psychology of *human* meanings, and it culminated in the work of Theodor Lipps and the later Dilthey (cf. Dilthey, 1961, p. 23), as well as in that of Ortega y Gasset. It led, as Dilthey understood, to the union of psychology, philosophy, and history, because it made human meanings central to all three disciplines. Ortega's words very well sum up this whole tradition:

> . . .[We] become aware of the necessity of another science which must investigate the actual setup of human con-sciousness, that base and clue to everything else. This science—fundamental because it deals with fundamentals— will therefore start out as psychology, but a psychology planned in a way to illuminate the general structure of consciousness and the generic system of its functioning,

in short, the reality of *living* consciousness in its typical
articulation. This science will, by the same token, be the
true philosophy. In Dilthey's opinion philosophy is empirical science; it is the last and decisive act in which
man *qua* intelligence takes possession of the *whole* reality
which is *his* reality. . . (Ortega y Gasset, 1963, pp. 162–163).

As we know, Dilthey and Ortega were hardly alone in this
realization. Along with them, Baldwin and Dewey also included the
organism in nature and focused on the primacy of human meanings.
Dewey set out to keep Kant's transactionalism, the organism transcended by nature, but still seeing nature from within its own experience. But Dewey criticized Kant specifically because, having developed the active transactionalism, he still remained glued to narrow
problems of epistemology, to the separation of subject and object,
of knower and known. The new psychology would absorb the problem
of epistemology within the larger dimension of meaning, and thereby merge the knower and the known. There would be nothing fixed
or absolute, either within the actor or outside him—nothing, that
is, that man need bother himself about, if he accepted the transactional limitation on knowledge. As far back as the turn of the century
William James had scoffed at Bertrand Russell's already outdated
atomistic epistemology. In a word, the new psychology had to have
the courage of its convictions, and be what it frankly was, namely, the
psychology of *human* meanings and not natural ones. Dilthey himself remained hung up in his exploration of the theory of knowledge
by what Ortega aptly termed the "epistemological mania" (1963, p.
181). Dewey saw both Kant's achievement and his failure more clearly,
and thus could elaborate a fully transactional esthetics, a naturalistic
psychology of human meaning.

Thus was solved a problem that had been outstanding since
Plato, and remained even after Kant. Plato had made a distinction
between the world of ideas and the world of material things, which
has come down to us as the distinction between science and philosophy:
science is supposed to be concerned with external reality, philosophy
with internal meanings or introspective reality (Merz, 1914, vol. 3,
pp. 23 ff.). Greek philosophy attached a higher value to the world
of ideas than to the world of things. Plato thought that the realm of
the idea, of the "pure" reality, is contaminated by its mixture with
material reality. Therefore, he could call the ideal the truly "real."
As Dewey complained, this was a false valuation that went to the
core of all of Greek culture, and prevented it from directing its full

creative energies to problems in the real world. Pragmatism, in fact, was an attempt to heal this two-thousand-year breach, by showing the intimate fusion of thought and things.

Full-fledged pragmatism arrived so late on the scene because it was not until after Darwin that we could get a convincing, naturalistic account of the nature of thought. Through the centuries, for example, theology could well account for the realm of the idea—or the "truly real." This was the Christian supernatural world that, like Plato's world of the idea, put the real material world to shame. At the decline of the medieval cosmology, Leibnitz reintroduced the Platonic dualism, and Kant accented it again: it was necessary to account for the limitation of human meanings. It was this limitation that Plato meant to accent when he said that the "real" was cheapened in its contact with the material. This was another way of complaining that man's ideal meanings, those which give him truly human dignity in a neutral world of nature, are superior to the everyday earthly things.

The historical problem was how to convert what Plato thought was a belittling situation into an ennobling one? How to accept that man's ideal meanings are hopelessly fettered to earthly things, and yet keep their ideality? Two things had to be done: the ideal had to be secularized, brought down to earth; and the manipulation of earthly things, the everyday business of science, had to be idealized, i.e., had to be put under the superordinate category of human meanings. Thus, when we take meaning as the superordinate category of a new science of Life, we put the Platonic dialogue onto a new level. Science then becomes concerned with the level of meaning, with the ideal; and, whatever science discovers is then automatically the concern of philosophy. By making a science of man the center, as Comte wanted, and making meaning the superordinate category of this science, as Dilthey saw, the realm of human meanings becomes the central concern of science. The merger of science and philosophy is complete, and man keeps his ideality by exercising it in the world. Human meanings become superordinate even in science.

The nineteenth-century convergence that led to this new and mature idealism was striking. It contained the following currents:

—The Platonic revival in Leibnitz and Kant;
—The "Idea of Humanity" in Herder, Goethe, Feuerbach, Lotze, Royce, et al.;
—The Geisteswissenschaften and the "Idea of Life" of Dilthey;

—The pragmatism of Peirce, James, and Dewey;
—The development of a mature, phenomenological psychology;
—The "esthetic reconciliation" in Kant, Schelling, Schiller, Baldwin, and Dewey.

The unique result was the complete secularization of human meaning, achieved without belittling man. The inevitable could be accepted: the ideal, or the "really real," is the *human creation of meaning*. It grows up in the transactional interplay with the material, everyday world. Its ideality can be no more than the continual fabrication of new meanings. By these meanings man enhances his life, and actually quickens the real in the material world. Not only are man's meanings not cheapened by being attached to things—on the contrary: this is the only way that the ideal can unfold. With esthetic mergers, with science and art, man fuses his meanings into the world of things. In this way he is led on to a revelation of his own ideal gropings, at the same time that the external world is increasingly unfolded for his use.

We can see what a superb thing the nineteenth-century convergence was, and we may wonder why it is only in the mid-twentieth century that we are turning toward it with an air of discovery. One of the reasons, we know, is that the "epistemological mania" was just that: it was a mania that ruled the field of psychology with a frenzy, and kept the experimental, mechanistic approach imperialistically enthroned; in fact, it sits there majestically still today. Another reason was that the conceptual scaffolding—as we might call it—for this nineteenth-century edifice was too shaky. When Merz called for the "new Idealism of the future" at the turn of the century, he knew it was indeed a thing of the future. It was not yet scientifically compelling. He also realized with B. G. Niebuhr that we lived in an epoch in which we would discover nothing radically new; the general conceptual framework was given. The only thing we could do—had to do—was to simplify, clarify, and synthesize the knowledge that had already accumulated, and so fit it coherently and economically into the loose nineteenth-century framework.

The science of man attacked this problem, but slowly and gropingly. Sociology very early gave voice to Dilthey's later discovery: that the science of man would have to be a science of the human consciousness, of human meanings and valuations. This is the notion of the social forces that Lester Ward introduced as the basic program for sociology. Other sociologists, such as Cooley and Small, shared

Ward's vision for a sociology of the broadest human scope. Cooley's words sound strange to us today, precisely because he saw sociology in the earlier vision:

> I think then, that the supreme aim of social science is to perceive the drama of life more adequately than can be done by ordinary observation. . . . Indeed one of the best things to be expected from our study is the power of looking upon the movement of human life in a large, composed spirit, of seeing in it something of ideal unity and beauty.

Albion Small, citing this quote, went on to observe, emphatically:

> The problem of knowledge in the field of social science reduces to this: *What is the meaning of human experience, and to what extent have we developed a technique which may be relied upon to ascertain more of that meaning?* (1923, pp. 410–411.)

But sociology as a discipline shunned this program; in its attempt for scientific respectability, it narrowed itself almost wholly into the objective approach that was popular at the time. Consequently it could no longer approach human behavior from within, and therefore could not be a science of consciousness or Being, a science that would come to grips with human meanings.[2] Having thus narrowed its scope, sociology had to wait for other disciplines to elaborate the nature of the social forces. Again, this was a long and halting development, precisely because the various disciplines had objectified man, and adopted mostly mechanical and mathematical measuring approaches to human behavior, looking at it from the outside.

The disciplines conquered the problem of the social forces, despite the Newtonian faddism, but the conquest came from unexpected areas. It was phenomenological psychiatry which supplied theories of sadism and masochism, by viewing them as constrictions on behavior; Scheler, Lucka, and later Sartre and Simone de Beauvoir revealed the nature of some of the forms of love as attempts to come into contact with life and to maximize private meanings in the world.

Then a whole sequence of thinkers saw that man had to place his consciousness at the center of life and history, in some kind of intimacy with the cosmic process, and in some kind of unified world schema. Feuerbach, James, Royce, Hocking—all contributed to this naturalistic interpretation of religious experience. Hocking showed beautifully that happiness itself was an ideal, an ideal which man could only hope to approach when he acted with a knowledge that his acts could *succeed and hold in history* (1912, p. 503). This was still another way of stating the pervasive logic of idealist esthetics, of man's need to see and understand his own purpose woven into the face of the earth and its history.

Then there was a whole tradition stretching from critics such as Ruskin in the nineteenth century to historians such as Huizinga in the twentieth, who showed how man's striving for rich self-expression is influenced by the historical epoch and the social context in which it takes place.

These lines of inquiry were given great critical weight and sharpness by the small handful of sociologists who still insisted on doing meaningful work. Thus, Veblen and Mills could show us how society, under certain kinds of distributional systems, leads individuals to constrict their behavior to certain hollow forms of self-display. Perhaps most important for our time, Mills could show further how a society devoted to the ideology of dignity and freedom could actually severely limit these things, and flirt with global war, in the interest of maintaining its unexamined and irrational economic-distributional prestige system. This took the basic problem of economics that Marx had raised and broadened it to an understanding of how the social forces function in a total social system; it allowed us to take the broadly descriptive ontology of human striving, and give it critical weight for our historical period.

Once this was accomplished, there was nothing to prevent us from appropriating the ideal-real framework fashioned by the nineteenth century, from linking up with the earlier tradition of the science of man. We can answer the question What does man want? And with this answer we have at the same time laid the basis for our anthropodicy and our ethical ideal.

As we promised earlier, by providing an answer to this basic question, a large part of the problem of the nature of the social bond was solved. But in order to have a truly complete picture, a really mature social psychology, we had to answer another question: how does the feeling of right and wrong grow up, and why is it so ingrained in the human spirit? Only by answering this second question would we be able to give full substance to an ethical idea. It was a difficult and long-outstanding problem, and it too took a whole tradition of our best thinkers to solve—the early German idealists, the French *idéologues*, Royce, Mead, Baldwin, Cooley, Dewey, Freud, Adler, and a host of thinkers. Actually, Diderot, Rousseau, and Hume were three of the first major figures here.

Diderot and Rousseau were very troubled by the problem of conscience; they wanted to understand its nature without reducing it to a mere reflex of the environment. As we saw in Chapter Two, Diderot was struggling against the subversion of morality by the extreme intellectualism of the time: he wanted to keep some sense of right and wrong anchored in the organism, in a human nature that would not be completely relative. Helvétius was the principal enemy, with his theory of extreme environmental determinism. Rousseau likewise attacked Helvétius, by insisting that there was an "innate principle of justice" at the heart of man (1762, p. 352). At the time it was put forth, Diderot's and Rousseau's protest was little more than a hope, a protest for the whole man against the facile and fragmented intellectualism of the century. But at least it allowed them to stress the total organismic nature of experience; and scientifically this was a great gain.

Hume carried this development further when he struck out against the easy rationalism of his age. He pointed out that the sense of right and wrong cannot be arrived at by rational analysis—that it was a question of convention as revealed in unanalyzable feelings. This was meant to be an attack on the Enlightenment optimism, on the faith in reading nature intellectually for moral prescriptions. But it was actually much more. By shifting the problem of morality from reason to total feeling preference and sentiment, Hume might be said to have begun the tradition of modern dynamic psychology. Much later than Hume, Rousseau, and Diderot it was left for Freud to show how, genetically, the child develops a sense of conscience, or superego, which remains more or less the same throughout life. Freud offered a theory of ego development based on a theory of anxiety and identification, which explained why the individual holds on so determinedly to his early learning. Thus he accomplished what neither Bain, Baldwin, Dewey, Scheler, nor any of the self-psychologists could do. This drew the full circle on Hume and on romanticism. At the beginning of this tradition, the sense of right and wrong was broadened from reason to feeling, but this tended to take it out of the realm of objective, scientific description. Freud helped to close the rationalist tradition right over the romanticist one, so to speak, by taking the problem of feeling back to its pre-Humian stage: it was now possible to talk about the *feeling* of conscience in *rational* terms, and a major scientific victory was accomplished.

By showing how the sense of conscience was built into the child, Freud performed the task that had been outstanding since Rousseau, and that had troubled Stendhal, Nietzsche and so many others, including Jean-Marie Guyau. How to get rid of the notion of fixed morality—of what Guyau called "the last dogma." Like thinkers of the Enlightenment, Guyau wanted a morality without the sense of obligation, and without a higher sanction, and he made a very comprehensive effort to work this out before his tragically premature death. But again, no one man could solve the ethical problem. The nineteenth century was little better off than the eighteenth in this respect.

Furthermore, Freud helped us see the great gulf that could exist between early learning and the demands of adult experience. By focusing on the dichotomy we could see how early training in the cultural ideology actually constricted cognition and behavior. This revelation could then be coupled with the work of the critics of society and culture, and the larger-scale analysts of society, that we sketched above. In sum, when we had supplied a complete theory of the nature of the social bond, we had at the same time a full-field theory of human alienation, a theory which we can now see united several levels of explanation: the phenomenological, the social-psychological, the historical-institutional, and the individual-genetic. All the currents flowed into one, and we could understand man's striving in its fullest, most neutral terms, and see clearly all the various constrictions on human choice. It was as complete an anthropodicy as the Enlightenment could have hoped for, and one for which we had been groping with increasing intensity these past decades (cf. Lippman, 1929; Mumford, 1951). It showed exactly what Comte had wanted: the fullest possible correlates of the dependence of private troubles on social issues.

Perhaps most important of all, the ethic of this new anthropodicy shined through as clearly as day. The problem for all the thinkers of the Enlightenment, and especially for Comte, was how to get social interest to predominate over selfish private interest. The new theory of alienation showed that ethical action could not be possible where man was not supplied with self-critical and socially critical knowledge, and with the possibilities of broad and responsible choices. Recurrent evils like sadism, militant hate, competitive greed, narrow pride, calculating self-interest that takes a nonchalant view of others' lives, mental illness in its extreme forms—all stem from constrictions on behavior and from shallowness of meaning; and these could be laid in the lap of society, specifically, in the nature and type of education to which it submits its young; and to the kinds of choices and cognition which its institutions encourage and permit. Man could only be ethical if he was strong, and he could only be strong if he was given fullest possible cognition, and responsible control over his own powers. The only possible ethics was one which took man as a center, and which provided him with the conditions that permitted him to try to be moral. The antidote to evil was not to impose a crushing sense of supernatural sanction, or unthinking obligation, or automatic beliefs of any kind—no matter how "cheerful" they seem. For the first time in history it had become transparently clear that the real antidote to evil in society was to supply the possibility of depth and wholeness of experience. Evil was a problem of esthetics—that is, esthetics understood in its broad sense as the free creation of human meanings, and the acceptance of responsibility for them. It had never been so well understood that goodness and human nature were potentially synonymous terms; and evil was a complex reflex of the coercion of human powers.

CHAPTER FOURTEEN

SELF-ESTEEM: THE SINGLE
PRINCIPLE FOR A GENUINE SYNTHESIS

We said in the last chapter that, having fashioned a full-field theory of alienation, there was now nothing to prevent the science of man from appropriating the ideal-real framework of the nineteenth century. Not quite: one problem yet remained. It is a problem that takes us back to where we left the failure of Lotze and his system, in Chapter Five. As we saw there, the first lesson of the failure was that we had not yet achieved a thoroughgoing theory of the nature of the social bond. The second lesson was that, even having achieved it, there was still something else to be had. And, on the level of a genuine synthetic theory, it was perhaps the thorniest problem of all. I mean, of course, *the single unifying principle* that would form an integrated and firmly centered science. For those readers whose thought tends to theory and whose organism is soothed by the vision of an elegant and simplified intellectual structure, this part of our story is perhaps the most exciting of all.

The principle that we are seeking emerged from the new theory of personality, from the lengthy accumulation of personal biographies compiled by Freudian psychoanalysis and its various offshoots and schools. It emerged from the study of the Oedipus complex—a phenomenon, as we have amply seen, that is not to be understood as a complex at all, but rather as a shorthand term for the whole early conditioning period of children. What it really describes is the formation of the individual character, a formation in which the child learns to keep his feeling of well-being by conforming his action to the dictates of those around him. He learns to act, and to avoid anxiety, by fashioning for himself a definite life style which others around him approve of, or at least tolerate. Thus, the Oedipus complex (or better: oedipal phase of behavior) is really *a law in the strict scientific sense*: it is *The Law of Character Development* in the symbolic animal.

Now, a scientific law has to be explained, and it can only be explained by principles, just as, for example, the law of evolution was explained according to Darwin by the principle of natural selection. The principle which explains the law of human character development is *The Principle of Self-Esteem Maintenance*. The whole early training period of the child can be understood in one simple way: it is the period in which he learns to maintain his self-esteem in more-or-less constant fashion by adapting his reactions to the dictates and the possibilities of his human environment. He maintains his self-esteem by avoiding anxiety; and anxiety comes from his human environment in the form of disapprobation or the threat of separation from the parents. Thus, he maintains his self-esteem precisely by forming himself into the type of person who need not fear disapprobation or the loss of his succoring objects. As I have explained in more detail elsewhere (1962), this means that he becomes human by learning to derive his self-esteem from symbolic performances pleasing to the adults rather than from continued physiological dependence, which becomes displeasing to them. The various styles of human character (or life styles) which result from this early training can then be considered as *variations in modes of self-esteem maintenance*. Thus, in the most brief and direct manner, we have a *law* of human development and its explanatory *principle*.

I do not think it would be possible to overestimate the magnitude of this achievement for the science of man. It is a universal principle for human action akin to gravitation in the physical sciences. In other words, we have arrived at a Newtonian maturity two hundred years after Hume and Hartley, but in a way that permits our science to be anything but mechanistic. The fundamental datum for our science is a fact that at first sight seems banal, or irrelevant: it is the fact that—as far as we can tell—*all organisms like to "feel good" about themselves.* Or, put in terms of existential ontology, self-feeling is at the heart of Being in nature. Need we say that, for a science of developing life, this central fact is anything but banal or irrelevant? (I have just recently learned that the importance of this idea was well appreciated by William James' friend Thomas Davidson, and it goes back to the nineteenth-century ontologists, Rosmini and Gioberti.)

On the human level, we find an organism that likes to feel good about itself in symbolic as well as organismic ways. And here is a universal datum which links all men and their individual conduct to the full reach of their social structure. Moreover, it is a universal datum that is far superior, in one way, to the universal datum of the physical sciences: that is, it is directly given in our own experience—we do not have to surmise it inductively. We *know* that we like to feel good about ourselves—this is basic, direct knowledge. As Vico saw at the very beginning of the new science of history and human experience, its truths are more certain than those of the objective Newtonian world, and they are loftier and more noble as well (cf. Manuel, 1962, p. 19).

Furthermore, like the principle of gravity—or any viable principle—our principle must explain apparently contradictory phenomena —which is exactly what it does: *it explains the most disparate life styles as variations around the single theme of self-esteem maintenance.* Just as gravity explains both the northward course of the Rhine and the southward course of the Rhone, so the principle of self-esteem maintenance "explains" both schizophrenia and depression, sadism and masochism, hypersexuality and homosexuality, passivity and aggressivity, and so on. Not, of course, "all by itself," but with a properly elaborated theoretical structure. Given the achievement of this very structure in modern times, we have a perfect synthetic and deductive principle for our science.

Finally, and not least, it is—like gravity—an *irreducible primary property.* Just as innate attraction and repulsion are the irreducible primary properties of matter, self-esteem is the irreducible primary property of *behaving organisms.* There is no need at this time to seek further for a valid, nonreducible unifying principle.

The question may now arise as to why such a simple and fertile principle had not been discerned previously. But the fact is that it had—and right at the beginning of modern theorizing on the nature of the social bond. As we know, the role of self-esteem in human action was a basic part of the seventeenth- and eighteenth-century theories of human nature. There were literally a host of writings on the love of fame, glory, approbation as principal motive powers of human conduct. Lovejoy, who gave us a nice summary of this vast work, concluded that "This conception . . . of the irrational approbativeness of men as the dynamic of good conduct was one of the favorite themes of social psychology from the 16th to the late 18th century" (1961, p. 156). Cicero and Dante had spoken of it earlier—Dante in some particularly beautiful words; but in the modern epoch it became the "motive of virtually all the modes of behavior necessary for the good order of society and the progress of mankind" (Lovejoy, p. 157). In this way, what had been the scandalous insights of Mandeville and La Rochefoucauld became accepted scientific theory. Not only these, but also Adam Smith, Helvétius, Hume, Kant, and Rousseau made central use of the self-esteem motive. Kant's words are typical of the whole theoretical social psychological movement, and are worth noting: "A craving to inspire in others esteem for ourselves, through good behavior (repression of that which could arouse in them a poor opinion of us), is the real basis of all true sociality . . ." (in Lovejoy, p. 193). And who insisted more resoundingly than Rousseau on the basic goodness and malleability of human beings, on the neutrality of the passions? "There is absolutely no original perversity in the human heart. . . . The only passion natural to man is the love of himself, or self-love understood in a broad [i.e., not mean] sense" (1762, p. 81).

Most of the thinkers in this tradition argued that since man could not possess reason or virtue, God ingeniously arranged society by implanting this special mechanism that would order behavior harmoniously. If reason and virtue cannot guide the affairs of men, then the seeking of self-esteem is the perfect substitute guide. As we would expect, it was Hume who was pivotal in this tradition. He devastated everyone by showing that not only do reason and virtue *not* control the passion for self-esteem, but that they cannot control it. As Lovejoy remarks, it was with this single coup that Hume seriously challenged the great tradition of moral philosophy, and paved the way for the new groping of the nineteenth century.

Now we can see better why we said that Hume was the father of modern personality theory. We now know that he was basically correct, that self-esteem comes to be maintained by automatic behavior designed to avoid anxiety—it is thus initially out of the range of reason and virtue. Only when each individual painfully examines his own life style, how it came into being and how it functions, is he capable of placing his self-esteem maintenance under some kind of rational control, and allowing for conduct that is *virtuous*—that is, conduct that attempts to meet each new situation on its own distinctive merits, and does not automatically reflect previous training.

All in all, we can say that the Enlightenment showed astonishingly acute insight into human action. Most of its thinkers thought highly of the self-esteem motive because it seemed to guarantee harmonious human sociality: it was only necessary for society to devise ways to make appeal to it, ways that would not lead to divisiveness and destruction. They saw that man needs a warm feeling about himself, and that he must address himself to his fellows for this feeling. Self-esteem seemed very naturally to be the surest basis for true selflessness and social harmony. Hume sharpened the problem further by showing that the self-esteem was not amenable to mere moral exhortation or to a facile cold sway of reason—that it went much deeper than these.

It remained for modern personality theory to bring this whole tradition to flower. We can now see that with the law of the oedipal transition and the principle of self-esteem maintenance, we have closed the circle on three hundred years of cogitation on the workings of human nature. By interpreting the oedipal transition in an Adlerian or a post-Freudian way, we also rejoin one of the views of the Enlightenment: we understand that the striving for self-esteem is essentially neutral (Rousseau, 1762, p. 247). We can see again that it is dependent on social appraisals, and not on the working-out of hostile inner drives. But we can also see that—for science—the Enlightenment insight was insufficient: it was merely an insight, unsupported by an extensive, documented, esoteric body of knowledge. In the work of Helvétius and Bentham the penalty for this lack had to be paid: the principle of self-esteem maintenance took the guise of the simple principle of hedonism; it was interpreted so narrowly, and unsupported by any understanding of its genesis or the range and breadth of the many things it related to, that it fell into an undeserved disfavor. It could only be salvaged and fully installed as a scientific principle when the full dimensions and modes of its operations had been traced out. When Marx compared Adam Smith to Mandeville he summed up the whole problem: it may have been meaningful to talk of self-love, but at the same time it overly simplified the broad relationships that had to be determined in order to make the principle truly productive. In science it is necessary to simplify exposition and investigation by leaving out some cooperative factors; but in the human sciences the risk is greatest that by leaving out cooperative factors we may falsify the whole investigation. The fiasco of Bentham's Panopticon venture showed how true this was. Deductions have to spring from a broad spread of data, which was unavailable at that time. Modern social psychology has completed the task begun by the inspired early theorists of the Enlightenment: we have spelled out not only the forms and dimensions of self-esteem needs and maintenance, but also have a thoroughgoing law of its genesis and sustenance in the early training period. The breakthrough at the very beginning of a science of man has now been completed by a full-field theory of self-esteem. Today we can see that Helvétius, despite the inevitable narrowness of his views, was the key figure in this whole tradition: it was he who proposed that all the passions be phrased in terms of the single principle of self-love; and in an insight of genius he said in one simple phrase in his notes that *this* was *the program for morality!* (See 1909, p. 280.) Later thinkers tried to fulfill precisely this mandate: Jouffroy in his important 1832 essay on "Self-Love," and, of course, Fourier in his inspired theory of the passions. But since they could only make the simplest of statements in their time, a *science* of *morals* based on this single principle had to wait until our day.

Looked at in another way, the whole history of the science of man since the Enlightenment has been an attempt to come to terms with some central dynamic principle with which to correlate the social dimensions of human consciousness. The intuition of the various thinkers was mostly correct, but the attempts were usually clumsy, precisely because the available knowledge was so scanty.

Perhaps the outstanding example of this was Lester Ward's extreme involvement with the "social forces," a conceptualization that we noted in some detail in Chapter Four. We can now understand with perfect clarity what Ward was driving at, and exactly why he failed. Thus we can add further support for the necessity of the disciplinary quest; it gave us, after all, a comprehensive theory of personality. But at the same time we can also add support for the systemic synthesis that Ward proposed. We can see that it was a correct vision because it included the dynamic principle; but the vision was not compelling because the principle was still in gross form. The "social forces," as Ward understood them, were an attempt to locate the mainsprings of action in each individual actor; Ward tried to subjectivize the science of man—exactly what Lotze wanted. But the social forces were something more than this. They represented not only the individual personality, but also the dynamic forces, or desires, of the personality. The social forces, in other words, represented the adumbration of the unifying principle for a complete science of man.

Ward, who understood well the problems of science, could not conceal his excitement over such a principle. He pointed out how the idea first appeared to him, how it seemed overly simple and not really the revolutionary and "exceedingly fertile principle" which he knew it to be (1893, p. 118). This simple principle was a "great truth" that had been neglected because it was not "adequately supported by scientific proofs" and because its causal relations had not been spelled out (p. 119). Ward knew that the scientific investigators of the time would not recognize such a principle because of the "rigid scientific method" they were accustomed to (p. 118). But Ward could only marvel at the simplicity and obviousness of the principle, which struck him "so forcibly," that he hesitated to try to demonstrate what to him was "an axiom" (p. 119).

In his elation, incredulousness, and regret, Ward sums up the whole history of the Enlightenment problem of the self-esteem that I sketched above. He saw how central this principle of symbolically mediated pleasure was to human action; he saw how difficult it would be to get narrow, traditional science to accept this kind of non-quantifiable deductive principle; and he also understood, finally, that its full range and dimensions would have to be spelled out before it could achieve scientific standing.

For one thing, Ward was upset that the critics of hedonism had discredited it (1918, v. 6, pp. 4–5). He saw that Bentham had made on overly simplistic formulation of the problem of human pleasure, that it was a symbolic and psychic phenomenon which took many shapes and extended over time. In today's jargon we would say that self-esteem is fundamentally tied up with the symbolic identity; it cannot be simplistically reduced to simple gratification, since it involves the total, cultural self. For example, even though one's present condition be miserable, one can gain a warm feeling of self-esteem, by a belief in a future reincarnation. Ward wanted to trace the dimensions of self-feeling in their full ramifications, and he wanted to make self-feeling the property of science rather than of art and religion. In his book *The Psychic Factors of Civilization* (1893), Ward had a chapter on the "Nature of the Soul." We recognize immediately that he was, like all the major thinkers of the nineteenth century, occupied with the *Seelenfrage*; and, like Lotze, he translated the idea of soul into the idea of personality. He too wanted to take it out of the realm of transcendental metaphysics and to make it central to a science of man. Ward says:

> The full definition of the soul therefore becomes: *the collective feelings of organic beings and their resultant efforts.* No subject can be thoroughly understood without prolonged investigation, and profound reflection. Down to the present century the soul, notwithstanding the amount of time and energy expended upon it, had never been the subject of any such critical study. . . . Thus

tabooed, the animated feelings, or true soul, could not
be expected to receive that penetrating criticism which
alone could yield a true conception of its nature, and the
whole subject remained philosophically and scientifically
speaking, a *terra incognita*. It was given over entirely to
other agencies, to art, literature, religion, and government,
all of which proceeded blindly and added nothing to its
extent or fruitfulness (1893, pp. 46–47, his italics).

It is obvious from this quotation that Ward's system was to the
science of man what Lotze's was to philosophy. Ward is here pleading
for a focus on the centrality of organic life as the proper subject
matter of the human sciences, and he understood the center of this
life as the soul, or the self-feeling that exists in nature.

Again, we must in all justice remember that Ward knew that his
position was premature because the causal relations of the self-feeling
were not spelled out. Critics such as E. C. Hayes and Morris Cohen,
as we noted in Chapter Four, found the idea of social forces fair
game. But now we can see that, while they were correct to criticize
Ward, they were also somewhat beside the point. True, Ward's social
forces represented an energizing of human volition that was bound
to get in the way of a social behavioral theory of the self. It had an
uncomfortable ring of instincts and vitalism, at a time when the full
relationships of the self to the social field had not been spelled out
(cf. Hayes, 1911). Ward seemed actually to be obscuring instead of
promoting the Enlightenment view of man, in the same way that
Freud later did, by accenting innate forces rather than social relations. And a mature social psychology, as we stressed, cannot use causes
wholly antecedent to social activity as explanations for the mainsprings
of behavior. Yet Ward had Lotze's correct vision of the need to find
a principle *within* each individual. Today, having plotted the dimensions of self-esteem in terms of a full-field theory of action, we can
support Ward's correct vision: in order to act one must develop socially
approved patterns of behavior; this gives one an identity based on
self-esteem, which is inseparable from the objects in one's field and
from the rules for behaving toward them. We can see, then, that
"pleasure" or self-feeling is a dimension of the social field, *and* it is
organismically based. That is to say, it *is* socially-conditioned, but it
also is *antecedent* to society: the infant's organism naturally experiences warm self-feeling, but only on condition that he is properly cared
for. The self-esteem mechanism thus links biology with culture because
it operates by avoiding anxiety for the *organism,* by teaching it to
maneuver in a *cultural* object world.

We can see that Ward was a level above his critics because we can now understand what he wanted to show: that the mechanism of self-feeling, or soul, is a fully social phenomenon which, at the same time, is firmly centered in the biological organism as a *non-reducible* property of organisms. Ward eagerly asked for criticism from his friends, but at a time when criticism could only be destructive of his intuitions since a theory of personality was lacking. He suffered the same weakness as Newton had earlier, when Newtonianism was rejected by many as a return of science to the Dark Ages, the time when man relied on "innate forces" as explanations (Kuhn, 1962, p. 162). The idea of "innate forces" could only be made palatable by a broadly relational and descriptive theory such as Newton provided.

But, once modern personality theory had plotted the correlates of self-esteem, we could see Ward fully vindicated. Self-esteem becomes one dimension of a full social field. As such, it is inextricably a matter of human values and personal valuations. Albion Small had very early understood Ward's social forces in the modern sense. Once again Small's vision of the goal of social science was prophetic. He saw that social science would have to explore the full dimensions of human action *as valuations,* and that Ward had designed this task. "For lifting this perception above the threshold of consciousness," says Small, "social science owes more to the author of *Dynamic Sociology* than to any other man." But Small could see the prematurity of Ward's effort: "I express this judgment in spite of the fact that in my opinion Professor Ward's elaboration of the thesis, *psychic forces are the true causes of all social phenomena,* makes the actual human process much simpler than it really is" (1910, p. 200, his italics).

Small saw, in other words, that the task of social science, once it was fixed on the centrality of human valuations and their workings, would have to spell out the full dimensions and correlates of these valuations. In our modern terminology we would say that social science would have to talk about life styles and their relation to the full social, institutional role structure. "Social forces" would have to convey a complete picture of self-esteem maintenance of the individual immersed in his full social milieu. But this was only to be possible when we had combined large-scale studies of the complex interrelationships of social values—of the type of Max Weber, Thorstein Veblen, and C. Wright Mills—with the personal biographies of a half-century of psychoanalytic patients. It then became possible to talk not only about the low self-esteem of a depressed patient, but about a depressed wife of an oil executive, whose shallow consumer life had lost all meaning. It only became possible, in sum, when we had a complete social-psychological theory of human alienation that was based on a single, unifying principle present in each individual. We could then talk about a society failing to provide for the self-esteem needs of its members, by limiting their critical awareness, limiting their role flexibility, confining their action to shallow, routine, and unconvincing performance.

Here we can also understand better how different Ward's orientation was from Freud's, even though they could both be accused of putting the accent on inner forces rather than social relations, as we noted above. Both Ward and Freud took some of their inspiration from Schopenhauer, but each had different things in view. Ward was particularly grateful to Schopenhauer for turning psychology "out of the old and hopeless channels of objective psychology into the new and promising channels of subjective psychology" (1893, p. 62). In other words, Ward saw the possibility of a subjective, value-centered approach to human behavior. Freud, on the other hand, evidently took Schopenhauer literally and seized upon the unconscious driving nature of the will, which firmly opposes man and society and makes man an object of nature, rather than a subject. Little wonder that Ward's sociology is inherently radical, and that Freud's theory played right into the hands of conservatives: it lent support to the idea that man was inherently beyond correction, and that therefore social reconstruction could never really make human happiness. This is certainly one explanation for the long popularity of Freud in anti-reconstructionist America. Freud is in the tradition of Hobbes and de Maistre, and not of Condorcet and Saint-Simon. Ward, on the other hand, saw Schopenhauer's will as "universal soul force"—which was quite another matter. He left open the possibility of a subjective science of man that was not pessimistic. In his book *Psychic Factors of Civilization,* the very next chapter following upon his discussion of Schopenhauer is titled "Refutation of Pessimism"; in it he says (like Fourier) that the "hostile social state" is responsible for the "woes of mankind" (p. 69)—and not the inner driving will. Here we have two inspirations from Schopenhauer, both of which correctly re-pivot human science on a universal subjective factor. But one draws a pessimistic lesson, by isolating the individual, and the other an optimistic one, by focusing more broadly on the social environment.

Finally, to support the idea that Ward's intuition went straight to the heart of the matter, we must mention that Ward refused to place ethics at the head of the sciences, in front of sociology—as Comte earlier did. And Ward insisted on this for a very crucial reason.

He understood that "all science is essentially ethical" (1918, v. 5, p. 281). The problem was merely to make of the invariant point of reference of a dynamic sociology a principle which would contain *in itself* an ethical imperative. In other words—and this is crucial— the single principle which unites the full-field theory of alienation would have to be *itself a measure of social criticism*. And it could only do this if it was centered on human psychology, in the individual actor. This is exactly what the principle of self-esteem maintenance does. It keeps the fundamental notion of hedonism, while relating human happiness to the whole social institutional structure. When we plot the correlates of human unhappiness, using self-esteem as the focal point of reference, *we have an automatic ethical imperative*. Thus the highest vision of Enlightenment science is fulfilled: science and ethics are shown to be inseparable, and a reading of nature in the service of man is realized in the most basic and direct way. The science of man in society, linking the individual subjectivity with the social, institutional roles via the principle of self-esteem maintenance, then becomes itself a wholly ethical edifice. There is no need to place ethics in front of sociology, as Comte did, precisely because this edifice is based on a continuing facilitation of human well-being. Lotze and Ward saw that life itself, "the great heart of nature," is the subject matter of science. To further human desires is to further nature, and a science devoted to this will be inescapably ethical and educative. "Human desires," to quote Ward again, ". . . constitute the only good from the standpoint of sociology" (1893, p. 115).

It is this that modern existentialism has had to rediscover as it focused on the centrality of *"Being."* But we can see that neither the old idea of Life, nor the modern revival of it in terms of Being, had any scientific meaning until we could bring them partly into the realm of objective science. And this is exactly what the principle of self-esteem maintenance does: it is the *specific descriptive* of Being; it brings Being into the world of science by *objectively correlating its dimensions*—first through the oedipal training period, and then through the roles provided by the social structure. Modern existentialism wants to maximize creative Being, exactly as Ward wanted. But the idea is neither existentialism's nor Ward's: it is the early Enlightenment option for man over things. One of the major pre-occupations of the Enlightenment thinkers who had broken away from Newtonian mechanism was, as we have repeatedly noted, to found a science with man as center. For Turgot, and the thinkers who came after him, this had a concrete meaning; the mandate of this science was the furtherance of Being in its highest and most complex reaches, namely: *the preservation of genius and the maximization of the talents of genius.* This was the central function of the good society, upon which the whole morality of the new science was based. The morality was then very simple: those forces which stifled genius were evil, those which allowed it to flower to full fruition were good (Manuel, 1962, p. 28). The idea of fostering genius continued through Condorcet to Saint-Simon, who evolved projects for the subsidization of genius. By the time we get to Ward, we can see that his urging of a full, critical education, as the core of the new science of man, was really a continuation of the Enlightenment mandate to foster *genius.* Translated into late nineteenth-century terms, this was a mandate to foster *the full evolution of Life or creative Being, up to the highest reaches of potential.* Little wonder that Ward wanted hedonism understood more broadly and revived as a program for science; and that he saw the fostering of human desires as the only good. He was prepared to carry through Schiller's proposal that man could try to make God, and the only way to do this was to maximize creative Being. The Enlightenment thus had very serious ambitions for science and life; they would be dumbfounded to see how we have trivialized them today. (In America the president of the National Association of Manufacturers recently proclaimed that the budget for education should be curtailed: it does not help business.)

It has been a long and difficult road to substantiate Ward's conception of sociology. All the disciplines have had to join in, to plot the basic correlates of the mere fact of human action and to dislodge the single principle which would unite these correlates. I have dwelt on Ward's sociology because it sums up the Enlightenment attempt to come to terms with this principle, and because it shows exactly what was lacking and what had to be done. Sixty years after Ward, R. S. Lynd echoed the perennial problem of a single principle, and the moral gap that had to be filled by it: "If social science is not to be forever stalemated in the face of the future, some point of reference must be established by which it can get beyond the present paralyzing question, 'But how are *we* to determine what *ought* to be? That can be of no concern of the scientist'" (1939, p. 201). We can see that Lynd tried to bring Ward up to date, and he tried to find the ethical imperative of science "within the human stuff of us all." He again proposed that science satisfy the specifically human cravings as he saw them, cravings for security, status, the expression of capacities, and so on. Only in this way would science be able to serve man, because it would enable us to ask: "What ones of our current institutions, appraised from this point of view, effectively support men's needs—and how effectively—and what ones block them? And what changes in these institutions are indicated?" (p. 201). Lynd saw very clearly, but he too was condemned to be premature; there was still no possibility of making out a compelling case for an invariant point of reference, twenty-five years ago, that would link the individual desires with the whole social structure. Lynd was loudly heckled by the little men in sociology and in other disciplines, who had no idea what the science of man was about; he thus suffered the same neglect as Ward. I have personally heard it reported that, at a talk to various disciplinarians at one of our purportedly better universities, Lynd was "made a fool of" without realizing it. Obviously he had bitten off more than they could chew. Only today is it possible to silence the irresponsible hecklers, as well as to satisfy the serious critics of prematurity in science. Over seventy years after E. A. Ross had signaled "jealousy" to Ward as an important social force, we are today in possession of a sufficiently thorough understanding of it, and of shame, guilt, the psychiatric syndromes (cf. E. Becker, 1964a), as well as the minutiae of the interaction ceremonial in society. Furthermore, and most important, we have succeeded in linking them all together by the single principle of self-esteem maintenance in the symbolic animal (cf. E. Becker, 1962). Ward could not have hoped for more.

The nineteenth century solved *Die Seelenfrage* and *Die Soziale Frage;* the twentieth century solved the problem of the true synthetic unity of the science of man. All the disciplines and all the disparate researchers could now—if they wanted to—join around the single focus: British analytic philosophy, Continental phenomenology, physiological and pathological psychiatry, positivist empiricism with humanist idealism—all could employ their energies to further the self-feeling in nature, as it is embodied in human striving. The twentieth century—like Lotze in the nineteenth—had finally made possible the highest form of eclecticism; but even more than Lotze it proceeded to a real, single-principle unification.

CONCLUSION: THE SHAPE OF THE UNIFIED SCIENCE

And so we have a splendid vision of an authentically unified science of man, an integral and broadly relational theoretical structure, held together by a centered single principle. Early in this book we made it a point to note how each of the innovators of the science of man styled himself a Newton, or a Columbus, etc., of the new science. We promised to give our own view of the matter, and now that we have been able to sketch the unified science in its entirety this is the place to do it. We can see that our science has had an altogether unique, prolonged, and halting development. It has taken several hundred years just to build up its analytic framework, and to substantiate its earliest intuitions. The uniqueness of its theoretical form and its constructs forbids any direct analogy to the development of the physical and natural sciences. Yet, if we have to talk about a science in its development, it is always necessary and instructive to compare it to older and better-established sciences in some ways. If we use the major figures of the science of man in analogy with some of the major figures of the physical and natural sciences, we get an idea of the complex nature of the science of man, and we get too an explanation of why it was so long in coming to maturity.

Saint-Pierre would be the Bacon of this science. He focused originally on what shape the science of man should take, and what its broad program should be: it should be a science employing reason in the service of human ends, implemented by academies of political and moral science. Leibnitz urged a similar program, and he could also share the Baconian laurels.

Vico, Diderot, and Rousseau would be its Copernicus. Vico was really the first to discover that culture and history were man-made; and he understood that all science properly centers on man's creation of symbolic meanings. Diderot too saw the need to man-center the sciences; and Rousseau offered an ideal-typology that would justify and carry the new centering. Rousseau saw that man was essentially neutral and uncorrupt, that society was at fault in shaping the human consciousness. Consequently he urged that we focus on man in an entirely new way, start from scratch, so to speak. Herder would have to be included in this group of striking innovators: his undertaking was similar to Vico's, and even though it took place later in the century it was evidently independent of Vico. Saint-Simon and Comte could share the Copernican honors, for a strong and comprehensive restatement of this position after the French Revolution.

Helvétius, Fourier, and Ward would be its Galileo. They saw that the passions or the social forces have to be the central core of the science, and urged that analysis must start from there, that the passions or desires were the empirical data which would serve as the base for the new experimental science. Fourier was the first complete experimentalist of the passions, of the basic law of human attraction.

He, and later Ward, wanted to base a science of man on self-feeling as it manifests itself in laws of operation. But he was a century ahead of his time, since we had to plot the correlates of the passions, or of the self. Bentham, of course, would share some of the honors here, but he was not as complete an experimentalist as Fourier, not as ready to make a clean slate.

Who, then, was to be the Newton of the new science? We can see that in the science of man we have to talk, not about a Newton, but instead about a *"Newtonian movement"*—which, in effect, took about a century to achieve. It remained to plot the correlates of the self, and the forces invariably involved in shaping it, before we could dislodge a single, unifying principle. Actually, the principle had been discerned as early as the beginning of the Enlightenment, but it could not be used scientifically until its relations had been broadly and clearly mapped. It was like finding the law of gravity before clearly making out that there was an interrelated solar system. Thus, a host of thinkers comprise the Newtonian movement: Marx, and all those upon whom he drew (especially Feuerbach), Weber, Veblen, C. Wright Mills—all contributed to plotting the large-scale social influences on the formation of the self. Idealist philosophers like Hegel, Fichte, and Schiller, then Baldwin, Royce, Cooley, George Mead, Dewey—all joined to show the genesis of the self in its interpersonal, interorganismic dimensions. Many other thinkers belong to this movement, and we have mentioned them in these pages—Wundt, Durkheim, Fouillée, William James, Georg Simmel. And of course Vico's and Rousseau's contributions are basic in this area also—as are Herder's. We would also want to include the early French "ego psychologists" and theorists on the power of early habit—Cabanis, Destutt de Tracy, and Maine de Biran.

It is very clear that here is a distinctive science, with a distinctive shape and history. But the most distinctive part of it is the single ideal-real principle which the whole Newtonian movement served to dislodge. As we saw, it was revealed most intimately as the result of a half-century of psychoanalytic case-history biographies. Here human behavior came to be studied in the detail of all its many general, gross forms and minute, subtle contortions, through the vicissitudes of the early training experience and the trials of adult life. We could understand how the self is constructed in microcosm, as the individual learns to avoid anxiety by performing in a ready-tailored world view. But *all the variations* of the life styles constructed in this process hinged around the single principle of self-esteem main-

tenance by an animal who needs affection, respect, and security. Here
was a single principle which linked the human self to the full field
of social influences: to the social roles as well as the culturally defined
appendages of the actor's own body, the traditional past as well as
the utopian future—there was apparently nothing distinctively human
which was not somehow directly contingent on the self-esteem principle. Furthermore, and not least, the principle was distinctive because
it was ideal-real: it was empirical, and yet it allowed for a science
that would be man-centered and hedonistic. This was truly an unprecedented combination for science.

And yet, with all this unprecedented distinction about the new
principle, it was precisely here that the science of man followed the
early path of many of the other sciences. I mean that *it had to draw
its decisive data from a technique or craft*. Just as technology and
medicine had played vital roles in the emergence of the earlier physical
and natural sciences, so now the professional technique of psychoanalysis dislodged the appropriate esoteric data for the new science.
At the beginning of any science, as Thomas Kuhn points out, all the
facts are likely to seem more or less alike. There is a reaching-out
for any facts that can be gained by casual observation, and recourse is
usually had to the facts which lie close at hand. But a science needs
esoteric facts, those *most difficult to discover,* and these are most readily
drawn *from sources that are not casual* (Kuhn, 1962, pp. 15–16). This
process was repeated exactly in the science of man, as psychoanalytic
technology gave us the esoteric data on self-esteem maintenance and
anxiety-proneness. In this way, we could affirm with authority the
straightforward and basically simple nature of human behavior.
Science uses esotericism only when absolutely necessary to give weight
to its clarifications, and not in order to obfuscate its theories under a
miasma of mystery.

But psychoanalysis has been around for quite some time, and yet
it is only now that we are fastening on the direct early Enlightenment
principle that it confirmed. What is the reason for delay? I think I
can convey the reason most forcefully by means of an autobiographical
note. When this final result of the Newtonian movement urged itself
on my attention, it seemed inconceivable that the science of man
could be so simply and easily unified. I repeated almost exactly
Lester Ward's reaction to the vivacity of the idea of the social forces.
The principle of self-esteem maintenance, like its precursor, the social
forces, seemed "overly simple" and not really the "exceedingly fertile
principle" that it was. It seemed a "great truth," so forcible and yet

so obvious, that it seemed axiomatic and hardly in need of demonstration (Ward, 1893, pp. 118–119). But, unlike Ward's social forces, this principle did not suffer neglect because it had been unsupported by scientific proofs or by the elaboration of causal relations. On the contrary, it was well supported by innumerable case histories, and connected to a host of varying manifestations of life styles. The problem with the principle of self-esteem maintenance was of another kind; namely, it was not adequately supported *by a subjective framework*. With all its empirical elaboration, modern science had entirely lost the nineteenth-century notion of a man-based value science in the service of human pleasure. It was thus necessary again to execute a "Copernican shift." The psychoanalysts, who had etched the principle in modern times, did not dislodge it and place it at the center of science. After all, how could they?—they were basically medical technologists. Instead, they talked about it as just another correlate, just another variable in a field of relationships. This was true of Otto Fenichel's orthodox encyclopedic treatment of psychoanalysis, which made prominent mention of self-esteem, as well as of Abram Kardiner's important works, which traced its variable workings in different societies. It was also true of Adler, who very early in the history of psychoanalysis made it prominent in his explanations. But it had not only to be recognized and broadly described, but again made pivotal, as the social forces had been with Ward.

It then became possible to have a science which would seek the maximization of the self-feeling, or the sense of Being. In this way, the whole nineteenth-century legacy was crowned, and its mandate was finally fulfilled. The full-field theory of alienation provided a comprehensive view of the constrictions on Life or Being. The nineteenth-century mandate to maximize Being could take place within a unified science of man in society. The sense of obligation that was felt by man was now transferred, as Guyau had wanted, from higher otherworldly sanctions *to the sanction of Life itself*. The science of Life would be based on the principle of self-esteem, and its moral sanction would be the expansion of Being. The moral sanction would not be specified in advance, in any "thou shalt" or "thou shalt not" manner. It was obvious from the theory that it would have to encourage an *autonomous morality of unspecified choices*. Otherwise it could not further the expansion of Life. The anthropodicy thus gave an open and broad ethical directive, which was, simply, the directive to create human meanings in the largest possible measure.

Thus the new science solved the knotty twofold problem of ob-

A SIMPLIFIED SYNOPTIC CHART TRACING THE DEVELOPMENT OF THE SCIENCE OF MAN SINCE THE DECLINE OF THE MEDIEVAL COSMOLOGY

Dominant Metaphysical Ideology	*Scientific Reaction*
1. Theological Synthesis: Scholastic Idealism. —Union of Reason and Faith, Reason and Nature, the Ideal and the Actual, Science and Theology.	Stress on the particular, the fact, on practice. Instead of the former theory, speculation, abstraction, universalism, there is a move toward decentralization, simplification, pragmatism, naturalism (e.g., *Bacon, Machiavelli, Montaigne*).
Duration: Roughly to mid-14th century	*Duration*: Roughly to 16th century
2. New Scientific Synthesis: The Newtonian World Machine. —Union of Reason, Nature, and Law, governing a natural theology, as well as ethical, social, and political theory.	Stress on man as center of nature; stress on human purpose and values, and on the products of thought as a human creation. Separation of Reason, Nature and Morality: stress on practice and pragmatism in morals (e.g., *Vico, Diderot, Hume, Rousseau*).
Duration: Roughly to mid-18th century	*Duration*: Roughly to 19th century
3. New Synthesis of Hegelian Idealism. —Union of the Ideal and the Actual, of Religion and Philosophy, of Reason and Nature.	Again, as in (1), stress on naturalism, empiricism, pragmatism, positivism (e.g., *Feuerbach, Darwin, Peirce, James, Dewey*).
Duration: Roughly to mid-19th century	*Duration*: Roughly to 1st quarter of 20th century
4. Projected New Synthesis of Logical Empiricism. —Attempt to find a unitary language for all the sciences, based on mathematics and symbolic logic, and using physical science precedents. Strict empiricism, behaviorism, separation of fact and value, eschewing of any idealism.	Again, as in (2), stress on man as center of nature, on values, on primacy of human purposes. Also, there is a similar protest against an over-eager rationalism that defeats true pragmatism.
Duration: Roughly from 1st quarter to mid-20th century	

Residual Emergent Ideas for a Science of Man	*Various Attempts at an Ideal-Empirical Synthesis Leading to a Science of Man as Anthropodicy*

—Naturalism
—Empiricism }

     A

Duration: Continuing

—Restoration of hypothesis to a dominant
  role in science
—The Idea of Progress
—The Idea of Liberty
—The projection of the ideal-type
—Acknowledgment of the centrality of human
  symbolic meanings }

     B

Auguste ———— Hermann ———— Lester
Comte ———— Lotze ———— Ward

Duration: Continuing

—Evolution
—Mature pragmatism
—Full transactionalism: the togetherness of
  subject and object in nature and history }

     C

Duration: Continuing

No new ideas emerged. Instead, an increasing groping and appraisal of what had already been achieved and thought through; clarification, simplification, and synthesis. The result was a true, empirical synthesis of all the cumulative, residual ideas of this long tradition: (A, B, & C).

(All three failed because the full theory of the nature of the social bond had not been achieved. When it was, Comte's historical overemphasis could be corrected; Lotze's continued separation of the subject and object repaired; and Ward's precursory adumbration of the "social forces" could finally be demonstrated as the central concern for an active science of man in society, one that would promote human well-being.

The anthropodicy was finally achieved by a clarification, simplification, and synthesis of the concepts of three additional major figures in this tradition—figures who themselves represented syntheses of many of the major currents: Marx, Freud, Dewey.)

jective naturalism: it could treat values as well as the problem of evil. It could further life as a value, and it could help overcome evil by furthering autonomous ethical choices. Evil can be overtaken by helping man maximize his own meanings, in a science centered on the furtherance of Life. From a theoretical point of view the outstanding problem of the nineteenth century had been solved, and from a point of view of logical consistency nothing could be simpler. The unified science of man was the anthropodicy that had been sought since the medieval decline. Furthermore, it was an anthropodicy directly in the tradition of one of the first postmedieval thinkers—Erasmus. It was he who first sought to combine sociological observation and spiritual vision into one organic whole (Salomon, 1963, pp. 396–397). Thus we seem to be able to say that the problem left outstanding by the decline of the medieval cosmology has now been theoretically resolved.[1]

CHAPTER FIFTEEN

THE PROBLEM OF PREMATURITY IN SOCIAL THEORY:

Comte's Failure Reappraised

> *Do we have to show expressly the profound inanity of trying to constitute a social science—intellectually and all at once— before we are able to rest it on a sufficiently broad experimental basis, and before we have rationally prepared our own intelligence for it?*
>
> AUGUSTE COMTE *(1830–1842, vol. 4, p. 125)*

Having thus spread before us a panoramic vista of the successful unification of the science of man, we can see why it had to fail to be unified in all the earlier attempts. We spoke of Ward at length in the last chapter, but no study of the science of man as a unified vision would be complete without lingering a bit on the greatest sociologist of all—Auguste Comte. We must understand with complete clarity why Comte failed, for only in this way can we pay proper tribute to his greatness. But, perhaps more important, only in this way can we do complete justice to the continuing rumblings of the problem that Comte left us, and to the repeated attempts to revive Comte as a central figure in the history of sociology.

The fact is that Comte has never been allowed wholly to expire in France; and recently an annual Comte lecture was inaugurated in England, which our best scholars have been invited to present (see Simon, 1963, for details on these activities). In 1953, De Grange published a major sociological treatise based on Comte, which seeks to bring him up to date with sociological theory since his time. And recently an English sociologist, Ronald Fletcher, has called for a reappraisal of Comte.

What, then, did Comte teach us? And what have we learned that he did not know? By answering this twofold question we might hope to contribute definitively to the solution of the "problem of Comte" in our time. Since we have already covered most of the ground, let us try to answer these questions directly and simply, in a summing-up way:

1. Comte fully understood what a science of man should be: a man-centered science of society, actively working to implement progress, according to some kind of ideal.

2. Only such a science could provide what we have always lacked, and what we had glimpsed during the Middle Ages: the possibility of the subordination of politics to morals. Even more, Positive science would give us something that we did not have during the Middle Ages: it would give us a *rationally and empirically demonstrated faith.* The medieval cosmology had a major failing: it was a theodicy that was not rationally and empirically demonstrable.

3. Comte understood that both systemic synthesis *and* disciplinary analysis were necessary in order to constitute such a science. But he thought that the disciplinary, analytic stage should last *only long enough* to dispel the old superstitions and to provide compelling rational knowledge. Once we had such knowledge, we should proceed at once to a man-centered synthesis, and begin social reconstruction under the aegis of the new superordinate science of society.

4. What would provide such compelling knowledge for the new synthesis? Comte thought he had the answer, the famous "Law of the Three Stages of Human Development." Comte based his whole system on this law which he called "the true Theory of human and social development" (1848, pp. 34–35). He considered that his age was supremely ripe to use this law to command allegiance to the new synthesis that he proposed. This law, he was profoundly convinced, provided the sufficient "rational preparation" on the basis of which man could opt once and for all for the new Positive social reconstruction. Once mankind saw how it had progressed from theology through philosophy, to positive knowledge in all *the various sciences,* it would choose to live by positive knowledge in society also. It would choose to live under social science. The final area for this progression was in social phenomena themselves. "Thus the foundation of Social science depends simply upon establishing the truth of this theory of development" (1848, p. 37).

He wrote the six volumes of the monumental *Cours de philosophie positive* to demonstrate this progression to positive knowledge in the various sciences, expecting that this would be compelling knowledge for all men of good will—the great work that would uphold the great idea. It did compel Stuart Mill and many other notable intellects, but as we know it left his age as a whole singularly undisturbed; and today in much of our lives we are still blissfully frolicking in the first two stages. Comte had erred in his reading of history.

We can see today that the failure of Comte's system revolves, really, on the sole pivot of that fatal word—"simply." The fact is that the Law of the Three Stages *simply* did not and could not support the foundation of social science. The distinction between science and ethics, which he sought to efface, continued to exist. Natural Philosophy (science) and Moral Philosophy had been separated since Aristotle and Plato, and they are still separated today. Comte saw that this separation was "provisional" (p. 37); still today we see that it is provisional. His only error was to imagine that the separation could be overcome by the three-stage theory of human development, that this alone would enjoin a value option for a science of man in society. Comte was a true Enlightenment man in that he believed that a thoroughgoing scientific demonstration of human ills would carry its own ethical imperative. But he was also a typical Enlightenment man in that he was too eager in his belief about what was sufficiently rationally "thoroughgoing."

Comte, of course, was a passionate man—he was not talking to the insipid specialists of our time. He was addressing the post-Revolutionary generation, and thought they all had the requisite historical experience and hence the passion to opt for his reasoned system. He thought that at no time had conditions been proper until *after* the French revolution; only then was man prepared to cogitate social and moral problems on a rational basis. He fully expected that broad social response and rational acceptance could be counted on because of the unique historical conditions and the extreme predicament of his time. Perhaps this is the error of the sensitive, passionate nature. After all, it is the same one Rousseau committed earlier when he expected everyone to sense the outrages of contemporary social morality as he had filtered them through his sensitive system. It is the same error Ward committed as he surveyed the idiocy and rampant anarchy of laissez-faire that had knocked about his organism during his trying youthful and Civil War experiences. He too must have been surprised when Americans did not opt for a society built on the exercise and infinite growth of directive reason and the flowering of the individual personality—"the great heart of nature." Finally, it is the same error committed by C. Wright Mills, who must have had experiences and indignations similar to Ward's, in the Texas oil fields, and in witnessing the stark plight of the new nations. Perhaps after all Mills' indignation was greater because he came upon the scene in the equivalent of a post-Revolutionary time. How could his fellow academicians stomach the bland inanity of the "overdeveloped" society in the face of the unprecedented needs and opportunities of this new industrial time?

Comte erred in his understanding of moral indignation, which partly explains his failure to appraise Rousseau correctly. He thought that man opts for a new morality when his intelligence has been "sufficiently prepared." But man squeezes his intelligence out of the total experience of his organism—and thus organisms vary in the indignation they can muster, as Ward and Mills must later have discovered to their bafflement. Comte offered an intellectualistic criterion of progress that seemed sufficient to him, but it was a criterion that seemed to others a facile historicism. It was simply insufficient to rally support for his new moral system. Dewey, when he read Comte, reacted not to Comte, but rather to what Comte himself had reacted against—to the social problem and the need for a scientific solution, but not to Comte's justification for action. In Dewey's words: "I cannot remember that his law of 'the three stages' affected me particularly; but his idea of the disorganized character of Western modern culture, due to a disintegrative 'individualism,' and his idea of a synthesis of science that should be a regulative method of an organized social life, impressed me deeply" (in Adams and Montague, 1930, p. 20). In short, Dewey was a sensitive man who did not have the particular historical experience that would have permitted him to espouse Comte's intellectual ideal.

The inadequacy of Comte's whole system lies in his failure to base it on a compelling ideal of man derived from a psychological understanding of human nature. What he did was to merge the idea of progress with a reading of history, and thus put forth an ideal that was historical and somewhat impersonal, rather than intimate and psychological. The omission of psychology in his classification of the sciences confirms this failure. We cannot reproach Comte for not possessing knowledge that his age had not prepared; he had to leave it to the future to discover the laws of human nature that would complete his system. He thus left himself open to the very same criticism that he leveled at all previous attempts to found a synthetic system—he tried to constitute such a system prematurely, intellectually, before any broad base of knowledge had prepared it.

Perhaps nowhere is the prematurity of Comte's system so strikingly summed up as in the "Synthetic" section of his Positivist Library (the "Great Books" of his synthesis): among its thirty recommended volumes are Gall's system of phrenology and Broussais's work on *La Folie* (Comte, 1851–1854, vol. 4). In view of what we have learned today in psychology and the theory of mental illness, we can see the stark prematurity of Comte's vision, and we can see it in terms of language that he himself would understand only too well: he was obliged to arrest a full-field theory of alienation at a truly "metaphysical stage" of individual and social psychology.

Although he was sharply critical of Gall, and especially of his phrenologist disciples, Comte rested on him for his psychology. Obviously he championed Gall in order to put psychology on a scientific basis and remove it from the realm of theology and metaphysics; he wanted to show that mind is behavior, and not supernatural soul (cf. 1851–1854, vol. 1, p. 541). Many of the major thinkers of the century—Renan, Dilthey, Brentano—were unhappy with Comte's psychology as was his own disciple, Littré (cf. Simon, 1963). Stuart Mill simply could not understand Comte's admiration for Gall, and the two ultimately fell out on this point.[1]

The option for biological psychology was fatal to Comte's vision. It led to the great contradiction which condemned his system to fail: he opted for a subjective systematization of all the sciences, but he continued to treat man's mind objectively. Thus he could not provide that great fruit that a union of philosophy and science would have to provide, namely, an ethics that was arrived at *from within human experience*. The result was that despite his correct vision and penetration into the problem, he offered a union of science and philosophy that was conservative and that concealed an authoritarian ethic. It was evidently embarrassment over this problem that was responsible for his adding the category of ethics to his system, as superordinate over all. It was an attempt to supply an ideal that a purely naturalistic treatment of human nature could not supply (see 1851–1854, vol. 1, chap. III; and De Grange, 1953, pp. 464 ff.). As De Grange carefully explains, this later addition had truly revolutionary implications for Comte's whole system, implications that Comte himself could no longer be expected to work out satisfactorily. We are reminded of Freud and his problem of reconciling his later ego-psychology with his earlier instinct-psychology—a reconciliation that he could no longer fully effect.

Today we very clearly understand Comte's dilemma: since he was unable to offer a psychological theory of the nature of the social bond, the ethics could not emerge *from* his sociology. He offered us a historical anthropodicy instead of a science of man truly centered on the individual and the unfolding of his powers. We can look at Comte as measuringly as he looked at Montesquieu, and make the same judgment of his prematurity. He dated the beginning of the science of man from Montesquieu's attempt to establish laws about the forms of political institutions. Whereas Comte gave Rousseau short shrift for supplying the divisive ideas that contributed to the Revolution, he thought Montesquieu was too far ahead of his time; and it was this very prematurity that explains why he was outshone by the more activist Rousseau (1830–1842, vol. 4). Comte thought that Montesquieu's undertaking was premature because the indispensable foundations for it—the scientific and historical ones—were far from complete. Neither the study of history proper, nor the various sciences that deal with the human environment and the biological and psychological adaptation to it, were sufficiently advanced at Montesquieu's time. Hence his plan for a science of society had to fail (G. Davy, 1960).

And now it should be obvious that we can make the same judgment of Comte as we did of Ward: these systems fell partly because of the immature state of the disciplinary quest, upon which alone they could seek solid support. And not only of Comte and Ward, but of all the precursors of an authentic science of man, who had brilliant intuitive visions, and who understood that the precise nature of the science of man was a moral problem. Durkheim, for example, saw all the components of the nineteenth-century dilemma: the prematurity of the systems, the lack of disciplinary knowledge, and the need for a new morality. But he stood off from all temptations: from the socialists, and from Saint-Simon and the Comteans. The socialists, he thought, did not pay enough attention to needed moral reform and concentrated only on economic reform, hoping that this would automatically solve everything—as the narrower Marxists and Communists still do today. He shunned Saint-Simon and Comte simply because they believed that they had *already* discovered the new morality required by society. Durkheim wanted a middle position. He continued to believe that social science could ultimately provide a basis for morality, that someday this would be possible. But he was realistic enough to see that science, at this time, had not sufficiently advanced to provide this (1959, p. xx). So he hedged between scientific objectivity and moral prescription—and to the critical observer seemed confused about the two (see Deploige's excellent discussion, 1912, esp. pp. 299–303). By temporizing, and trying to accommodate to the conditions of his time, Durkheim reminds us of Bentham: supremely conscious of his work as a moral problem, yet condemned to be morally insufficient because of the need to go along with the spirit of the epoch. Thus, his Bentham-like proposal that we try to cultivate the natural emergence of morality in industry, by developing new forms of occupational corporations (1959, pp. xx–xxii, of Gouldner's excellent Introduction).

Another brilliant precursor whose intuitions had to fail was Alfred Vierkandt; and his failure was all the more poignant because of the already advanced state of psychology in his time, as compared to that of Comte, Durkheim, and Ward. And of course when Vierkandt asked for a recentering of social science on the human subjectivity, he was wholly misunderstood. When Vierkandt came upon McDougall and his analysis of the sentiments, he glimpsed the possibility of approaching man from within, and linking him actively to the social system. He saw McDougall, quite logically in his view, as the new Copernicus. In other words, Vierkandt wanted to effect a belated Copernican shift—as Diderot and Lester Ward had done—utilizing the knowledge of human nature gained by disciplinary psychology. He called for a new phenomenological sociology that would unite McDougall with Husserl and Simmel. McDougall would give the proper centering on organismic striving, Husserl would provide the phenomenology of object relations, and Simmel would provide the descriptions of formal, social regularities. Howard Becker found this a quite amusing view of sociology (Barnes and Becker, vol. 3, p. 914), but Vierkandt saw very clearly and incisively that sociology needed a man-centered synthesis utilizing the new disciplinary knowledge. Alfred Shuetz later proposed a thesis similar to Vierkandt's, suggesting too that Husserl provides the necessary foundation for the social sciences.

Today this thesis is beginning to be entertained by a few lonely voices in American sociology, but not at the time Vierkandt put it forth. Howard Becker can hardly be blamed for scoffing at Vierkandt, since the current of objective sociology was in full swing, and is still running its fatal course. The thinkers who frankly understood sociology as a moral problem were replaced by the newer disciplinary men; the visions of Comte, Ward, Durkheim, Small, Vierkandt, Oppenheimer, and Freyer were allowed to lapse. Different names came to dominate sociological thought: Hobbes, Spencer, Weber, Pareto. When there was any talk of a theory of the social system, it included their names, and it was conceived in objective terms. These were the people, for example, who Parsons claimed had provided the basis for an analytic theory of society (Parsons, *et al.*, 1961, vol. 1, pp. 85 ff.). And Durkheim, who was included in the group, now presented only an objective problem, the problem of linking the institutional level of theory with the individual level. It was Parsons who offered his own synthesis of Durkheim and Freud, which showed how values were built into the human actor; it was a historically necessary task, brilliantly executed. It gives, as Parsons wants, a unified theory of the social system. But alas, it is a far cry from what sociology wanted and needed—a subjective, value synthesis, that would form a critical moral science.[2]

CONCLUSION

It was Whitehead who opined that all of philosophy was merely an extended footnote to Plato; by the same token, we can now see that all of sociology is merely an extended footnote to the failure of Comte's system. Comte's problem, as we now know so well, was to subordinate politics to morals, as the Middle Ages had attempted. And to do this we had to reconstruct society on the basis of a new ideal of man. It remained for the various disciplines to converge on such an ideal, and thus to breathe the necessary life into Comte's system. Only today is this possible. We can accomplish what Comte wanted, without committing his fatal error: that of subjugating the individual to the new social synthesis. Let us close our discussion of Comte by reminding ourselves how this is theoretically accomplished. It will help us draw together all the major threads of the problem of the prematurity of Comte's vision.

Comte drew down the wrath of the believers in liberty in the nineteenth century because of his attack on the thesis of individual rights. As he understood it, the only way of subordinating politics to morals was to attack the spurious and divisive ideal of individual rights. Comte saw that in the Middle Ages individual rights had been somewhat balanced by public duties, but that with the rise of commercial-industrial society, the public duties had dropped right out: one could have the rights of land without the duties of land; individual rights stood alone in all their egotism and social divisiveness. Comte saw that the thesis of individual rights was important historically because it destroyed the idea of Divine Right. It was thus important *destructively*, but not constructively, since it ushered in a period of liberalist anarchy. The function of Positivism, then, was to give a systematic demonstration of the fallacy of the individual-rights thesis, "based on the sum of our scientific knowledge" (1848, p. 403).

But, as we have now seen, this "sum of scientific knowledge" was precisely what Comte could not offer; and his hope was drowned in the upsurge of new and real human liberty in the nineteenth century. As one Englishman observed to another, watching one of the first trains pass, "It is an ugly thing, but it is the death of Feudalism" (Whitehead, in Johnson, 1959, p. 68). To have denied the individualist surge of the new society would have nipped man in the bud, just as he was emerging from the yoke of traditional society, and it would have placed him back into that yoke. We would never have been able to aim for a truly autonomous man, with powers over his own destiny; we would have nullified the positive effects of the French Revolution. The whole problem is nicely summed up in a statement by Burke, and one by Comte. Burke said that natural rights were fictitious, but that human wants and needs are primary, and that to allow for these primary needs requires a deep knowledge of human nature (Nisbet, 1952–1953, p. 170). Exactly—but it has taken us 150 years to get this knowledge. At the time the conservatives put forth this plea, a "deep knowledge of human nature" could not be anything more than a hope or a belief; it did not have any scientific footing, and served only as a mystique against social change. Today we realize that a "deep knowledge of human nature" means something like what Burke and others hoped it meant, but it also means something more. It means that man's psychological needs for dignity and conviction could not be satisfied by a mere laissez-faire scramble for goods. In this we can agree with Burke: man needs support by society for the fullest expression of human freedom and meanings. But "deep knowledge" means something more than Burke or Comte suspected. It means giving over to the individual himself the full control over his ethical decisions and life choices, which is exactly what Emerson meant in his thesis on "Self-Reliance," when he said that "Whoso would be a man, must be a nonconformist." Comte, for example, was against uncontrolled experiments by Positivism; and his argument was that, since everything is related to everything else, experiments can only change everything, since they change one thing. And, since man can never know everything, and since social order is very important, then experiment can only succeed in making the world more irrational and uncontrolled.

Now, this much must be said: in a society of powerless individuals, in which science and ethical decisions are hopelessly disparate, Comte's thesis has validity. Perhaps more today than at the time he put it forth. We have only to look at the problems raised in our time by the uncontrolled development of chemical insecticides, food preservatives, dyes, etc.—not to mention military weapons. Also, since we have very little intelligent control over the processes of decision making, since our local and national politics merely perpetuate the unthinking profit system, then our world *does* become more irrational with the advance of science. But this whole picture would be sharply altered if we had a unified science of man in society, one that would try to maximize life by maximizing individual choice. This kind of science would control irrationality, even while permittng broader behavior. In the first place, it would be based on a continual exploration of the interrelatedness of all things in society, continually further refining and extending the comprehensive social theory of alienation. In the second place, this knowledge, placed increasingly in the hands of *responsible* ethical decision makers, scientists and citizens who are not separated from a common ideal, would control the social disruption. In a word, one could promote idiosyncratic exploration without fear *only* in a society in which people are treated as ends, and in which they are given the power over their own destinies.

Thus we can say that Comte may have been right about restricting science, subordinating it to the conditions of his time. But this very subordination would have sacrificed true possibilities of developing a new kind of ethical man—it would have frustrated the very thing Comte wanted: a society devoted to mankind and based on love. Such a society can only come by freeing the individual, and all his unexpected energies.

Little wonder that he came under the attack of those like Proudhon and Renouvier for smothering individuality. Everyone was concerned, as was Comte, with the problem of social solidarity, but the word "solidarity" meant different things to different people. The word became a broad platform for French politics right up to World War I. It gradually faded under the shock of the war, perhaps because the war created its own solidarity, and when it had slaughtered a million of the cream of French youth there were fewer people to keep alive the nineteenth-century vision. In the nineteenth century the problem of the new society was very much alive, and intellectuals wanted a new society that would have solidarity and freedom both. Proudhon and Renouvier could criticize the solidarity proposed by Comte, Lamennais, Fourier, and Louis Blanc, for example, precisely because it was an organic solidarity that submerged individual liberty—the contractual liberty to be a free agent, that was so hard won from the old traditional society. The champions of liberty wanted to stress contract as well as general will, they wanted to fuse organicism and contractualism, and they felt that Comte had failed—which indeed he had (cf. Hayward, 1963).

Alfred Fouillée, who devoted his life to just such a reconciliation of individualism and social solidarity, considered Renouvier, for his part, too personalistic; Fouillée was trying for a true *juste milieu*. The full historical continuity of a unified science of man is given further support by one striking fact: that Fouillée actually had the proper insight for true social solidarity, that he saw what was wrong with Comte's system *in the same terms that we can now apply*. In his words:

> The more we live personally, the more we are able to achieve collective solidarity. On the other hand, the more personality is pauperized, the more it is subordinated to a purely natural solidarity, which . . . far from leading to harmony, love and peace, may lead to antagonism, hate and war (quoted in Hayward, 1963, p. 208).

In other words, we would say today that to deprive the individual of the aegis over his own responsible executive powers is to bring about the very calamities that we want to avoid. To tuck the individual back into the submissive and protective folds of traditional society, with its natural solidarity, cannot promote the kind of world we want. Even worse, what Fouillée seems to have foreseen, to deprive the individual of aegis over his own powers, in divisive commercial society, was destined to have more disastrous effects: it would result in the blind submission of whole societies to their bureaucratic machines, and its issue would be Nazi gas ovens and Hiroshima.

Today we can understand that Fouillée's vision of the *juste milieu* for social solidarity was the correct one. That the new society must achieve *social* cohesion by maximizing the possibilities of *personal* living. This must have sounded like an odd contradiction to strict political logicians, at the time it was put forth. It had the same anarchistic ring as the earlier Emersonian doctrine on "Self-Reliance," which threatened to "overturn society, and resolve the world into chaos" (Rusk, 1949, p. 284). But now we can understand how right both Emerson and Fouillée were. In fact, today we can do something truly unprecedented in the history of political theory and factional antagonism, namely, unite the radical and conservative factions within one agreed platform.

The reason is that for the first time we truly understand what "personal living" means, and how it is best accomplished. It means the free creation of meaning, and it is best accomplished in a community devoted to the achievement of superordinate purposes—purposes that transcend narrow, everyday selfishness. Now, the conservative wants real personal integrity, and so does the radical. Each also wants maximum social harmony. The problem has been how to get both at the same time—how to get *real* individual freedom and true community living without sacrificing one to the other. The answer is that truly autonomous choice must be encouraged, and that to do this means living in a community devoted to man as an end—man as an individual, and mankind as a whole. This would give man the sense of belongingness that he had in traditional society, but it would permit him a freedom he did not have.

Furthermore, with a full-field theory of alienation, both the left and the right can agree about what is constricting human energies. A good scientific theory of human ills would be compelling to any reasonable person who examined the evidence—no matter what personal persuasions he might feel; that is, by definition, what science does: it presents compelling evidence that triumphs over the personal prejudice of the single observer. He accepts the fact that the world is round even though it appears flat. Thus, the real problem of freedom versus coercion in society is a *scientific* and not primarily a *political* problem. That is, it is scientific primarily and political only instrumentally. "But what is government itself," said James Madison, "but the greatest of all reflections on human nature?" (Quoted in Crocker, 1963, p. 437.) The parliamentary approach to freedom, with science off to one side minding its own value-free business, is a historical anomaly. It has been the outstanding anomaly since Saint-Pierre. In Rousseau's prose:

> . . . tant que la puissance sera seule d'un côté; les lumières & la sagesse seules d'un autre; les savants penseront rarement de grandes choses, les Princes en feront plus rarement de belles, & les Peuples continueront d'être vils, corrompus & malheureux (1750, p. 161).

Bentham's failure did not prove that the union of science and politics was incompatible; it showed only that the hypothetico-deductive science of man was still immature, and it provided a striking example for the need to make scientific counsel the equal—and not the junior—partner in the association of government and science. Parliamentary maneuvering, in the absence of a science of human behavior that would advise on the reasons for evil in society, has always been beside the point of the good life. At worst, it has served as a dodge for failing to institute a rationally governed society; at best, it has performed patchwork operations, and has skillfully juggled competing self-interests. But a scientific theory of the causes of human ills would overcome political relativity, and compel agreement on values. This was Saint-Pierre's, Rousseau's, Saint-Simon's, and Comte's vision, re-iterated by Lester Ward, and again by Albion Small, and by Dewey. A science of man intending to help mankind at every step should not mean different things to different people (Chugerman, 1939, p. 533). As Small said, this agreement on human values would be science stripped of cant, science cleared for action. Or, we might better say, politics stripped of cant, politics cleared for action (cf. Gray, 1963).

Granted that scientific knowledge is relative to the human observer, it is not relative to *particular and concrete contexts*. Certain kinds of political and social systems permit certain kinds of choices and not others. For example, it is becoming clear that we cannot handle the problem of juvenile delinquency with a commercial-industrial distributional system; there is no free way we can use youth's energies without making them competitively productive with the adult labor market. Likewise, it is very clear that a society founded on a dogmatic Marxist historicism cannot opt for people as ends, cannot permit the free expression of individual meanings. It refuses to examine evidence which threatens its ideology, even though human energies are sacrificed in the process. A compelling theory of human ills in society, in sum, should rally men of good will to the same general program of action no matter what the ideology. Finally, in our time, and with our cumulative anthropodicy, we can perform Comte's task in the way suggested by Fouillée, without the errors of authoritarianism, without a social physics or a narrow positivism, without a shallow and self-defeating individualism. We can unite the radical rationalist and the conservative romanticist traditions, out-standing since the nineteenth century, on a high level of scientific synthesis. We can finally go beyond both the emotional and the abstract philosophical handling of the issues that these positions con-tain. Rather, let us hasten to modify all these optimistic statements and say that we "could" do them, and not that we "can." There remains one great paradox in all this, to which we must now turn.

CHAPTER SIXTEEN

THE ENLIGHTENMENT PARADOX

*In the conflict among scientific points of view and the living
personalities it was not merely what was empirically and logically
equally correct for everyone which played a role. The difficult
task . . . proved to be: to work out what is thus compellingly
valid.*

KARL JASPERS *(in Schilpp, 1957, p. 25)*

One of the reasons the politician scorns the academic intellectual is
that he knows that to work things out in elegant theory is not to
work them out at all. The theoretical problem of a science of society
is a case in point. How do we finally establish a synthetic science of
man? The answer is now common intellectual property: we establish
this synthetic science when the diverse analytic activity of the various
disciplines has given us enough knowledge of our human subject
matter to make the new synthesis compelling. We establish it, in other
words, by agreeing on the rationally compelling nature of the new
anthropodicy, of what makes people act the way they act, and why
they are unhappy. Comte thought he had arrived at such a time, that
mankind was unhappy because it had not applied the scientific
method to social morality; but we have seen that he lacked a science
of human nature, and so suffered the same blemish of prematurity as
he noted in Montesquieu. This is the lesson of late Enlightenment
science: each thinker offered up his own *personally* compelling paradigm for a new anthropodicy, but none of the paradigms were really

360

socially compelling enough to enjoin a new moral option, and without this broad allegiance these anthropodicies were worthless. Rousseau, Saint-Simon, Comte, Marx, Fourier, Ward, Freyer—all suffered the same failure in their time.

At this point we come up against an uncomfortable realization. When does a paradigm for a new anthropodicy become compelling enough, so compelling that the scientific world uses it actively to champion the institution of a socially experimental science of man? *We realize that the answer to this question can be: never.* In the first decades of the nineteenth century Comte was convinced that the disciplines had already done their analytic activity well, and dispersed the metaphysics enough so that a new synthesis was justified. He thought the pre-paradigm stage in the science of man was over—to borrow Thomas Kuhn's concept. But now we see that he was wrong, *and he was wrong only because no large consensus supported him.* He would have been "correct" had a science of man in society, on his model, been inaugurated. Science progresses from the pre-paradigm to the paradigm stage *by convention* of the scientists themselves. They declare the new stage by consenting to work according to the new theoretical model. We noted in Chapter Four that William Strong observed, in 1870, that a synthetic science could only emerge, in America, after the disciplines had reached their full development. Durkheim, too, held that unity would come after the disciplines matured enough so that they could form one natural, organic whole, intimately sharing their undivided subject matter. But what can "fully developed" mean in science? Here is the rub. Science is never "fully developed." Thomas Kuhn, in his very important monograph (1962) on the development of physical and natural science, has shown that science is not only a cumulative activity, as we had always thought. On the contrary, it can also be a saltatory and radically changeable activity: that is to say, the advance of science can be traced to new and daring, often outlandish theoretical paradigms, which gradually compel the allegiance of the workers in the various sciences. Scientists counter theory to theory and the competition among theories is often close, sometimes bitter, usually a struggle that takes decades. The theory that finally wins support is the one that is most compelling. In other words, a theory is a persuasive, propagandistic symbolic device that wins loyalties in the field. From Kuhn's history we can see strikingly how much a matter of conventional agreement science is, how much it depends on *commanding loyalty,* on its *historical appropriateness,* on *active personal choice.* Hence, no science is ever "fully developed"—nor can it be. Its claim to maturity rests only on the fact that it has offered up an agreed paradigm which is compelling enough to group the loyalties of a majority of workers in the discipline. It then becomes "the" theory, and everyone proceeds "to do" science on its model.

Suppose that Stuart Mill had been able to develop a science of character or ethology. Suppose that he had delineated a careful and correct picture of many of the "constant elements" in human nature. Would this have guaranteed the founding of a science of man? Obviously not. We can now assess the full problem of analysis versus synthesis in science. Even if the nineteenth century had been able to elaborate the necessary psychology, it would not have been enough. *The founding of a science is never a cognitive problem alone: it is always inseparably a moral problem, a problem of gaining broad agreement to act on the basis of a theory.* Furthermore, as far as psychology is concerned, laws of human nature can never be complete. There is no such thing as a complete scientific world picture, even in the disciplines taken together. We can see then that the Enlightenment thinkers, from Rousseau on, were basically correct to opt for an active commitment on the basis of a limited ideal-typical projection. Any ideal-typical projection will always be limited. The problem for morality is always this: how much of a picture is necessary to command agreed action?

In the human sciences the problem of gaining wide loyalty to a paradigm is no different than in any of the other sciences—as Albion Small already understood in 1915. Only, a subtle new factor magnifies the problem immensely, and gives it entirely new proportions: *in the human sciences it is sharpened to an extreme degree, because the agreement cannot be disguised as an objective scientific problem.* That is to say, in the natural and physical sciences, paradigm agreement looks like a disinterested matter of option for an objectively compelling theory. It does not look like an active social and historical (moral) problem. In the human sciences, on the other hand, *the same kind of option for a compelling theory looks unashamedly like a wholly moral option,* because of the frankly moral nature of its subject matter. The physical sciences, when they opt for an attack on reality, also set in motion massive social and institutional changes of a moral nature. Only, there is a difference between this kind of change and that projected by the human sciences: the process of change is indirect; it does not call immediately into play the deep-seated reaction to the habitual human world. This helps physical science assume the disguise of a spurious kind of detachment since its reality is removed from immediate repercussions on the human realm.

And so we can see that we would have every reason to use the same language as the other sciences, and insist that paradigm agreement in the human sciences is just as much a conventional agreement based on compelling rational grounds as the paradigm agreement is in the physical and natural sciences. Paradigm choice, in sum, in the human sciences, differs in no way from that of the other sciences except that the willful, moral nature of the option cannot be disguised.[1] The human sciences, just like the others, read nature in the Enlightenment tradition and vision: in order to find compelling reasons for agreed action. The reading can never be complete, hence the action must always be willful. All of science, as the Enlightenment understood, is thus a moral problem.

If this is so, we can understand how important the historical context is in determining the shape of a science. Scientists will choose only those theoretical paradigms for which they are historically ready: it is never merely a matter of abstract, objective, rational compellingness. In the science of man the problem is infinitely sharpened: since the paradigm in the science of man is in effect an anthropodicy which enjoins a new morality, an option for it will be almost wholly influenced by the historical context in which the new anthropodicy would be set to work. Thus, we can understand that in Rousseau's time the "primitive man" ideal-typology had no chance of being espoused and implemented by a social science; it could therefore only be used as propaganda for a revolution. We saw that in the nineteenth century the idea of the "social forces," of implementing human desires and passions, was hardly rationally compelling because of the rudimentary state of the disciplinary quest. Now we have to stress again the other part of the reason, the social and moral problem, which we played down at that point: Ward's paradigm failed because he was immersed in a laissez-faire society which had other visions of promoting the human passions, namely, by surfeiting them with consumer goods. The same held true in Freyer's time: the system was not compelling enough to command allegiance *in that particular historical and social context*. This must always be added as the complement of the requirement that a theory be rationally compelling. If a society does not want to opt for necessary changes demanded by its ideal-typical projection, *there can never be a science of man*. Perhaps we could say that Rousseau drew the first lesson, and Bentham the next. Today we have even more graphic lessons.

For example, C. Wright Mills tried in the mid-twentieth century to give sociologists the task that Comte had tried to give them in the mid-nineteenth, namely, to translate "personal troubles of milieu" into "the public issues of social structure." But for many sociologists the time was still not ripe for this. One sociologist, who evidently would not adopt Mills' paradigm, said: "There is already enough silliness in public life without the addition of Professor Mills's 'improvements'" (Shils, 1960–1961, p. 619). Mills died an outsider to his own profession, largely because it did not find his scientific disclosures compelling enough to accept as good theory.

But in these kinds of disagreements, it would be wrong to imagine that the acceptance or rejection of a theory is a matter of "cold" intellect, or that every scientist is a wise and impartial judge. William James noted this long ago in his essay on "The Will to Believe." In every field the acceptance or rejection of a theory is a complex matter, compounded of vested interests, personal beliefs, scientific habit—in short: total organismic esthetic preference. In the science of man the problem is magnified immensely, almost certainly outside the bounds of cold reason alone. To opt for a theory of human ills is not only to opt for the kind of person one is going to have to pay deference to professionally; it is also to opt potentially for the kind of world *one is going to wake up in,* the kinds of human beings that one will have *to come across in the street.* To opt for a particular theory of human ills is very much like falling in love in the strictest sense: it is to opt for the presence of a certain kind of being in the world, and hence for a certain kind of world. It is complicated immensely for the scientist of man because it depends not on how he feels about cold physical reality or about flower petals, but about real flesh-and-blood human actors, with all their capacity to cause harm and suffering. In other words, I am saying no less than this: that to opt for a full-field theory of alienation is an act of courage. It takes a strong person because it means opting for man as an end, and this means introducing indeterminacy into the world. One has to have a firm faith in man, in his potential for increasingly ethical action. Perhaps this is why Jefferson was so hostile to the Church—he believed in human good, trusted man's motives.

Of course there is another side to the coin. Every theory is "conceptually sadistic," it imposes its own conceptual mold on a world of concrete reality. In the science of man a theory is "sadistic" not over external physical reality, but over *people.* To shun such a theory is to say that it does not have enough right to disturb the human reality.

Thus, the sociologist who did not find Mills' theory of human ills acceptable, went on to say:

> Why should only troubles and issues be investigated . . . and why should public opinion be led to think so? . . . The image of our own society which his [Mills'] program would create would be a false one, and the public opinion into which it would enter would be no less distorted than that which prevails today, so full of wrongheaded notions as it is. He would generate, by this false picture of society, an apathy greater than that which he regrets so much today, and a fanatical Prometheanism far more devastating than that to which even he aspires (Shils, 1960–1961, pp. 619–620 *passim*).

The sociologist hesitates to move the human reality, even though he has no high opinion of it: the sentiment is certainly not Jeffersonian; nor is the easy global prediction congruent with careful empirical sociology. It seems clear that to opt for a theory of alienation in the science of man is to opt for a kind of world, and that the way one sees theories depends partly on the way he sees people.

This illuminates another crucial difference between the physical scientist's approach to reality and that of the human scientist, and it is not a difference that is apparent, namely, that the physical or natural scientist *trusts* in the *basic neutrality* of his subject matter. If he thought that the world of atomic particles was inherently evil or malicious, this would cripple scientific advance, take it back to the stage of alchemy. Now the human sciences are just emerging from this stage, partly because it has taken us a long time to see human striving in all its neutrality. Freudian theory was the last and longest hurdle that we had to overcome to rid our subject matter of the taint of inherent evil, and only thus could we get back to the previous Enlightenment neutrality about man and his motives. But we have not been able to get rid of the fear of our subject matter, and hence our reluctance to open society up by putting the power back into the hands of individuals.

We are now in a position to appreciate fully what we noted earlier, that the unity of science is a social problem, as Dewey so well understood. Furthermore, we can see with complete clarity that the science of man began as a moral problem, and that it must always remain one. Rare thinkers have seen this, that "the supreme unity of social science" cannot be sought in the widest law of causal sequence, but must rather come about by getting agreement on ultimate social ends (Cohen, 1959, p. 343).

We can see, then, the question we must ask of a science: "Is the theoretical picture offered by it enough, at a particular stage in history, to gain support for its active moral implementation?" "Or are the socially (or scientifically) conservative forces so strong that even the most compelling paradigm will fail to rally support?" In the case of this failure, we would have to say, paraphrasing Comte, that the positive theory has not "sufficiently succeeded" in dispelling the "previous metaphysics," that there is still a need for "more complete" knowledge. We can always judge whether this is so, *post facto*, by seeing whether the various professional disciplines withdraw into their shells of "further research." Indeed, this is the only way we can judge.

This, then, is the continuing "Enlightenment paradox" in science, the creative moral dynamic of all the sciences, sharpened acutely in the science of man. We can now rephrase the paradox in terms of two necessary contradictions:

We must have an abstract, full-field theory of human nature in order to compel agreement on a new science of man in society, a new anthropodicy. But we cannot wait for such a theory, since it will never be "full."

(And)

We must use our reading of nature as a guide to the paradigm which will be offered up for option, but we cannot continually lean on a passive reading of nature: we must make a willful option that is at all times based on incomplete knowledge.

Put this starkly, we can well understand that the Enlightenment paradox is like a haunting curse over social science. When we talk about the "alienation" of the intellectual in modern society, we are really referring back to the basic paradox that has dogged him since he emerged from the medieval time with his bright new hopes. The philosophers of the Enlightenment were in the same isolated and heroic position as was Erasmus earlier: they were budding scientists in a pre-paradigm age. Hence they had to look both heroic and pathetic: heroic personally, like Condorcet, Diderot, Rousseau; pathetic scientifically, with a trust in reason that has provided succeeding generations with much cause for scoffing. On a flimsy basis they had to lean to a social activism that makes them look naïve to the present generation of social scientists.

But today's intellectual is alienated exactly as was his Enlightenment prototype: he is caught in the identical bind between abstruse analyses of his subject-matter and the impotence of his active powers. Unless we understand this acute similarity between the Enlightenment intellectual and today's social scientist, we will not be able to understand today's drama in social science. In fact, we are still continuing the Enlightenment today so it is small wonder that we are plagued with its problems. The recent bitter disputes in sociology reflected a re-enactment of the Enlightenment struggle, and issued in the same Enlightenment paradox. C. Wright Mills, for example, along with others, attacked Talcott Parsons' sociology in an attempt to induce its retreat from its analytic and abstruse advanced position—just as Enlightenment rationalism had to do. Mills wanted a more concrete social analysis, and wanted to continue Park's "Big News" paradigm for social research. This was an enjoinder to opt for some kind of action, and to abandon the passive posture of eternally reading nature. Mills thought there was enough compelling data to enjoin such an option; for example, he analyzed the contemporary social structure to show how the military, the corporate bureaucracy, and the government are becoming part of an identical power structure. He was again demonstrating the thesis that commercial-industrialism causes wars, and it does this even though the intentions of the country, and its traditions, are for peace and anti-militarism. He thought that this was a serious enough matter to enjoin an option for moral action on the part of the contemporary social scientist—that it was compelling enough as a theory.

So far it has not been compelling and Mills seemed to his colleagues, in the true Enlightenment vein, both heroic and pathetic. But now we must ask: why should the social scientist continue, at this late date in the development of the Enlightenment, to demand that all the facts be in? Why should he continue to hesitate to opt for doing, even with an insufficient reading of nature? One major reason is that we have still not learned the Enlightenment lesson: that social science cannot be in the service of ideology. Mills' paradigm would have meant that social science actively turn itself into social criticism of its own society. And at this stage in history we are still not prepared to do this.

But, if I accomplish nothing else with the present work, I hope at least to have pulled the mask down, or to have left a piece of writing that shows how the mask can be pulled down. Sociologists should no longer imagine that it suffices "to do" science; that in order to have a science of man, they need only work piling up data, and trying to "tease out" (horrid positivist word) social laws for eventual use. They may turn their backs on a paradigm; they may shun a theory that seems only to reflect historical accident, but they cannot shun an active option for man as an end. If they continue to do so, they will not have any science. The reason is, simply, that the science of man is an ideal-typical science, or—there is no science of man. This must be grasped wholly and digested once and for all. An ideal-typical science is an inseparable union of *liberty, progress,* and a scientifically-etched *ideal-type.* This means that all social scientists must work toward a projective vision of the good life, which the whole society works toward in unison. This was the nineteenth-century understanding of social science, and it is the same one that will have to be recaptured today. No one stated the ideal-typical nature of sociology better than T. Ernest Allen, before the long period of modern disciplinary fragmentation, the divorce of social science from social life. His words still hold for us today:

> The nature of man is the supreme fact of sociology. . . . [Its task is] to postulate an ideal man, and to derive sociological laws and social institutions from his nature. . . . [T]he method which is destined to be of most value, in the development of higher social states, consists in studying the nature of the ideal man and in elaborating therefrom a social state adapted to his nature and supplying the condition for a complete and harmonious exercise of all his faculties and functions. . . . As two points determine the position of a line in space, so does the statement of social conditions as they are to-day, and of an ideal society, present to our view the pathway over which the race is destined to travel in that grand development called social evolution (quoted in Bernard, 1943, pp. 704–705).

The nineteenth century, decidedly, was the century of grand visions which we have since lost. But today we have the material for the vision, material which the nineteenth century did not have; we are able to provide a solid scientific structure for the indispensable Utopian method of an ideal-typical science.

What does an ideal-typical science mean for us today? It means that we have to recognize three essential things in order for us *to have* a science. In the first place, we must actively opt for furthering the ideal-type projected by the science. In the second place, we must realize that such a science deals on superordinate levels—it is a science of human meanings, human becoming—it is not and cannot be a reductionist science, except to derive data that will be used to serve free human development. Finally, and inseparably, the science is characterized by a natural fusion of fact and value, which will repair the split that was begun by the decline of the medieval cosmology and was intellectually justified by Kant. Let us consider each of these questions briefly, as a conclusion to our retrospective discussion.

The ideal-type projected by the science of man is the vision of the kind of man we would have if we could banish evil in the social realm. It is thus an ideal-type designed by the science of man as anthropodicy. We have learned that alienation means the constriction of individual, responsible self-powers. Our ideal-type, therefore, is an autonomous, ethical man, who would represent the increasing development of human powers. Thus, there can be no "autonomous man," or "ethical man," or "normal man," as a finished product; he represents a value *option*, an ideal-type toward which we must continually aim. If we accepted any definition of "normal" as a finished product, we would be without a science since we would be deprived of a man-centered ideal-type. This makes it very clear why we cannot tolerate any fear of the human subject matter. We have to choose man as an indeterminate end, and opt for the furthering of his powers on the basis of scientific knowledge about what is constricting them.

By the same token, we cannot tolerate any theoretical approaches to man which take a dim view of human nature; nor can we avoid planning society to absorb the changes that would take place by the fuller release of individual human energies. Democracy and liberty, in other words, are also ideal-typical, along with the image of man. Alienation, neurosis, democracy, autonomy, and so on, are always relative terms, terms about which the science must at all times be valuational. The reason is that it approaches man *from within* his behavior primarily, and only secondarily does it approach him objectively. The purpose of the science is to provide conditions for man's development, and to trust in the limitlessness of that development. It cannot seek to "adjust" man to any fixed forms, either scientific or institutional.

Here we understand why a pan-reductionist approach has utterly failed to produce a science of man. Pan-reductionism has been beside the point, first, because man operates on superordinate levels, and microscopic data do not reflect what is truly characteristic about human action. A second reason why pan-reductionism has failed to produce a science of man is that its option is always for a continued "reading" of nature. It looks forward to an unlimited future of scientific research, with an ever more precise approach to a smaller and smaller segment of reality. Now both of these emphases are fallacious enough, but there is a still more powerful reason that pan-reductionism misses the science of man. By objectivizing man, and seeking to reduce him to deterministic laws, pan-reductionism *fouls the entire nature* of an ideal-typical science. This has been one of the outstanding fallacies in social science since the early Newtonian mechanical philosophers, their descendants the Associationists, and even someone like Fourier (Bernard, 1943, p. 700). They wanted a science of man that would draw its laws and principles from a knowledge of human nature —a knowledge of man achieved once and for all. They simply did not see clearly that the subject matter of such a science would then be a determinate thing. There would be no science of man in society, but rather a parceling out of man to the physical and natural sciences. Many—even most—scientists and philosophers of science still envisage this today as a desired goal of science.

But this is to fail utterly to think through the implications of such a program. Granted that the deterministic and pan-reductionist study of man should succeed beyond the fondest hopes, and that all levels of behavior are firmly linked into causal laws. Granted that science, working diligently, comes into possession of the knowledge to control and determine man, to do what it will with him. The next question is the crucial one: when this knowledge for controlling man is finally in, when we can manipulate him by physical, chemical, and genetic means—*who is going to exercise* this control, and in the name of *what*? What "democracy" is going to use this knowledge? Obviously none; we should have to renounce the knowledge, and the science that accumulated it, and keep the scientists themselves under close surveillance. A fine end to the Enlightenment venture, and to the billions of research hours and dollars. Charles Beard foresaw and lamented this very thing: he said that even if narrow scientific method were to reach its impossible goal, its victory would be defeat for mankind (Beale, 1954, p. 22). In other words, the pan-reductionists, and those who fear man and want to control him, would subvert two out of the three interdependent and indispensable elements of an ideal-typical science, namely, *liberty* and the *ideal-type*. They imagine that the third element, progress, can have some kind of meaning particular to itself. But without liberty (democracy) and the ideal-type, there can be no progress that could possibly have any humanly desirable meanings. With no ideal that seeks to further man's own inner freedom and development, and no liberty by which to do it.

how would progress be determined? We can thus see how vital this triad is, and how it is fouled at the base when man is not taken as a free, indeterminate center of the science (cf. Tillich, 1961; Burtt, 1962).

Do we wonder that modern sociology has ceased to have any vital relationship either to science or to man? Here are the words of a well-known and conscientious sociologist, which reflect with incredible eloquence the interdependent nature of a belief in man, in human freedom, and a science which would further both:

> Our knowledge is always going to be inadequate in some degree, and we shall never be able to demonstrate universal determinism, for even if we got to the place where we thought that in principle we could predict everyone's behavior, it would cost more to do it than the result would be worth. Money, not doctrine, will be the savior of free will. I myself have always been utterly convinced that every single bit of human behavior is determined down to the last sneer (Homans, 1963, p. 100).

The unfortunate thing is that this world view is not idiosyncratic; it is popular, and has been stamped on part of a social-science discipline: man is a determinate object who characteristically sneers, and the god Money makes the world go round. Contemporary sociology has not only failed to understand Enlightenment science, it has also forgotten the lesson of Giddings' whole career, his gradual change of faith, after a lifetime of belief that science might reduce everything to formulae if only we could know enough. Giddings did not give up his faith in a scientifically controlled society because there might be a shortage of money; rather, he came increasingly to see that psychological happenings are not reducible to physio-chemical laws, that man operates on a level of choice (Douglas G. Haring, personal communication). Social cause-and-effect depends on human knowledge and decision—it may be mostly blind and blundering, a reflex of cultural conditioning, but it exists on a level of its own, not relentlessly determined by mechanics or explainable in physio-chemical terms. One has to conclude that a sociology without any sense of its own history will also be a sociology without any knowledge of what its own illustrious scientists have already lived and thought through; it will be a sociology without any sense of its own achievement, a sociology of the "utterly convinced" beliefs of each new generation of graduate students. Thus for all its methodological pretentions to "hard" scientific standing, it will be unscientific.

The third and final thing which an ideal-typical science means for us today is the fusion of fact and value. This fusion obviously follows from the entire structure of the science. The problem dates from the decline of the medieval cosmology, thus, from the rise of the science of man. What was needed was a science which hopefully would fuse fact and value in a new way, and not in the theological synthesis which had declined. Fact and value *had* to split, so that science could proceed unfettered in its investigations. But the split was a temporary one, pending the discovery by the Enlightenment of a new scientific structure which could reinstate the fusion of fact and value in an entirely new way. Kant was the pivotal figure here: he wanted to keep a predominant place for morality, and also for science; and thus he intellectually legitimated the separation of fact and value by marking off the internal world of morality from the external world of the senses. This is the crucial problem that we are still hung up on today. It led Dewey to criticize Kant for closing off the realm of nature and experience as a guide to moral action. In Kant's system, said Dewey, "Every attempt to find freedom, to locate ideals, to draw support for man's moral aspirations in nature, is predoomed to failure" (1915, p. 21). We continue to pay the price of this artificial separation, since we have *neither* Enlightenment science *nor* Christian morality.

But it must be added that Kant was the tragic figure here, as well as the pivotal one. One can argue that the criticism of Dewey and others are not fair to the whole body of Kant's work, and the thrust of his thought: that Kant did not leave man separate from nature or condemn the moral world to remain empty of precepts drawn from experience. Kant proposed that we can read nature up to a certain point, and that point is the one at which *we decide* that moral action is justified by the facts at hand; moral action thus becomes an empirically supported ideal. Kant's dilemma, as we mentioned earlier, reflected that of the whole Enlightenment: he outlined a program of empirical study of man, a true anthropology, which would be used to buttress a moral ideal; but at that time the program was only at its beginning, and consequently his moral enjoinders had to remain merely formalistic and "empty."

Of course the fusion of fact and value is very troubling; it weakens the authority of both science *and* traditional morality. Science becomes more human and indeterminate, and morality becomes more humanly determinate. Little wonder that so many have held on so tenaciously to the separation of fact and value. Without this separation, man is thrown back on his own decisions. But we must realize that there is no alternative to this; we must begin again to trust man, as the early Enlightenment did. And this will mean learning to live with a tentativeness in both ethics and science. This would be a secularized ethics which those like Saint-Simon, Matthew Arnold, Guyau, Dewey, and others wanted; it would go beyond all absolutisms toward a true human freedom. And this relativist ethics would keep the best of Kant—it would be tentative and transactional; it would keep the best of Hegel—the emphasis on process and historical changeability that he so timidly put forth.

Surely this is as compelling a picture as we need to show how distinctive the science of man is, and how resolute we must be to insist on its radically different structure. Since the nineteenth century, exact science has gotten along very well without opting for man as an end, but man himself is now beginning to pay the full toll. How will we institute a new science unified around man? This is the massive problem, and it is impossible to predict how it will come about. For one thing, the whole structure of science will have to repeat something similar to what Marx did to Hegel; it will have to be "turned on end." Comte thought that each science rested on those anterior to it, and utilized all their truths. But if the science of man is nonreductionist, it must use its own superordinate laws. Anterior sciences are not directly causal in the realm of human meanings, and thus they are downgraded. They contribute their knowledge to a structure which must be crowned by some kind of superordinate, generalizing discipline—call it sociology or anthropology. This discipline will draw together the data of all the other disciplines, and use these data to formulate and revise the generalized anthropodicy: psychiatry, social psychology, and so on, will all contribute data for the broadest possible generalizations on the question of evil in the social sphere. This is what Comte meant when he said that if sociology were focused on man all the other sciences would become "sociological facts" subordinated to the supreme idea of humanity (Lévy-Bruhl, 1903, p. 350). Finally, we must repeat that this kind of unification, if it did come, could not come about passively. Action will not necessarily follow concepts, no matter how industriously they are fabricated —we have only to look at the disciplines today. As Comte understood so well, each discipline could work from now to eternity, following out its single line of inquiry, and we would never have a science of man in society; we would only, as Diderot feared, bury man under mountains of data. Our knowledge will always be limited; many of us will always fear unknown human energies; others will never be comfortable with a tentative evolutionary structure of science and morality. But let us know this one thing, for the signs of it may already be in the air: if we do not institute a unified science that promotes human freedom and well-being, mankind itself may grow tired of this dangerous plaything called social science. In many countries, and for the same reason, many people are already tiring of their dogmatic Marxist social science. Eventually man tends to rebel against efforts that deprive him of freedom and dignity, as today we are beginning to rebel against the social and legal abuses of organized psychiatry and against a consumer-oriented sociology. The unfortunate thing is that disillusionment tends to condemn the whole structure of social science, and so might end one of the most promising ventures in human thought. Nothing less than the whole Enlightenment tradition is at stake.

With the curse of our Enlightenment paradox, and with the ponderous problem of giving reason half a chance in our staggeringly irrational world, we have cause to feel wistful over the prospects of a science of man as anthropodicy. We might well echo Erasmus' complaint: "Although I am aware that this custom is too long accepted for one to hope to be able to uproot it, yet I thought it best to give my advice in case things should turn out beyond my hopes" (1936, p. 243). But today there is no one man who is giving advice, or hoping beyond hope that the habits of centuries be uprooted. The whole Enlightenment speaks potentially through the voice of every social scientist, trying fumblingly to praise man. This is the soul, as Durkheim so well put it, that lives in the conscience of scholars, the soul of a science that has long been ignorant of itself.

The Merger of Science, Philosophy, and Religion

When Auguste Comte offered the world his Religion of Humanity and proposed that it worship Mankind as the Great Being, most of the thinkers of the nineteenth century turned away with a shudder. As it turned out, it seemed like a prophetic shudder: the twentieth century taught us that when a nation worships itself and its people there are no limits on the tyranny that may be unleashed. And yet, from the vantage point of a more calm appraisal, Comte's vision is hardly so terrible. No nation has yet worshiped the *spirit* of man, or treated *each individual* as an end. If they did, there would be no tyranny. The worst that could happen was seen with a brilliant flash of insight by Dostoievski: the worshipers of the Great Being, of man as an end of creation, would be . . . lonely and sad in an empty universe.

Comte offered his Religion of Humanity simply because he understood what the science of man was in its broadest scope: that if it was to fulfill its historical role it had to shoulder the task it inherited from the decline of the medieval cosmology. It had to provide what religion had provided—and even more: it had to provide what religion itself failed to provide, since religion itself had gradually failed. This means that the science of man would have to do three things that were formerly assured by religion:

It would have to explain evil credibly, and offer a way to overcome it;

It would have to define the True, the Good, and the Beautiful;

And it would have to re-establish the unity of man and nature, the sense of intimacy with the cosmic process.

375

Taken in its broadest scope, the science of man can in large part assure these very things, as we have seen in these pages. It is a Faustian science, and within the limitations of life on earth it could propose to do great things. It is a Kantian science, and a Deweyan one: it is bounded by man's limitations, and it is dependent on man's active transactions with his environment. It doesn't take over the full task of religion since the anthropodicy is not a theodicy: it would limit itself to the use of human powers effecting whatever they can to overcome avoidable evil. Man would abandon otherworldly gropings for unrealizable ideals, and consent to make his meanings unfold in the material, everyday world.

If we thought that Comte was discredited, Dewey forgotten, Kant merely a painful episode in the training of an academic philosopher— we were wrong. Today many thinkers are again turning to a Faustian science of man. Frank P. Chambers, for example (1961), calls for these very things. Since there is no rational solution to the whole problem of evil, no way of understanding all the imperfection in the world, Chambers also would have us work within the problem. Since we cannot have the promise of another world, we can have our revelation in this one. This would be a revelation "by works" rather than "by words," a vision shared by the social group as a whole. In the manner suggested by Comte, the revelation would "proliferate down the centuries, express itself in great symbolic arts, and prove its logic in the illogic of living history. . . . It is the Revelation that would create a world and a way of life, and nourish epochs and civilizations" (Chambers, 1961, p. 269).

BEAUTY, EVIL AND REVELATION

Earlier in this century, it was James Mark Baldwin who taught us what the True, the Good, and the Beautiful must mean for a vision of life working within Kantian limitations and centered on man. He saw that Truth and Beauty could not be abstract concepts in a post-Darwinian world. And he was one of the first to show that human abstraction must exist in behavior; it is organismic primarily, conceptual only secondarily. This means that the Good, for an animal who strives within nature, must be the inwardly satisfying; the True must be the outwardly proven—that which shows the acting subject that his thoughts do indeed make accurate connection with the material reality; the Beautiful, then, must be the union of the Good and the True (Baldwin, 1915, p. 287) because only thereby is the organism's Being heightened. In other words, the Good is relative to organismic needs; the True is relative to organismic perceptions; the Beautiful is relative to its peculiar modes of making satisfying contact with the world. The Real, then, is all of this taken together: the world as seen from within behavior—the only Real that an organism can know.

This was Baldwin's once well-known theory of Pancalism, which had a place in Hasting's famous *Encyclopedia of Religion and Ethics*, but which dropped out of history because there was no social vision to use it. With Pancalism, Baldwin tried to declare that the science of man was an esthetics that could take over the problem of religion and provide the organism with an awe-inspiring universe partly of its own making. Thus Baldwin offered a truly secular definition of Beauty and Ugliness, a definition which is still basic to a man-centered science: he saw that the Beautiful is the free, the Ugly is that which is contingent, determinate, caused (1915, p. 287). When the organism uses its own distinctive energies in effecting its esthetic mergers with the external world, the Beautiful comes about. The Beautiful, then, always derives from the free potential, from the proper matching of means to effect self-chosen ends. Dewey saw that the work of art is beautiful because it contains in itself the perfect matching of means and ends. Furthermore, the work of art is, par excellence, a product which is caused for its own sake, and is thus beautiful by Baldwin's definition. Baldwin saw that the Ugly was something whose existence is the causal result of something else, thus, a slack pile, a rubbish heap: partial, determinate, contingent on something else, finished. We are beginning to find automobiles ugly because their effects are contingent: they choke our cities, wreak slaughter on the highways, fill our lungs with gases. And yet they were not made for this: they were made for money gain and the pleasures of personal manipulations and convenience. We find houses ugly when they are built for utility living only—when they are contingent upon something else. In a world of organisms and objects, in sum, the Beautiful is defined by the free interplay of subjective energies in a determinate world of matter.

This kind of behavioral definition of the Beautiful and the Good also gives us support for the ethical imperative that we have needed for a science of man, namely, that we have only to maximize self-powers and freedom, allow man to be other than determinate, contingent, caused. Thus modern man is also ugly in his alienation, because he is unfree, because he is not the seat of his own responsible, executive powers. For a science which would aim at an ethical ideal of freedom, each individual who lives in automatic and uncritical response to the forces that shaped him is ugly. He has a life style that is contingent and caused by the unthinking social facilitation of the business of life.[1] For the acting organism, the Good and the Beautiful must always be a function of the exercise of self-powers. For the acting *human* organism, the Good and the Beautiful must always be a function of the exercise of his *distinctive* self-powers, namely, responsible choice based on the fullest possible exercise of *critical* powers. Thus all actions which are reflexively forced will seem ugly, except perhaps to those who find open and free choice a threat to their existence. They have to make a different kind of closure with the world, in order to feel satisfaction. Hence, the Good, for them, will be the automatic and the coerced. These people will also be insensitive to the unusual esthetic object, because its meaning will be private, integral to itself, and indeterminate. But these kinds of people are precisely the ones that an ideal-typical science seeks to educate and free.

We have, then, a way of judging degrees of Good and Beautiful. And it is a behavioral standard which is ethically superior in some ways to religious versions of the Good and the Beautiful. That is to say, it is not partially fantasy and otherworldly and only partially this-worldly. We can judge the Good in virtue of whether it allows free human energies to unfold in this world, whether it liberates man from automaticity, whether it decreases the coercion of man against man. It is a Good that is based on and measured by developing human potential. It supports an ontology of spontaneity and love like the one Stendhal put forth.

Baldwin was hardly alone in these views: they are part of a whole current of organismic thinking that grew out of the fusion of naturalism and idealism in the late nineteenth century. Dewey put forth similar views, as did Whitehead, and all of them provided a basic ontology for the science of man. Whitehead's understanding of the "real" was the same as Baldwin's and Dewey's: it was firmly based on the distinctive capacities of each type of organism in a neutral world. Thus, he held that "the sense of reality is the sense of effectiveness"—a beautifully transactional statement of the problem of experience (1958, p. 167). In this kind of segmented life situation, organismic striving must be an esthetics, it must be a process wherein the organism tries to put more and more of the external world together so it can have a greater "real." The organism can be aware of its own presence only in terms of the reality it addresses itself to. Hence, the more reality, the more sense the organism has of itself. Consequently, organismic striving attempts to come into possession of more external objects, and thereby creates a greater "real" both inside and outside itself. In this kind of esthetics (to use Whitehead's words), " 'actuality' is in its essence 'composition.' Power is the compulsion of composition. . . . The final actuality has the unity of power. The essence of power is the drive towards aesthetic worth for its own sake" (1958, p. 163). In other words, the organism "composes" the real or the actual out of the powers it exercises over sense-data. Dewey would say that the organism keeps action moving by converting a problematic situation into an organized whole or an esthetic unity.

What kind of universe does this philosophy offer to a science of man? One in which all goodness is the imposition of modes of order; which is another way of saying that in a world of organisms the world achieves meaning as it is placed under use and control. The ultimate grandeur of the world, then, arises out of the slow process of unification. Whitehead sees this as a slow and solemn process in which all the diversities of existence are utilized, although they are never lost (see Levi, 1959, p. 531). In terms of esthetic theory, this would mean that the concrete world is ordered into meaningful wholes, while the peculiarities of its parts are retained. This is the great counterfictional triumph of the esthetic object: it represents the weaving of unifying human purpose into a pluralistic but neutral world. The world is enriched by the unifying esthetic object, but the object itself is never completely possessed or determined. It retains all of its natural diversity and richness, and ultimate freedom. The esthetic object is thus the highest object because it adds concreteness and freedom to the world, at the very same time. It thus overcomes both disunity and determinism.

When we get to the problem of evil in organismic ontology, it seems that the possibility of a merger of this philosophy with the science of man is at an end. For Whitehead, evil is implicated in the very nature of reality; for the science of man, evil must be somehow amenable to human control. Thus, for Whitehead, the two great sources of evil are that "things fade" and that "alternatives exclude." In the world, objects alone, and their unique organization, allow for the birth of one's powers, and allow for building in human meaning. Hence, when they fade, man experiences his greatest undermining. Furthermore, the creation of objects and meaning is continually in progress in a unilinear time stream; this means that to take one course of action is to miss any other possibilities; it also means that the course one chooses is an irrevocable self-creation. Hence the Care that visited Faust when he took over the house on the hill from Philemon and Baucis is the natural plague of man's condition.

But there is no divergence between organismic ontology and the science of man, even on the evil that is implicated in the very conditions of existence itself. To some extent, this evil can be put under human control. There is a way for man to alleviate the burden imposed by the exclusion of alternatives. And that is by depriving alternatives, as much as possible, of randomness or of determinism. Man shifts the weight of natural happenings from the external world and its laws and randomness, to the internal world of his decision and execution. Choices should be under free, human control. This means that man must strive to have as much of a critical and self-aware command of his action as possible, exactly as Spinoza had proposed. Which is the same as saying that man promotes the Good by promoting the organism's capacity to dispose freely of its uniquely creative energies.

As for the evil of things fading, the only thing that man can do is to strive to create more and more esthetic objects of lasting significance—to leave a historical record of human purpose woven almost indelibly into the world of nature. A Greek temple against the sky, or the inscription of the Spartans at Thermopylae, is a distinctive human victory over evil. A spirit has been woven into the world by the only animal in nature than can overcome the evil of things fading. Thus we quite properly date the appearance of the distinctively human on earth from the first signs of ceremonial burial of the dead. It was then that an apelike animal first became concerned with the fading of things, and was able to do something distinctive about it: he created a ritual, artistic event-object for a natural one that faded. Both concreteness and freedom were purposively introduced into nature.

So much, then, for a brief sketch of how intimately the science of man can merge with philosophy on the problems of the Good, Beauty, and Evil. As for the remaining problem it inherited from the medieval cosmology—revelation—we should not now be surprised that there is much room for convergence here too between traditional thought and the workings of the new science. It was the brilliant Max Scheler who pointed the way here by showing us how the latest findings of social psychology are linked with the thought of Augustine. For example, we have seen that liberating love takes root from strength and flexibility of character; and that, conversely, narrow or fetishistic love is due to rigidity and weakness. Strong individuals can freely choose to relate to more and more of the object, and more and more on *its* terms; weak individuals must try to coerce the object to react in those limited ways which they have rigidly and automatically learned.

In Augustine's thought, the function of love was precisely to develop more and more of the object world for our own interest and attention, and for its own unfolding. Love is a going-out to the object, a venture in discovery of the new and the unexpected. Love deepens and broadens our sphere of perception and interest, and so enlarges our image of the world. It attunes us to aspects of the object that are unique and private, and that do not fit into any expected perceptual patterns. Augustine saw that love was this, and something more besides. It was not just a narrow subjective path to the world, a way that humans use to discover it, or a replacement of animal instinct as we today understand it. For Augustine, love was intimately tied to revelation: he saw that *things themselves* do not acquire their full existence and value except in being revealed in nature. And so he had the beautiful thought that plants have the tendency "to be seen" by man (Scheler, n.d., pp. 174–181).

We can understand, then, that a science of man as anthropodicy also appropriates itself some of the burden of revelation. The more we create free, confident, and self-aware individuals, the more of the object world, in its fullness and uniqueness, will be revealed to man. We can put "revelation" to some extent under human control by educating the freest kind of citizen. We would consider that anything that works against human perception is evil since it narrows man down to a determinate, quasi-instinctual level, and at the same time closes off the world in its potential richness. In other words, we would aim for a standard of ethics that would itself enhance natural revelation as a struggle against natural evil. Neither the Middle Ages nor even the Enlightenment could have foreseen how well man would one day theoretically unite an ontology of natural revelation with a reliance on reason.

This is the healing of the rupture between poetry and science that Goethe and Herder so ardently yearned for. We can see why the rupture has continued so long, and why it is still gaping today. There was no science of man to take on the burden of helping to create a new world. We needed a science that would help us "live the dream" better than it was lived in the Middle Ages, or in "primitive" society—a science that would seek to develop the conditions of life enhancement. In default of this science, man has seen his world become poorer and poorer, more irrational, more violent. This is the lesson of the first half of the twentieth century, if there is any lesson.

Furthermore, in default of a science of man in society, devoted to creating a new moral community of free men, our best thinkers had to strain to explain the utter degradation of the modern human condition. No wonder we had the wave of religious pessimism in the 1930's with Barth and Niebuhr, the new prophetic voices of man's fall. We had never been able to get started on creating a moral society. The attempts to do this all petered out after World War I: the great Walter Rauschenbusch's Social Gospel, Harry F. Ward's New Social Order. No wonder we turned to a pessimistic view of man: we had failed to give him a chance in a new equalitarian social order—and *this* was the real failure of the 1930's, as the wise Harry F. Ward so well understood (cf. 1919; 1940).

As history has taught us, theory luxuriates when man is prevented from acting. If the Russian Revolution had not occurred, Lenin would undoubtedly have spent the rest of his days annotating Hegelian manuscripts. This explains at least partly the disputes between theologians—the religious Absolutists, Realists, Naturalists, Pragmatists: man's fate and the true path of his salvation have to be worked out on the head of a pin, since they are not actively fashioned by his own creative energies. If man had been able to get started on a new social order, much of the wind of these disputes would be carried away. We would have a sort of empirical theological laboratory, so to speak. Then we could see if Kierkegaard was right: if we helped in the freeing of men, would they grow naturally into a personal relationship to God? Would men in a free community of equals turn naturally to an alliance with the cosmic process, simply because they have nowhere else to turn—no narrow and trifling meanings that would contain their strivings toward rich experience, and the highest, ultimate support? This is what Hocking claimed they would do (1912, p. 489) and Scheler (1921, pp. 268–269), and Simmel in his *Sociology of Religion*. If this came about, it would melt, as we said, many of our most acrid disputes between religious theists and naturalists.

We might call this the true social laboratory for the distillation of the human spirit—but a peculiar kind of laboratory in the traditional image of science: it would be the laboratory of a community of free men, trying to express the unknown and the unpredictable. The whole current of post-medieval thought has been stirring for just such a creation, ever since Leibnitz proposed the creation of scientific and religious academies that would group minds together in the discovery of the highest truth. This was the attempt to unite Augustine and science, by aiming for a natural revelation instrumented by man. It would be a way of effecting Spinoza's grand vision, too—of reason working confidently and growingly within a self-transcending cosmic mystery. While it may not seem obvious today, Comte's Re-

ligion of Humanity was in this same tradition, as was Mazzini and
his "new religious synthesis." By the time of the late nineteenth century, many thinkers saw that the task of man was to help realize the
ideal in nature, and that this could only come about by fulfilling the
early Enlightenment vision of the Religion of Science, the natural
unity of modern science and religious values (cf. Burtt, 1951). This
is what Josiah Royce aimed for with his philosophy of the Great
Community, what Rauschenbusch and Harry Ward wanted, and
Max Scheler with his union of otherworldly Christianity and this-
worldly socialism; William P. Montague stated it in his *Promethean
Religion* (1930)—it was the program of Faustian science, as we have
called it; and what about Russian thinkers like Soloviev? And not
least, John Dewey and his *Common Faith* (1934), in which he defined
God as the active relation between the ideal and the actual.

In a sense, Dewey was one of the last great Enlightenment men,
one who gave fitting voice to the centuries of human yearning and
stumbling over man's dispossession of himself and the world. He saw
God as the idealizing possibility in life, that calls upon the best
natural energies, and by means of which self and world are given
heightened significance. The quintessentially religious comes into play
as man envisages the ideal as a call to his highest efforts: the vision of
the possible, to be realized by the best intelligence of the whole
community of man. This alone justifies human effort in nature and
in history: it unites divine possibility at least somewhat with human
purpose.

It seems fitting to close our vision of the science of man by
reminding ourselves that the mandate of a half century of American
sociology is the mandate of the whole Enlightenment; and by letting
the founder of scientific sociology itself, the many-sided Albion Small,
give us a candid and clear statement of the problem of the scientific
and the holy in the community of man:

> . . .the more science we have [said Small] the more are we
> awed and lured by the mystery beyond our ken; the
> more do the unsatisfied longings in us yearn for larger
> interpretation. And this is the heart of religion. It is the
> investment of such values as we have along with the
> best labor in our power to make them productive. We have
> no other scope for this work but in our intercourse with
> our fellow-men. In this view social science carried into
> the creative stage is the only conceivable body in which
> religion can be vital (1910, pp. 275–276).

Some Observations on the Method and the Philosophy of the Science of Man as Anthropodicy

Durkheim understood something we now see clearly in the science of man: that the method of a science cannot be established before the science begins to take form—the method follows from the shape of the science (1960, p. 14). If the science of man is uniquely based on a unified theory of alienation, what kind of method would it use? What relationship would this method have to traditional notions of scientific method? In this Appendix I want to touch briefly on some of the major areas of difference between this science and the more traditional ones.

THE PROBLEM OF THE "IS" AND THE "OUGHT"

If the science of man is an ideal-type science, then the problem of the "is" and the "ought" is automatically solved; I noted this in an early chapter, but there is so much continuing argument on this point that it seems well to set it down here in a special section. An ideal-type science works within a creative duality, a tension between the way things are and the way they ought to be. Those who have made the facile linguistic separation of "fact" and "value," of "is" and "ought," have completely overlooked the heart of the human sciences. On strictly logical grounds they claim you cannot deduce an "ought" statement from an "is" (cf. Gillispie, 1959, p. 282). As soon as you jump from an "is" to an "ought," so they say, you lose the "is." I hope that we have seen with enough historical evidence that this is exactly what the science of man *should attempt* to do, working within an ideal-typical model of man. The "ought" is part of the guiding morality of a science whose very spirit and purpose is moral. Without it there can be no science of man. We have no other reason for studying nature except to use it for cues to our own happiness. Of course we cannot "logically deduce" value from fact, but why split logic from life? As Dewey so conclusively taught us, man is not a disembodied thinking machine. Science has no meaning apart from life, just as "is" has no meaning apart from "ought." For a science of man as anthropodicy, once we discern the evil which makes for human misery, we have an imperative to act. (See also Lewis Mumford's recent wise and comprehensive synthesis of such a vision, 1951).

THE PROBLEM OF DISCIPLINARY FRAGMENTATION

Ever since the proliferation of scientific disciplines in the early part of the nineteenth century, the yawning separation of fact and value began. And this was logical because the disciplines themselves aggravated the artificial separation. They loudly clamored that they could not make value judgments on the basis of their knowledge, that their inquiry was neutral. In a sense they were correct. Since each discipline arbitrarily chops up the whole of the human subject matter, and confines its attention to a narrow segment only, it is impossible to make any kind of value judgment on the basis of the part. We cannot prescribe for the whole man with a knowledge of only, say, kinship groupings on Amami Oshima or class consciousness in a Detroit suburb. We would expect the physical sciences to be value-free since we cannot make prescriptions for social man in his everyday world on the basis of our knowledge of the stars. For the physical scientists, the mixture of fact and value truly seems like bringing back astrology into science. But the issue of values becomes inescapable as soon as a superordinate social science begins to design the outlines of human misery on the basis of a comprehensive theory of alienation in society and in history. Once we cover the whole field of human behavior, it is no longer possible to agree that because the single disciplines separate fact and value then *science* has no business talking about values. Let the disciplines speak for themselves: they can maintain that they cannot prescribe values, but they are not entitled to speak in the name of an entire science.

In von Wiese's and Becker's *Systematic Sociology* there occurs the famous phrase which most sociological workers had adopted; it is sounded on a note of triumph: "Value-judgments, Adieu!" (1932, p. 8).

Now we must understand that when we make sociology, as von Wiese and Becker do, a mere formal discipline, the eschewing of values is the correct thing to do. They are right when they disavow that they can shed light on "human nature" (p. 2) since they have chosen not to be able to, by limiting their understanding of human nature to a very small area. They fail to understand that it is precisely this restricted focus that guarantees value neutrality because it limits humanly relevant scope. Without a comprehensive vision of man, to preach values is fraud. They are sensitive to the fraud, like truly conscientious scientists, but they have lost the need for a vision. This holds true for people from all disciplines—economics, political science, and so on. They disqualify themselves from "judging" man; and on the basis of their limited picture of man this is the correct disclaimer.

In sum, then, the disciplines have simply rendered themselves incapable of approaching the problem of values because it is only when you get a thoroughgoing view of the ensemble of man in his full field of social relationships that value judgments become possible and compelling. This again is the Enlightenment lesson of a unified theory of alienation.

THE PROBLEM OF "SCIENTIFIC METHOD"

This clears the air, too, on the problem of method. As soon as a discipline decided on its method, it claimed itself a science on the basis of it, and at the same time urged its separation from values. The whole process was circular and self-reinforcing: method = scientific stature = value neutrality. Many of the disciplines, unable to employ the hypothetico-deductive method, cast about for new definitions of science. Anthropology, for example, argued that "science is description," and that as long as one describes faithfully the observed facts of the external world, he is doing valid science. This is of course true: in the first place, all science is description and can be nothing but the description of regularities in nature. But the point is that description takes place under different conditions: it can be careless, sporadic, accidental, piecemeal, accumulated very slowly—or just the opposite. The best description takes place within the experimental hypothetico-deductive method, for here it is most careful, continuing, controlled, integrated, and it is accumulated very quickly and thoroughly because nature is being manipulated under pointed inquiry. Therefore we have gotten into the habit of considering the experimental method as "true" science, whereas in reality it is merely "better" descriptive science.

In the second place, as we have seen, the Enlightenment vision of science was description for a *purpose*, for the purpose of freeing man. As scientists of the nineteenth century got away from this vision, they modified their definition of science. It is all summed up in the change that came over the early *Wissenschaft* view of science as a total social and moral problem. Gradually, as the disciplines groped for scientific respectability on the model of the physical sciences, they came to favor a narrower view of science: they leaned to method and precision in place of systematic unity and scope—which the *Wissenschaft* ideal had been. Then only the limited area which the Germans called *exact Wissenschaft* came to qualify as science. The result was that when more accurate description was made possible, no one any longer knew what the description was to be used for. Gumplowicz, Ward, and Small were among the last to know that some generalizing discipline had to gather together the descriptions of the other disciplines in order for science to make any sense.

Again we are brought up against the realization that in the science of man the subject matter cannot be compartmentalized. This is another criticism of positivism. The narrow positivist program, which seeks to analyze separate and distinct items of information without relating them to the whole in which they belong, was bound to fail in the science of man. It is plausible in physics, but already in biology it runs into difficulties (Ritchie, 1958, p. 186). In the human sciences man must be seen at all times in the total social-cultural-historical context, precisely because it is this that forms his "self" or his nature, as the nineteenth century discovered. True, science has always had the mandate of arbitrarily separating off a certain area for intense study and of suspending research into its relationships to the larger contextual area. But in the science of man this has great dangers because it is precisely the broad range of relationships which is characteristic of every human act. In all science the relationships between data are as important an object for science as the data themselves. In fact, the relationships *define* the data. Whitehead has cautioned on this very problem, which is a crucial one for the science of man. When we abstract an internal system from an external system which we ignore, we may very well fail to understand the changes in the internal system which depend on the changes in the external system (1958, p. 192). In the language of the science of man, we can say, for example, that the identity is constructed of the total social performance world, and to talk of self-esteem in the absence of all the objects which constitute it is to fail to understand its changes. For these reasons you cannot really have a theory of "individual" behavior, a "personality" theory in the strict scientific sense in which psychology has sought it. You can only have a theory of man in society. This should be abundantly clear.

The narrow positivist fallacy has always been that one can somehow know the object in itself, that it exists as a thing in nature and must be isolated and defined. But this is a species of essentialism, in an age where science has come to be occupied not with things but with space-time connections. We come to know a thing, furthermore, only in terms of its relationships, never in itself. For example, a fire hydrant cannot be really "understood" in terms of its form or red color, or even less by breaking it down into metallurgical components. It can only be understood in terms of its relationships to a number of human hopes, fears, and activities embodied in such things as buildings, water mains, and raincoated men in red trucks. The broader the context of cogitation, the better we know a thing. To atomize the world is to lose the possibility of really understanding it. We can actually see that too much precision does not aid understanding and may even obscure it. There is a difference, in other words, between "significant precision" and "maximum precision": the degree we need depends on the *intent* of the actor. To continue with the hydrant example: For the purpose, say, of someone who was merely walking down the street, it would be enough to define the hydrant merely as a "hard, immovable object." For a city planner, interested in a tested and inexpensive hydrant, the brand name would be important. For the production manager interested in duplicating it, the cast-iron content, etc., might be important. Precision actually drowns out clarity if we push it beyond the point of establishing the optimum context for action. For example, if the *passer-by* were to insist on the brand name of the hydrant merely in order to avoid bumping into it, he would be uselessly adding precision to his world, and obscuring the relational, contextual understanding of the object.

In the scientific investigation itself, we can thus see that, beyond a given point of clarification, nothing worthwhile can be established by mere definitions, *unless experimental inquiry is pressed.* Then the clarity of definition can be played off against experimentally changed circumstances. My point is that in social science, since we do not press experimental inquiry, we tend to pursue precision for its own sake: and this does not necessarily give us knowledge worth having. In science, jargon gives us distinctness, but common sense gives us contextual understanding. This is why jargon pushed to extremes obscures understanding. We need *some* jargon in order to achieve precise cognition; but the advocates of common sense are right to argue for the importance of context in order to get true understanding. (On all this see Pasch, 1958, pp. 207–209).

If science has any meaning, then, it refers to broad understanding and not narrowly to "kinds of approach" to the subject matter. Today, happily, we no longer have to argue against the unthinking pan-reductionist posture which is obviously puerile to every serious student. We are coming to see that science deals with structure in process, and that structure is destroyed when it is analyzed into mere aggregates (Cassirer, 1961b, pp. 171–172). And the structure of human relationships in society and history defies any scientific "gimmicking." As Hugh Miller so well put it: "Science is the creator of techniques, not their creature" (1949, p. 578). It is only a matter of time before the younger generation comes to work comfortably within newer approaches and comes to see that the old models which captivated their elders are unnecessarily sterile and limiting; they will then overthrow creature science.

Perhaps we might even hope to see the day that the various disciplines will call themselves according to what they study. I mean that someone who studies the behavior of pigeons would not call himself a psychologist, since the pigeon has no psyche, self, or identity. Instead of this almost willful fraud, this kind of "psychologist" could call himself frankly a zoologist, who may be finding out things important for the study of human behavior—just as the present-day ethologists so honestly do. This would clear much of the air for prospective students, and lead to much less disillusionment in our universities, where students interested in man sign up for courses to find that they have been sentenced to study rats. Of course, this new honesty can only be helped by the downgrading of the fetish of method: the disciplines would be able to permit themselves a new ease, and could be less strident in their claims about being "true" sciences because they follow the correct method, etc.

The Problem of the Relativity of Values

Finally, what does the science of man as anthropodicy have to tell us on the long-outstanding problem of relativity of values? It troubled Diderot, as we saw, and it troubles us still today—is there no dependable standard anywhere, is everything relative to time, place, observer, custom, habit? The Enlightenment already taught us that the best we could do was to compromise on this problem. They began by trying to read nature in the hope of finding a dependable natural basis for moral action. But it was accepted, after Hume, that man could not find values in nature; the most he could do was to look for cues upon which to base his action. In other words, man looks to nature as a guide to *his own* creation of value. There is an area of dependability—the natural regularities in the external world; but there is also an area of chance and risk: the human decision to act on the basis of only a partial picture of the world.

Enlightenment thinkers from Helvétius on drew the lesson from this problem, and urged a frankly experimental approach to values. In modern times it was that late Enlightenment man Dewey who brought it all up to date. Let us experiment with values, said Dewey, so that we may have ever more dependable ones, just as physical science has an ever more dependable world by its experimentation. And so he defined human values as something *achieved*, rather than something *had*. How does man *achieve* value? By taking fuller control of the objects of his world: the more connections he ascertains about the objects, the more he *knows* them; the more he knows them, the more meaning and validity they have; the more he possesses them by knowing them, the more control he has over a world that is richer (Dewey, in Konvitz and Kennedy, 1960, pp. 208–211).

So far as we can tell, animals experience the world more in terms of fleeting feelings, sense perceptions, qualities in isolation. On the human level, man begins to establish broad connections between the objects of experience by the use of imaginative concepts and rigorous experimentation. We cannot say that the animal does not possess values, that only man does. They do possess some immediate qualities of the object: in this way we can say that they *have* values. But Dewey wanted to draw a distinction between values as *had* and values as *achieved* in order to attack antique notions of absolute, pre-existing values. This still leaves human values unique in the world, just as man is unique in the animal kingdom. But it does not set values above human vision and human effort. For Dewey, the rise of modern experimental science meant that man set out to discover the world and place it under control, and it was logical to conclude that the lesson of anti-authoritarian, experimental science extended to all realms: if nonexperimental knowledge had no authority, there was only one area to look for dependable values—values grow up as man learns the broad interrelationships of objects. This means that value grows *as man's power of action and choice grows*. It is achieved as objects are possessed in their greater fullness, rather than experienced as passing sensations and pleasures—accidentally and blindly. In other words, value must reflect man's possession of the world. Dewey's position represents the full flowering of the late Enlightenment emphasis on purposive manipulation of all realms of experience, whereby "all is within the realm of human vision and purpose."

What is the relevance of this pragmatism of values for the science of man? Simply that it enables us to cut through the long-standing problem of relativity of values in the sphere of culture. When the anthropologists finished tallying up the variations in customs and institutions over the face of the globe, we had striking evidence for the plasticity of human behavior and belief. It seemed as though societies could provide for the human feeling of self-value by the most disparate kinds of behaviors: anything from cannibalism to hot-car racing. This led to the conclusion that, since man derived the possibilities of action from a wide variety of customs and seemed quite content in doing so, there was no superordinate standard by which to judge. Values seemed hopelessly relative to the society in which they were practiced.

Now some anthropologists themselves were not comfortable with the idea of complete relativity. It seemed to destroy the possibilities of finding scientific regularities upon which to base some kind of moral action. Again, the Enlightenment groping in modern guise. Robert Redfield thought that cannibalism was an antihuman institution, and that it could be shown to be an aberration on the norm of human nature. Clyde Kluckhohn, continuing along the same lines, thought that values could not be wholly relativistic, but must rest on uniformities responsible for the peculiar human condition. Both Redfield and Kluckhohn are recommitting the early Enlightenment error of searching for the normal in the reasonable, the desirable, and the apparent universal. For example, when the Newtonian world picture was on the ascendancy, it was immensely popular to turn to the newly discovered Oriental societies, to try to find which laws and institutions they held in common with the West (Randall, 1940, p. 277). If scientific laws were general and uniform—so they thought— then what was lawful and natural in human affairs would also be universal, would lie under the surface of apparent diversities. The modern anthropologist continues this same unfruitful historical quest when he looks to far-flung human institutions as a guide to overcome extreme value relativity.

But Kluckhohn was not concerned merely with customs or institutions that might change over time; he was attempting to probe more deeply to the facts of human biology and gregariousness; what he wanted was to find "certain invariant points of reference" upon which to compare cultures (Kluckhohn, 1962, p. 294). This would give him a "modified Absolutism of values" with which to replace utter relativism. Like Redfield, Kluckhohn found some forms of value that man seemed to share across cultures; and while these universal values also seemed to be "commonplace," he nevertheless felt that they form some basis for human agreement on what is desirable for the furtherance of life.

Human agreement, unfortunately, is not had so easily, precisely because man uses descriptive data on nature in order to build *his own* values. Take the matter of slow infant development: could we indeed get agreement on the forms of life that should be furthered between an American fascist, a Stalinist, and a New Guinea native, even though they share the knowledge of infant helplessness? Would they be in accord on what was desirable? We can see what the confusion is here: that Kluckhohn did not probe deeply enough for the invariant point of reference; and neither did he progress from the early Enlightenment passive posture to the late Enlightenment activist one. He is looking over the surface of nature for cues for morality instead of looking for broadly relational cues *upon which to build values*; he has stopped at passive, comparative, neutral, inductive science, and has not proceeded on to an active, critical, hypothetico-deductive one.

Only when we look at values transactionally, and see them as emergents, can we understand the problem of relativity and absolutism. In this we could compare values with sense-data perceptions, for example. The less an animal knows about the interrelationships of the objects in his world, the more he is a slave to the accidental, single object, to the random sense-data. The same holds with values. We could say that the less man knows about the interrelationships of the objects in his world, the more variation there will be in his cultural valuations. Thus, cultural relativity would exist in its pure form *precisely where there is a minimum of transactional control* over the environment. This is evident for the kinds of behavior which are usually cited as evidence of the extreme relativity of human customs, for example, the Eskimo killing of parents who cannot survive the winter, Australian aborigine cannibalism of children, and so on. But as man comes to control a greater area of the external world he can slough off behaviors such as these—and he usually does. This is probably what led Redfield to imagine that man's abandonment of

cannibalism represented a universal: it was a *developed* universal—
it grew up as man's mastery of the world grew up, as he included
larger and larger areas within his experience and understanding. So
there gradually developed the situation in which he could take vitamin
pills and shots for strength instead of pieces of his enemy's body, and
so on. (Also, cf. Lévi-Strauss, 1961, pp. 385–386, on the positive aspects
of cannibalism, and on the question whether we have more respect
for the dead in our society.)

Furthermore, if we were to apply scientific method to all realms
of human activities we would be able to establish even broader interrelationships between the things of society, and consequently we would
diminish further the area of relativity of values. We would have, so
to speak, a "tightened transactionalism" in the cultural realm that
would be similar to that in the realm of physical theory. The area
of relativity in the choice among physical theories is narrow, precisely
because man uses them to build himself transactionally into the
physical world by means of experimentation and application. In this
way, physical science becomes a "universal" science: it is the same
for all those who employ its techniques for the manipulation and
control of matter. By the same token, with considerably more variation, when science is applied to society and when social and ethical
phenomena become the object of experiment under a regnant theory
of alienation, then it is reasonable to expect that morality will tend
to standardize and universalize. After all, the idea of a complete
relativity of values is partly based on the belief that values somehow
exist "in a realm apart" from behavior and action. But this is of
course utter nonsense: as Mannheim saw, certain values are inseparable from certain given situations (1953, p. 212). Contextually,
values lose their absolute relativity. The idea that values exist in a
realm apart had some foundation only when there was a minimum of
transactional control over the objects of the external world. Then,
indeed, values were somewhat disembodied from situations. If you
had no idea of meteorology, for example, you might try to induce rain
by either human sacrifice, blood letting, fasting or what not. The
range of relativity was large, and the statistics of success were similar.
Once you begin to place the weather under some kind of conceptual
control as an object of scientific experience, you are bound to establish
a uniformity around the rain-making technique, whether you are
communist, capitalist, or aborigine.

The idea of the historical inevitability of socialism is based on the
same thesis. If man extends the area of his rational control over

economic life, he will not fail to socialize it in some way. Hence, if man will be rational, some form of socialism is inevitable: he must make economics into a firmly possessed object of experience. This will tend to universalize economic values as *created* values, created precisely because they have been shaped and brought under experimental control.

Thus we see that value relativity becomes narrower when man begins operating experimentally under an acceptable general theory of alienation, a theory that includes a criticism of major social institutions. We can then start asking questions about social organization, questions about the specific kind of actions that various kinds of organizations inhibit. Or, as Deutscher put it (1960, p. 105), we must ask which kinds of social organization will allow man to be more expansive in broad human terms. Then value relativity will shrink, as we come to understand how and why certain types of social structures constrict man.

This is probably what the Enlightenment thinker d'Holbach meant when he voiced the hope that true morality should be the same for all the inhabitants of the globe. In the nineteenth century the idea was echoed by the remarkable and tragically short-lived thinker Jean-Marie Guyau, in his famous book *The Non-religion of the Future* (1897). And today we supply the deeper scientific understanding and can say with Alfred Weber that a universal morality is one that is achieved, not one that is found in nature (Barnes and Becker, 1961, vol. 2, p. 775). As man comes into ever firmer possession of the various realms of experience, he will tend to create possibilities of freer, broader action. Values, then, will universalize around those life ways which permit such action. This, finally, is the accusation of the immaturity of social science, as Morris Ginsburg saw: its findings could be used for supporting contradictory policies (1953, p. 30); which means that it has not yet succeeded in carrying out the Enlightenment mandate.

And so we see how Dewey is exonerated from the charge of some of his critics—that the instrumental position he represented was one of expediency (see Lepley, 1949, and Kluckhohn, 1952). Now we can understand that the argument is an unnecessary one, that there is no incompatibility between the instrumental and the intrinsic position on values. The instrumental people are right: values are created in action, they are not ready-made in the human spirit. But the intrinsic people are also right: we can easily agree that there is a mandate in the human spirit for the kind of values we should further.

Values may be created in experimental living, yet we must place the highest priority on those values which permit free and creative human action. In other words, there is an intrinsic ethical mandate for human becoming. And we also know that human nature is best served where the potential of action and control is greatest. Pragmatic, tentative values guarantee precisely such potential for broader action, and hence we can say that they are the most spiritual in a humanistic sense.

Furthermore, as we have abundantly seen in this book, even values which we ordinarily think of as "intrinsic"—such as love and esthetic creativity—depend heavily on the free exercise of reason and on the possibility of a broad range of action. We ascribe them to the "spirit," but they draw on the possibilities of action and self-mastery. Free choice is genuinely intrinsic to responsible human action, and it is this freedom that experimental morality makes possible. The opponents of instrumental morality need not fear that it will lead to chaos; on the contrary, it is the major source of dependable order.

Finally, we can calm the fears of those who think that "universality" of values means necessarily authoritarianism of values. The extreme relativists championed their position precisely because it seemed to guarantee a freedom from the right set of values. Thus they argued for an "open" society and for social pluralism, imagining that this alone could assure unrestricted human development. Today we are not so sure about this; pluralistic society is uncomfortably monolithic in its irrationality; it is plural without a guiding rational plan. As a result, it is an "overdeveloped" growth (to use Mills' term) that actually is stifling the human spirit. The fallacy is to imagine that disorder in the external world guarantees multiplicity in the realm of individual personalities. We imagine that the more our institutions are problematic and competitive in their diverse ideologies, the freer we are.

But what if uniform institutional arrangements that respond to intellectual, critical control are the only way of guaranteeing a multiplicity of personal values? What if this were really the best way to liberate individual energies? (Cf. Ayres, 1961.) These are questions that could be answered in the active laboratory of free social experimentation.

NOTES

CHAPTER TWO

1. Today we might lament the loss of potentially good physicists, from among the army of narrow-focused technicians who have invaded disciplines like psychology and sociology, which need the broadest and most daring thinkers. George Sarton has given us a modern, stinging restatement of Rousseau's complaint, to support the conclusion that the problem is now worse than ever: "I am not thinking now of the men—alas but too numerous! —who are doing scientific work without a real vocation for it (the man of science without vocation is as pitiful a creature as the minister or the priest without an inner call). These wretched individuals help to darken the picture. . . . This fact witnesses against science in general. There is far more room for mediocrity of every kind in the house of science than in the house of arts and letters" (Sarton, 1962, pp. 180–181).

2. For an argument among authorities on this problem, see Gay, 1964, p. 204, footnote 5. I am hardly qualified to enter this dispute on Hume, but it seems to me there is something to be said on both sides, and that Gay does not settle it. I would like, however, to register strong agreement with Gay in his general criticism of Carl Becker's book: to orient the whole Enlightenment as a yearning toward a new "heavenly city" is grossly to distort the emphasis of the period—as I hope myself to show in this work.

3. There is of course a *third* tradition of progress, that I am forced to leave out of the purview of this study: I mean the fusion of man's action and God's powers, in the spiritual sects that grew out of the Reformation (see Rufus Jones' classic studies). Indeed, this "third" idea of progress may well outlast the first two: it extends, in modern times, from Boehme through

396

Schelling and Kierkegaard, up to Tillich. I hope elsewhere to show that this tradition may well be the proper one for a truly unified science of man. It is implied in the conclusion of the present work.

CHAPTER THREE

1. Alvin Gouldner makes a suggestive speculation on why Comte is preferred by modern sociologists over Saint-Simon as the father of the discipline. He says that Saint-Simon is too tinged with the subsequent development of socialism, that it might be too professionally damaging to sociology today to see socialism as part of the impetus to the development of sociology. By going back to Saint-Simon sociology would acquire not only a father, but, as Gouldner says, a "black sheep brother" as well (Introduction to Durkheim, 1959, p. ix, footnote 5). But I would go even further, and suggest that to acknowledge Saint-Simon not only carries a taint of socialism, but an *even worse* taint: namely, Saint-Simon lacked disciplinary and scientific respectability. He was a dilettante, self-taught, an adventurer, a financial speculator, a sometimes very irrational man who failed in a suicide attempt when the world ignored his program. In addition, he attacked science viciously, and his urging for a Science of Man in Society was unpretentiously moral and not scientifically inspired. Saint-Simon reveals the basic value nature of sociology, as a protest against social disruption and current conditions, to an extent that Comte does not. Comte was a trained scientist and a careful, patient thinker; by the time we get to his system we can breathe a purely intellectual as well as a basically reformist air—hence his use by the conservatives. Saint-Simon, then, is not only a socialist, but he is so ridden through with values, irrationalism, untempered volition, strident protest, rank amateurishness, that sociological respectability would be fouled at the base by acknowledging him as a father. Sociology would have to work itself into a wholly new image as a value-laden science striving to correct basic problems in the real world. Perhaps now we are ready for such a self-revaluation, but we certainly have not been in the last fifty years.

CHAPTER FOUR

1. I am quoting at length, here and elsewhere, on the early notions of the social forces, partly because later I will want to refer back to the problem of the social forces, in order to clarify the history and nature of a unified theory.

CHAPTER FIVE

1. The reasons for this demand an extensive study of the sociology of science in our time. One of the contributing facts, without doubt, is that many of the social scientists themselves underwent Freudian analysis; which meant that they then had a vested personal interest in the integrity of the Freudian world view.

CHAPTER SIX

1. I do not mean to imply that Baldwin was without precursors, or that he was alone in this feat. What he did was to crown a century-long development on the origins of abstraction and language. Vico was one of the first to observe his children carefully in this regard; and Kant posed the problem of why the child sees himself first as an object, and only later as a subject. Perhaps the earliest "scientific" study of child development was the one undertaken in 1803 by the Society of the Observers of Man, in Paris; but as the century wore on the volume increased. A noted study, prior to Baldwin and on similar lines, was Bernard Pérez' *La psychologie de l'enfant,* which went into two editions in the 1870's.

2. The problem of judging what types of social creativity are more humanly desirable, and thus superior to others, is one that my whole work is addressed to in a general way. The problem for social theory is to make the analysis more specific; it is already safe to predict that if we have a science of man worthy of the name this problem will be its central one: "What kind of society is best fit for the fullest possible development of free human meanings?"

CHAPTER NINE

1. See Chase's excellent study for Melville's penetration, and for his solutions of the problem. Melville had to learn to live "at the lower level of ecstasy." Only in this way could he achieve the esthetic integrity of his life, in the face of the disjunction between his ideas and the times. As we know, it is not enough for the ideas to be great, the times must also be right, as Goethe observed. The innovator knows the value of his work; how is he to keep from being torn apart by its disjunction with the world around him? Many, like Stendhal, take comfort in predicting that they will be recognized by a future age, that their ideas will find conjunction with a future time. But this still leaves the problem of the present life. Biography would be

greatly enriched if more explicitly animated with this point of view. For example, it is interesting to see how Veblen met the problem of esthetic incongruity—apparently by keeping his "level of ecstasy" down to zero and below. C. Wright Mills, with a message similar to Veblen's a generation later, did not want to or could not repeat Veblen's feat; and he seems to have been particularly torn by not lowering the pitch of meaning of his work, even though it was still in sharp disjunction with the times. These observations, while coarsely speculative, still seem to me biographically very meaningful. Cf. the closing sections of this chapter.

2. I do not wish to mar the happy ending, but it is important to note that nature's triumph in this case was massively aided by the almost world-wide export of childish, commercial-industrial, consumer culture.

CHAPTER TEN

1. Even the so-called "fighting instinct" of man seems largely a derivative of social learning. We find it especially developed where the individual is forced to create a sense of his own value with limited social means; or where society specifically values the fight as a game, as a means of creating meaning (cf. Huizinga, 1955, p. 65). In this light, it would be important to restudy some of our data on primitive societies, where we had previously applied psychoanalytic categories like "unconscious hate and aggression." I think we would find it more productive to talk in terms of different types of standardized agonism (cf. E. Becker, 1962, chap. 9). But this new approach would raise havoc with the small but tenaciously dedicated group of "psycho-analytic functionalists" in social science.

2. As modern man lost the sense that he was making his weight meaningfully felt in a ritualized present, he had to seek substitute forms of self-assertion. The consumer fetishism that we will touch on below is one "natural" answer to this problem; the new sex fetishism of our time is another. Society, in other words, encourages and provides substitute forms of self-assertion for impoverished modern man; so does biology. These two substitutes taken together amount to a fairly complete slavery of the human spirit. Students of the problem will have to show in detail the intercon-nections of the generalized meaning loss of modern society, and the new meaning games it provides as substitutes. As we will note below, this study is precisely the one begun by Marx, Veblen, and C. Wright Mills.

CHAPTER ELEVEN

1. Cf. his very revealing paper (1936). In it, Freud is almost explicit about meaning as a more superordinate thing, about man's fear of losing a

self-transcending locus of dependable meaning. He does not talk narrowly about the fear of castration, but rather he refers to the troublesome incident as actually a matter of "piety" (p. 312) in reference to his father. But we can understand that one does not need to talk *only* about his father at times of meaning crisis: the whole world screams out the relativity of one's meanings, and the fragility of one's rights to offer them. For Freud, on the Acropolis, there was all the past of Greece—the old stones and all their history, the immediate world of the Oedipus myth which he had so conclusively appropriated as his distinctive domain. One might even say that Freud was met, on the Acropolis, with a veritable historic din, the whole past of Western man confronting the right of a Viennese Jew to offer meanings that undercut so much of what man had always taken for granted as higher and unquestionable values.

This late paper by Freud raises many interesting questions: there is an "underside" to Freud's life, where we see many astonishing things that his adulatory biographers gloss over, for example, his lack of courage in the face of death, compared to that of William James. On the face of it, Freud seems to have had more sure support than did James, but this is only on the face of it (cf. Sykes, 1962, p. 136, and see Freud and Pfister, 1963, esp. pp. 115–116). The whole matter deserves serious study, especially when we remind ourselves that great historical figures are the ones we turn to precisely to help us define our ideal of man. We will see some clues to the problem of Freud's life as our discussion develops.

2. There are many figures who contributed to aspects of this tradition, a few of whom we might mention in passing: Santayana, of course (see 1953, pp. 140–211); W. E. Hocking (1912, esp. pp. 167 ff. and chap. 33; also, 1944); J. B. Pratt (1920); E. S. Ames (1929); and Leuba (1912; 1933).

CHAPTER TWELVE

1. We should not be surprised, then, that scholars who use Freud's theory skew their understanding of their own subject matter. Thus Crocker (1963), in his study of the French Enlightenment, is obliged to lean on the shallow expertise of modern psychiatry (as does also the brilliant scholar Marcuse, 1956). This legitimates a narrow and pessimistic view of human motivation, and leads Crocker to conclude erroneously that the views of some Enlightenment thinkers—who saw man's basic motives as aggressive, sexual, and egotistic—are "confirmed" by "modern science." It is quite logical for Crocker to conclude that Freud makes a full circle with the musings of the Marquis de Sade (pp. 415 ff.). But the reason is not that mature science is confirming the correct early adumbrations on the nature of man. Rather, *both* de Sade *and* Freud are equally fetishistic and sexually reductionist in their explanations. This is the last vestige of nineteenth-century reduc-

tionism doing its (hopefully) final harm, by giving support to early views on human nature that were erroneous. Today we are in a position to realize that the narrower thinking of both the Enlightenment and modern psychiatry must be abandoned. We have had to make a tremendous circle back to the one thinker who really characterizes the Enlightenment and what it stood for—Rousseau: he saw with almost unbelievable clarity and subtlety that such behavior as aggression is not a "natural drive" in the child, but rather that it represents his fumbling for activity (1762, esp. pp. 48–49).

2. The failure of professional psychoanalysts to proceed to a scientific critique of society had some notable exceptions—especially Wilhelm Reich. Of all the psychoanalysts he is outstanding in his early effort to broaden psychoanalysis into social criticism by allying it with Marxist social reconstruction. The outcome of this attempt was what we might expect: Reich was drummed out of the psychoanalytic corps (to assure its professional respectability?); he was hounded by German fascism, and of course scorned by Stalinist communism. Neither professional nor social dogma allows any place for the free, reconstructionist thinker (see De Marchi's excellent brief appreciation of the political dimension of Reich's early work [1961]). A full generation was to pass before another psychoanalyst, Erich Fromm, frankly turned again to Marxist social reconstruction as the natural and logical complement to a nondogmatic psychoanalysis. And he could do this without being hampered, as were Reich and Freud, by basic medical allegiances. After all, the search for "Orgone" was Reich's attempt to find a *medical* standard for social-critical action. It represented Reich's search for an irreducible common property of organisms, in order to have a unifying principle for a science of man. But the search for this common property is not a medical project; it cannot be approached reductively and biologically, as Reich tried in his option for "Orgone." The reason is, as we will see in a later chapter, that this common irreducible property of organisms must embody *in itself* a measure of social criticism; at the same time, it must be a *free* and *subjective* principle. Reich's search for an irreducible common property of organisms was correctly inspired, but the specific scientific hope was fallacious. Even if it could somehow be shown that our "society" led to a "deficiency" of "Orgone," and we succeeded in isolating this substance, the matter would remain medical and *socially neutral*: we could line people up, big-brother fashion, and give them their "booster shots" of "Orgone." It is after all not without social-institutional significance that the Russian approach to mental illness has remained essentially reductive, physio-chemical, and based mainly on Pavlovian conditioning principles. We must realize once and for all that the whole research orientation of the science of man is guided by an implicit vision of man: if we find data that, in our conscience as scientists, we cannot use or permit to be used, then we had better adopt a more productive orientation in our search for data; either that, or we will busily forge a science that no one wants—or worse, forge ourselves into the

kinds of persons who would use it. These conclusions are not just a dry exercise in logic (cf. also Duncan, 1962, pp. xxx, 324).

CHAPTER THIRTEEN

1. This is not quite fair to Kant: it would be better to say "necessarily abandoned." Actually, he adopted Rousseau's activist solution to the problem of theodicy, and he subscribed to the program of finding an empirical foundation for the development of social morality—whence his admiration of Rousseau. But of course this empirical quest had only *begun* in Kant's time; in this sense, he suffered the same fate as the early Marx with the problem of alienation.

2. The only exception to this development is, of course, the tradition of "action theory" which extended from Ward's sociology. But after Ward, and after sociology had lost its Enlightenment mandate, action theory was too timid, as we can see even in its fullest development with Parsons (see Hinkle, 1963).

CHAPTER FOURTEEN

1. See the synoptic chart for a simplified summary presentation of the gradual emergence of the science of man since the Middle Ages.

CHAPTER FIFTEEN

1. This whole problem is very complex, and cannot be treated adequately in any summary way. Comte was not a biological reductionist; he held firmly to a full transactionalism of organism and environment, and insisted that biology was subordinate to sociology in its laws. But he was antagonistic to subjective psychology. Thus, even though Comte tried to keep his psychology transactional, he lost the individual in the transaction, since there was no way for him to rise above it. In this sense, Comte's pragmatism suffered the same loss of the ideal as did later pragmatism, and for the same reasons. Of all the critics of Comte, Stuart Mill was perhaps the clearest on what overall shape the new science of man in society would have to take. He understood that history was not enough, since it gave only "empirical laws." He saw that these historical laws would have to be connected with psychological laws and laws of human character ("ethological" laws, as he called them). In other words, Mill understood that a mature science would have to go beyond the descriptive stage, to the hypothetico-deductive one (cf. 1950, pp. 345–346). In the language of today's concepts, we would say

that Mill understood that for a science of man, history has to be merged with functional theory, with social psychology at its core. Unlike Comte, he saw that history alone was inadequate, because it did not give an answer to the scientific question "How do things work?" It can only answer it in part, by showing "how things have come to be as they are" (Teggart, 1960, p. 165). Only a fully hypothetico-deductive science of character ("ethology") would show the "constituent elements" of things, and give a full answer to the "how things work" question. Mill himself hoped for many years to make a substantial contribution to the new science of ethology, which he correctly saw was the basic one for the social sciences. But, as Ribot later lamented, nothing came of Mill's efforts, or his hopes: during his time he was fated— like Comte—to seek the laws of the mind in a bogus psychology—atomistic association.

2. Parsons did attempt to get at action from the inside, with his scheme of "pattern variables" (Parsons and Shils, 1952). It was a curious attempt to reflect human subjectivity objectively, and has not borne real fruit because it is still too mechanical and static. See Scott, 1963, for Parsons' struggles in this area, and for a hint of his courageous new stirrings to rejoin his earlier, frankly philosophical and idealistic position—which he held briefly during the late 1930's. Like so many other social scientists, Parsons seems to have been badly influenced by the Freudian framework and by scientistic psychology, in their mechanistic and physicalistic aspects. But, unlike most other social scientists, Parsons has himself worked through the Freudian theory of the Oedipus complex to an almost thoroughgoing sociological restatement. Having done this, it is in a sense only logical that he attempt frankly to rejoin his own earlier idealistic position on values and meaning.

CHAPTER SIXTEEN

1. Perhaps I might note here that in my opinion the problem of paradigm choice in the human sciences is immersed in a larger, cumulative development. The science of man shows a development somewhat different from the history of the physical and natural sciences—at least as Kuhn has traced them (although many historians of science do not agree with Kuhn's reading). If my own history of the science of man withstands major critical attack, it shows that the competition between theories or paradigms was at all times very sharp—Marx versus Malthus, Ward versus Sumner, Weber versus Marx, and so on; almost every major thinker was in opposition to someone. But, all this opposition took place against *a background development* of ideas—a development that was in large measure cumulative. Furthermore, the main framework for the whole development—the Enlightenment triad of progress, liberty, and the ideal-type—has remained the constant vehicle for the cumulatively mature science.

EPILOGUE

1. I might mention here, for the student interested in following up these suggestions, Spiegel's important study of the concept of beauty in children (1950), which bears out many of the points made about beauty, innovation, and personal freedom. Spiegel found, for example, that beauty exists in reference to expected behavior; for the child, who has not yet well learned to use abstract categories, beauty tends to have a more obvious total organismic reference—it tends to be "morally real" in Piaget's sense (1932). Since beauty resides in a physical readiness to respond, according to one's experience, we can better understand why it is usually the "maladjusted" person in a particular society who develops new forms of beauty. He must create an esthetic object on his terms, terms which are not standardized into the usual body-set modes of abstraction. One might say that the innovator creates a new art because he is able to reformulate experience with a minimum of acculturated sense perceptions, set in a preformed mold. He has not well learned to "act" beauty, as has everyone else.

BIBLIOGRAPHY

ABEL, T. (1959): "The Contribution of Georg Simmel: A Reappraisal," *American Sociological Review*, Vol. 24, pp. 473-481.

ADAMS, G. P. and MONTAGUE, W. P. (eds.) (1930): *Contemporary American Philosophy: Personal Statements* (New York: Macmillan), Vol. 2, pp. 13-27.

ADLER, FELIX (1918): *An Ethical Philosophy of Life* (New York: Appleton).

ALLPORT, F. H. (1927): "The Present Status of Social Psychology," *Journal of Abnormal and Social Psychology*, Vol. 21, pp. 372-383.

AMES, EDWARD S. (1929): *Religion* (New York: Henry Holt).

ANTONI, CARLO (1959): *From History to Sociology: The Transition in German Historical Thinking*, trans. Hayden V. White (foreword by Benedetto Croce) (Detroit: Wayne State University Press).

ARENDT, HANNAH (1958): *The Human Condition* (Chicago: University of Chicago Press).

AYRES, C. E. (1961): *Toward a Reasonable Society, the Values of Industrial Civilization* (Austin: University of Texas).

BAILLIE, JOHN (1950): *The Belief in Progress* (New York: Oxford University Press).

BALDWIN, JAMES MARK (1915): *Genetic Theory of Reality* (New York: Putnam's).

——— (1926): *Between Two Wars* (Boston: Stratford), 2 vols.

BARNES, HARRY ELMER (ed.) (1948a): *An Introduction to the History of Sociology* (Chicago: University of Chicago Press).

——— (1948b): *Historical Sociology, Its Origins and Development* (New York: Philosophical Library).

———, and BECKER, HOWARD (1961): *Social Thought from Lore to Science* (New York: Dover), 3rd edition, 3 vols.

BARNES, HAZEL E. (1959): *The Literature of Possibility: A Study in Humanistic Existentialism* (Lincoln: Nebraska University Press).

BARZUN, JACQUES (1958): *Darwin, Marx, Wagner: Critique of a Heritage* (New York: Doubleday Anchor Books).

—— (1956): *The Energies of Art: Studies of Authors Classic and Modern* (New York: Harper).

—— (1961): *Classic, Romantic and Modern* (New York: Doubleday Anchor Books).

BEALE, HOWARD K. (ed.) (1954): *Charles A. Beard: An Appraisal* (Kentucky: University of Kentucky Press).

BECKER, CARL (1935): "The Dilemma of Diderot," in *Everyman His Own Historian: Essays on History and Politics* (New York: Crofts), pp. 262–283.

—— (1959): *The Heavenly City of the 18th Century Philosophers* (New Haven: Yale University Press).

BECKER, ERNEST (1962): *The Birth and Death of Meaning: A Perspective in Psychiatry and Anthropology* (New York: The Free Press).

—— (1963): "Personality Development in the Modern World: Beyond Freud and Marx," in *Education and the Development of Nations*, ed. Hobert W. Burns (Syracuse: Syracuse University Press), pp. 83–105.

—— (1964a): *The Revolution in Psychiatry: The New Understanding of Man* (New York: The Free Press).

—— (1964b): "Mills' Social Psychology and the Great Historical Convergence on the Problem of Alienation," in *The New Sociology: Essays in Social Science and Social Theory in Honor of C. Wright Mills*, ed. Irving L. Horowitz (New York: Oxford University Press).

—— (1965): "Fetishism, Sadism, Masochism: Dimensions of Human Experience" (forthcoming).

BELLAH, R. N. (1959): "Durkheim and History," *American Sociological Review*, Vol. 24, pp. 447–461.

BENEDICT, RUTH (1938): "Continuities and Discontinuities in Cultural Conditioning," *Psychiatry*, Vol. 1, pp. 161–167.

BERGER, PETER L. (1961): *The Precarious Vision: A Sociologist Looks at Social Fictions and Christian Faith* (New York: Doubleday).

BERNARD, LUTHER L., and BERNARD, JESSIE (1943): *Origins of American Sociology* (New York: Crowell).

BORING, E. G. (1950): *History of Experimental Psychology* (New York: Appleton-Century-Crofts), 2nd edition.

BORN, MAX (1964): "What Is Left to Hope for?" *Bulletin of the Atomic Scientists*, April, pp. 2–5.

BOSANQUET, BERNARD (1927): *Science and Philosophy and Other Essays* (New York: Macmillan).

BOSS, MÉDARD (1949): *Meaning and Content of Sexual Perversions* (New York: Grune & Stratton).

——— (1954) : "Mechanistic and Holistic Thinking in Modern Medicine," *American Journal of Psychoanalysis,* Vol. 14, pp. 48–54.

BRAND, RICHARD B. (1941) : *The Philosophy of Schleiermacher* (New York: Harper).

BUBER, MARTIN (1955) : *Between Man and Man* (Boston: Beacon Press).

——— (1957) : "The William Alanson White Memorial Lectures, Fourth Series," *Psychiatry,* Vol. 20; "Distance and Relations," pp. 97–104; "Elements of the Interhuman: the Social and the Interhuman," pp. 105–113.

BURKE, KENNETH (1945) : *A Grammar of Motives* (New York: Prentice-Hall).

——— (1950) : *A Rhetoric of Motives* (New York: Prentice-Hall).

BURNHAM, JOHN C. (1956) : *Lester Frank Ward in American Thought* (Washington, D.C.: Public Affairs Press).

BURTT, E. A. (1932) : *The Metaphysical Foundations of Modern Science* (New York: Doubleday Anchor Books).

——— (1946) : *Right Thinking: A Study of Its Principles and Methods* (New York: Harper).

——— (1951) : *Types of Religious Philosophy* (New York: Harper), revised edition.

——— (1962) : "The Value Presuppositions of Science," in *The New Scientist: Essays on the Methods and Values of Modern Science,* eds. P. C. Obler and H. A. Estrin (New York: Doubleday Anchor Books), pp. 258–279.

BURY, J. B. (1955) : *The Idea of Progress* (New York: Dover).

CARLYLE, THOMAS (1829) : "Signs of the Times," *Essays: Scottish and Other Miscellanies* (London: Everyman's Library Edition, 1915).

CASSIRER, ERNST (1949) : " 'Spirit' and 'Life' in the Philosophy of the Present," in *The Philosophy of Ernst Cassirer,* ed. Paul Arthur Schilpp (Evanston: Library of Living Philosophers), pp. 857–880.

——— (1954) : *The Question of Jean-Jacques Rousseau,* ed. and trans. Peter Gay, with Intro. and additional notes (New York: Columbia University Press).

——— (1955) : *The Philosophy of the Enlightenment* (Boston: Beacon Press).

——— (1961a) : *Rousseau, Kant, Goethe* (Hamden, Conn.: Archon Books).

——— (1961b) : *The Logic of the Humanities,* trans. C. S. Howe. (New Haven: Yale University Press).

———, KRISTELLER, P. O., and RANDALL, J. H., JR. (1948) : *The Renaissance Philosophy of Man* (Chicago: University of Chicago Press).

CHAMBERS, FRANK P. (1961) : *Perception, Understanding and Society: A Philosophical Essay on the Arts and Sciences and on the Humane Studies* (London: Sidgwick and Jackson).

CHAMBLISS, ROLLIN (1963) : "Mead's Way Out of the Basic Dilemma in Modern Existential Thought," *The Journal of Social Psychology,* Vol. 60, pp. 213–220.

CHARLTON, D. G. (1959) : *Positivism in France During the Second Empire, 1852–1870* (Oxford: Clarendon Press).

CHASE, RICHARD (1949) : *Herman Melville: A Critical Study* (New York: Macmillan).

CHUGERMAN, SAMUEL (1939) : *Lester F. Ward: The American Aristotle* (Durham: Duke University Press).

CLARK, ROBERT T., JR. (1955) : *Herder: His Life and Thought* (Berkeley: University of California Press).

COHEN, MORRIS R. (1954) : *American Thought: A Critical Sketch,* edited with a foreword by Felix S. Cohen (New York: The Free Press).

——— (1956) : *A Preface to Logic* (New York: Meridian).

——— (1959) : *Reason and Nature* (New York: The Free Press).

COLLINGWOOD, R. G. (1924) : *Speculum Mentis,* or *The Map of Knowledge* (Oxford: Clarendon).

COMTE, AUGUSTE (1830–1842) : *Cours de philosophie positive* (Paris: Schleicher edition, 1908), 6 vols.

——— (1848) : *Discours sur l'ensemble du Positivism* (Paris: Société Positiviste Internationale edition, 1907) ; English translation: *A General View of Positivism* (Stanford: Academic Reprints, n.d.).

——— (1851–1854) : *Système de politique positive* (Paris: Librairie Positiviste edition, 1912), 4 vols.

COTTON, JAMES HARRY (1954) : *Royce on the Human Self* (Cambridge: Harvard University Press).

CROCKER, LESTER G. (1963) : *Nature and Culture: Ethical Thought in the French Enlightenment* (Baltimore: The Johns Hopkins Press).

DAVY, GEORGES (1960) : "Durkheim, Montesquieu and Rousseau," in Emile Durkheim, *Montesquieu and Rousseau,* trans. Ralph Manheim (Ann Arbor, Michigan: University of Michigan Press).

DE GRANGE, MCQUILKIN (1953) : *The Nature and Elements of Sociology* (New Haven: Yale University Press).

DELVAILLE, JULES (1910) : *Essai sur l'histoire de l'idée de progrès jusqu'à la fin du XVIIIe siècle* (Paris: Alcan).

DEMARCHI, LUIGI (1961) : *Wilhelm Reich* (Genova: Rivoluzione Libertaria).

DEPLOIGE, SIMON (1912) : *Le conflit de la morale et de la sociologie* (Paris: Alcan), 2nd ed.

DEUTSCHER, ISAAC (1960) : *The Great Contest: Russia and the West* (New York: Oxford University Press).

DEWEY, JOHN (1891) : *Outlines of a Critical Theory of Ethics* (Ann Arbor: Inland Press).

——— (1910) : *The Influence of Darwin on Philosophy* (New York: Holt).

——— (1915) : *German Philosophy and Politics* (New York: Holt).

——— (1934) : *A Common Faith* (New Haven: Yale University Press).

DIAMOND, STANLEY (1963) : "The Search for the Primitive," in *Man's Image in Medicine and Anthropology,* ed. Iago Galdston (New York: International Universities Press), pp. 62–115.

———— (1964): "The Uses of the Primitive," Introduction to *Primitive Views of the World*, ed. Stanley Diamond (New York: Columbia University Press).

DILTHEY, WILHELM (1961): *The Essence of Philosophy*, trans. S. A. Emery and W. T. Emery (Chapel Hill: University of North Carolina Press).

———— (1962): *Pattern and Meaning in History: Thoughts on History and Society*, edited with an Introduction by H. P. Rickman (New York: Harper Torchbooks).

DORFMAN, JOSEPH (1934): *Thorstein Veblen and His America* (New York: Viking Press).

DUNCAN, HUGH DALZIEL (1953): *Language and Literature in Society: A Sociological Essay on Theory and Method in the Interpretation of Linguistic Symbols* (Chicago: University of Chicago Press).

———— (1962): *Communication and the Social Order* (New York: Bedminster Press).

DURKHEIM, EMILE (1947): *The Division of Labor in Society*, trans. George Simpson (New York: The Free Press).

———— (1959): *Socialism and Saint-Simon*, with an Introduction by Alvin Gouldner (London: Routledge and Kegan Paul).

———— (1960): *Montesquieu and Rousseau*, trans. Ralph Manheim (Ann Arbor: University of Michigan Press).

EASTON, L. E. (1961–1962): "Alienation and History in the Early Marx," *Philosophy and Phenomenological Research*, Vol. 22, pp. 193–205.

ELLWOOD, CHARLES A. (1933): *Methods in Sociology: A Critical Study* (Durham: Duke University Press).

———— (1936–1937): "The Social Philosophy of James Mark Baldwin," *The Journal of Social Philosophy*, Vol. 2, pp. 55–68.

———— (1938): *A History of Social Philosophy* (New York: Prentice-Hall).

EMERSON, RALPH WALDO (1904): "Self-Reliance," in *Essays: First Series* (Boston: Houghton, Mifflin), pp. 45–90.

ENGELS, FRIEDRICH (1946): *Dialectics of Nature*, ed. and trans. Clemens Dutt. (with a Preface and Notes by J. B. S. Haldane). (London: Lawrence and Wishart).

ERASMUS, DESIDERIUS (1936): *The Education of a Christian Prince*, trans. with an Introduction on Erasmus and on ancient medieval political thought, by L. K. Born (New York: Columbia University Press).

FEUER, LEWIS S. (1963): *The Scientific Intellectual: The Psychological and Sociological Origins of Modern Science* (New York: Basic Books).

FEUERBACH, LUDWIG (1841): *The Essence of Christianity*, trans. George Eliot (New York: Harper Torchbook edition, 1957).

FINGARETTE, HERBERT (1962): "A Fresh Perspective on a Familiar Landscape," *Journal of Humanistic Psychology*, Vol. 2, pp. 75–89.

———— (1963): *The Self in Transformation: Psychoanalysis, Philosophy and the Life of the Spirit* (New York: Basic Books).

FISCH, MAX HAROLD, and BERGIN, THOMAS GODDARD (eds. and trans. with an

Introduction and Notes, and Chronological Table) (1944): *The Autobiography of Giambattista Vico* (Ithaca: Cornell University Press).

FLINT, ROBERT (1904): *Philosophy as Scientia Scientiarum and a History of the Classifications of the Sciences* (London: Blackwood).

FOLLETT, MARY P. (1924): *Creative Experience* (New York: Longmans, Green).

FOURIER, CHARLES (1901): *Selections from the Works of Fourier*, trans. Julia Franklin, Introduction by Charles Gide. (London: Swan Sonnenschein)

FREUD, SIGMUND (1936): "A Disturbance of Memory on the Acropolis, an Open Letter to Romain Rolland on the Occasion of His Seventieth Birthday," in *Collected Papers*, ed. Ernest Jones (London: Hogarth Press, 1956) Vol. 5, pp. 302–312.

FREUD, SIGMUND, and PFISTER, OSKAR (1963): *Psychoanalysis and Faith: The Letters of Sigmund Freud and Oskar Pfister* (New York: Basic Books).

GAY, PETER (1964): *The Party of Humanity: Essays in the French Enlightenment* (New York: Knopf).

GERTH, HANS, and MILLS, C. WRIGHT (eds. and trans.) (1946): *From Max Weber: Essays in Sociology* (New York: Oxford University Press).

GIDDINGS, FRANKLIN H. (1922): *Studies in the Theory of Human Society* (New York: Macmillan).

GILLISPIE, C. C. (1959): "The *Encyclopédie* and the Jacobin Philosophy of Science: a Study in Ideas and Consequences," in *Critical Problems in the History of Science*, ed. M. Clagett (Madison: University of Wisconsin Press), pp. 255–289.

GINSBURG, MORRIS (1953): *The Idea of Progress: A Revaluation* (Boston: Beacon Press).

GOFFMAN, ERVING (1953): "Communication Conduct in an Island Community," (Unpublished Ph.D. dissertation, University of Chicago).

——— (1961): *Encounters* (Indianapolis: Bobbs-Merrill).

GOLDENWEISER, ALEXANDER (1948): "The Psychosociological Thought of Wilhelm Wundt," in *An Introduction to the History of Sociology*, ed. H. E. Barnes (Chicago: University of Chicago Press), pp. 216–226.

GOODMAN, PAUL (1962): *Growing Up Absurd* (New York: Vintage Books).

GOUHIER, HENRI (1933): *La jeunesse d'Auguste Comte et la formation du Positivism* (Paris: J. Vrin), Vol. 1 (of 3 vols.).

GRAY, ROBERT F. (1963): "Political Parties in New African Nations: an Anthropological View," *Comparative Studies in Society and History*, Vol. 5, No. 4, July, pp. 449–461.

GREEN, F. C. (1950): *Rousseau and the Idea of Progress* (Oxford: Clarendon Press).

GUMPLOWICZ, LUDWIG (1963): *Outlines of Sociology*, ed. with an Introduction and Notes by Irving Louis Horowitz (New York: Paine-Whitman).

HALÉVY, ELIE (1960): *The Growth of Philosophic Radicalism*, trans. Mary Morris (Boston: Beacon Press).

HAMILTON, ROBERT S. (1874): *Present Status of Social Science* (New York: Hinton and Co.).

HARING, DOUGLAS G. (compiler and editor) (1956): *Personal Character and Cultural Milieu* (Syracuse: Syracuse University Press), 3rd revised edition.

HARRIS, VICTOR (1949): *All Coherence Gone* (Chicago: University of Chicago Press).

HAYDN, HIRAM (1950): *The Counter-Renaissance* (New York: Scribner).

HAYES, EDWARD CARY (1911): "The Social Forces Error," *American Journal of Sociology*, Vol. 16, pp. 613–625.

———— (1925–1926): "Some Social Relations Restated," *American Journal of Sociology*, Vol. 31, pp. 333–346.

HAYWARD, J. E. S. (1963): " 'Solidarity' and the Reformist Sociology of Alfred Fouillée," *American Journal of Economics and Sociology*, Vol. 22, Part I, pp. 205–222.

HEBERLE, RUDOLF (1948): "The Sociology of Georg Simmel: The Forms of Social Interaction," in *An Introduction to the History of Sociology*, ed. H. E. Barnes (Chicago: University of Chicago Press), Chapter 11.

HEGEL, G. W. F. (1920): *Philosophy of Fine Art* (London: Bell and Sons), 4 vols.

HELLER, ERICH (1959): *The Disinherited Mind: Essays in Modern German Literature and Thought* (New York: Meridian).

HELVÉTIUS, C. (1909): *"Collection des plus belles pages"* (includes De l'esprit, De l'homme, Notes, Maximes, etc.) (Paris: Mercure de France).

HINKLE, ROSCOE C. (1963): "Antecedents of the Action Orientation in American Sociology Before 1935," *American Sociological Review*, Vol. 28, October, pp. 705–715.

HOCKING, WILLIAM ERNEST (1912): *The Meaning of God in Human Experience: A Philosophic Study of Religion* (New Haven: Yale University Press).

———— (1944): *Science and the Idea of God* (Chapel Hill: University of North Carolina Press).

HOMANS, GEORGE C. (1963): "Commentary on Schlesinger," *American Sociological Review*, Vol. 28, No. 1, February.

HOOK, SIDNEY (1962): *From Hegel to Marx: Studies in the Intellectual Development of Karl Marx* (Ann Arbor: Michigan University Press).

HOUSE, F. N. (1925–1926): "The Concept 'Social Forces' in American Sociology," *American Journal of Sociology*, Vol. 31, pp. 145–799, *passim*.

———— (1936): *The Development of Social Theory* (New York: McGraw-Hill).

HUIZINGA, JOHAN (1924): *The Waning of the Middle Ages: A Study of the Forms of Life, Thought, and Art in France and the Netherlands in the XIVth and XVth centuries* (New York: Doubleday Anchor Books, n.d.).

———— (1955): *Homo ludens: A Study of the Play-Element in Culture* (Boston: Beacon Press).

———— (1957): *Erasmus and the Age of the Reformation* (New York: Harper Torchbooks).

———— (1959): "The Problem of the Renaissance," in *Men and Ideas* (New York: Meridian).

HUME, DAVID (1739): *A Treatise of Human Nature: Being an Attempt to Introduce the Experimental Method of Reasoning into Moral Subjects* (New York: Doubleday Dolphin Books, 1961).

———— (1766): *Exposé succinct de la contestation qui s'est elevée entre M. Hume et M. Rousseau* (avec les pièces justificatives, traduit de l'Anglais par Suard, à Londres).

IZOULET, JEAN (1895): *La sainte cité, ou l'anti-marxisme* (Paris: Alcan) A. Michel edition, 1930, 2 vols.

JAMES, WILLIAM (1902): *The Varieties of Religious Experience: A Study in Human Nature* (New York: Longmans Green) (Mentor and Modern Library editions).

JOHNSON, A. H. (ed. with an Intro.) (1959): *Whitehead's American Essays in Social Philosophy* (New York: Harper).

JOUFFROY, T. (1823): *"De l'amour de soi," Mélanges philosophiques* (Paris: Hachette), fifth ed., 1875.

KARIEL, HENRY S. (1961): *The Decline of American Pluralism* (Stanford: Stanford University Press).

KELLER, A. G. (1903): "Review of Lester Ward's *Pure Sociology*," in *Yale Review*, Vol. 12, pp. 315–318.

KLUCKHOHN, CLYDE (1952): "Values and Value-Orientations in the Theory of Action: an Exploration in Definition and Classification," in *Toward a General Theory of Action*, eds. T. Parsons and E. A. Shils (Cambridge: Harvard University Press), pp. 388–433.

———— (1962): *Culture and Behavior*, ed. Richard Kluckhohn (New York: The Free Press).

KOLLE, K. (1957): "Jaspers as Psychopathologist," in *The Philosophy of Karl Jaspers*, ed. P. A. Schilpp (New York: Tudor).

KONVITZ, M. R., and KENNEDY, GAIL (eds.) (1960): *The American Pragmatists* (New York: Meridian).

KUHN, T. S. (1962): *The Structure of Scientific Revolutions*, International Encyclopedia of Unified Science Publication (Chicago: University of Chicago Press).

LAING, R. D. (1962): *The Self and Others: Further Studies in Sanity and Madness* (Chicago: Quadrangle Books).

LANDHEER, BARTHOLOMEW (1948): "The Universalistic Theory of Society of Othmar Spann and His School," in *An Introduction to the History of Sociology*, ed. H. E. Barnes (Chicago: University of Chicago Press), pp. 385–399.

LAVROV, PETER (1891): *Historical Letters*, translated with an Introduction and Notes by James P. Scanlan (Berkeley: Univ. of California Press, 1967).

LEFEBRE, LUDWIG B. (1957): "The Psychology of Karl Jaspers," in *The*

Philosophy of Karl Jaspers, ed. P. A. Schilpp (New York: Tudor), pp. 467–497.

LEHMANN, WILLIAM C. (1930): *Adam Ferguson and the Beginnings of Modern Sociology* (New York: Columbia University Press).

LEMING, A. (1952): "The Origins of the Popularization of Science," *Impact of Science on Society*, Vol. 3, pp. 233–257.

LEPLEY, RAY (ed.) (1949): *Value: A Cooperative Inquiry* (New York: Columbia University Press).

LEUBA, JAMES H. (1912): *A Psychological Study of Religion: Its Origin, Function and Future* (New York: Macmillan).

———— (1933): *God or Man? A Study of the Value of God to Man* (New York: Holt).

LEVI, ALBERT W. (1959): *Philosophy and the Modern World* (Bloomington: Indiana University Press).

LÉVY-BRUHL, L. (1903): *The Philosophy of Auguste Comte* (London: Swan Sonnenschein).

LÉVI-STRAUSS, CLAUDE (1961): *A World on the Wane*, trans. John Russell (New York: Criterion Books).

LINDNER, ROBERT (1962): *Prescription for Rebellion* (New York: Grove Press).

LIPPMANN, WALTER (1929): *A Preface to Morals* (New York: Macmillan).

LOUGH, J. (ed.) (1954): *The Encyclopédie of Diderot and D'Alembert, Selected Articles* (Cambridge: University Press).

LOVEJOY, A. O. (1960a): *The Great Chain of Being* (New York: Harper Torchbooks).

———— (1960b): *Essays in the History of Ideas* (New York: Capricorn Books).

———— (1961): *Reflections on Human Nature* (Baltimore: Johns Hopkins University Press).

LUCKA, EMIL (1922): *The Evolution of Love*, trans. Ellie Schleussner (London: Allen and Unwin).

LUNDBERG, G. A. (1944–1945): "The Proximate Future of American Sociology—The Growth of Scientific Method," *American Journal of Sociology*, Vol. 50, pp. 502–513.

LYND, ROBERT S. (1939): *Knowledge for What?* (Princeton: Princeton University Press).

MANHEIM, ERNEST (1948): "The Sociological Theories of Hans Freyer: Sociology as a Nationalistic Program of Social Action," in *An Introduction to the History of Sociology*, ed. H. E. Barnes (Chicago: University of Chicago Press), Chapter 18.

MANN, THOMAS (1932): "Goethe and Tolstoy," in *Three Essays* (London: Secker).

MANNHEIM, KARL (1936): *Ideology and Utopia: An Introduction to the Sociology of Knowledge* (New York: Harcourt, Brace).

———— (1944): *Diagnosis of Our Time* (New York: Oxford University Press).

—— (1953): *Essays on Sociology and Social Psychology* (London: Routledge and Kegan Paul).

—— (1954): *Man and Society in an Age of Reconstruction* (New York: Harcourt, Brace).

—— (1958): *Systematic Sociology*, eds. J. S. Eros and W. A. C. Steward (New York: Philosophical Library).

MANUEL, FRANK E. (1956): *The New World of Henri Saint-Simon* (Cambridge: Harvard University Press).

—— (1962): *The Prophets of Paris* (Cambridge: Harvard University Press).

MARCUSE, HERBERT (1956): *Eros and Civilization: A Philosophical Inquiry into Freud* (London: Routledge and Kegan Paul).

MARX, KARL (1844): *Economic and Philosophical Manuscripts*, reprinted in *Marx's Concept of Man*, edited, with an Introduction by Erich Fromm (New York: Ungar).

MATSON, FLOYD W. (1964): *The Broken Image: Man, Science and Society* (New York: Braziller).

MCRAE, ROBERT (1961): *The Problem of the Unity of the Sciences: Bacon to Kant* (Toronto: University Press).

MEAD, GEORGE H. (1956): *The Social Psychology of George Herbert Mead*, edited, with an Introduction by Anselm Strauss (Chicago: University of Chicago Press).

MERZ, J. THEO. (1914): *A History of European Thought in the 19th Century* (Edinburgh: Wm. Blackwood and Sons), 3rd edition, 4 vols., 1907–1914.

MEYER, R. W. (1952): *Leibnitz and the 17th Century Revolution* (Cambridge: Bowes and Bowes).

MILL, JOHN STUART (1950): *Philosophy of Scientific Method*, edited with an Introduction by Ernest Nagel (New York: Hafner).

MILLER, HUGH (1939a): "Philosophy of Science and History of Science," *Isis*, Vol. 30, pp. 52–64.

—— (1939b): *History and Science: A Study of the Relation of Historical to Theoretical Knowledge* (Berkeley: University of California Press).

—— (1949): *An Historical Introduction to Modern Philosophy* (New York: Macmillan).

MILLS, C. WRIGHT (1959): *The Power Elite* (New York: Oxford University Press, Galaxy Books).

MINKOWSKI, EUGENE (1962): "Aperçu sur l'évolution des notions en psychopathologie," *Toulouse Medical*, April, pp. 337–362.

MONTAGUE, WILLIAM PEPPERELL (1930): *Belief Unbound: A Promethean Religion for the Modern World* (New Haven: Yale University Press).

MUMFORD, LEWIS (1951): *The Conduct of Life* (New York: Harcourt, Brace).

NISBET, R. A. (1952–1953): "Conservatism and Sociology," *American Journal of Sociology*, Vol. 58, pp. 167–175.

NORTHCOTT, C. H. (1918): "The Social Theories of F. H. Giddings," *American Journal of Sociology*, Vol. 24, pp. 1–23.

OPPENHEIMER, FRANZ (1922): *The State: Its History and Development Viewed Sociologically*, trans. J. M. Gitterman (New York: Huebsch).

—— (1932): "Tendencies in Recent German Sociology," *Sociological Review*, Vol. 24 in 3 parts: pp. 1–12, 125–137, 249–260.

ORTEGA Y GASSET, JOSÉ (1956): *The Dehumanization of Art and Other Writings on Art and Culture*, trans. W. R. Trask (New York: Doubleday Anchor Books).

—— (1957): *On Love: Aspects of a Single Theme*, trans. Toby Talbot (New York: Meridian).

—— (1963): "A Chapter from the History of Ideas—Wilhelm Dilthey and the Idea of Life," in *Concord and Liberty* (New York: The Norton Library), pp. 129–182.

PACI, ENZO (1963): *Funzione delle scienze e significato dell'uomo* (Milano: Il Saggiatore).

PADOVER, SAUL K. (1956): *A Jefferson Profile as Revealed in His Letters* (Selected with an Introduction), (New York: The John Day Co.).

PARSONS, HOWARD L. (1964): "Value and Mental Health in the Thought of Marx," *Philosophy and Phenomenological Research*, Vol. 24, March, pp. 355–365.

PARSONS, TALCOTT (1954): "Certain Primary Sources and Patterns of Aggression in the Social Structure of the Western World," in *Essays in Sociological Theory* (New York: The Free Press).

—— and SHILS, E. A. (eds.) (1952): *Toward a General Theory of Action* (Cambridge: Harvard University Press).

—— ET AL. (eds.) (1961): *Theories of Society* (New York: The Free Press), 2 vols.

PASCH, ALAN (1958): *Experience and the Analytic: A Reconsideration of Empiricism* (Chicago: University of Chicago Press).

PETERS, R. S. (ed. and arranger) (1962): *Brett's History of Psychology* (London: Allen and Unwin), 1 vol. edition.

PFUETZE, PAUL E. (1961): *Self, Society and Existence: Human Nature and Dialogue in the Thought of George Herbert Mead and Martin Buber* (New York: Harper Torchbooks).

PIAGET, JEAN (1932): *The Moral Judgment of the Child*, trans. Marjorie Gabain (New York: The Free Press).

PRATT, JAMES B. (1920): *The Religious Consciousness* (New York: Macmillan).

RANDALL, JOHN HERMAN, JR. (1940): *The Making of the Modern Mind* (Boston: Houghton, Mifflin).

RANK, OTTO (1932): *Modern Education: A Critique of Its Fundamental Ideas* (New York: Knopf).

RENAN, ERNEST (1890): *L'Avenir de la science: pensées de 1848* (Paris: Calmann-Lévy).

RENOUVIER, C. (1883–1884): "La philosophie de Fourier," *La critique philosophique*, Vol. 12, Parts I and II, *passim*.

RIBOT, THEODULE (1903): *The Diseases of the Will* (Chicago: Open Court), 3rd English edition.

RICE, STUART A. (1931–1932): "What Is Sociology?" *Social Forces*, Vol. 10, pp. 319–326.

RICHARDS, I. A. (1925): *Principles of Literary Criticism* (New York: Harvest Books).

RIGNANO, EUGENIO (1928–1929): "Sociology, Its Methods and Laws," *American Journal of Sociology*, Vol. 34, pp. 605–622.

RITCHIE, ARTHUR D. (1958): *Studies in the History and Methods of the Sciences* (Edinburgh: The University Press).

ROSS, E. A. (1908): *Social Psychology* (New York: Macmillan).

ROUSSEAU, JEAN-JACQUES (1750): *Discours sur les sciences et les arts,* edited, with an Intro. and Commentary by George R. Havens (New York: The Modern Language Association of America, 1946).

——— (1762): *Emile ou de l'éducation,* with an Intro., Bibliography, notes and analytic index by François and Pierre Richard. (Paris: Garnier Frères, 1961).

ROY, CLAUDE (1962): *Stendhal par lui-même* (Paris: Editions du seuil).

ROYCE, JOSIAH (1901): *The World and the Individual* (New York: Macmillan), 2 vols.

——— (1919): *Lectures on Modern Idealism* (New Haven: Yale University Press).

RUSK, RALPH L. (1949): *The Life of Ralph Waldo Emerson* (New York: Scribner).

RUSSELL, BERTRAND (1926): *On Education, Especially in Early Childhood* (London: Allen and Unwin).

SALOMON, ALBERT (1963): *In Praise of Enlightenment: Essays in the History of Ideas* (New York: Meridian).

SANTAYANA, GEORGE (1953): *The Philosophy of Santayana,* selections from all the works, edited with a Preface and Introductory Essay by Irwin Edman (New York: Scribner).

SARTON, GEORGE (1962): *The History of Science and the New Humanism* (Bloomington: Midland Books).

SCHELER, MAX (1921): *On the Eternal in Man,* trans. Bernard Noble (New York: Harper, 1960).

——— (1954): *The Nature of Sympathy,* trans. Peter Heath, with a General Introduction to Max Scheler's work by Werner Stark (London: Routledge and Kegan Paul).

——— (n.d.): "Amour et connaissance," in *Le sens de la souffrance* (Paris: Fernand Aubier), pp. 174–181.

SCHELLING, FRIEDRICH (1942): *The Ages of the World,* trans. with an Introduction and notes by Frederick de Wolfe Bolman, Jr. (New York: Columbia University Press).

SCHILLER, F. C. S. (1921): "Hypothesis," in *Studies in the History and*

Method of Science, ed. Charles Singer (Oxford: University Press), Vol. 2, pp. 414–446.

SCHILPP, PAUL ARTHUR (ed.) (1951): *The Philosophy of Alfred North Whitehead* (New York: Tudor).

—— (1957): *The Philosophy of Karl Jaspers* (New York: Tudor).

SCHNEIDER, HERBERT W. (1946): *A History of American Philosophy* (New York: Columbia University Press).

SCOTT, JOHN FINLEY (1963): "The Changing Foundations of the Parsonian Action Scheme," *American Sociological Review,* Vol. 28, October, pp. 716–735.

SHANAS, ETHEL (1944–1945): "The American Journal of Sociology Through Fifty Years," *American Journal of Sociology,* Vol. 50, pp. 522–533.

SHILS, EDWARD A. (1960–1961): "Professor Mills on the Calling of Sociology," *World Politics,* Vol. 13, pp. 600–621.

SHOBEN, EDWARD JOSEPH, JR. (1960): "Personal Responsibility, Determinism, and The Burden of Understanding," *Antioch Review,* Vol. 20, pp. 405–416.

SIMMEL, GEORG (1959): "The Aesthetic Significance of the Face," trans. Lore Ferguson, in *Georg Simmel, 1858–1918,* ed. Kurt H. Wolff (Columbus: Ohio State University Press), pp. 276–281.

SIMON, W. M. (1963): *European Positivism in the Nineteenth Century: An Essay in Intellectual History* (Ithaca: Cornell University Press).

SMALL, ALBION W. (1905): *General Sociology: An Exposition of the Main Development in Sociological Theory from Spencer to Ratzenhofer* (Chicago: University of Chicago Press).

—— (1910): *The Meaning of Social Science* (Chicago: University of Chicago Press).

—— (1911–1912): "Socialism in the Light of Social Science," *American Journal of Sociology,* Vol. 17, pp. 804–819.

—— (1923): "Some Contributions to the History of Sociology," *American Journal of Sociology,* Vol. 28, pp. 385–418.

SMITH, JOHN E. (1957): "The Question of Man," in *The Philosophy of Kant and Our Modern World,* ed. C. W. Hendel (New York: Liberal Arts Press).

SMITH, T. V. (1939): *The Democratic Way of Life* (Chicago: University of Chicago Press), revised edition.

SOROKIN, PITIRIM (1928): *Contemporary Sociological Theories* (New York: Harper).

—— (1936–1937): "Improvement of Scholarship in the Social Sciences," *Journal of Social Philosophy,* Vol. 2, pp. 237–245.

—— (1956): *Fads and Foibles in Modern Sociology and Related Sciences* (Chicago: Henry Regnery).

SPENCER, HERBERT (1888): "Reasons for Dissenting from the Philosophy of M. Comte," in *Recent Discussions in Science, Philosophy and Morals* (New York: Dutton).

SPIEGEL, LEO ANGELO (1950) : "The Child's Concept of Beauty: a Study in Concept Formation," *Journal of Genetic Psychology*, Vol. 77, pp. 11–23.

STERN, B. J. (ed.) (1938) : "The Ward-Ross Correspondence," *American Sociological Review*, Vol. 3.

STIRNER, MAX (1844) : *The Ego and His Own*, trans. S. T. Byington, with an Intro. by J. L. Walker (New York: Benjamin R. Tucker, 1907 edition).

STUCKENBERG, J. H. W. (1903) : *Sociology: the Science of Human Society* (New York: Putnam), Vol. 1 (of 2 vols.).

SYKES, GERALD (1962) : *The Hidden Remnant* (New York: Harper).

SZASZ, THOMAS S. (1961) : *The Myth of Mental Illness: Foundations of a Theory of Personal Conduct* (New York: Harper-Hoeber).

—————— (1963a) : "Psychiatry in Public Schools," *The Humanist*, Vol. 23, pp. 89–93, May-June.

—————— (1963b) : "The Concept of Transference," *International Journal of Psychoanalysis*, Vol. 44, pp. 432–443.

—————— (1963c) : *Law, Liberty and Psychiatry: An Inquiry into the Social Uses of Mental Health Practices* (New York: Macmillan).

TEGGART, F. J. (1960) : *Theories and Processes of History* (Berkeley: University of California Press).

THOMAS, J. (1883–1884) : "Les théories sur le progrès," *La critique philosophique*, Vol. 12, Part II, pp. 103–112.

TILLICH, PAUL (1960) : *Love, Power and Justice* (New York: Oxford University Press, Galaxy Books).

—————— (1961) : "The Meaning of Health," *Perspectives in Biology and Medicine*, Vol. 5, pp. 92–100.

URBAN, W. M. (1949) : *Beyond Realism and Idealism* (London: Allen and Unwin).

VAIHINGER, HANS (1952) : *The Philosophy of "As If,"* trans. C. K. Ogden (London: Routledge and Kegan Paul).

VARTANIAN, ARAM (1953) : *Diderot and Descartes: A Study of Scientific Naturalism in the Enlightenment* (Princeton: Princeton University Press).

VICO, GIAMBATTISTA (1744) : *New Science of Giambattista Vico*, edited and translated with an Intro. by T. G. Bergin and M. H. Fisch (New York: Doubleday Anchor edition, 1961).

VON BERTALANFFY, LUDWIG (1960) : *Problems of Life* (New York: Harper Torchbooks).

VON HUMBOLDT, WILHELM (1963) : *Humanist Without Portfolio: An Anthology of the Writings of Wilhelm von Humboldt*, trans., with an Intro. by Marianne Cowan (Detroit: Wayne State University Press).

VON WIESE, LEOPOLD, and BECKER, HOWARD (1932) : *Systematic Sociology* (New York: Wiley).

WALLAS, GRAHAM (1923) : "Jeremy Bentham," *Political Science Quarterly*, Vol. 38, pp. 45–56.

WARD, HARRY F. (1919) : *The New Social Order: Principles and Programs* (New York: Macmillan).

—————— (1940) : *Democracy and Social Change* (New York: Modern Age Books) .

WARD, LESTER F. (1883) : *Dynamic Sociology* (New York: Appleton, 1902 edition) , Vol. 1 (of 2 vols.) .

—————— (1893) : *The Psychic Factors of Civilization* (Boston: Ginn & Co.) .

—————— (1896) : Letter to Franklin Giddings, *Social Forces,* Vol. 10, 1932, p. 317.

—————— (1901–1902) : "Contemporary Sociology," Part II, *American Journal of Sociology,* Vol. 7, pp. 629–658.

—————— (1909) : *Pure Sociology* (New York: Macmillan) .

—————— (1918) : *Glimpses of the Cosmos* (New York: Putnam) , 6 vols.

WEINGARTNER, RUDOLPH H. (1962) : *Experience and Culture, the Philosophy of Georg Simmel* (Middletown: Wesleyan University Press) .

WELLS, G. A. (1959) : *Herder and After: A Study in the Development of Sociology* (The Hague: Mouton & Co.) .

WHITEHEAD, ALFRED NORTH (1958) : *Modes of Thought* (New York: Capricorn Books) .

—————— (1959) : *Symbolism* (New York: Capricorn Books) .

WILLEY, BASIL (1961) : *The 18th Century Background* (London: Chatto and Windus) .

WOLFF, KURT H. (ed.) (1959) : *Georg Simmel, 1858–1918* (Columbus: Ohio State University Press) .

WRONG, DENNIS H. (1963) : "Human Nature and the Perspective of Sociology," *Social Research,* Vol. 30, pp. 300–318.

INDEX

❦

Subject index

Action theory in sociology, 90, 94, 170
Aggression, 159
   art as, 193
   Rousseau vs. Freud on, 151, 154, 303,
     401n.
Agonism, "agonistic rituals," 231–236,
   237, 262
Alienation, synthetic theory of, 98–248
   in Enlightenment tradition, 249–303,
     365–369
   Freud's contribution to, 143–154
   Marx's contribution to, 129–130
   and progressive education, 284–289
Anthropodicy, 45, 52
   critical, 148
   historical, 313–314
   as "secular" theodicy, 18, 24–25, 57,
     107, 310
   and theory of alienation, 98–248, 314–
     325
   see also Science of Man
Anthropomorphism, 264
Anxiety, 187, 328
   and cognition, 258–259
   in modern life, 17
Associationism, 23, 36, 101, 115
Authority, and human meanings, 192–194
Autonomy, 30
   individual support for, 258–259
   progressive education for, 294
   social support for, 259–270

Beautiful, the, as scientific problem,
   223–225, 375, 376–378

Behaviorism, 74, 121
"Being-in-the-world," 114
Bentham's system
   basic characteristics of, 35–36
   genial insights of, 36
   weaknesses of, 21, 36–37, 102–103, 331
Bureaucracy, 17, 139, 238, 242, 274

Charisma, 252–253, 257
Child development
   historical study of, 123–124, 128, 147
   and psychoanalysis, 147–151, 285–290
Class conflict, 6, 66, 139
Cognition
   neurosis as problem in, 258–259
   progressive education for, 289
Comte's system
   basic characteristics of, 43–51
   genial insights of, 218–226 *passim*
   weaknesses of, 80, 251–252, 345, 347–
     359 *passim*
Conformity, 208–209
Consumer, man as, 235–236, 241
Conviction, as esthetic problem, 174–176
Darwinism, 60–61, 82–83, 100, 108, 328
Death, comparative attitudes toward,
   246–248
Democracy, 39, 40
   education for, 286, 291–293
   as ideal-type, 291–292, 369, 370
   and science, 32
Depression (psychological), 162, 172, 182,
   329

420

Name index

DATE DUE	
# 8674,965	3/25/99